A Guide to Discursive Organizational Psychology

Edited by

Chris Steyaert

Doctor in Psychology and Professor in Organizational Psychology, University of St. Gallen, Switzerland

Julia Nentwich

Doctor and Associate Professor in Psychology, University of St. Gallen, Switzerland

Patrizia Hoyer

Doctor in Organization Studies and Cultural Theory, University of St. Gallen, Switzerland

 Edward Elgar
PUBLISHING

Cheltenham, UK • Northampton, MA, USA

Published by
Edward Elgar Publishing Limited
The Lypiatts
15 Lansdown Road
Cheltenham
Glos GL50 2JA
UK

Edward Elgar Publishing, Inc.
William Pratt House
9 Dewey Court
Northampton
Massachusetts 01060
USA

A catalogue record for this book
is available from the British Library

Library of Congress Control Number: 2016944272

This book is available electronically in the **Elgar**online
Business subject collection
DOI 10.4337/9780857939296

ISBN 978 0 85793 928 9 (cased)
ISBN 978 1 78643 171 4 (paperback)
ISBN 978 0 85793 929 6 (eBook)

Typeset by Servis Filmsetting Ltd, Stockport, Cheshire
Printed and bound by CPI Group (UK) Ltd, Croydon, CR0 4YY

Contents

Images and figures

Tables

Contributors

Pascal Dey is a Senior Research Fellow at the Institute for Business Ethics, University of St. Gallen. Much of Pascal's work has focused on the intersection of entrepreneurship, politics and society. Informed by (critical) sociological and philosophical theories, Pascal has placed particular heed on phenomena pertaining to discourse, power or identity, and, more recently, fantasy, time and ignorance.

Claudine Gaibrois is a Lecturer for Culture, Society and Language at the Zurich University of Applied Sciences and an External Lecturer for Language Diversity in Organizational Contexts at the University of St. Gallen, Switzerland, and the Ecole de Management Strasbourg, France. She received a PhD from the University of St. Gallen for her thesis on the discursive construction of power relations in multilingual organizations. Her research interests include linguistic and cultural diversity, communication and power relations.

Anna-Katrin Heydenreich is an External Lecturer for Environmental Psychology at the University of St. Gallen, Switzerland and for Business Ethics at the Duale Hochschule Stuttgart, Germany. She received a doctorate in Organizational Psychology for her discourse-analytic study of paradox in multi-stakeholder processes. She is interested in the psychology of sustainability and societal change and in the ambiguities of corporate social responsibility.

Patrizia Hoyer is a Postdoctoral Researcher at the Research Institute for Organizational Psychology, University of St. Gallen, Switzerland and Visiting Fellow at Lund University, Sweden. Her research interests include discursive and narrative approaches to identity, elite working contexts, resistance, global career mobility and career change. Patrizia's work has been published in journals such as the *British Journal of Management* and *Human Relations*.

Claus D. Jacobs is Professor of Public Management and Organization at the KPM Center for Public Management, University of Berne, Switzerland. His research focuses on organizational identity, organizational change and strategy work in pluralistic, multinational organizations and has been published in *Journal of Management Studies, Organization Studies* and *Strategic Organization*. He is Visiting Professor of Strategy and Organization at the University of St. Gallen and an Associate Fellow of Oxford University.

Christoph Michels is a Postdoctoral Researcher at the School of Humanities and Social Sciences at the University of St. Gallen, Switzerland. He has published in international journals and edited books in the field of organizational theory, geography and urban studies. His research addresses a range of issues relating to architecture and organizing, including participatory politics in the organization of public spaces and the production of atmospheres in cultural and educational institutions.

Julia C. Nentwich is Associate Professor in Psychology at the University of St. Gallen, Switzerland. She is interested in social and discursive practices of doing gender and diversity, organizational change, change agency and resistance. Her work has been published in international journals and books on organization studies, psychology and gender studies.

Anja Ostendorp received her doctorate in Psychology for a discourse analytical study on diversity management in Switzerland. Her main focus since the year 2000 is on organizational communication and discursive psychology. Currently, she uses her experience for coaching managers, groups, and teams. In addition she teaches courses on the psychology of group and leadership at the University of St. Gallen.

Roland Pfyl is Head of the Audit Office in the canton of Schwyz, Switzerland. Formerly, he has worked in internal audit of a major international banking group and gained a doctorate in Economics from the University of St. Gallen, Switzerland. His main academic interests concern regulation, control and compliance in organizations.

Dörte Resch is Professor of Human Resource Management and Organizational Behaviour at the School of Business, University of Applied Sciences and Arts Northwestern Switzerland. Her work focuses on post-structural organization theory and its application in human resources and change management. Most recently, she has been exploring the relationship between images of professions and the constructions of identities.

Florian Schulz is a Postdoctoral Researcher at the University of St. Gallen, Switzerland. He is interested in the organization of emotions as well as the effects of new forms of work practices and interventions in professions with a high degree of self-management.

Chris Steyaert is Professor for Organizational Psychology at the University of St. Gallen, Switzerland. He has published in international journals and books in the area of organizational theory and entrepreneurship. His current interests concern creativity, multiplicity (diversity) and reflexivity in organizing change, intervention and entrepreneurship.

Florian Ueberbacher is a Lecturer and Postdoctoral Research Fellow at the University of Zurich, Switzerland. Florian is an organization theorist and focuses on how organizations achieve power and influence over their stakeholders and how they gain and maintain legitimacy. His research has been published in the *Journal of Management Studies* and *Organization Studies*.

Preface and acknowledgements

This book aims to be a guide to discursive organizational psychology. It is based on a series of doctoral and postdoctoral projects conducted at the research institute for organizational psychology (OPSY) of the University of St. Gallen (Switzerland) over a period of roughly ten years and completed between 2006 and 2014. What is a guide? Often a person or a manual that brings people to, and leads them through, a museum or exhibition or neighbourhood to introduce them to unfamiliar objects, artefacts and ideas. In that spirit, we hope this book will guide those interested in discursive approaches to organizational phenomena and processes through the ideas and practices of discursive psychological analysis. Though a guidebook can never be as good as the experience itself, we have tried to write about the research projects in accessible and concrete ways, so readers can recognize the practices and practicalities of research. But this book is not meant to be methodological: if this sounds like a disclaimer, we want to emphasize that there are many ways to undertake discourse analysis, and that each research project needs to 'find' its own synthesis, one that interweaves processes of gaining research access, the conceptual framing, data gathering and analysing, and coming to a substantial interpretation and/ or theoretical contribution. Still, travel guides can become 'good friends' during the years one travels with them. So we hope this book – covered with coffee stains and traces of dust and sunscreen, and full of scribbled comments – can become a trusted support as readers and users explore the possibilities of discursive approaches to research in organizational psychology (OP) and organizational research in general.

The book opens with two introductory chapters, which respectively situate the book's contributions within the development of discursive approaches (mostly in organization studies) in Chapter 1 and in the history of organizational psychology in Chapter 2. Then, we present 12 chapters in four thematic sections: participation, resistance, creativity and intervention. Each chapter presents an independent and original empirical study that has been carefully composed in the context of a doctoral or postdoctoral project (see list below). As a result, the coverage of this book is boldly diverse. And yet, as we map out a different view on the field of organizational psychology through a lively collection of contributions, we do not aim – or claim – to present an exhaustive list of (emerging) OP themes. Rather, as one can expect from a research guide, we aim to illuminate some stimulating 'pieces' of OP work that exemplify how an interest in discursive dynamics can help to alter the ways we understand certain organizational themes.

Given our location in the German part of Switzerland, we must point out that much of the data collection was done in German or in Swiss German – but also in English, French and Spanish, as documented in Chapters 3, 6, 8, 10 and 11. As most of the studies have not been written or published in the native language of their authors and research participants, the discourse analysis has to be considered in light of the translation work that comes along with it. In other words, the chapters in this book contain empirical material that at some point in the analytical process has been translated into English. When working with translations, more than with so-called 'first-hand material', we must be careful to read transcriptions as material that has already been 'interpreted'. Recording what our research partners have 'said' and 'done' is quite different from recording the sayings and doings we have witnessed or been part of as researchers. This implies that discourse (analysis) is not just about text ('naturalized' as transcription), nor does it have to be inscribed in its linguistic context; instead, it forms a social research construct that gives expression to a social sentiment and life experience. The liveliness and emotion of the voices we hear are as much a part of discourses as of the specific language idioms that people draw upon in social interaction, such as research interviews.

In editing this book, we have been lucky to be supported on many levels. First, we are grateful to the (co-)authors of the various chapters for their valuable texts, and also for responding generously during the revision process and for giving our queries the fullest attention. We also thank the authors for providing feedback on each other's chapters; we are also grateful for feedback from other colleagues at the OPSY: Laurent Marti, Björn Müller, Martin Müller and Ursula Offenberger. In particular, we received excellent expert reviews from Martin Kornberger (Copenhagen Business School), and Art Dewulf (Wageningen University) who acted as external reviewers for some of the chapters.

Furthermore, as all of the chapters (except for the introductions) are based on empirical data collection, we would like to thank all those who participated in the empirical studies for their time and openness. While many of them stay 'anonymous' in our presentations, we are fortunate to have had collaborations with people, organizations and communities in a wide range of settings. These range from voluntary and non-profit organizations to (Swiss-based) multinationals in industries such as banking, pharmaceuticals and food, to local research institutes, global research organizations (such as CERN) and gatekeeping organizations (at UN summits); they also include citizens in local neighbourhoods and individual storytellers who simply took part in our research without any organizational connection.

In particular, we are grateful for a few people who assisted us in the process of editing this book. First of all, there is Helen Snively who for many years edited single manuscripts from members of our institute but who took up the challenge to language-edit each page of this book with care for detail and understanding of our context. For the best language editing ever, thank you, Helen, not in the least for your patience with us on this last piece! Claudia Biri was a great help in taking care of all the nitty-gritty work on formatting and reference-checking. Finally, we can never say thanks enough to Christina Ihasz-Riedener, who as secretary of our institute always supports us and even helps us get the details of our projects right. Also, we recognize the professional guidance of our publisher Edward Elgar, in particular Francine O'Sullivan and Aisha Bushby. Last but not least, we thank our partners and families. Editing this book would have been impossible without their generous support and patience.

The majority of chapters were written especially for this book; in addition, with a few research projects we opted to draw upon and adapt already published journal articles. In particular, we include seven doctoral projects:

Chapter 3: Anna-Katrin Heydenreich, 'Organising a multi-stakeholder process: Creating a paradoxical collaborative identity', Spring 2008.

Chapter 4: Christoph Michels, 'Räume der Partizipation – Wie man ein Kunstmuseum inszeniert', Autumn 2010.

Chapter 6: Pascal Dey, 'On the name of social entrepreneurship: Business School Teaching, Research, and Development Aid', Winter 2007.

Chapter 9: Roland Pfyl, 'Formality at work: Organizational discourses of formality in everyday management practices in a Swiss private bank', Spring 2009.

Chapter 11: Patrizia Hoyer, 'Careers in transition: Continuity, complexity and conflicting desires in the discursive identity construction of ex-consultants', Spring 2014.

Chapter 12: Anja Ostendorp, 'Human resource and corporate social responsibility concepts: Between fashionable luxury, old conflicts of interests, and new lines of flight', Spring 2006.

Chapter 13: Florian Schulz, 'The psycho-managerial complex at work: A study of the discursive practices of management coaching', Autumn 2012.

Four other chapters are based on previously published articles:

Chapter 7 is an adapted version of a manuscript published in the *British Journal of Management*: Nentwich, Julia and Patrizia Hoyer (2013), 'The power of counter-arguments: Part-time work as practising resistance', *BJM*, **24** (4), 557–570.

Chapter 8 is a language-edited adaptation of the article published in the *Journal of World Business*: Steyaert, Chris, Anja Ostendorp, and Claudine Gaibrois (2011), 'Multilingual organizations as "linguascapes": Negotiating the position of English through discursive practices', *JWB*, **46** (3), 270–278.

Chapter 10 is a language-edited version of the article published in *Technology Analysis & Strategic Management*: Jacobs, Claus D., Chris Steyaert and Florian Ueberbacher (2013), 'Anticipating intended users: Prospective sensemaking in technology development', *TASM*, **25** (9), 1027–1043.

Chapter 12 is a language-edited adaptation of the article published in the *Scandinavian Journal of Management*: Ostendorp, Anja and Chris Steyaert (2009), 'How different can differences be(come)?: Interpretative repertoires of diversity concepts in Swiss-based organizations', *SJM*, **25** (4), 374–384.

We thank the respective publishers – Wiley, Elsevier, and Routledge (Taylor & Francis) – for granting permission to reprint (partly adapted versions of) these articles.

We received financial support for the publishing of this book and especially for the language editing from the University of St. Gallen's Bühler-Reindl-Fonds. Furthermore, we are grateful for the grants we received for conducting the research projects reported in the following chapters:

Chapter 5: This text is based on a postdoctoral project that was funded by the Canton of St. Gallen, the Swiss Federal Fund for Integration (Integrationskredit des Bundes) and the Basic Research Fund of the University of St. Gallen's Research Commission.

Chapter 8: The Swiss National Science Foundation, NRP 56.

Chapter 10: The Basic Research Fund of the University of St. Gallen's Research Commission.

Chapter 12: The Swiss National Science Foundation's Marie Heim-Vögtlin Programme and the Basic Research Fund of the University of St. Gallen's Research Commission.

Chapter 14: This project was funded by the organization that had chosen Annette Kluge, Dörte Resch and Pascal Dey to implement this change process.

PART I

Introduction

1. Towards a discursive research agenda for organizational psychology

Patrizia Hoyer, Chris Steyaert and Julia C. Nentwich

> No genuinely critical work can emerge from within psychology that does not scrutinize the disciplinary location from which it emerges. (Hook, 2007, p. 3)

INTRODUCTION

The purpose of this book is to introduce and illustrate a multiplicity of discursive approaches applied to a range of classical and newer organizational themes in the field of organizational psychology (OP). By creating continuity within a given research tradition and also exploring new directions, the book is designed for a range of audiences. It may serve as a guide for researchers who are new to discourse analysis in the field of organization and management studies and who would like to learn about discursive approaches inspired by discursive psychology and investigate OP themes from a discursive angle. At the same time the book may serve as a starting point for those organizational psychologists familiar with the discipline, but less familiar with the epistemological and methodological underpinnings, and the empirical challenges, which offer plenty of chances for scholars in OP to generate various questions and perspectives. It might provide inspirational reading for scholars already contemplating or even conducting discourse analytical research in the field of organization studies/OP and for those who would like to enhance their conceptual and/or methodological understanding of it and critically reflect upon the discursive inquiry of organizational phenomena. Finally, this book addresses the broader community of organizational scholars (some of them quietly holding a degree in OP) as it draws attention to a number of discursive studies which clearly address OP themes, but have thus far often had to find 'a home' in the broader arena of organization studies, as the discipline of OP has been rather slow to embrace discursive approaches.

With the aim of suggesting such an agenda, we have broadly divided this first, introductory chapter into two parts. In the first part we briefly introduce the more general emergence of discourse analysis in the study of organizational phenomena, and then review how discourse analysis has been applied to date in analysing OP themes. We show how this emergence is aligned with several historically situated waves of psychology which have shown various levels of openness to discursive approaches to organizational phenomena. In the second part, we highlight the core contributions which the family of discourse methods brings to our understanding of OP topics, and also indicate key areas of debate that may pose challenges to the field but also set the direction and scope for its future research trajectory. In speculating on emerging trends and reflecting upon new developments, we try to sketch out how discourse analysis may become a key element in launching a consistent and substantial research agenda in the field of OP.

TRACING THE OPENINGS FOR A DISCURSIVE ORGANIZATIONAL PSYCHOLOGY

The Linguistic Turn in Organization Studies

The upsurge of interest in discursive approaches may have occurred as organizational scholars became disillusioned with a number of mainstream theories and methodologies (Grant, Hardy, Oswick and Putnam, 2004). As these scholars attempted to move beyond modernist and univocal accounts in the study of complex organizational processes (Oswick, Grant, Marshak and Wolfram-Cox, 2010), 'organizational discourse' emerged with a new terminology that invited alternative understandings of organizational and inter-organizational phenomena (Iedema, 2011). With the 'linguistic turn' in the 1980s (Deetz, 2003), a new perspective on the relationship between language and reality was introduced to the social sciences (Alvesson and Kärreman, 2000). This new perspective was grounded in the (meta-)-theoretical assumption that language is constitutive of social reality (Grant et al., 2004).

The epistemological postulation of the discourse project, however, signified much more than a simple shift in attention to matters of language. It became a shorthand for an entire philosophical tradition influenced by scholars such as Wittgenstein, Barthes, Foucault and Derrida (Mumby, 2011). Traditionally, language was considered to be a passive descriptor of pre-existing objects – it was 'true' when it correctly reflected reality and 'false' when it did not – but the 'linguistic turn' marked a radical departure from the view that language simply mirrored or revealed a pre-existing social reality (Phillips and Oswick, 2012). Instead, it suggested that, through the production and dissemination of text and talk (Berger and Luckmann, 1967), or more concretely, in the process of 'differentiating, fixing, naming, labeling, classifying and relating' (Chia, 2000, p. 513), discourse may construct whatever phenomenon we are interested in. This new insight greatly unsettled the conventional wisdom of language as being unproblematic (Alvesson and Kärreman, 2011a).

The linguistic turn took some time to find its way into the study of organizations, but eventually organizational discourse became a prominent area of analysis (Leclercq-Vandelannoitte, 2011). As they employed a social constructionist epistemology (see Chapter 2), researchers became sensitized to the discursive dynamics that were also pertinent in the construction of organizational reality. Now that organizations were no longer considered as objects to be counted and measured (Phillips and Oswick, 2012), discourse analysis opened up possibilities for re-imagining the everyday practices of organizing in a processual way. As discourse analysis took a particular interest in how texts became meaningful in relation to other texts, and how collections of texts could affect the social context in which they occurred, close attention was given to organizational discourses that defined what was to be considered as normal, acceptable and standard behaviour, thereby reproducing and institutionalizing certain practices (Hardy and Maguire, 2010).

Hence, by recovering the intrinsically political nature of discourses that may privilege one reality construction over another, organizational discourse studies problematized power relations and conceptualized organizations in performative terms, bringing issues of knowledge, power and resistance to the core of organizational analysis (Phillips and Oswick, 2012). As they engaged in interpretation and deconstruction, scholars began to realize how much routine organizational interactions were taken for granted; they also saw how discursive closure was being reified in the form of marginalization or naturalization (Mumby, 2011). At the same time discourse provided the means to point out that things could also be different, thereby exposing the effects of acculturation and habituation (Iedema, 2011) and even inviting competing discourses that held the potential for bringing about institutional change (Hardy and Maguire, 2010). Built on these premises, organizational discourse inspired a variety of analytical and interpretive moves that were considered particularly suitable for studying the complexity and processuality of organizational phenomena (Alvesson and Kärreman, 2011a; Chia, 2000).

Whereas other qualitative approaches were tailored towards understanding and revealing organizational reality, discourse analysis investigated how language constructed the experience of reality in the first place

(Phillips and Oswick, 2012). In particular, this discursive conception of reality brought with it practical implications for researchers' methodological choices about the way they would identify, collect and analyse data (Phillips and di Domenico, 2009). Over the past two decades then, organizational discourse expanded into such a well-established theoretical and methodological framework for organizational analysis that the continued proliferation of discursive studies turned it into a veritable 'shooting star'; it quickly became 'a mainstream, conventional, institutionalized and (almost) canonical "field" of study' (Rhodes, 2005, p. 793), granted space for special issues even in top tier journals (Phillips and di Domenico, 2009; Phillips and Oswick, 2012). For instance, Grant et al. (2004, p. 1) could claim that '[it] is now difficult to open a management or organizational journal without finding that it contains some sort of discursive-based study'. In fact, many books, special journal issues, edited collections and even conferences – such as the international conference on organizational discourse, meeting biannually since 1994 – have been dedicated to the topic of discourse and discursive studies in the field.

The Stalemate in (Organizational) Psychology

Though discourse studies have generally been gaining prominence in the social sciences, discursive work in the more specific field of organizational psychology has received little attention to date. As many scholars within the field of OP have moved their locus of commitment and publication to other so-called 'neighbouring fields' such as organization studies and critical management studies, few have noticed the potential in the contributions that organizational psychologists have made to these seemingly expansive and all-encompassing fields. This is particularly pertinent since OP has provided widely applied and popularized concepts that up to now shape organizational discourses and practices. Indeed, our starting point is the considerable impact of work and organizational psychology, as many of its concepts have come to centre stage in both everyday discourse and professional language since its conception in the early 20th century.

The application of psychological notions to the field of work and organization has had a great impact, as the language of psychology has considerably shaped the discourse of corporate selfhood: 'The psychological discourse was enormously successful because in the background of the rise of the professions, psychologists offered a language – of persons, emotions, motivations – which seemed to correspond to and make sense of the large-scale transformations of the American workplace' (Illouz, 2007, pp. 16–17). Thus, OP notions such as intelligence, personality, identity and motivation, as well as practices like collaboration, participation, coaching and teambuilding, have travelled and become part of organizational theory and practice. To understand how psychology in general and organizational psychology in particular have allowed for a discursive investigation of these topics, as this book tries to illustrate, we will first take note of a number of alternative positions which have developed within these fields.

A key reason psychology has been such a successful discipline is that its ideas, concepts and practices have had a widespread impact on all parts of society, including work, education, health care, sexuality, family, criminality, and security. As psychological concepts and practices were adopted in everyday life and found widespread application during the 20th century, psychology 'prospered by becoming a protean profession, responsive to the needs of any and all' (Capshew, 1999, p. 264). Driven by the demands of the marketplace, Capshew explains, '[p]sychological knowledge became a cultural commodity that was easily manufactured and widely distributed by a self-sustaining community of technoscientific professionals'.

This increasing success, however, brought with it mounting scrutiny, analysis and critique. Ironically, psychology became a discipline in search of its self. Since the early seventies the discipline of psychology has received strong critiques both from inside its own community and from external analysts. Within the discipline, various alternative strands were developed in the interpretive (Held, 2007; Tappan, 1997), critical (Fox and Prilleltensky, 1997; Fox, Prilleltensky and Austin, 2009; Hepburn, 2003), social constructionist (Burr, 2003; Gergen, 1985) and feminist (Burman, 1998; Gergen, 2001a; 2001b; 2010; Wilkinson, 1986; Wilkinson and Kitzinger, 1996) psychological approaches. Psychology was criticized for its one-dimensional attachment to neo-positivist scientific models and for celebrating the methods and logics of the natural sciences. Even though the narrowly defined and positivist boundaries had expanded over the years, the 'traditional' discipline of psychology continued to be strongly associated with theories and methods that systematically excluded non-quantitative perspectives (Weatherall, 2012). Moreover, psychology was criticized for failing to consider ideological and political differences, and even for reproducing them, and for imperialistically imposing a heroic and phallocratic individualism on people and cultures across the world (Gergen and Davis, 1996).

From the outside, but not independent of these internal comments, psychology tried, but failed, to stay out of the interpretive, critical and poststructuralist upheavals in the human and social sciences since the late sixties. Multiple approaches – Habermas' analysis of interests in knowledge-seeking, Foucault's understanding of the power/knowledge nexus in the construction of our ideas and identities, and Derrida's deconstruction to analyse binaries and to reveal contradiction and suppressions of meaning – scrutinized and questioned the ways the psychological discipline proceeded in scientific knowledge production and in authoring all things called psychological problems and interventions in society at large (Hepburn, 2003).

Psychology did no longer 'count' as a neutral scientific endeavour; rather, it became clear, as Hook explained (Hook, 2007, p. viii), that 'both through its practices and through the concepts that justify its practices', psychology 'operates for the most part as an ideological apparatus'. As a result, 'its array of discourses and activities constructs and sustains systems of domination and oppression even as they appear to support self-understanding and well-being'. As they operate, '[t]herapy, counseling, assessment, research, self-help, prevention work, clinic spaces, case studies and all forms of psy-work construct specific forms of understanding and experience'. In light of this growing critique, some psychologists did try to enter new premises by developing alternative perspectives and approaches, thereby, reinventing themselves. In the following section we will draw particular attention to the rise of discursive psychology.

The Entry of Discursive Psychology

Discursive psychology – as it explored the possibilities of discourse theory to analyse psychological phenomena – was based on a critique of the old paradigm, in which psychology rarely included itself in the phenomena that it described. Instead, it preferred to study those outside the discipline by promoting an abstract model of behavioural and cognitive mechanisms that was in line with the rigid methodologies employed for studying them (Parker, 2012). So, not long after the 'crisis in social psychology' during the 1970s, discursive psychology emerged in the late 1980s and early 1990s as a promising and dynamic new enterprise that did not simply provide another critique, but instead offered an alternative to social psychology, one that was both theoretically and methodologically coherent. Given social psychology's fetishism for experimentation, this may be considered a revolutionary turn (Augoustinos and Tileagă, 2012); indeed, it has been the centre of many controversial debates (Stokoe, Hepburn and Antaki, 2012).

In seeking out the intellectual and historical origins of the discursive project in social psychology, three seminal books – all published in 1987 – were said to actually predate the establishment of the term 'discursive psychology' (Augoustinos and Tileagă, 2012). These books all mark a critical body of work on language and social psychology; they are *Discourse and Social Psychology* by Jonathan Potter and Margaret Wetherell, *Common Knowledge* by Derek Edwards and Neil Mercer, and *Arguing and Thinking* by Michael Billig. Some scholars see the intersection between these three books as the birthplace of discursive psychology. Though other accounts on the rise of discursive psychology do not view all three books as equally significant (Billig, 2012), there is a wider agreement that the Potter and Wetherell book, cited over 4,000 times in over 250 different journals, has had a major impact across various social and human sciences (Potter, 2012).

Much of the success of *Discourse and Social Psychology* may be attributed to its setting out a clear and detailed vision of how research might be done (Potter, 2012) in terms of a systematic, empirical analysis of everyday recorded talk (Edwards, 2012). Especially by introducing and drawing on 'interpretative repertoires', which became a central tool for analysis, the authors investigated how people employed common-sense descriptions as rhetorical resources for explaining and preserving moral and social orders (see also Weatherall, 2012).

Content-wise, discursive psychology took the topics of the social psychology textbooks of that time (Potter, 2012) – attitudes, cognition, attribution, persuasion, identity, prejudice, and so on – and offered alternative ways to analyse these topics as they were produced in formal or informal everyday talk (Augoustinos and Tileagă, 2012). In this way discursive psychology offered an alternative perspective for apprehending the mutual relationship between people, practices, and institutions; it also introduced a coherent set of concepts and methods for investigating these relationships (Augoustinos and Tileagă, 2012).

When considering its development over the past few decades, however, critics have argued that discursive psychology is no longer driven by its initial political impetus to unsettle the disciplinary concerns and practices of mainstream psychology, as it now makes few, if any, critical references to other kinds of psychology (Billig, 2012; Edwards, 2012; Parker, 2012). Instead, by working in partnership with the mainstream, discursive psychology has become a distinct and popular 'way of doing psychology'. Based on this harmonization, Stokoe et al. (2012) have even accused the field of having lost its critical edge for engaging in emancipatory projects and for potentially bringing about social change.

Despite these objections, there remains little doubt that discursive psychology has made a considerable contribution in terms of redefining social psychology and other areas (Dickerson, 2012; Van Dijk, 2012). This 'new field' within psychology has generated a considerable network of scholars who by now identify as 'discursive psychologists' with a growing number of postgraduates who engage in this type of work (Augoustinos and Tileagă, 2012), and a wealth of introductory textbooks to this new psychology (for example, Burr, 2003, 2015; Dickerson, 2012; Hepburn, 2003; Tuffin, 2004). This achievement of discursive social psychology is not to be underestimated, given that it moved from being at the margins of 'politically motivated critique' to now sit comfortably within the tradition of western psychology (Augoustinos and Tileagă, 2012).

The Potential for a Discursive Research Agenda in Organizational Psychology

In contrast to the noteworthy development of discursive approaches in (social) psychology, quite a different story must be told for the neighbouring field of organizational psychology. First of all, OP has not been considered a stable arena as it has continuously been evolving. In fact, OP is rarely seen as its own field; it is usually presented in connection with personnel psychology (Steffy and Grimes, 1992), industrial psychology (Islam and Zyphur, 2009) or work psychology (Chmiel, 2008), which blurs its boundaries and obscures its actual contributions. Second, and in contrast to some other social sciences, the canon of theories, methodologies and methods that constitute this subfield of psychology have been rather static, as one can see by comparing its textbooks over the years. As a consequence, many of the OP scholars who take a more critical approach have shifted their focus to the wider field of organization studies. That field, 'which is distinct from, but in many ways parallel to, IO psychology, has a rich and growing critical and postmodern tradition . . . but has been more strongly represented in business schools and in sociology departments than in IO psychology departments' (Islam and Zyphur, 2009, p. 122). It is not surprising then that much of the OP research to date continues to be highly interdisciplinary and aligned with research in the areas of sociology and management (Parker, 2012).

OP's lack of critical and reflexive engagement with its own research processes, which encompassed neither neutral nor innocent activities of knowledge and reality productions, has triggered a growing series of critical analyses and attempts to reframe its research agenda. For example, in a critical review of personnel and organizational psychology, Steffy and Grimes (1992) retraced the self-regulating code of discourse which constitutes the discipline. In describing the set of rules that reflect its ontological content, epistemological strategy and methodological tactics, they observed that 'psychology in general and [P]OP in particular have not witnessed the schisms and debates that characterize other organizational and social sciences' (Steffy and Grimes, 1992, p. 183). As ontological and epistemological questions were mostly assumed to be irrelevant in the neo-positivist approaches of OP, self-critique and reflection have thus far been mostly limited to considering whether researchers have adequately followed the normative rules of method and proper validation procedures.

Drawing upon the work of Habermas and Foucault, Steffy and Grimes

(1992) called for a critical research agenda that would imply greater reflexivity in knowledge production. Wendy Hollway (1991) took this initiative a step further in what is by now almost a classic: *Work Psychology and Organizational Behaviour*. Hollway reframed 80 years of history of work psychology based on the perspectives of Althusser and Foucault. Her analysis showed that the research in OP has mostly been tied to the goals of regulation by management, but she pleaded for research that would focus on the 'multiple and competing discourses which contribute to people's positioning' (Hollway, 1991, p. 188).

In response to these criticisms, one aim of our book is to retrace some lines of OP and to re-invigorate and make visible its specific contributions to the field of organizational studies. At the same time we aim to connect to the critical tradition of studying how psychological concepts and practices are enacted in organizational contexts. Moreover, by drawing on multiple logics of organizing and reflecting upon the paradoxical ways in which these logics become maintained or changed in research processes, this book aims to draw attention to more innovative developments in OP that have so far remained dispersed and thus not noticed in the wider field of organization studies.

Consequently, with the current book we draw attention to the discursive analysis of classical as well as crucial themes in OP. By doing so we place into perspective OP's potential – thus far mostly neglected – to contribute to the broader discursive movement in organization studies. In that way, the book follows one important line of research: tracing how discursive studies can be established as a different form of analysis in OP, one that presents and reflects upon its own performance in the course of studying a broad range of research topics. Discursive endeavours in OP mark a noticeable development of distinct forms of studying and explaining language based on taking up discourse-analytical, rhetorical and deconstructionist ways of proceeding. In the following section we delineate what a more explicit discursive agenda in the field of OP could possibly look like.

DISCOURSE ANALYSIS IN OP: CHALLENGES, DEBATES AND FUTURE POTENTIALS

When they look ahead, organizational scholars still expect to see growth in discourse oriented work (Oswick et al., 2010); they argue that the potential scope for its application has not yet been realized (Grant et al., 2004). As we have tried to maintain in this introductory chapter, this expectation for growth is particularly apposite for discursive studies in the field of OP; we believe a substantial research agenda for discursive contributions could soon gain considerable momentum. Despite this optimism for such an agenda, we are also quite aware of current challenges and debates around the discourse project which can certainly create obstacles to further establishing a discursive research trajectory in OP. Thus we also address some of the future potentials – along with these challenges and debates – for further opening up the field of discourse studies, thereby turning the call for discursive work in the area of OP into a more thought-provoking and daring venture.

Therefore, in the pages to come we address several issues of debate and concern. First, we look at the problem of broad definition, which renders 'discourse' and 'discourse analysis' as two loosely defined concepts that for better or worse have resulted in a huge variety of different research approaches over a vague common denominator. Second, and in line with this concern about the variety of approaches, we shed light on a debate around conceptual clarity and methodological rigour which has divided the community of scholars into proponents of more standardization and consistency on the one side and advocates for open, trans-disciplinary and multi-methodological analysis on the other. Third, we warn about overemphasizing and privileging language and discourse at the expense of other non-discursive elements such as materiality and affect that also mark important ingredients of organizational life and meaning making. In our closing thoughts we delineate how these challenges and debates may – after all – inform rather than jeopardize the goal of strengthening the link between OP themes and discourse studies by making that link more explicit and thereby more prominent.

Variety in Theories: Discourse Analysis as a Fuzzy Concept

The first issue of debate revolves around the critique that 'discourse analysis', like the term 'discourse' itself, lacks a simple definition that clearly delineates its boundaries (Phillips and di Domenico, 2009; Phillips and Oswick, 2012). As a consequence, discourse analysis has been criticized for being a poorly defined, vague, ambiguous and fuzzy concept, encompassing a bewildering array of disparate perspectives, methods and approaches. As discourse may mean a broad range of different things, it may above all be considered an umbrella term that accommodates an enormous diversity of ways that people talk about and analyse organizational discourse (Grant et al., 2004).

Different academic disciplines have drawn on the term 'discourse analysis' to describe what they do and how they proceed to do it (Bargiela-Chiappini, 2011). This eclecticism may be explained by the way that organizational discourse analysis has evolved over time from an array of distinct disciplinary antecedents (Phillips and Oswick, 2012), including the traditions of sociology, anthropology, psychology, social theory, linguistics, sociolinguistics, communication and literary-based studies (Bargiela-Chiappini, 2011; Grant et al., 2004). For instance, intertextual analysis derives from the work of Bakhtin (1981; 1986) and is grounded in literary studies, while Foucauldian discourse analysis, as the name suggests, emanates from Foucault's (1972; 1980; 1984) work, which itself was nested within philosophy, history and social theory (Phillips and Oswick, 2012). Alvesson and Kärreman (2011a), among other scholars, express their discontent with this variation, suggesting that it 'overpacks' the concept of discourse, makes it clumsy to use, clouds awareness of different theoretical and analytical options and thus leads to confusion. As they see it, the only thing that unites much discourse work is the (over)use of the discourse label. By not using this signifier in a nuanced way, they say, some researchers have applied it rather uncritically to cover up muddled thinking.

While other commentators share this critical view, seeing the varied use of organizational discourse analysis as problematic (Van Dijk, 1997), others in fact see it as a healthy sign of pluralism which serves as a source of strength and has the potential to be further exploited for meaningful contributions to the study of organizations (Grant et al., 2004; Phillips and Oswick, 2012). This is especially the case for scholars who, in a poststructuralist or processual mode of engagement, embrace concepts of multiplicity, plurivocality and paradoxicality; they subscribe to an understanding that there is never just one (understanding of) discourse that characterizes organizational life, but a multitude of relatively autonomous yet overlapping organizational discourses, each of which allows for a variety of possible readings. From this perspective, a given research endeavour provides only a limited appraisal of the multitude of 'organizational realities', depending on the conceptual perspective and the methodological choices that determine the study (Grant et al., 2004). Considering the organization itself as a fluid and polyphonic entity, several scholars try to avoid definite readings of discourses that would reify the concept 'organization' (Chia, 2000) and thereby exclude notions of incoherence and inconsistency. These notions are key however for understanding the escalating demands of globalization and the increasing unpredictability of markets (Grant et al., 2004).

In the course of suggesting a discursive research agenda in the field of OP, we go along with those who advocate for multiplicity and hospitality towards discursive approaches that have different disciplinary roots. Hence, in the chapters of this book you will find a varied mix of discursive endeavours – but what aligns them all is the idea that language (together with other social practices) constructs organizational reality. Many upcoming studies lean towards a discursive psychology approach, where concepts of interpretative repertoires and rhetorical arguments or strategies come to centre stage. Several others take an explicitly critical perspective that is influenced by the work of Habermas, Gramsci or Foucault, while still others draw on more recent debates and understandings, where discourse is framed for instance as 'practice' or 'intervention'. While allowing for such a broad understanding of discourse in the suggested research agenda in OP, we also emphasize the need to strive for conceptual clarity and transparency when conducting and writing up empirical studies. We have therefore encouraged the authors included in this book to be quite careful and explicit in demarcating the boundaries for their specific use and understanding of the term discourse. It is exactly this combination of multiplicity on the one hand, and definitional clarity on the other, that we find promising for a future research trajectory in the field of OP.

Variety in Methods: Between Methodological Rigour and Flexibility

Some see another 'problem' that goes along with the high degree of diversity and heterogeneity in the field: the variety of methods applied in discourse studies. This has led to a debate around conceptual clarity and methodological rigor, which is nicely exemplified in a point-counterpoint exchange between Leitch and Palmer (2010) on the one hand and Chouliaraki and Fairclough (2010) on the other (see also Antaki, Billig, Edwards and Potter, 2003). Leitch and Palmer have looked sceptically at the loose application of concepts and methods, particularly in the area of critical discourse analysis (CDA), but also in the broader field of discourse studies; they argue that the field needs at least some area of commonality underpinning a methodological approach. They fear that researchers may draw on CDA as a rhetorical sleight of hand, thereby omitting a detailed description of the methods they used in their analysis of discourse. Doing so could limit the inherent potential of discourse work, and it could mean that researchers are actually combining paradigmatic assumptions unreflexively. Hence, Leitch and Palmer (2010) make the case for more definitional clarity as well as for greater consistency and rigor in the methodological application of discourse analysis. They suggest nine 'methodological protocols' that can help researchers to systematically address three stages where they must decide on their methods: defining concepts, selecting data, and analysing data.

In contrast to that view, Chouliaraki and Fairclough (2010) have clear reservations about the ability of universal methodological protocols and rigid rules to guarantee consistency and regularity. They see such regulation, based on tight definitions and single protocols, as undesirable, as it puts limits on CDA as a methodology and thereby restrains the dialectical relations between discourse and other elements of 'the social'. Instead they argue for leaving analysis deliberately more flexible and even porous, so it can remain versatile and contingent on the specific research questions at hand. In that way, new space can be created for an alternative conception of discourse. Novel research designs in the field may then become transdisciplinary and integrationist, privileging a spectrum of desirable methodological variation over rigour (Bargiela-Chiappini, 2011; Chouliaraki and Fairclough, 2010).

We concur with the editors (2010) of this point-counterpoint debate who note that both Leitch and Palmer (2010) and Chouliaraki and Fairclough (2010) raise valid points. While the former are concerned with the dependability of discursive research, the latter are worried that an overemphasis on strict methods may make it harder for researchers to use discourse work flexibly in both theoretical and critical ways. Thus, to begin unfolding a discursive programme in OP we suggest keeping a fruitful balance between both positions. Rather than supporting strict adherence to predefined research protocols, we promote methodological variety and urge researchers to develop the flexible methodological approaches they believe are most appropriate for, and even tailored to, the characteristics of their area of interest and research questions. On the other hand we have urged the authors in this book to act as guides for their readers, and thus to be as explicit and detailed as possible when describing their empirical setup, their unit of discursive analysis, and the various steps they took during their analysis. In this way we have allowed for a broad variety of analytical approaches that are still transparent and unambiguous regarding their methodological choices.

Expanding the Focus on Discourse: The Relevance of Materiality, Affect and Aesthetics

The third issue we would like to draw attention to is a critique: with the widespread adhesion to a social constructionist epistemology, some organizational scholars have overvalued the significance of language, meanwhile not paying sufficient attention to other facets of organizational life (Bargiela-Chiappini, 2011). This critique addresses researchers who uncritically reproduce some taken-for-granted assumptions that underlie the discourse project (Bargiela-Chiappini, 2011). Within such a discourse-driven mindset, so the argument goes, organizational complexity has been converted into text, no questions asked (Iedema, 2011). When most activity in organizations is considered to be discursive in nature (Grant et al., 2004), there is little evident need to study anything 'outside' of discourse. This emphasis, some say, has greatly diminished the value of discourse analysis, which is not sensitive enough to non-linguistic aspects of organizing (Mumby, 2011) or misunderstood the materiality of discourse (Prasad, 2005; Hardy and Thomas, 2015).

In line with this argument, Robert Chia (2000), despite his passion for the social constructionist ontology, acknowledged that some areas of experience within organizations are not so easily captured in discursive endeavours (Bargiela-Chiappini, 2011). Critics of discourse have particularly flagged the topics of affect, aesthetics and other more embodied versions of sensemaking as being beyond the reach of textual analysis, and have called for different modes of engagement (Potter, 2012). Assuming that affect is continuous, pre-personal and pre-conscious (Anderson, 2014), researchers concerned with it tend to focus on movement, change and ephemeral action; meanwhile discourse is limited to dealing with experiences that are discontinuous, and capable of being located and owned. Addressing affect in a non-discursive way would make it possible, though, to study the not-yet-said, thereby engaging with phenomena that would otherwise be disdained as matters of intuition, suspicion, or magic. When they are simply ignored, however, these dimensions of embodied affect may undermine rather than enrich the project of discourse studies, and render it 'immaterial' to the contemporary study of organizations (Iedema, 2011). Hence, scholars with an interest in a 'post-linguistic turn perspective' (Mumby, 2011) would appreciate better ways to attend to the material, the physical, and the affective, as well as to the aesthetic qualities of work-related experiences (Bargiela-Chiappini, 2011; Kenny and Fotaki, 2012; Putnam, 2015). For instance, Margaret Wetherell (2012) has undertaken an encompassing attempt to align affective and discursive dimensions of practice; she called the affective turn the wrong turn because, as she observed, the discursive becomes almost entirely separated from conceptualizations of affect.

Rather than making a case for affect and materiality in replacing discourse, we have a different suggestion for a future research trajectory in OP: bring the interface between the discursive and the non-discursive into a meaningful balance (see also Alvesson and Kärreman, 2011a; 2011b; Wetherell, 2012; Putnam, 2015). Looking into the future, we believe that, if discourse analysis were explored to its full extent, it might reach its limits in terms of contributing new understandings. Hence it might be more farsighted to begin exploring some potentially fruitful methodological pairings that would combine discursive approaches with non-discursive ones; this would mean a shift from focusing only on linguistic methods to including methods that invite complementary understandings of organizational processes (Phillips and Oswick, 2012). Ethnography, as one example, may well have the potential to bring together text and context, that is, to combine discourse with the material, the nonverbal and the relational (Bargiela-Chiappini, 2011; Nentwich, 2014; Steyaert and Van Looy, 2010; Wetherell, 2007; Hardy and Thomas, 2015).

By concurrently applying discursive and non-discourse approaches – and then eventually letting go of this unfruitful binary – the field of OP might be able to move beyond the discursive isolationism that has kept some neighbouring fields from developing multidisciplinary approaches and connecting to the more material world of organizations (Phillips and Oswick, 2012).

CONCLUSION AND FUTURE OUTLOOK

To date, strict 'gate-keeping' practices in the mainstream field of OP have forced researchers with an interest in discursive approaches to go outside of the discipline where critical and alternative perspectives are less marginalized, but considered relevant and hence more publishable. In this introductory chapter we have tried to sketch out a discursive research agenda that would allow OP studies that are so far widely dispersed in the broader field of organization studies to become more visible. Having said this, we are not necessarily suggesting that discourse analysis in OP 'become a coherent alternative tradition' (Parker and Burman, 2008, p. 102; see also Symon and Cassell, 2006). Instead, we would like to draw attention to discursive OP work as a complementary form of qualitative and critical inquiry; rather than becoming a new standalone approach we believe it enlightens the existing research project in OP and widens its scope.

Moreover, we call for a more conscious and daring engagement with some of the roots of OP themes that currently go unnoticed in the wider context of organization studies, where studies in the intersection between discourse work and OP topics are being published. Above all, we see the possible contribution that lies in developing a discursive research agenda in OP, a promising direction for future research that continues to open up new ways of exploring organizational psychological phenomena. In the next chapter we provide an overview of the chapters of this book; they illustrate ways to combine a range of (post-)discursive approaches with various OP themes and phenomena.

REFERENCES

Alvesson, Mats and Dan Kärreman (2000), 'Taking the linguistic turn in organizational research: Challenges, responses, consequences', *Journal of Applied Behavioral Science*, **36** (2), 136–158.

Alvesson, Mats and Dan Kärreman (2011a), 'Decolonializing discourse: Critical reflections on organizational discourse analysis', *Human Relations*, **64** (9), 1121–1146.

Alvesson, Mats and Dan Kärreman (2011b), 'Organizational discourse analysis – well done or too rare? A reply to our critics', *Human Relations*, **64** (9), 1193–1202.

Anderson, Ben (2014), *Encountering Affect: Capacities, Apparatuses, Conditions*, Farnham: Ashgate.

Antaki, Charles, Michael Billig, Derek Edwards and Jonathan Potter (2003), 'Discourse analysis means doing analysis: A critique of six analytic shortcomings', *Discourse Analysis Online*, **1** (1).

Augoustinos, Martha and Cristian Tileagă (2012), 'Twenty five years of discursive psychology', *The British Journal of Social Psychology*, **51** (3), 405–412.

Bakhtin, Mikhail M. (1981), *The Dialogic Imagination*, Austin: University of Texas Press.

Bakhtin, Mikhail M. (1986), *Speech, Genres and Other Late Essays*, Austin, TX: University of Texas Press.

Bargiela-Chiappini, Francesca (2011), 'Discourse(s), social construction and language practices: In conversation with Alvesson and Kärreman', *Human Relations*, **64** (9), 1177–1191.

Berger, Peter and Thomas Luckmann (1967), *The Social Construction of Reality: A Treatise on the Sociology of Knowledge*, Garden City, NY: Anchor Books.

Billig, Michael (1987), *Arguing and Thinking: A Rhetorical Approach to Social Psychology*, Cambridge: Cambridge University Press.

Billig, Michael (2012), 'Undisciplined beginnings, academic success, and discursive psychology', *British Journal of Social Psychology*, **51** (3), 413–424.

Burman, Erica (1998), *Deconstructing Feminist Psychology*, London: Sage.

Burr, Vivien (2003), *Social Constructionism* (Second Edition), New York: Routledge.

Burr, Vivien (2015), *Social Constructionism* (Third Edition), New York: Routledge.

Capshew, James H. (1999), *Psychologists on the March: Science, Practice and Professional Identity in America, 1929–1969*, Cambridge: Cambridge University Press.

Chia, Robert (2000), 'Discourse analysis as organizational analysis', *Organization*, **7** (3), 513–518.

Chmiel, Nik (2008), *An Introduction to Work and Organizational Psychology*, Oxford: Wiley/Blackwell.

Chouliaraki, Lilie and Norman Fairclough (2010), 'Critical discourse analysis in organization studies: Towards an integrationist methodology', *Journal of Management Studies*, **47** (6), 1213–1218.

Deetz, Stanley (2003), 'Reclaiming the legacy of the linguistic turn', *Organization*, **10** (3), 421–429.

Dickerson, Paul (2012), *Social Psychology: Traditional and Critical Perspectives*, New York: Pearson Education.

The Editors (2010), 'Critical Discourse Analysis (CDA) in context: Alternative perspectives on the analysis of discourse', *Journal of Management Studies*, **47** (6), 119–21193.

Edwards, Derek (2012), 'Discursive and scientific psychology', *British Journal of Social Psychology*, **51** (3), 425–435.

Edwards, Derek and Neil Mercer (1987), *Common Knowledge: The Development of Understanding in the Classroom*, London: Routledge.

Foucault, Michel (1972), *The Archaeology of Knowledge*, New York: Pantheon.

Foucault, Michel (1980), *Power/Knowledge: Selected Interviews and Other Writings 1972–1977*, New York: Pantheon.

Foucault, Michel (1984), 'The order of discourse', in Michael Shapiro (ed.), *Language and Politics*, Oxford, UK: Blackwell, pp. 108–139.

Fox, Dennis and Isaac Prilleltensky (1997), *Critical Psychology: An Introduction*, London: Sage.

Fox, Dennis, Isaac Prilleltensky and Stephanie Austin (2009), *Critical Psychology: An Introduction*, London: Sage.

Gergen, Kenneth (1985), 'The social constructionist movement in modern psychology', *American Psychologist*, **40** (3), 266–275.

Gergen, Mary (2001a), *Feminist Reconstructions in Psychology: Narrative, Gender, and Performance*, vol. vii, Thousand Oaks, CA: Sage.

Gergen, Mary (2001b), 'The emergence of Feminist Postmodern Psychology', in Mary Gergen (ed.), *Feminist Reconstructions in Psychology: Narrative, Gender, and Performance*, vol. vii, Thousand Oaks, CA: Sage, pp. 9–51.

Gergen, Mary (2010), 'Teaching psychology of gender from a social constructionist standpoint', *Psychology of Women Quarterly*, **34** (2), 261–264.

Gergen, Mary and Sara N. Davis (1996), *Toward a New Psychology of Gender: A Reader*, London: Routledge.

Grant, David, Cynthia Hardy, Cliff Oswick and Linda L. Putnam (2004), 'Introduction: Organizational discourse: Exploring the field', in David Grant, Cynthia Hardy, Cliff Oswick and Linda L. Putnam (eds), *The Sage Handbook of Organizational Discourse*, London: Sage, pp. 1–37.

Hardy, Cynthia and Steve Maguire (2010), 'Discourse, field-configuring events, and change in organizations and institutional fields: Narratives of DDT and the Stockholm Convention', *Academy of Management Journal*, **53** (6), 1365–1392.

Hardy, Cynthia and Robyn Thomas (2015), 'Discourse in a material world', *Journal of Management Studies*, **52** (5), 680–696.

Held, Barbara S. (2007), *Psychology's Interpretive Turn: The Search for Truth and Agency in Theoretical and Philosophical Psychology*, Washington, DC: APA books.

Hepburn, Alexa (2003), *An Introduction to Critical Social Psychology*, London: Sage.

Hollway, Wendy (1991), *Work Psychology and Organizational Behaviour*, London: Sage.

Hook, Derek (2007), *Foucault, Psychology and the Analytics of Power*, Basingstoke: Palgrave Macmillan.

Iedema, Rick (2011), 'Discourse studies in the 21st century: A response to Mats Alvesson and Dan Kärreman's "Decolonializing discourse"', *Human Relations*, **64** (9), 1163–1176.

Illouz, Eva (2007), *Cold Intimacies. The Making of Emotional Capitalism*, Oxford: Wiley/Blackwell.

Islam, Gazi and Michael Zyphur (2009), 'Concepts and directions in critical

Industrial/Organizational Psychology', in Dennis Fox, Isaac Prilleltensky and Stephanie Austin (eds), *Critical Psychology: An Introduction*, London: Sage, pp. 110–125.

Kenny, Kate and Marianna Fotaki (eds) (2014), *The Psychosocial and Organization Studies: Affect at Work*, New York: Palgrave Macmillan.

Leclercq-Vandelannoitte, Aurélie (2011), 'Organizations as discursive constructions: A Foucauldian approach', *Organization Studies*, **32** (9), 1247–1271.

Leitch, Shirley and Ian Palmer (2010), 'Analysing texts in context: Current practices and new protocols for critical discourse analysis in organization studies', *Journal of Management Studies*, **47** (6), 1194–1212.

Mumby, Dennis K. (2011), 'What's cooking in organizational discourse studies? A response to Alvesson and Kärreman', *Human Relations*, **64** (9), 1147–1161.

Nentwich, Julia (2014), 'Puppen für die Buben und Autos für die Mädchen? Rhetorische Modernisierung in der Kinderkrippe', in Gerlinde Malli and Susanne Sackl-Sharif (ed.), *Wider die Gleichheitsrhetorik. Soziologische Analysen – theoretische Interventionen. Texte für Angelika Wetterer*, Westfälisches Dampfboot, pp. 50–61.

Oswick, Cliff, David Grant, Robert J. Marshak and Julie Wolfram-Cox (2010), 'Organizational discourse and change: Positions, perspectives, progress and prospects', *Journal of Applied Behavioral Science*, **46** (1), 8–15.

Parker, Ian (2012), 'Discursive social psychology now', *British Journal of Social Psychology*, **51** (3), 471–477.

Parker, Ian and Erica Burman (2008), 'Critical psychology: Four theses and seven misconceptions', *Hellenic Journal of Psychology*, **5**, 99–115.

Phillips, Nelson and Maria Laura di Domenico (2009), 'Discourse analysis: Methods and debates', in David Buchanan and Alan Bryman (eds), *The Sage Handbook of Organizational Research Methods*, London: Sage, pp. 549–565.

Phillips, Nelson and Cliff Oswick (2012), 'Organizational discourse: Domains, debates and directions', *Academy of Management Annals*, **6** (1), 435–481.

Potter, Jonathan (2012), 'Re-reading *Discourse and Social Psychology*: Transforming social psychology', *British Journal of Social Psychology*, **51** (3), 436–455.

Potter, Jonathan and Margaret Wetherell (1987), *Discourse and Social Psychology*, London: Sage.

Prasad, Pushkala (2005), *Crafting Qualitative Research: Working in the Postpositivist Traditions*, New York: M.E. Sharpe.

Putnam, Linda (2015), 'Unpacking the dialectic: Alternative views on the discourse-materiality relationship', *Journal of Management Studies*, **52** (5), 707–716.

Rhodes, Carl (2005), 'Book review of *The Sage Handbook of Organizational Discourse*', *Organization Studies*, **26** (5), 793–804.

Steffy, Brian D. and Andrew J. Grimes (1992), 'Personnel/Organizational Psychology: A critique of the discipline', in Mats Alvesson and Hugh Willmott (eds), *Critical Management Studies*, London: Sage, pp. 181–201.

Steyaert, Chris and Bart Van Looy (2010), *Relational Practices, Participative Organizing. Advanced Series in Management Vol. 7*, Bingley: Emerald.

Stokoe, Elizabeth, Alexa Hepburn and Charles Antaki (2012), 'Beware the "Loughborough School" of Social Psychology? Interaction and the politics of intervention', *British Journal of Social Psychology*, **51** (3), 486–496.

Symon, Gillian and Catherine Cassell (2006), 'Neglected perspectives in work and organizational psychology', *Journal of Occupational and Organizational Psychology*, **79**, 307–314.

Tappan, Mark B. (1997), 'Interpretive psychology: Stories, circles, and understanding lived experience', *Journal of Social Issues*, **53** (4), 645–656.

Tuffin, Keith (2004), *Understanding Social Psychology*, London: Sage.

Van Dijk, Teun A. (1997), *Discourse as Social Interaction: Discourse Studies – Volume II*, Newbury Park, CA: Sage.

Van Dijk, Teun A. (2012), 'A note on epistemics and discourse analysis', *British Journal of Social Psychology*, **51** (3), 478–485.

Weatherall, Ann (2012), 'Discursive psychology and feminism', *British Journal of Social Psychology*, **51** (3), 463–470.

Wetherell, Margaret (2007), 'A step too far: Discursive psychology, linguistic ethnography and questions of identity', *Journal of Sociolinguistics*, **11** (5), 661–681.

Wetherell, Margaret (2012), *Affect and Emotion: A New Social Science Understanding*, London: Sage.

Wilkinson, Sue (1986), *Feminist Social Psychology: Developing Theory and Practice*, Milton Keynes: Open University Press.

Wilkinson, Sue and Celia Kitzinger (1996), *Representing the Other: A Feminism & Psychology Reader*, London: Sage.

2. Mapping the field: key themes in discursive organizational psychology

Julia C. Nentwich, Patrizia Hoyer and Chris Steyaert

INTRODUCTION

In the first, introductory chapter of this book we provided an overview of how discourse analytical approaches have entered the domain of social sciences including the arena of (discursive) psychology, and we suggested what a discursive research agenda could look like for studies in organizational psychology (OP). In this second introductory chapter, we provide an overview of the key themes of organizational psychology that this book addresses from a discursive perspective. Further, we show how these themes relate both to more traditional stances and to more recent developments in the field of OP. Having explored how discursive approaches both reframe and introduce different themes to the 'map' of OP, we have arranged the 12 chapters according to four major themes: participation, resistance, creativity and intervention. Furthermore, we have identified change as a bridging theme across all the chapters, to conform to discursive psychology's 'potential for bringing about social change or engaging with emancipatory projects' (Augoustinos and Tileagă, 2012, p. 6). The focus on social change (McNamee and Hosking, 2012) might well be the book's adage, considering our effort to situate discursive organizational psychology within a generative ecology (Gergen, 1978).

More concretely, we take a particular interest in theorizing social change from a discourse perspective (Barrett, Thomas and Hocevar, 1995; Berger and Luckmann, 1966; Gergen, 1991; Rabinow and Sullivan, 1979); this approach has gained credibility over the past few decades as a useful alternative method for studying the phenomenon and for illuminating the social construction of its meaning (Oswick, Grant, Marshak and Cox, 2010). It has been argued that discourse theory helps to move beyond conventional conceptions which depict organizational change as a systematic or rational process; by focusing on how discourses create, sustain and transform organizations, it emphasizes the complexity of change (Barrett et al., 1995). Discursive studies on change also highlight the importance of taking context into account, by connecting to discourses that were produced before and after the one in focus (Marshak and Grant, 2008); this process makes transparent the complex interplay of socially and historically produced texts which unfold in a non-systematic, iterative and recursive manner (Hardy, 2001).

Thus, in this chapter, we recreate the context of OP in which we think discursive approaches can be fruitfully inscribed. What can push forward OP, so we argue, is the careful identification of those intellectual threads and conceptual ideas that stem from and are in alignment with the discursive turn; we can use them to intervene in the ways we address themes and topics as crucial in the field of OP (Augoustinos and Tileagă, 2012). Therefore, we will first briefly sketch how OP's modernist project became increasingly questioned for denying the paradigmatic changes that took place elsewhere in the social sciences and even in its most adjacent fields, such as management and organization studies. Second, we will enumerate some of the alternatives that were developed to place OP on postpositivist rails (Prasad, 2005), through which discursive approaches in OP could begin to be investigated and applied. Then, we will introduce each of the four main themes – participation, resistance, creativity and intervention – through which we want to illustrate how OP theories and practices can be re-thought, and explain each time how change is a crucial dimension of this reframing. In discussing those themes, we will also situate the subsequent chapters of this book within the developing landscape of discursive studies in OP.

ORGANIZATIONAL PSYCHOLOGY IN RETROSPECT

For over a century, OP has been an independent field of psychology (Reichman, 2014). It has commonly been defined as the study of human behavior in the context of the workplace (for example, Katz and Kahn, 1978) where psychological theories are applied to problems facing organizational systems (Heidbreder, 1961). Historically, OP has played an important role in attaching meaning to paid work and thus to the identities of individuals who are involved in organized work practices. In pre-industrial times wage labor was not considered a superior form of work, but the industrialization of capitalist societies brought about a distinction between work and non-work which is still reflected in today's over-simplified demarcation between a public and a private sphere of life (Pahl, 1988). OP, as a scientific ally to industrialization, soon became associated with practices of human resource management and job enrichment, which modified the physical and organizational variables of factory work (Lawthom, 1999). While organizational forms and practices have changed considerably over the last century, OP as a pragmatic and vocational discipline is still enmeshed in its original concerns with human resource practices including job design, career development and training, issues of organizational development and change, leadership, decision-making, well-being at work, employee engagement, motivation, retention and work–life dynamics (Donaldson and Dollwet, 2013).

In a critical reading (Hollway, 1991), the (above) historical narrative of OP can be seen as a modernist parable. While OP presents itself as an ideologically neutral domain of technical expertise, many of its interventions were subtly driven by the interests of the organization (Lawthom, 1999). Influenced by the school of functionalism, aspects of employee health and safety, job satisfaction, motivation and work–life balance were usually evaluated by measuring how well they served the goals of the organization (Reichman, 2014). Even seemingly humanistic concerns with the well-being of employees were tailored toward increasing organizational effectiveness (Donaldson and Dollwet, 2013; see also Gorgievski, Bakker and Schaufeli, 2010; Harter, Schmidt and Hayes, 2002), namely by means of increasing employee engagement, participation and productivity, while at the same time decreasing turnover rates, absenteeism and deviance. Because of this focus, OP practitioners were critiqued for often being servants of business and the powerful, as they were seemingly paying only lip service to the well-being and rights of the workers. In this regard, it was noted that scholars of OP increasingly moved to business schools or management departments, giving priority to business issues and organizational concerns (Highhouse and Schmitt, 2012) at the expense of public and social welfare issues (Spink and Spink, 2015). For instance, Highhouse (2006, p. 205) questioned this trend in the following comment: 'We should not be a field that merely services organizational problems, and we should not allow research programs to be dictated by rapidly fluctuating economic conditions and management whims.'

Not surprisingly then, OP research seemed to follow a similar 'functionalistic' logic, showing little effort to examine and develop the field's underlying epistemological assumptions that influence how studies are undertaken, constructed and evaluated (Johnson and Cassell, 2001). Many social science and managerial disciplines have put themselves through a period of critical analysis in which they questioned their own foundations, but OP seems to have mainly missed this moment of disciplinary self-questioning, neglecting significant insights from 'alternative' perspectives such as interpretivism, postmodernism or critical theory (Symon and Cassell, 2006). In this it is much like the discipline of psychology which has been predominantly entrenched in a positivistic paradigm.

Even if a considerable number of OP scholars have engaged with these alternatives (Hollway, 1991; Hosking, Dachler and Gergen, 1995) apparently these attempts were not enough to alter the positivist status quo, buried within the sediments of history (Johnson and Cassell, 2001). This situation led Peter Herriot and Neil Anderson (1997, p. 13), to note this about personnel psychology (seen as an elementary part of OP):

> No other sub-discipline in the organizational sciences has exhibited such a paucity of theoretical perspectives, such a lack of debate over guiding paradigmatic assumptions and such unquestioned conformity to naive, managerialist positivism. And if the discipline fails to stimulate a diversity of theoretical perspectives and epistemological approaches, then it runs the risk of becoming an overheated engine house of remote, blind empiricism.

As many OP scholars seemed to cling to the mainstream position of their field, other scholars, feeling increasingly uneasy with this status quo, formulated heartfelt pleas to open up the scope of the discipline. For instance, Phil Johnson and Catherine Cassell (2001) suggested more epistemological reflexivity in OP, inviting scholars to explore their own thinking and their epistemological pre-understandings, as well as the possibility of alternative commitments. This would require that organizational psychologists become skeptical about how they engage with the world, what categories they deploy and what assumptions their interpretations are based on. As the authors suggest, reflexivity 'encourages irony and humility as well as rebellion against the imposition of any totalizing meta-narrative which erases plurality through discursive closure' (Johnson and Cassell, 2001, p. 137). Such a reflexive engagement would make OP scholars aware of the choices available to them for confronting and challenging their epistemological and methodological commitments, and thus, for developing OP into a critical, mature and pluralistic research-based discipline where several alternatives can flourish.

ALTERNATIVES IN ORGANIZATIONAL PSYCHOLOGY

The title of the book by Dian Marie Hosking, Peter Dachler and Kenneth Gergen (1995), *Management and Organization: Relational Alternatives to Individualism*, neatly reflects how scholars were urgently considering alternatives to break through OP's paradigmatic conformity (Symon and Cassell, 2006). What quickly became obvious was that work and organizational psychology was actually a very fertile playing field for experimenting with new paradigmatic positions, and the different conceptual and methodological alternatives on offer, not in the least as it gained support from parallel developments in organization studies. Illustrative for this joint pioneering work were the qualitative handbooks by the organizational psychologists Catherine Cassell and Gillian Symon (Cassell and Symon, 1994; 2004; Symon and Cassell, 1998; 2012) who also inaugurated a new journal in 2006: *Qualitative Research in Organizations and Management.*

The search for alternatives led OP scholars to become familiar with new 'traditions' (Prasad, 2005), including social constructionism, critical theory, feminism and poststructuralism; these have all been crucial to understand the emergence of a discursive organizational psychology. Inspiration for what these alternatives could look like was drawn from the ground-breaking work by several scholars. Among them, Kenneth Gergen (1985) outlined a social constructionist approach to (social) psychology, Nikolas Rose (1985) undertook a historical reconstruction of the psychological complex, and Ian Parker and John Shotter (1990) edited a volume in which poststructuralist ideas were applied to deconstruct social psychology. What connected these various radical reformulations was their focus on possibilities of change and the effort to instigate the political engagement of psychology with society. More concretely, while they were concerned with the social conditions of life more generally, these alternative psychologies also began to inquire into the ideological project of psychology as a discipline; they uncovered how theories of psychology are culturally and historically constructed, how a psychological culture operates beyond academic and professional practices, how surveillance and self-regulation operate in everyday life, and how everyday activities can provide the basis for resistance to contemporary disciplinary practices (Parker and Burman, 2008).

First, an important alternative was developed around the much-debated rise of a social constructionist epistemology. Social constructionism attracted attention across the social sciences, embracing a variety of discursive approaches (Burr, 2003; 2015). Also scholars from OP were smitten by social constructionism, which was increasingly debated in workshops and at conferences in the area of organizational psychology and organizational research in general. Illustrative of this spillover was the book collaboration between organizational psychologists Dian Marie Hosking and Peter Dachler with Kenneth Gergen as one of the pioneers of social constructionism in psychology. But other social constructionist thinkers such as John Shotter (1993) were also influencing the view on organizations as conversational realities (Cunliffe and Shotter, 2006; Holman and

Thorpe, 2002). The social construction of organization was explored in thematic books (Hosking and McNamee, 2006) as well as in special issues on, for instance, learning (Hosking and Bouwen, 2000) or community and applied social psychology (Hosking and Morley, 2004). In the meantime, many of the themes in these social constructionist understandings of organizations have become expanded into processual approaches to organization (Cooren, Vaara, Langley and Tsoukas, 2014). Considered as a 'meta-theory' about relationality for communal organizing, social constructionism has opened up processual, relational and dialogical understandings of work and organization (Gergen and Thatchenkery, 2004; Shotter, 2008; Steyaert and Van Looy, 2010) which shared similar critical stances on methodology, knowledge creation, and the relationship between theory and practice, as well as a strong alignment with feminist and poststructuralist theory.

Second, even if OP might seem to be a natural home for critical theory, critical perspectives have remained on the periphery of the discipline, contrasting strongly with the way critical psychology (Parker, 2015) expanded in general. Revisiting the history of OP, Spink and Spink (2015) argued that OP was much more involved with public debate than usually assumed, as it also took an interest in public organizations, being more concerned with societal than business interests (Spink and Spink, 2015). Following such early attempts at keeping a distance from OP's managerialist position, a whole range of themes in organizational behavior and work psychology have been analyzed over the years from a critical perspective (Wilson, 2014) in an attempt to nurture more equal employment relations. Nevertheless, as Islam and Zyphur (2009) argue, there is still much room and potential for critical work and thus for new and interesting debates in all the major subfields of OP. Critical theory in this area would invite an analysis of the socioeconomic parameters which frame and condition people's (working) lives and which, in the worst case, enchain them. Critical OP scholars taking a discursive stance might for example erode the apparently self-evident meta-narratives of mainstream OP by emphasizing how phenomena such as stress, motivation or personality, which organizational psychologists take to be 'real', are rhetorically produced linguistic constructs (Johnson and Cassell, 2001). They might additionally question and reframe social categories such as careers, organizational culture and work-related stress as being power-relevant (Islam and Zyphur, 2009). By doing so, they would deconstruct the scientific status that has been accorded to seemingly neutral OP discourses but they might also suggest new routes to make work meaningful again.

Third, feminist theories and pedagogies have paved the way for a discursive organizational psychology. Feminist theories shed valuable light on the gendered nature of organizations and the wider societal power relations that are reproduced in the workplace. But they also allow researchers to do far more. Drawing upon the seminal article on the 'F-word' by Marta Calás and Linda Smircich (1992), Rebecca Lawthom (1999) undertook a similar analysis, in which she took issue with the dialectic relationship between theory and practice by breaking down the hierarchy which separates the two. In Lawthom's view, feminist approaches form core 'attempts to de/reconstruct and alter/change societal contexts such as organizations, contexts in which traditional psychological links have reigned with the effect of disempowering employees' (Lawthom, 1999, p. 65). With a particular focus on the idea of *praxis*, feminist understandings can indeed offer insights into the practical activities of organizational psychologists by reconstructing and changing organizational and societal spaces.

OVERVIEW OF THE BOOK

In providing an overview of the book, we want to plot how the various empirical studies in this book address and adapt the key themes that belong to the to-be-expected repertoire of OP, thereby helping to expand its horizon. More concretely, the chapters to follow in this collection report on some exemplary studies that have been developed in the intersection between OP themes and discursive understandings. They include empirically rich discussions of both traditional and widely studied topics such as resistance, participation, inclusion and exclusion, along with multi-stakeholder collaboration and diversity management, as well as newer research topics such as language negotiations, work time arrangements, technology development and discourse analysis as intervention. The authors have used a range of discourse analytical devices to address these phenomena, including interpretative repertoires, discursive practices, modes of ordering, rhetorical strategies and sensemaking narratives. Furthermore, some chapters have an interventionist character in that they expose or critique certain forms of domination in order to arrive at more equal and agreed upon social relations (see also Symon and Cassell, 2006), or they draw upon discourse analysis to intervene in the context of a change intervention (see Dey and Resch, Chapter 14 this volume). Hence, in the following few pages, we give a brief description of each chapter, elaborating issues of change in the context of the four more specific themes of participation, resistance, creativity and intervention.

Participation and Change

Participation in organizational change and decision-making processes was one of the earliest interests of organizational psychologists (French and Bell, 1999), and today the concept continues to grow more popular. The early rationale for participation was grounded in the expectation that employees are more likely to accept decisions in which they were invited to participate (Austin and Bartunek, 2012). And indeed, the most widely shared understanding of participation is that it circumvents power relations by giving voice to those who are normally marginalized and by representing their interests in the design, implementation, and outcomes of certain (change) programs (Kesby, 2005). Moreover, some suggest that this redistribution of power can help to establish more reciprocal relationships and eliminate hierarchy among participants, thereby making space for 'participatory democracy' (Healey, 1997, p. 5). As participative forms of organizing can redefine and reopen existing boundaries, they may lead to relational practices that are 'naturally' more inclusive (Steyaert and Van Looy, 2010).

And yet, amidst this plethora of largely positive accounts, there are several critical interpretations of the concept (Kesby, 2005). Critics have argued, for instance, that very often the goal of participation is an instrumental one: to orchestrate multiple and opposing voices, stakeholders and interests into a widely shared consensus. In that case, rather than overcoming power relations, participatory approaches may impose a new system of domination (Michels, Chapter 4 this volume) and thus produce a new subject position of 'compliant participant' (Henkel and Stirrat, 2001). Moreover, while participation makes claims to inclusivity, its orthodoxy may in fact help to exclude those who refuse to participate (Cleaver, 2001; Kothari, 2001). Likewise it could be argued, however, that rather than being a new form of power that should be resisted, participation can also be interpreted as a practice that enables resistance namely through radical, transformative and political praxis (Kesby, 2005).

In this book, based on the chapters that follow, we take the stance that the project of participative organizing, when oriented toward social change and emancipation, needs (and continues) to be an ongoing endeavor (see also Steyaert and Van Looy, 2010). Moreover, three of the chapters around the theme of participation help to expand the original focus of employee participation by addressing different, and creative, modes of participating which take note of aesthetic and affective dynamics (Michels, Chapter 4 this volume), or which require the ability to endure paradoxes instead of opting for consensus (Heydenreich, Chapter 3 this volume). Moreover, the critical debate around participation is advanced by carefully zooming in on the intricate relationship between 'ideal' discourses of inclusion and 'actual' practices of exclusion that are formed around practices of (non-) participation (Nentwich and Ostendorp, Chapter 5 this volume). What connects these three chapters is that they are all concerned with understanding the relationship between discursive enactments and democratic forms of organizing, whether in the context of planning multi-party collaboration (Heydenreich), planning a new museum (Michels) or keeping a community's sports club thriving (Nentwich and Ostendorp).

In Chapter 3, Anna-Katrin Heydenreich explores aspects of participation in the context of multi-stakeholder collaboration. More concretely, by questioning the paradigmatic assumption that convergence has to be achieved in order to collaborate successfully, she examines how people tackled the paradox of divergence and convergence during the preparation phase for the UN World Summit on Sustainable Development in Johannesburg, South Africa in 2002. The conference itself aimed at a collaborative agreement on environmental issues through 'stakeholder action'. Basing her analysis predominantly on a series of meeting conversations, Heydenreich shows that both convergence and divergence are created through five different discourses, all contributing to a different understanding of what it means to collaborate. Through shifting between these discourses, different interplays are produced that manage the paradox between divergence and convergence in different ways and with different consequences. With this analysis Heydenreich contributes to research exploring how collaboration as a participatory process can be organized.

In Chapter 4 we move from planning on a global scale to a more local planning endeavor, as Christoph Michels describes the planning process for a new art museum which involved the participation of many different stakeholders. By introducing a new understanding of participation as 'performative', he draws special attention to the different affective modes and dynamics among human and non-human participants, which all evoke distinctive versions of a future museum. For his analysis of affective dynamics, Michels mainly drew on his auto-ethnographic vignettes and on photographs taken during his field research to reconstruct his aesthetic experience and to reflect upon the aesthetic qualities encountered in different spaces that were chosen as key sites for interaction during the planning process.

In the analysis of this material he then zooms in on what John Law (1994) refers to as 'modes of ordering'. These are large-scale ordering patterns that share similarities with the notion of discourse, but that reach beyond language by explicitly attending to the performances of sociomaterial and bodily practices. Michels then distinguishes three modes that respectively co-enacted the identities of their participants. The insight gained through this (post-)discursive engagement is that different logics and practices of organizing, anchored in the aesthetic performance of places, invite different forms of participation and different imaginations of a future (museum). With this study he contributes to a call for more reflexivity regarding which performances one wishes to participate in and which ones are preferably to be resisted.

In Chapter 5, Julia Nentwich and Anja Ostendorp look at dynamics of participation in the context of a women's sports club. More concretely, they investigate the paradoxical relationship between the ideal of 'inclusion' and practices of 'exclusion'. Their in-depth analysis of a group discussion with women of a particular sports association illustrates how exclusion is practiced and inclusion inhibited through complex moves of what the authors term 'manoeuvring acts': a well-orchestrated interplay of creating positive in- and negative out-groups. In these manoeuvring acts, which allowed group participants to produce exclusion in a legitimate and hence politically correct manner, people shifted continuously between three interpretative repertoires: 'harmony with like-minded people', 'open-minded cosmopolitism' and 'the problematic Other'. Rhetorical strategies of 'categorization', 'generalization', 'creating facticity' and 'denying racism' moreover helped them to camouflage and stabilize the exclusion. By understanding participation through examining how exclusion and inclusion are discursive effects, the authors indicate that neither of them represents a static state, as people negotiate their feelings of (not) belonging to an in-group, along with the resulting in- and out-group identities, in everyday talk.

Resistance and Change

In the next section we move to the theme of resistance that often gets associated with change. Depending on the discursive context in which it appears, resistance can have either positive or negative connotations. Throughout the 20th century, employee 'resistance to change' – as an almost unchallenged notion – was consistently conceptualized as a dysfunctional phenomenon and a barrier to well-intended and desirable change (Bauer, 1991). A large body of management research was therefore concerned with how to minimize, overcome or eliminate such resistance (Collinson, 1994). While this negative framing reflects the historical context in which the concept of resistance was introduced to the organizational literature on change, Mumby (2005) noted that over the past few decades (and we can add another one since his publication), organization and management studies evolved around an implicit binary which either privileged organizational processes of control – such as those exhibited in top-down change initiatives – or which cele-brated and partly romanticized employee efforts to resist these control mechanisms.

Rather than following the binary, in this research guide we try to shift the focus toward more processual understandings of how resistance and change are in fact co-productive. More concretely, contemporary OP studies, which explore possibilities of resistance, such as Chapters 6 to 8 of this collection, often aim to de-naturalize dominant constructions of reality, including those that have been reified and naturalized as OP concepts and practices. These studies are based on the understanding that realities are not fixed and that the major site for challenging and changing them is, once again, language (Collinson, 1994). From this perspective, new meanings, negotiations and in(ter)ventions become possible through the re-opening of marginalized and repressed discourses. Even if power takeovers by dominant or hegemonic discourses make it almost impossible to imagine alternative discourses and practices, there is also an apprecia-tion that every dominant discourse or practice makes space for contradic-tions, and this in turn helps to challenge an existing status quo and to support alternative reality constructions.

By shedding more light on how dominant constructions are produced and to what effects, and how they can possibly be resisted, we believe that the following three chapters make a valuable contribution. At the same time, these studies do not fall for a naïve depiction of change as being simply a matter of speaking differently about something (see also Parker, 2002; Parker and Burman, 2008). Acknowledging that change is not a matter of easily talking oneself out of oppressive social relations or damaging identity constructions, the authors remain sensitive to the possibility that resistance may actually reinforce the power effects that it tries to defy. And yet, by zooming in on the micro-dynamics of everyday practices – whether resisting the entrepreneurial discourse in the context of aid organizations (Dey, Chapter 6 this volume), countering the norm of full-time work in a research institution (Hoyer and Nentwich, Chapter 7 this volume) or questioning the dominant position of English in a mul-tinational company (Steyaert, Ostendorp, and Gaibrois, Chapter 8 this volume) – the authors invite some optimism that resistance can and will continue to happen.

In Chapter 6, Pascal Dey adopts discourse analysis as a way to denatu-ralize and develop an immanent critique of the solidified discourse on entrepreneurship and thus to tease out the power of this discourse by looking at resistant forms of it in which its meanings are received differ-ently and appropriated. Drawing on interviews with practitioners from a range of Swiss non-governmental organizations, he investigates how the discourse of entrepreneurship, as it becomes increasingly infused into the field of development aid, is adopted, altered or resisted. Using the micro-discursive approach developed by Potter and Wetherell (1987), his analysis offers a clearer understanding of how NGO practitioners interpret the entrepreneurship discourse from their local position, and he discloses the situated agency of the NGO practitioners as they are increasingly hailed as entrepreneurs. The analysis identifies and juxtaposes the interpretative repertoires of 'benevolence', 'professionalism' and 'enterprising', and their respective subject positions of 'ideal-type helper', 'down-to-earth professional' and 'autonomous and risk-taking self-starter'. This investigation is important because it demonstrates convincingly how micro-discursive approaches permit us to pinpoint the inherently critical capacity of language to create socially pertinent meaning that resists dominant discourse. According to Dey, a micro-discourse analysis illustrates that people already have the potential for resistance and, by implication, change, as part of their everyday existence.

In Chapter 7, Patrizia Hoyer and Julia Nentwich present a study on the possibilities of change in everyday organizational realities, namely in the form of part-time work. More concretely, they investigate rhetorical strategies that aim to legitimize part-time work as a valid alternative to the norm of full-time work. Based on interviews conducted with both part-time and full-time workers at a science and engineering research institution, their analysis focuses on the rhetorical interplay between arguments which construct the dominant discourse of full-time work and counter-arguments which contest exactly these arguments, thereby suggesting alternative reality constructions. Concerning the discursive framework, the authors make visible a line of history, showing how the work of Bakhtin (1981; 1986) came into psychology through Billig's (1987) work on rhetorics. By taking a rhetorical perspective on resistance, the authors aspire to contribute to a micro-discursive understanding of how organizational logics may gradually shift over time, when the dominant discourses that shape these logics are persistently being undermined and altered in minor rhetorical moves. By focusing in on these rhetorical nuances, the authors show that resistance is not necessarily a matter of grand opposition, but rather an achievement of minor rhetorical moves. They illustrate in detail how certain reality constructions were 'reified' and made rhetorically persuasive and how other arguments were 'ironized' in an equally convincing way, thus challenging or even changing the assumptions that underlie the argument.

In Chapter 8, Chris Steyaert, Anja Ostendorp and Claudine Gaibrois address the complex theme of multilingualism by discursively investigating the different ways in which people account for the use of language in multi-lingual settings. This question is particularly interesting considering the controversial debate around English as an emerging lingua franca which possibly calls for resistance. Empirically, they examine how multilingualism is negotiated within the context of two Swiss-based yet multilingual companies which differ in their degree of global orientation and thus their relationships to the use of English. In the discourse analysis the team of researchers distinguished six discursive practices (Wetherell, 2001), revealing how people accounted differently for the use of languages. Inspired by the work of Appadurai (1996), they frame the combinations of accounts as 'linguascapes'. The notion of linguascape points to the discursive dynamics among a plethora of discourses that negotiate language use across a specific organizational space. Applying the term in a socio-political sense, the authors draw attention to the complex processes and the potential (im)balances that can be found in the multilingual composition of organizational communication. Overall, the study documents that a discursive perspective is useful for helping to understand how people deal with language diversity, including the possible effect of 'overthrowing' the hegemony of English as a lingua franca.

Creativity and Change

If the easiest way to change something is probably to create something different, creativity is seen to be crucial to deal with the many changes we are confronted with (Glaveanu, 2010). Also, creativity is not something that starts from a tabula rasa situation but is situated in a socio-cultural context of existing practices, ideas and values. This implies that current practices and ideas need to be questioned and changed but often not totally dismissed or 'destroyed'; rather there is a form of continuation, while other parts are rewritten, or re-contextualized. In contrast, in OP, the approach to creation has predominantly been characterized by a focus on heroic and individual creativity (Bilton, 2007). In his overview of paradigms of creativity in psychology, Glaveanu (2010) underlines how psychologists study creativity in an elitist and essentialist way, only slowly turning to understand it as an ordinary and everyday event that comes into being through relational, cultural and material practices. In this book, we engage with such a socio-cultural view on creativity (Steyaert, 2014) which is enacted in dialogical (Pfyl, Chapter 9 this volume), sensemaking (Jacobs, Steyaert and Ueberbacher, Chapter 10 this volume) and narrative (Hoyer, Chapter 11 this volume) ways.

Therefore, in the section on 'creativity and change', we consider the notion of creativity in relation to change by taking a particular interest in processes of organizing creativity which may result in the creation of new technologies (Jacobs, Steyaert and Ueberbacher) or taking an inventive leap in the unfolding of one's career (Hoyer) but which may also be about small changes that allow us to adapt to the ongoing rules and regulations of everyday business life (Pfyl). Consequently, the empirical focus on creativity has been elaborated in such diverse contexts as banking regulation, technology development and (individual) career change. In relation to discourse, then, creativity is not a spectacular one-time action; instead, it implies an interest in the multiple, plurivocal and sometimes even contradictory foundations of organizing. As Kuhn (2009) notes, studies which examine the multiplicity and heterogeneity of discourses across particular work settings provide a richer and more contextualized conception of organizational phenomena; they do so by emphasizing that organizational life – including change – is often influenced by an array of different discourses and their interplay.

Each of the following three chapters illustrates such a multiplicity of discourses or narratives, which creatively constitute, maintain and possibly alter the heterogeneity and complexity of organizational processes. Creativity, then, is not the invention of something new; instead it forms an effect, a way to handle the tensions between discourses. Whether it is in the form of a centrifugal variation (Pfyl), or in the form of anticipating the (not-yet-existing) user of a new technology (Jacobs, Steyaert and Ueberbacher), or in the imagination of a different career move (Hoyer), the existing practice, identity or self-conception cannot be erased totally; rather it remains at work in the dialogical creation between discourses.

In Chapter 9, Roland Pfyl describes a study which links the OP theme of (non-)compliance toward banking regulations with the investigation of everyday convergent and divergent discursive practices surrounding these regulations. The study brings to our attention a gap between the rationalistic expectations of what banking regulation should ideally perform and the practical realities that failed to prevent the banking system from collapsing into an unprecedented financial crisis. Theoretically, the study is grounded in the Bakhtinian (1981) conception of organizations as heteroglossic. That is, different discourses – in a dialogical way – simultaneously contradict and mutually constitute each other in a struggle between convergent (centripetal) and divergent (centrifugal) discursive forces. In the context of an international bank, the analysis reveals a rationality discourse which claims there exists an objective best way to do everyday work. In seeming opposition to this stance, Pfyl identified three additional discourses – the myth, game and fate discourses – all of which displayed a dynamic struggle with the hegemonic rationality discourse of regulations.

While managers consistently upheld the rationalistic concept of regulations when talking about abstract organizational themes, they immediately switched to one of these other discourses when speaking about concrete and particular situations of everyday practices. Pfyl's analysis shows that centripetal forces tended to mimic and to standardize the hegemonic rationality discourse, while their centrifugal counterparts resisted discursive closure by offering alternative and counter-hegemonic worldviews that would de-couple the rationality discourse from actual working practices. According to Pfyl it is exactly this simultaneous presence of centripetal and centrifugal forces which explains the existence, and the persistence, of the expectations gap of banking regulation.

In Chapter 10, Claus Jacobs, Chris Steyaert and Florian Ueberbacher investigate the discursive processes through which 'intended users' are identified by different key stakeholders within the broader context of technology and systems development. To do so, they conducted a case study at the European Organization for Nuclear Research (CERN) on the development of a not-yet-stabilized technology: grid computing. They followed a project for establishing a pan-European multi-science grid infrastructure; the project involved four distinct communities including high-energy physicists, scientists from other disciplines, and IT service providers as well as the European Commission as funder of the project.

Assuming that a given technological artifact has no singular, inherent user, the authors took a particular interest in the variety of user concepts that people constructed through a number of different prospective sense-making narratives. Their analysis identified four distinct such narratives that the communities drew upon to conceptualize both the technology of grid computing and the intended users. As the authors maintain, these concepts may in fact have broader relevance and contribute to a more fine-grained understanding of prospective consumers and clients, not only in the context of grid computing but also in other areas where potential users need to be anticipated in processes of innovation, strategy formulation, or entrepreneurial creation.

In the last chapter of this section, Patrizia Hoyer addresses the question of why some people may be more successful than others at creating an alternative identity in the course of a career change. Taking a narrative perspective, she draws particular attention to a variety of transition narratives which function as legitimizing resources for people to distance themselves from previous self-concepts, while at the same time allowing them to experiment with new sources of meaning and to create alternative identities. Her analysis, of how former management consultants narrated the story of their career shift, focuses on four particular transition narratives (re-invention, alteration, re-enactment and stagnation) which help to account for some of the variation observed in career change experiences.

Her analysis also reveals a good indicator of how successful speakers will be in achieving alternative identity constructions in a new work environment: the radicalness of the career change and the contextual resources those speakers can call on to tell more or less compelling transition narratives. Thus we see that choices around a career change are dynamic and relational, as they are socially constructed in dialogue with others.

Intervention and Change

When looking at the relationship between intervention and change it is worth noting that – from its very beginnings – organizational psychology has been characterized by several approaches to intervention (Austin and Bartunek, 2012). This implies that, unlike other social science disciplines, OP takes the role of practice into account and has an identifiable practitioner community (Johnson and Cassell, 2001). We find one form of intervention particularly interesting: the discursive and narrative interventions which highlight the role of language and rhetoric in organizational change endeavors (Ford and Ford, 2008; Oswick et al., 2010). Theoretically, these interventions are rooted in sensemaking (Weick, 1995) and interpretive approaches to organizations (Boje, 1991). They are based on the assumption that discourse is not only a means for understanding organizational change, but in fact a way to generate and shape it.

As Heracleous and Barrett (2001) note, discourses guide people's interpretations of events, thereby also prompting their everyday behaviors and work routines. In fact – in addition to strategies, structures and rewards – discourse may become an important lever for organizational change (Marshak and Grant, 2008). Considering change as an element of social interaction (Bushe and Marshak, 2009; Ford and Ford, 2009; Phillips, Lawrence and Hardy, 2004), Gergen, Gergen and Barrett (2004) particularly emphasize the transformative capacity of dialogue. They argue that it can create space for new meanings, generate shifts in attitude and behavior when organizational members start to operate under new assumptions, and transform the knowledge base and practices upon which an organization rests; thus it can produce conditions conductive to organizational change (Marshak and Grant, 2008). In that sense, organizational change can be facilitated or even generated by developing new stories and building consensus around a shared vision for an alternative future (Austin and Bartunek, 2012; Ford and Ford, 2008). In other words, new ways of talking about something can generate possibilities for new actions (Barrett et al., 1995).

While discursive and narrative interventions are becoming more popular, thus far few scholarly researchers have theorized them in the context of change processes (Austin and Bartunek, 2012). In addressing this gap, the final three chapters illuminate how change can come about through a variety of interventions; their approach is to focus on the discursive negotiations which each intervention elicits. By doing this, the chapters help to document and explain both the discursive and the post-discursive enactment of (change) interventions in which the organizing process remains open, thus allowing for new and sometimes surprising possibilities to emerge. In these three chapters, classical interventions such as diversity initiatives (Ostendorp and Steyaert) and coaching conversations (Schulz) are critically considered for the kind of changes they effect, while discourse analysis itself becomes an intervention in a process of consulting for change (Dey and Resch).

In Chapter 12, Anja Ostendorp and Chris Steyaert present a study on how difference is constructed and enacted in the context of organizational diversity initiatives. As the authors note, 'diversity' is currently perceived as a fashionable concept which companies imitate until they increasingly resemble each other around the globe. At the same time, the notion of 'diversity management' may be re-interpreted and translated differently into various local contexts and their micro-political sensemaking processes. To discursively investigate such local sensemaking processes, the authors conducted interviews with employees and with diversity professionals participating in diversity interventions in six Swiss-based organizations. Following a discourse psychological approach to analyze the interview data, the authors identified four specific interpretative repertoires that interviewees drew upon in order to make sense of various diversity initiatives and of the notion of difference more generally. Three of these repertoires framed diversity interventions as irrelevant for the organization, as designed only for specific minorities, and as potentially causing conflicts over resources among different minority groups. Within these constructions, difference became positioned as a taboo, as a need, or as a source for dispute. In contrast, a fourth interpretative repertoire reframed diversity engagements as a necessary element to be included in the overall hybridized organization; this conception overturns the dominant logic around the 'ideal worker' and the understanding that difference is a topic to be dealt with only by diversity professionals. By showing the implications of each repertoire for either enabling or foreclosing difference, this study helps to explain the dilemma of managing diversity. That is: the more that diversity management tries to explicitly nurture differences, the more diversity may become situated at the margins rather than the center of organizations.

In Chapter 13, Florian Schulz investigates a particular form of HRM intervention: individual-centered management coaching which is organized and paid for by the coachee's employer. By investigating the dynamics and potential effects of coaching practices, Schulz seeks to expand the critical-reflexive understanding of how employees are managed through these practices. Empirically, the chapter is based on an in-depth analysis of the opening sessions of coaching conversations which aim to increase people's self-awareness, self-regulation and relationship management skills.

Based on a discursive psychology framework, the analysis documents how the managers showed variations in their interpretations of problems, while the coach persistently promoted a 'psychic dynamics' repertoire, thereby enacting a classical psychotherapeutic framework. This observation suggests that the coach partly ignored the variety of concerns the managers initially presented, and instead, conducted the conversation in a routinized form, seeing problems as internalized and emotionalized and more or less neglecting contextual variables. While management coaching has mostly been framed as a space for reflection, this study highlights how HRM interventions such as coaching may also be understood as new forms of management which help to shape and control people's emotions and thereby produce more intense regimes of the self.

In the final chapter of this book, Pascal Dey and Dörte Resch illustrate the interventionist potential of discourse analysis to change organizational realities rather than just analyze and interpret them. Situated in the context of a consultancy project for a large German voluntary organization, the authors describe how they intervened in a conflict between managers and employees of that organization. The conflict revolved around the introduction of a new accounting system which entailed strict controls over all operations. While managers considered these reforms crucial to ensure the organization would survive financially, employees experienced these new arrangements as a threat to the social, humanistic mission of the organization.

Overall, the project involved a series of steering committee meetings with key stakeholders, and a thorough effort to seek opinions from employees via questionnaires, followed by several workshops where members of the organization were updated about the insights gained during the project. The authors' intervention consisted of two interrelated steps. Considering discourse analysis as a vehicle for conflict resolution, they first created democratic, discursive spaces that offered members of the organization an opportunity to vent their frustration and to create awareness of antagonistic discursive practices – namely the activation of either a social or managerial repertoire – which triggered tensions and conflict. Second, they initiated a generative dialogue between the opposing parties to allow for more affirmative re-interpretations of the changing process, and thus, for a more affirmative mode of exchange. By emphasizing the practical value of discourse analysis, the authors illustrate how an interventionist usage – such as one in the context of a consultancy project – can make competing discourses within an organization more transparent, thereby helping organizational members to re-evaluate these discourses and to ultimately suspend organizational conflicts.

CONCLUSION

In this book on discursive organizational psychology we have developed an understanding of contemporary OP that lets us create a bridge between psychological and social theory for the investigation and problematization of organizational phenomena. While we have been keen to reflect critically on the ways people use psychological concepts in contemporary life, we also aim for a discipline informed by what Brown and Stenner (2009) call 'reflexive and creative foundationalism'. That means we are eager to develop a way of thinking about organization(s) that affirms the creative possibilities of a life. Therefore, we also see this book as enabling 'interventions-that-make-a-difference' in how organizations co-constitute and alter society. As we have zoomed in on many engaged, critical and also creative projects, we hope that this book can offer a taste of a contemporary discursive OP, including a broad variety of themes that can be studied in the future along these imaginative trajectories.

REFERENCES

Appadurai, Arjun (1996), *Modernity at Large. Cultural Dimensions of Globalization*, Minneapolis, MN: University of Minnesota Press.
Augoustinos, Martha and Cristian Tileagă (2012), 'Twenty five years of discursive psychology', *The British Journal of Social Psychology*, **51** (3), 405–412.
Austin, John R. and Jean M. Bartunek (2012), 'Organization change and development: In practice and in theory', in Irving Weiner, Walter C. Borman and Daniel R. Ilgen (eds), *Handbook of Psychology, Volume 12: Industrial and Organizational Psychology* (Second Edition), Somerset, NJ: Wiley, pp. 309–327.
Bakhtin, Mikhail M. (1981), *The Dialogic Imagination*, Austin, TX: University of Texas Press.
Bakhtin, Mikhail M. (1986), *Speech, Genres and Other Late Essays*, Austin, TX: University of Texas Press.
Barrett, Frank J., Gial F. Thomas and Susan P. Hocevar (1995), 'The central role of discourse in large-scale change: A social construction perspective', *The Journal of Applied Behavioral Science*, **31** (3), 352–372.
Bauer, Martin (1991), 'Resistance to change – a monitor of new technology', *Systems Practice*, **4** (3), 181–196.

Berger, Peter and Thomas Luckmann (1966), *Social Construction of Reality*, New York: Doubleday.

Billig, Michael (1987), *Arguing and Thinking: A Rhetorical Approach to Social Psychology*, Cambridge: Cambridge University Press.

Bilton, Chris (2007), *Management and Creativity: From Creative Industries to Creative Management*, Boston, MA: Blackwell Publishing.

Boje, David (1991), 'The storytelling organization: A study of story performance in an office supply firm', *Administrative Science Quarterly*, **36** (1), 106–126.

Brown, Steve D. and Paul Stenner (2009), *Psychology Without Foundations: History, Philosophy and Psychosocial Theory*, London: Sage.

Burr, Vivien (2003), *Social Constructionism* (Second Edition), New York: Routledge.

Burr, Vivien (2015), *Social Constructionism* (Third Edition), New York: Routledge.

Bushe, Gervase and Robert Marshak (2009), 'Revisioning organization development: Diagnostic and dialogic premises and patters of practice', *Journal of Applied Behavioral Science*, **45** (3), 348–368.

Calás, Marta and Linda Smircich (1992), 'Using the "F" word: Feminist theories and social consequences of organizational research', in Albert J. Mills and Peta Tancred (eds), *Gendering Organizational Analysis*, London: Sage, pp. 222–234.

Cassell, Catherine and Gillian Symon (1994), *Qualitative Methods in Organizational Research: A Practical Guide*, London: Sage.

Cassell, Catherine and Gillian Symon (2004), *Essential Guide to Qualitative Methods in Organizational Research*, London: Sage.

Cleaver, Frances (2001), 'Institutions, agencies, and the limits of participatory approaches to development', in Bill Cooke and Uma Kothari (eds), *Participation: The New Tyranny?*, London: Zed, pp. 36–55.

Collinson, David (1994), 'Strategies of resistance. Power, knowledge and subjectivity in the workplace', in John M. Jermier, David Knights and Walter R. Nord (eds), *Resistance and Power in Organisations*, London: Routledge, pp. 25–68.

Cooren, Francois, Eero Vaara, Ann Langley and Haridimos Tsoukas (2014), *Language and Communication at Work: Discourse, Narrativity, and Organizing*, Oxford: Oxford University Press.

Cunliffe, Anne J. and John Shotter (2006) 'Wittgenstein, Bakhtin, management and the dialogical', in Dian Marie Hosking and Sheila McNamee (eds), *The Social Construction of Organization*, Oslo: Liber CBS Press, pp. 226–239.

Donaldson, Stewart I. and Maren Dollwet (2013), 'Taming the waves and wild horses of positive organizational psychology', *Advances in Positive Organizational Psychology*, **1**, 1–21.

Ford, Jeffrey and Laurie Ford (2008), 'Conversational profiles: A tool for altering the conversational patters of change managers', *Journal of Applied Behavioral Science*, **44**, 445–467.

Ford, Jeffrey and Laurie Ford (2009), *The Four Conversations: Daily Communication that gets Results*, San Francisco, CA: Berrett-Koehler.

French, Wendell L. and Cecil Bell (1999). *Organization Development* (Sixth Edition), Englewood Cliffs, NJ: Prentice Hall.

Gergen, Kenneth J. (1978) 'Toward generative theory', *Journal of Personality and Social Psychology*, **36** (11), 1344–1360.

Gergen, Kenneth J. (1985), 'The social constructionist movement in modern psychology', *American Psychologist*, **40** (3), 266–275.

Gergen, Kenneth J. (1991), *The Saturated Self*, New York: Basic Books.

Gergen, Kenneth J. and Tojo Joseph Thatchenkery (2004), 'Organization science as social construction', *The Journal of Applied Behavioral Science*, **40** (2), 228–249.

Gergen, Kenneth J., Mary M. Gergen and Frank J. Barrett (2004), 'Dialogue: Life and death of the organization', in David Grant, Cynthia Hardy, Cliff Oswick and Linda Putnam (eds), *The Sage Handbook of Organizational Discourse*, London: Sage, pp. 39–60.

Glaveanu, Vlad-Petre (2010), 'Paradigms in the study of creativity: Introducing the perspective of cultural psychology', *New Ideas in Psychology*, **28** (1), 79–93.

Gorgievski, Marjan J., Arnold Bakker and Wilmar Schaufeli (2010), 'Work engagement and workaholism: Comparing the self-employed and salaried employees', *Journal of Positive Psychology*, **5**, 83–96.

Hardy, Cynthia (2001), 'Researching organizational discourse', *International Studies of Management and Organization*, **31** (3), 25–47.

Harter, James K., Frank L. Schmidt and Theodore Hayes (2002), 'Business-unit-level relationship between employee satisfaction, employee engagement, and business outcomes: A meta-analysis', *Journal of Applied Psychology*, **87** (2), 268–279.

Healey, Patsy (1997), *Collaborative Planning: Shaping Places in Fragmented Societies*, Basingstoke: Macmillan.

Heidbreder, Edna (1961), *Seven Psychologies*, Englewood Cliffs, NJ: Prentice Hall.

Henkel, Heiko and Roderick Stirrat (2001), 'Participation as spiritual duty: Empowerment as secular subjection', in Bill Cooke and Uma Kothari (eds), *Participation: The New Tyranny?*, London: Zed, pp. 168–184.

Heracleous, Loizos and Michael Barrett (2001), 'Organizational change as discourse: Communicative actions and deep structures in the context of information technology implementation', *Academy of Management Journal*, **44** (4), 755–778.

Herriot, Peter and Neil Anderson (1997), *International Handbook of Selection and Assessment*, Chichester: John Wiley.

Highhouse, Scott (2006), 'Commentary – the continental divide', *Journal of Occupational and Organizational Psychology*, **79** (2), 203–206.

Highhouse, Scott and Neal W. Schmitt (2012), 'A snapshot in time: Industrial-Organizational Psychology today', in Irving Weiner, Walter C. Borman and Daniel R. Ilgen (eds), *Handbook of Psychology, Volume 12: Industrial and Organizational Psychology* (Second Edition), Somerset, NJ: Wiley.

Hollway, Wendy (1991), *Work Psychology and Organizational Behaviour*, London: Sage.

Holman, David and Richard Thorpe (2002), *Management and Language. The Manager as a Practical Author*, London: Sage.

Hosking, Dian Marie and René Bouwen (2000), 'Organizational learning: Relational-constructionist approaches: An overview', *European Journal of Work And Organizational Psychology*, **9** (2), 129–132.

Hosking, Dian Marie and Sheila McNamee (eds) (2006), *The Social Construction of Organization*, Oslo: Liber CBS Press.

Hosking, Dian Marie and Ian E. Morley (2004), 'Social constructionism in Community and Applied Social Psychology', *Journal of Community and Applied Social Psychology*, **14** (5), 318–331.

Hosking, Dian Marie, Hans P. Dachler and Kenneth J. Gergen (1995), *Management and Organization: Relational Alternatives to Individualism*, Aldershot: Avebury.

Islam, Gazi and Michael Zyphur (2009), 'Concepts and directions in critical industrial/organizational psychology', in Dennis Fox, Isaac Prilleltensky and Stephanie Austin (eds), *Critical Psychology: An Introduction* (Second Edition), Thousand Oaks, CA: Sage, pp. 110–125.

Johnson, Phil and Catherine Cassell (2001), 'Epistemology and work psychology: New agendas', *Journal of Occupational and Organizational Psychology*, **74** (2), 125–143.

Katz, Daniel and Robert L. Kahn (1978), *The Social Psychology of Organizations*, New York: Wiley.

Kesby, Mike (2005), 'Retheorizing empowerment-through-participation as a performance in space: Beyond tyranny to transformation', *Signs*, **40** (1), 2037–2065.

Kothari, Uma (2001), 'Power, knowledge, and social control in participatory development', in Bill Cooke and Uma Kothari (eds), *Participation: The New Tyranny?*, London: Zed, pp. 139–52.

Kuhn, Timothy (2009), 'Positioning lawyers: Discursive resources, professional ethics and identification', *Organization*, **16** (5), 681–704.

Law, John (1994), *Organizing Modernity*, Oxford: Blackwell.

Lawthom, Rebecca (1999), 'Using the "F" word in organizational psychology: Foundations for critical feminist research', *Annual Review of Critical Psychology*, **1**, 65–78.

Marshak, Robert J. and David Grant (2008), 'Organizational discourse and new organization development practices', *British Journal of Management*, **19** (1), 7–19.

McNamee, Sheila and Dian Marie Hosking (2012), *Research and Social Change: A Relational Constructionist Approach*, London: Routledge.

Mumby, Dennis K. (2005), 'Theorizing resistance in organization studies: A dialectical approach', *Management Communication Quarterly*, **19** (1), 19–44.

Oswick, Cliff, David Grant, Robert Marshak and Julie Wolfram Cox (2010), 'Organizational discourse and change: Positions, perspectives, progress and prospects', *Journal of Applied Behavioral Science*, **46** (1), 8–15.

Pahl, Ray E. (ed.) (1988), *On Work: Historical, Comparative and Theoretical Approaches*, Oxford: Blackwell.

Parker, Ian (2002), *Critical Discursive Psychology*, New York: Palgrave Macmillan.

Parker, Ian (ed.) (2015), *Handbook of Critical Psychology*, London: Routledge.

Parker, Ian and Erica Burman (2008), 'Critical psychology: Four theses and seven misconceptions', *Hellenic Journal of Psychology*, **5** (1), 99–115.

Parker, Ian and John Shotter (1990), *Deconstructing Social Psychology*, London: Routledge.

Phillips, Nelson, Thomas B. Lawrence and Cynthia Hardy (2004), 'Discourse and institutions', *Academy of Management Review*, **29** (4), 635–652.

Potter, Jonathan and Margaret Wetherell (1987), *Discourse and Social Psychology*, London: Sage.

Prasad, Pushkala (2005), *Crafting Qualitative Research: Working in the Postpositivist Traditions*, New York: M.E. Sharpe.

Rabinow, Paul and William M. Sullivan (1979), *Interpretive Social Science*, Berkeley, CA: University of California Press.

Reichman, Walter (2014), 'Industrial and Organizational Psychology encounters the world', in Walter Reichman (ed.), *Industrial and Organizational Psychology Help the Vulnerable: Serving the Underserved*, Basingstoke: Palgrave Macmillan, pp. 1–11.

Rose, Nikolas (1985), *The Psychological Complex: Psychology, Politics and Society in England 1869–1939*, London: Routledge and Kegan Paul.
Shotter, John (1993), *Conversational Realities. Constructing Life through Language*, London: Sage.
Shotter, John (2008), 'Dialogism and polyphony in organizing theorizing in Organization Studies: Action guiding anticipations and the continuous creation of novelty', *Organization Studies*, **29** (4), 501–524.
Spink, Marie J.P. and Peter K. Spink (2015), 'Organizational psychology and social issues: The place of place', in Ian Parker (ed.), *Handbook of Critical Psychology*, London: Routledge, pp. 155–163.
Steyaert, Chris (2014), 'Going all the way: The creativity of entrepreneuring in the Full Monty', in Chris Bilton and Stephen Cummings (eds), *Handbook of Management and Creativity*, Cheltenham, UK and Northampton, MA, USA: Edward Elgar Publishing, pp. 160–181.
Steyaert, Chris and Bart Van Looy (2010), *Relational Practices, Participative Organizing. Advanced Series in Management Vol. 7*, Bingley: Emerald.
Symon, Gillian and Catherine Cassell (1998), *Qualitative Methods and Analysis Organizational Research*, London: Sage.
Symon, Gillian and Catherine Cassell (2006), 'Neglected perspectives in work and organizational psychology', *Journal of Occupational and Organizational Psychology*, **79** (3), 307–314.
Symon, Gillian and Catherine Cassell (2012), *Qualitative Organizational Research: Core Methods and Current Challenges*, London: Sage.
Weick, Karl E. (1995), *Sensemaking in Organizations*, Thousand Oaks, CA: Sage.
Wetherell, Margaret (2001), 'Themes in discourse research: The case of Diana', in Margaret Wetherell and Stephanie Taylor (eds), *Discourse Theory and Practice*, London: Sage, pp. 14–28.
Wilson, Fiona (2014), *Organizational Behaviour and Work. A Critical Introduction*, Oxford: Oxford University Press.

PART II

Participation and change

3. Divergence and convergence in multi-party collaboration: 'moving the paradox on'

Anna-Katrin Heydenreich

MULTI-PARTY COLLABORATION FOR SUSTAINABLE DEVELOPMENT

Today, most people agree that humankind faces serious, interrelated problems and challenges on a global scale. Many agree on the urgent need for societal change to avoid further aggravating environmental and developmental problems. And we are increasingly aware of the ways that different actors have become interdependent within global social and economic domains (Bouwen and Steyaert, 1999). Accordingly, multi-party collaboration has come to be appreciated as a valuable method for achieving strategic change in response to such complex and weighty societal problems (Hardy, Lawrence and Phillips, 2006). The more these 'metaproblems' become intractable (Lewicki, Gray and Elliott, 2003), the more it is worth crossing traditional boundaries, bringing together multiple stakeholders who can engage collaboratively, using their broad range of expertise and resources (Trist, 1983) to tackle the challenges and jointly explore new and creative ways of organizing.

Multi-party collaboration (Bouwen, Craps and Santos, 1999; Bouwen and Taillieu, 2004; Gray, 1989; 2011; Henttonen, Lahikainen and Jauhiainen, 2014; Huxham and Vangen, 2005; Vangen and Huxham, 2012) also referred to as multi-stakeholder processes (Hemmati, 2002) or multi-stakeholder initiatives (Zeyen, Beckmann and Wolters, 2014) are intended to serve this goal. The aim is to bring actors from diverse societal sectors and backgrounds into constructive engagement, dialogue and decision-making so they can collaboratively improve a situation characterized by common and conflicting interests. Each stakeholder, whether an individual, group or organization, has a unique appreciation of and a particular interest or stake in that issue (Gray, 1989; Hemmati, 2002).

The greatest asset of a multi-stakeholder process is its potential to

47

assemble diverse interests, stakes and logics – and that is also its greatest challenge. These processes face a basic paradox: they simultaneously involve both divergence and convergence. The divergence arises as actors assemble heterogeneous expertise and outreach of the diverse stakeholders, in order to find creative and sophisticated answers to the pressing questions of our time. Thus it can be very hard to engage constructively and make sound decisions, given the variety of interests and worldviews involved. Hence, if they are to succeed, these processes require convergence: the coming together of different perspectives in concrete steps of action. Handling this paradox between convergence and divergence is the most demanding task in organizing multi-party collaboration. In this chapter I present an in-depth case study of people negotiating this very paradox throughout the unfolding of a multi-stakeholder collaboration process in the run-up to the World Summit on Sustainable Development in Johannesburg, South Africa in 2002. Adopting a discursive perspective, I theorize the paradox between divergence and convergence as organized through five distinctive discourses and also through the specific ways those discourses interacted throughout the multi-stakeholder process.

The chapter is organized as follows. First, I elaborate on multi-party collaboration as an inherently paradoxical activity. As I introduce a discursive perspective on collaboration, I place on centre stage two of its key characteristics: it is constructed through interaction, and because of that it has a processual character. This perspective makes it possible to explore what I depicted as the 'paradox of convergence and divergence' (Heydenreich, 2008). I then describe my methodological approach in the study, and present my results. The paradox between divergence and convergence is enacted first through five discourses of collaboration. Second, the paradox is re-enacted by different interplays between these five discourses. In the next section I discuss the subsequent discursive conceptualization of multi-stakeholder collaboration resulting from the five discourses and their interplays. Thereby I am looking at how the paradox is 'moving on' (Beech, Burns, de Caestecker, MacIntosh and MacLean, 2004). Finally, I consider the theoretical, practical and methodological implications of my findings.

THE FUNDAMENTAL PARADOX OF COLLABORATION: A DISCURSIVE VIEW

When it comes to collaboration, issues of divergence and convergence are at the fore. Diversity is *the* defining feature of multi-party collaboration and usually the very reason people choose to collaborate in the first place. Through assembling diverse stakeholders, organizers can broaden the range of expertise, perspectives, available resources and outreach. Furthermore, the participation of diverse stakeholders is seen as crucial if societal change agendas are to succeed and is usually an explicit aspect of the sustainability agreements to be implemented. Of course, from the perspective of those managing a multi-party collaboration that includes representatives of all those diverse backgrounds, interests and viewpoints, divergence poses a considerable challenge. Accordingly, Huxham and Vangen (2005) and Hardy et al. (2006) have noticed a tendency in the literature to emphasize the importance of convergence in the sense of having common aims, a well-defined purpose, shared values and so on. Agreeing on joint goals is seen as a major precondition for successful multi-stakeholder processes. Vangen and Huxham (2012) point out that the same literature paradoxically describes the many difficulties that arise along the path to such agreement in practice. Clearly, then, the literature only addresses paradox in an implicit way and it deserves more explicit investigation.

Huxham and Vangen (2005, p. 82) refer to this constellation as the 'fundamental paradox' of collaboration: the need for a collaboration to reach congruence and simultaneously maintain diversity in its goals. On the one hand the diverse stakeholders come together primarily because of their diverse interests, views, expertise and resources; on the other hand precisely those divergent interests engender different and potentially contradictory conceptions and purposes that lead the stakeholders to approach the collaborative venture. While it is important to cultivate the inherent diversity, the divergent forces need to be coordinated and organized in a way that allows enough convergence to permit effective joint action.

Besides Huxham and Vangen, who studied the role of paradox as inherent in multi-actor collaboration within the collaboration management research stream, Connelly, Zhang and Faermann (2008) and O'Leary and Bingham (2009) did so within the field of public and policy networks. Despite a growing body of theoretical reflections on this issue, hardly any empirical studies have focused on the role of paradox in multi-party collaboration and on how it is being addressed by the actors, as Ospina and Saz-Carranza (2010) noted. Their work, although not discourse analytic, is an important exception. Looking at the 'inward work' of collaboration, they identified a main paradox between 'unity' and 'diversity' and hence the paradox that is also important for my more process oriented analysis of 'convergence' and 'divergence'.

In this study I use the term paradox in the sense of challenging contradictions, oppositions and tensions that occur in practice (Beech et al., 2004; in line with Poole and van de Ven, 1989) and that are characterized by the simultaneous presence of contradictory yet interrelated elements (drawing on Cameron and Quinn, 1988; Clegg, da Cunha and Cunha,

2002; Schad, Lewis, Raisch and Smith, 2016). Traditional approaches either aim at 'resolving' the paradox, or seek win–win outcomes (Lewis, 2000), or avoid emerging tensions. But these approaches result in other problems (Beech et al., 2004; Hardy et al., 2006; Huxham and Beech, 2003) and inevitably lead to disappointment as actors encounter insurmountable obstacles in the collaborative process. Instead of removing, resolving or denying the existence of paradox, the paradox could be 'kept open' for 'working with or through it' (Beech et al., 2004, p. 1314). In this dynamic, circular understanding, engaging actively with the paradox is viewed by Beech et al. (2004, p. 1315) 'as an essentially creative or transformative phenomenon'. Since the paradox is a constitutive feature of multi-party collaboration, the more promising approach is probably 'to accept the paradox and learn to live with it' (Poole and van de Ven, 1989, p. 566; see also Smith and Tracey, 2016).

Accepting the paradox does not by any means suggest ignoring it. Rather, we can appreciate the contrast provided by the opposition and actively pursue the implications of the paradox (Poole and van de Ven, 1989). Hence, paradox becomes an 'invitation to act' (Beech et al., 2004). Adopting a paradox lens (Smith and Lewis, 2011; Smith and Tracey, 2016) then means that collaboration depends on fostering divergence and convergence simultaneously as they mutually reinforce one another. Without divergence, the participants cannot converge on the multi-stakeholder approach, and without convergence, they cannot bring the divergent logics into fruitful interaction. These simultaneous yet contradictory demands make multi-party collaboration what Hardy et al. (2006, p. 108) call a 'juggling act'.

To study paradox as a 'juggling act', I draw on a discourse-analytical approach. With my empirical work I build on Hardy et al. (2005) who contributed important discourse-theoretical reflections on the significance of sustaining tensions in collaboration through an ongoing interplay of discursive constructions, thereby addressing what Putnam, Fairhurst and Banghart (2016) consider as a gap in the paradox literature. The collaborative activities are constructed interactively, through the use of various specific ways of talking (discourses), each of which engenders specific effects on the tangible characteristics and outcomes of the collaboration. The discursive view focuses on the way that talk constitutes the foundations for collaborative action (Hardy et al., 2005), as participants draw on discursive resources to achieve practical consequences (Wetherell and Potter, 1988). The potential of a discursive view lies in its focus on processual aspects of collaboration: how the various conceptions of collaboration as inherently paradoxical come into being, how they are interactionally modified or sustained, or how they disappear (Phillips and Oswick, 2012). Hence, the discursive view looks at how language, as a form of interaction, is *creating* collaboration with its inherent tensions as a social reality rather than simply reflecting it (Gergen, 1999; Hardy, Lawrence and Grant, 2005; Putnam et al., 2016).

Studying these processual aspects of collaboration from a discursive perspective emphasizes the contextual embeddedness, as discourse is situated in three ways (Potter, Tileagă and Hepburn, 2011, p. 44). First, discourse is organized sequentially, in interaction: what is said in a collaborative setting is contextualized by what has been said before, and this prepares the ground for what comes next. Second, collaborative talk is situated in a specific institutional context. Third, discourse is situated rhetorically, as it may justify, resist or counter actual or potential discursive constructions on how to organize collaboration (Billig, 1996). In a nutshell, the discursive view facilitates a strong interactional orientation (Wood and Kroger, 2000) and responds perfectly to the suggestion by Smith and Lewis (2011) that process-oriented and contextualized methods are most appropriate for the study of paradox.

In this analysis I assume that the paradox is being nurtured in a productive manner as long as the actors conceptualize their collaborative activities in ways that ensure both sufficient divergence and sufficient convergence to enable the development of joint action pertaining to external actors and targets. Summing up, from a discourse perspective, multi-actor collaboration becomes a continuous 'juggling' act (Hardy et al., 2006, p. 108) of creating and addressing the countervailing tendencies of divergence and convergence (Heydenreich, 2008).

From this perspective, the main question is how the paradox of divergence and convergence is discursively constructed and addressed and what kind of consequences this has for the collaborative process. Hence the first part of my analysis is guided by the question: 'What are the various discourses of collaboration that the stakeholders interactively develop and use in order to deal with the divergence and convergence paradox?'; followed by a second part guided by the question: 'How does the interplay of the various discourses (re-)constitute the paradox and the way it is being addressed?'

The different discourses of collaboration that are developed and used by the participating actors are studied as discourse with a small 'd' (Alvesson and Kärreman, 2000); that is, they are studied with 'a close-range interest in a local-situated context'. In contrast, discourse with a capital 'D' refers to 'a long-range interest in a macro-systemic context' (Phillips and Oswick, 2012, p. 21). By taking discourse with a fairly small 'd' as my unit of analysis, in the sense of a discursive construction situated in the specific context of this specific multi-stakeholder collaboration, I emphasize the characteristics of discourse as construct*ed* and construct*ive* (Potter et al., 2011).

The discourses of collaboration are identified around controversial issues (Wetherell, 2006) such that each enacts a specific 'logic' comprising basic assumptions, often about constraints, problems and their solutions around this controversial issue. The specific logics of the discourses of collaboration need to be discernibly different so we can identify them as specific constructions of collaboration, but they may be modified as people use them in interaction. Each of the discourses of collaboration presents a specific way of addressing the divergence and convergence paradox. With the discourses in interplay, though, it may occur that two opposing discourses each represent one pole of the paradox. On a meta-level, the very plurality of discourses nurtures divergence, and, especially when situations become confusing or conflictive, it will provoke a demand for sufficient convergence. Hence, the paradox is addressed by either a single discourse, the interplay of two opposing discourses or the interplay of a plurality of discourses.

THE CASE: THE MULTI-STAKEHOLDER 'IMPLEMENTATION CONFERENCE'

My empirical investigation of the major paradox of divergence and convergence in multi-stakeholder collaboration is based on an in-depth analysis of the stakeholder-initiated Implementation Conference that took place at the World Summit on Sustainable Development, in Johannesburg, South Africa. The conference aimed to implement international environmental agreements through 'stakeholder action'. In this study I focus on the preparation phase and the kick-off conference at which various collaborative multi-stakeholder projects were launched; hence I study a multi-stakeholder collaboration in its formative stage.

In 2002, ten years after the UN Conference on Environment and Development (UNCED) in Rio, delegates met in Johannesburg to review what had been achieved since then and to discuss how to move forward on implementing Agenda 21, a 40-chapter programme of action adopted in Rio. The World Summit on Sustainable Development (WSSD) was until then the second-biggest UN conference ever; the 18 months of run-up to the summit featured an extensive preparatory process with four preparatory committees (PrepComs). However, it became clear quite early in that phase that no major breakthroughs were to be expected. The official outcome documents, the Johannesburg Declaration and the Johannesburg Plan of Implementation, mainly reaffirmed existing commitments instead of agreeing on new goals, targets and timetables. While this summit threatened to fail in terms of producing strong agreements, many stakeholders urged action towards at least implementing existing agreements.

During this process, many parallel events were taking place alongside the official UN negotiations. One of those was the multi-stakeholder conference process that I focus on here. In line with the strategic vision in which collaborative multi-stakeholder processes help to advance the implementation of international environmental agreements and to refresh governance processes, the convening organization had shaped a coherent agenda linking multi-stakeholder processes to sustainable development action. The multi-stakeholder Implementation Conference (IC) Process was an important project on that agenda. It culminated in a three-day conference immediately preceding the WSSD in Johannesburg after a year-long preparation phase. It involved 400 participants from the nine major groups as defined at UNCED in Rio: business and industry, farmers, indigenous peoples, local authorities, non-governmental organizations, the scientific and technological community, women, workers and trade unions, and youth, along with intergovernmental organizations like the World Bank and the WHO, and some government representatives.

At the final event, all these groups joined together to launch more than twenty action plans that would help to fill the implementation gap in the following issue areas: freshwater (the focus of this study), energy, food security and health. For each issue strand, a multi-stakeholder issue advisory group was pulled together to design and guide the process, draft issue papers and collaborative action plans, identify potential partners and choose participants for the final Implementation Conference. The participants representing specific stakeholder groups were all engaged in some way in the official WSSD process in order to represent their constituent organizations.

METHODOLOGY

Entering the Field

Through searches on the internet I learnt about the Stakeholder Forum's activities on multi-stakeholder processes. Then, thanks to the convener of the IC process who acted as my 'gatekeeper', I was given the opportunity to attend the Implementation Conference at the WSSD and its preparations. I entered the process, which had been running since the end of 2001, in spring of 2002 at PrepCom III in New York. This conference served as my first orientation: the Stakeholder Forum team and I got to know each other, and I was immediately immersed in the UN conference sphere. In the basement of the UN headquarters I listened to various meetings of PrepCom III, most of which were not related to the IC process but formed its background. Having gained an initial overall impression of the process, I chose, in consultation with my gatekeeper, a specific issue strand and action plan group to follow.

Data Sampling Strategies

Given the processual character of the case study, in which I followed a sequence of different events in a highly complex setting, I accrued a huge amount of data. I attended and taped the main preparatory events (meetings at PrepCom III in New York and PrepCom IV in Bali, a smaller preparatory meeting in Switzerland, and a telephone conference) up to the three-day final Implementation Conference at the WSSD in August 2002. The data I collected include documents (produced by the Stakeholder Forum, by participants, and by other organizations in the context), correspondence, participation in meetings (taped, thoroughly transcribed and enriched with field notes) and 13 interviews. Ultimately, I concentrated on the meeting transcripts and the documents, the data that was 'naturally occurring' in the ethnographic sense (Marshall and Rossman, 1989), as they captured in detail the richness and variety of available discourses and their interplay. I also gained access to minutes and notes from meetings that had taken place before I entered the process; I used those data, plus my interviews, to enhance my contextual understanding.

Data Analysis

The discourse analytical approach was deeply grounded in and guided by the empirical material; however, my initial understanding of the supposed relevance of paradox and its conceptualization as produced in discourse served as a 'sensitizing concept' (Blumer, 1954). The first phase of the analysis allowed me to make sense of the overall process. As I assembled and retraced the different sources of material and the references to previous and later events, I reconstructed how the process, themes and difficult or conflictive issues developed over time.

In the second phase of the analysis, I carved out the categories the participants employed as they structured their process, according to their core activities and main concerns. This phase of analysis was largely led by a focus on 'trouble points' (Tracy and Ashcraft, 2001). Trouble points are a pragmatic point of departure for identifying and analysing paradoxical tensions, as they serve as analytical markers. They can be regarded as a first indication of the paradox inherent in the process and can be identified straightforwardly as they are marked by obvious discussions, for example those for and against a point, along with disagreement, anger or any kind of difficulty. Other indications of trouble points are issues that consistently reappear as subjects of discussion or repeated questions about a specific topic. As one of the core collaborative activities I identified the joint development of their conception of collaboration, since two of the major concerns and troubles in the formative stage of the collaboration were the question of who they were as a group and how they related to one another. This conceptual definition of themselves as a group is consistent with what Ospina and Saz-Carranza (2010, p. 425) term the 'inward work of building community', compared to the 'outward work' that is directed towards external actors. As I assembled the trouble points concerning this core collaborative task in which the collaborating stakeholders cultivated their relations I was able to carve out the basic paradox of divergence and convergence. Tied to this core collaborative activity, the trouble points became apparent as tangible embodiments of the paradox.

In a third phase of the analysis, I identified the various discourses addressing the paradox that were made relevant throughout the inward work of the collaboration. Here again the trouble points served as points of departure for identifying the discourses of collaboration, as this is where inconsistencies came into play most obviously. I clustered the key terms and arguments assembled around a specific trouble point according to two indicators: internal *coherence within* a specific discourse and *variation between* the discourses (Potter and Wetherell, 1987; 1994, p. 55; Wood and Kroger, 2000).

In a fourth phase of the analysis I figured out how the various discourses were used over the course of the process: at what stage which discourses became relevant and how the various discourses interacted, for example if they were used in an oppositional or complementary manner, and how the paradox was (re-)constituted throughout the interplay of the discourses.

DISCOURSES OF COLLABORATION

A first version of the paradox between convergence and divergence surfaced with the tension between two concurrent concerns: should the group – including a wide variety of relevant stakeholders – cover the breadth of their suggested issues through a joint vision, or should it focus on separate action plans that were concrete and realizable but diverse and not entirely coherent? From the beginning, the challenge was to identify the key issues within the broader range of issues. The entire preparation phase of the conference process was characterized by this paradox between the attempt to reach completeness and the simultaneous criticism of this attempt as being too broad and diffuse, as lacking an action orientation, and as hampering the manageability of integrating diversity. The preparation phase was managed by developing an issue paper, and here the paradox became obvious. The issue paper grew longer and longer, since the participants 'want to put all the important points in there, so it's just been swelling even though we didn't want that', as the coordinator put it. As the Issue Advisory Group coordinator suggested, 'we might be an awful lot wiser, if we pursue all these things, but we won't actually be any closer to doing anything'.

Hence, the divergence–convergence paradox became manifest in a pair of simultaneous and contradictory demands: on the one hand, to foster and integrate diversity, and on the other, to narrow down the complexity to achieve focused action through concrete action plans. Over the course of the process, a variety of collaborative relations were enacted in five different discourses for addressing this paradox. These were (1) collaboration as a normative-holistic relation; (2) collaboration as an issue-driven relation; (3) collaboration as a partnership relation; (4) collaboration as a learning-sharing relation; and (5) collaboration as a passionate-transformative relation. Each discourse offers a distinct way of conceptualizing and balancing divergence and convergence and can hence be depicted as a specific way of organizing collaboration with regards to the contradictory demands of the paradox.

In the remainder of this section, I introduce the five discursive constructions in detail (see Table 3.1), illustrating them with excerpts from participants' talk in the meetings and from the documents produced within the collaborative process.

Collaboration as a Normative-Holistic Relation

The normative-holistic discourse predominated when people were defining stakeholder collaboration. It came to the fore mainly in the initial outline for the process, which built heavily on the organization's expert book on multi-stakeholder collaboration (Hemmati, 2002), and it was taken up again during the final conference. With this discourse, people conceive of multi-stakeholder collaboration as a process in which they acknowledge each other's roles and values within a holistic frame, and in which those whose roles and values are not yet acknowledged are being empowered. It refers in a normative way to what is expected from participants, to criteria for the outcomes as well as to principles of the stakeholder collaboration. According to the outline brochure the participating stakeholders were expected to demonstrate 'commitment', 'ownership', 'accountability' and 'responsibility' as they 'should play their part in delivering sustainable development'. Consequently, the process outcomes should include

Table 3.1 *Discourses of collaboration*

	Normative-holistic discourse	Issue-driven discourse	Partnership discourse	Learning-sharing discourse	Passionate-transformative discourse
Divergence	Stakeholders with specific roles and responsibilities.	Distinct positions, more or less reconcilable or oppositional.	Diverse actors, diverse projects, diverse ideas, partners with specific strengths, puzzle pieces.	Experts, specialists with specific experiences, diverse case studies.	Inspirational diversity of actors, ideas, emotions, and so on.
Convergence	Importance of common ground: very important. Significance of common ground: common ground lies in the joint recognition of the normative-holistic picture of sustainable development with its specific roles and responsibilities.	Importance of common ground: important. Significance of common ground: position paper process in order to maximize common ground through analysing and synthesizing positions.	Importance of common ground: less important. Significance of common ground: neutral space, platform, marketplace of ideas, clearing house, jigsaw puzzle, consultative council, consortium.	Importance of common ground: less important. Significance of common ground: learning hub. Beyond the mutual respect and acknowledgement of the diverse approaches, no common ground is needed.	Importance of common ground: important. Significance of common ground: holistic vision, shared experience. Participants act together, assuming a holistic vision. The holistic vision is not specified though, as this is not of so much importance.
Integrating diversity	Stakeholders each play their roles and meet their responsibilities for sustainable development. Roles and responsibilities are given and specific and they are integrated into a holistic picture. Balanced representation is important.	Differences need to be negotiated to reach agreement.	Networking, partnering with agreed differences on a few issues; differences are recognized and can be juxtaposed.	Participants respect and acknowledge each other mutually for their specific experience and expertise.	Diversity is celebrated. Roles are fluid. Diversity is melded in an unspecific manner within a holistic vision.

'increased commitment of stakeholders towards taking their role in implementing international and regional sustainable development agreements'. The process was based on several 'principles of stakeholder collaboration' including 'equity', 'inclusiveness', 'legitimacy', 'societal gains' and 'transparency'.

Overall, people used the normative–holistic discourse mainly when they discussed the committed engagement of the participants, urged balanced participation and aimed to reduce the power differences between the participants. The discourse enacts divergence through the diversity in the specific roles and responsibilities for each stakeholder group. The full range of diversity is integrated in the holistic worldview with values like inclusiveness, empowerment, equality and balanced participation (in terms of region, gender and stakeholder group). In it, diversity is seen as given, but not yet brought together; hence the process aimed at moving 'from fragmentation to integration' (outline brochure). This kind of convergence was ensured as people committed to contribute to the holistic picture of sustainable development according to their specific roles and responsibilities, presupposing equal power and mutual respect. Within this discourse, the respective roles and responsibilities and the meaning of sustainable development seem to be given; they simply need to be taken up and realized.

Collaboration as an Issue-Driven Relation

Once the group secured a normative basis, using the normative-holistic discourse, the issue-driven discourse came to dominate the first part of the process. It was used in the outline to sketch the collaborative procedure: the group was to produce a 'synthesis of stakeholder positions' by 'identifying differences and common ground'. The group organized an issue-paper process through which a 'rolling paper' was developed further from one meeting to another. Accordingly, the coordinator promised from one meeting to the next: 'to review all the submissions of members and identify "Common Ground" – areas on which people are in agreement; identify differences – areas on which people are not in agreement; identify any emerging themes' (outline brochure).

The issue-driven discourse conceptualizes divergence in terms of different stakeholder positions. These positions might represent fundamental differences and might need to be integrated by a method that includes synthesizing and focusing on common ground while analysing, clarifying and negotiating the differences. It is important to ascertain those differences in detail and negotiate the changes over the course of the process. Hence, convergence is a result of this synthesizing process which should, despite some remaining differences, yield the broadest and most solid possible base of agreement for identifying focus areas and formulating a joint vision and mission. The main aim of this procedure however is not to produce issue papers per se but to derive from them the action initiatives, according to the Issue Advisory Group coordinator:

> This freshwater issue paper is just really a sort of scoping exercise, for us as a group to find out what are the focus areas that we think are really relevant to think about when we want to go forward towards action. (Coordinator)

A thorough base of agreement coming out of the issue paper process is important to participants before heading towards the action initiatives:

> What happened at the last meeting was that we drafted some . . . specific action plan, and people said, we want our joint picture first. We want . . . to do more work within this group to structure a vision amongst ourselves, and that's why we listed comments and inputs into this issue paper. (Coordinator)

Collaboration as a Partnership Relation

The project outline also prepared the ground for a partnership discourse, as 'partnerships between various stakeholder groups, as well as between stakeholders, governments and intergovernmental bodies' were part of the 'desired outcome' of the Implementation Conference. The partnership discourse nourishes divergence as differences are recognized and can be juxtaposed; thus the diverse partners can each bring their strengths to bear. This discourse gained momentum at a meeting halfway through the process, where the quotes in the remainder of this section are from. As a group, the 'water partners' would form a 'consultative council', 'consortium', or 'clearing house'. One participant invoked the metaphor of a marketplace: 'So it becomes the marketplace where we all come with our little baskets. . . . Putting it all together. And then we go shopping.' Another spoke of their differences as 'kind of a jigsaw puzzle picture' and used the metaphor to avoid any claim of completeness, as they are 'not gonna fill it all in'. Within this discourse only a minimum of common ground is required; the emerging consensus is used to build partnerships not around issues, but around themes, questions and areas of concern and concentration. Instead of concentrating on finding agreement, the use of subgroups is preferred:

> If there are three, four organizations that want to go ahead and do something, you know, then this is what they should do. We don't need fifty people involved in everything, you know, they will have their own networks, and they should pursue these initiatives . . . build subgroups, and let them develop their ideas. (Coordinator)

Hence, in this discourse the participants would achieve convergence by providing a common platform and engaging in brokering and networking activities. The role of the conveners, then, was to broker the various initiatives:

> It's gonna be up to us to do a lot of brokering on the basis of the information you bring in, you know, this organization might be interested in this, contact them and put them in touch and so on and . . . we're going to be a broker facilitating team. (Coordinator)

Collaboration as a Learning-Sharing Relation

Drawing on the learning-sharing discourse, collaboration is conceived as sharing experiences and learning from each other's expertise. 'Shared experience and expertise' were among the 'desired outcomes' listed in the outline. Within this discourse, diversity is a precondition for mutual learning. The collaboration process is capitalizing on diversity in two ways: it brought in a wide range of expertise and allowed them to distribute tasks, as each participant was supposed to choose his or her 'specialist area'. Divergence is conceived as opportunity and is used for cross-fertilization; whereas convergence is conceptualized as a learning hub offering mutual learning: 'All groups represented within the IC have both something to contribute to this issue as well as something to take from it' as one participant put it. Moreover, participants were mutually respected and acknowledged for their diverse expertise and experience. Instead of trying to maximize common ground and striving for completeness, within this discourse convergence is achieved through the case study approach, which helped to reduce the complexity. Accordingly, the collaboration is also characterized as moving 'from leading by rules to leading by example' (outline brochure).

Collaboration as a Passionate-Transformative Relation

Finally, the passionate-transformative discourse excels in portraying a strong, energetic, passionate and inspiring stakeholder movement. This discourse featured considerably in the project outline. The vision of the project was formulated in this 'from–to' style: 'To plant seeds for cultural change – from words to action, from static to dynamic, from competition to collaboration; stakeholders collaborating – spinning into action – towards new horizons', transforming previously negative conditions into desirable ones almost magically: for example, the collaboration effort was expected to produce a 'shift towards the desired stakeholder culture' (outline brochure). It also touched on the question of who should participate and in what way. During the process, it was used to substantiate the selection of participants: 'And we've approached *this* group because we knew you might not shoot each other anymore. So there is a dynamic here, one that is positive and action-oriented.' The idea is that the participants are collaborating enthusiastically as they have overcome long-established antagonism. Accordingly, issues were to be chosen in a way that would allow the group to gain from 'a broad-based leadership among stakeholders with an active, enthusiastic "core"' (outline brochure). The use of the passionate-transformative discourse framed the conference process: it was used mainly at the beginning (to inspire potential participants) and at the end (to celebrate the participants). At various points during the process participants used it to deal with conflictive situations by praising the distinctiveness of the group:

> it was remarkable how much of a consensus we were able to achieve. We still niggle at each other [group: some laughter], we still have slightly higher priorities here and there [points towards another participant; group: laughter, clapping]. But you know in fact . . . we're not really shooting each other like we used to shoot each other [group: consent] . . . nothing is perfect in the world, but it is fantastic progress! (Participant)

The coming together of diverse actors from around the globe was also celebrated around the meetings during the process by providing enough 'space for gathering socially' (outline brochure), but especially as a highlight at the final conference. The IC event culminated in an amazing 44-minute drumming session for all the participants, led by a South African drum group, which developed into a magical, timeless moment of togetherness. This discourse fostered divergence, as diversity was celebrated as inspirational – as long as the diverse actors took a mutually positive stance. Convergence was ensured through a shared vision and the enthusiasm about working together and through shared experiences, especially about having overcome oppositional relations. Furthermore, in this discourse diversity is beauty; it is celebrated, enjoyed and melded within a holistic vision. A participant enthuses: 'This group is a fantastic group, you know we have a fantastic group and within this group we could try to establish a certain common denominator.'

THE DISCOURSES OF COLLABORATION IN INTERPLAY

With the first part of my analysis I identified five discourses of collaboration. Each discourse offers a distinct way of conceptualizing and balancing divergence and convergence and hence organizes the paradox differently.

Both the normative-holistic discourse and the passionate-transformative discourse tend to do so by settling issues of belonging (compare Smith and Lewis, 2011) in terms of balanced and equally empowered participation by committed, enthusiastically collaborating stakeholders; hence they form a larger frame of reference about how diversity unfolds and is being integrated. In contrast, the issue-driven discourse, the partnership discourse, and the learning-sharing discourse embody a concrete methodology for integrating the diverse positions, ideas, initiatives and the like. They came to the fore when the process headed to the more concrete discussion of developing the project initiatives. I will now describe these interplays in detail. In this second part of my analysis I am guided by the question of how the divergence-convergence paradox is (re-)constituted and addressed as the various discourses interact with one another.

At the beginning the project participants were invited to engage in 'collaborative stakeholder action' in order to implement global sustainable development agreements. The project outline offered the space for engagement on the basis of a normative-holistic understanding of stakeholder collaboration with a strong tendency towards an issue-driven approach, embedded in an enthusing passionate-transformative rhetoric. Though it placed more emphasis on an issue-driven discourse, the project outline already vaguely envisioned a partnership discourse; it combined the two in a complementary way. It presented concrete ideas for the collaborative work, but retained enough vagueness and ambiguity to allow the participants to shape the process jointly. On the one hand this allowed people to explore various ways of relating; on the other hand, the outline did not provide clear distinctions along the range of approaches, and this caused considerable confusion among the participants.

It was the issue-driven discourse that mainly guided the phase of identifying priority areas for action. When those priority areas were to be translated into concrete action plans, the group entered a difficult transition stage. Through the discussions at a meeting about halfway through the process, the partnership discourse emerged as a vital alternative, through which the two discourses were constructed as oppositional and mutually exclusive. The partnership discourse suggests that diversity can be assembled on a neutral platform, where different initiatives can be networked and brokered. The suggestion is, as the convener summed up the discussion, that the group brings onto this platform 'things that you're doing anyway and you say . . . we're looking for partners . . . something that's already out there . . . that you would like to see extended'; that existing and evolving partnerships can be strengthened, enriched, broadened and replicated. Furthermore, this pragmatic approach can attract more participants, as it is much more interesting and people are enthusiastic about it. Thus, those who are not yet part of the circle can be included:

> What you could do in the run up to Johannesburg is to get . . . all the developing partnerships and joint initiatives and ideas for implementation and to broker the networking, so that you have a virtual platform. Then many of those that are not necessarily part of the circle, can find out that X, Y and Z have this idea, they're committed to doing it, and we basically contribute that to the implementation networking, and others can, you know, say, that's really interesting, we want to be a part of it. (Participant)

As a result, the discussion at this meeting served both to introduce the sharp difference between the two main approaches and to get rid of the issue-driven approach, which was then constructed as unrealistic and overly ambitious and therefore as limited to 'diplomatic blabla'. This indicates that the issue-driven discourse was also thrust aside by the partnership discourse because of the developments in the official UN conference process, which suffered from deadlock. Participants believed it was important to use partnerships, because the stakeholders had engaged in an enormous amount of activity and wanted to demonstrate that to the delegates at the summit. They also wanted to form a contrast to the negotiation approach:

> How I could envisage the Implementation Conference . . . is if you're trying to profile basically partnerships and the commitments that all sorts of stakeholders . . . are putting forward to it. . . . By the time we come to Johannesburg, what we're doing is no longer negotiating, you're profiling, you're presenting it to the summit, because quite frankly, I think, we will actually have far more outcomes coming out of the non-governmental-slash-partnership dimension and dynamic than the governments . . . and then, when we're there, we all come together and say, look, we have fifty organizations that have come together behind this initiative, twenty here, add them all up and suddenly we have a world of action that might even shake governments to maybe be a little bit more courageous at the summit. Also, because they're gonna be so locked into this terrible process. (Participant)

The development in the official negotiations as well as their own experiences with the relations among the stakeholders in the water sector so far resulted in challenging and finally rejecting the issue-driven discourse:

> we've come up with this idea of the water partner meeting, that's very distinctly different than an issue paper driven process. And I think we've got to make a decision as to whether we're going ahead, issues or partnerships. Cause these are very, very, very different things! And I think what [another participant] put forward, was a probably more workable framework by shifting from issues to partnerships, then, you got a completely different spin on it, it's much more

comprehensible to people, it's much less confrontational, and you get magnets on the table to draw people together. (Participant)

Moreover, participants often combined the partnership discourse with the learning-sharing discourse, as some exchange occurred both within partnerships and between different partnerships to transfer experience and cross-fertilize ideas in order to inspire and innovate:

> And this can be a wonderful platform of brilliant goals, initiatives, lessons learnt . . . this can be a platform for a broader network for the future. And then it has a value. Because it brings everyone together on specific issues. (Participant)

People can share good practices and lessons learnt and also identify and fill in gaps. Accordingly, the IC process aimed to collect, review, and promote good or even best practices to derive those lessons learnt, or to substantiate or replicate them:

> Start with positive things, of bringing some of the best examples . . . so that we can learn from that together, have a learning exercise, and then we draw some lessons out of it . . . then going into countries and exhibit a road show with people from those examples. (Representative of convening organization)

At times, people also used the passionate-transformative discourse to support the partnership discourse, which was constructed as being far more inspirational and action-oriented:

> While much can be achieved by individual organizations, working in partnerships can often be more effective. . . . The IC was aiming to contribute to harnessing their energy, creativity and courage, and thus delivering real change on the ground. (IC executive summary)

Hence, the passionate-transformative discourse, which was used most prominently at the beginning and end of the process and in a supporting manner throughout, was important because it could embed the more specific discourses that enacted the methodology to be used for selecting priority areas and partnership initiatives. Five years later, when participants shared their memories of the IC and the drumming session on the internet, the convenor made use of the passionate-transformative discourse by writing this to the organizing team and the many volunteer helpers:

> The IC was such an intense experience . . . I have many many memories, and the [drumming] videos bring more back to life . . . You all were such a team! . . . I am still unsure where and when exactly to say NO to a project that is

half-funded but double-fun . . . but I still do know that all ideas and ideals and strategies and tools are worthless if they are not coming from the warmth of people and their love for each other and the planet . . . I also learned that from and with you. (Convener's email)

From the very beginning, the project was shaped by all the five discourses. The passionate-transformative and the normative-holistic discourses featured especially strongly in the beginning and towards the end of the conference process. The other three were refined during the first half of the process, after which the issue-driven discourse was replaced by the partnership discourse, which then was combined with the learning-sharing discourse. It was through this interplay that the discourses were mutually sharpened and developed distinctive ways of constructing and addressing the paradox of collaboration. In particular, the oppositional encounter between the discourses made their differences more clear; this became obvious with the interplay of the issue-driven discourse and the partnership discourse. Having first been combined in a rather complementary sense, they came to be constructed as oppositional and mutually exclusive. However, the interplay did more than simply influence the development of each individual discourse; it also allowed the participants to transform the paradox. In the next section, I discuss how this came about.

DISCUSSION

The analysis of the interplay between discourses reveals the fluid shifts in the prevalence of the different discourses as they unfolded during the process, often operating simultaneously. Sometimes certain discourses were more prevalent during specific stages of the process, sometimes they were pursued in parallel in complementary ways and sometimes they competed. With these shifts, the divergence-convergence paradox of collaboration was 'moved on', as shown in Table 3.2. Each discourse constituted and addressed the paradox in its own specific way. The interplay between the discourses sharpened the characteristics of each individual discourse. Recall that the issue-driven and partnership discourses only became oppositional as they were used in controversial ways. Once that happened, the partnership discourse turned out to be much more inclusive, as it assembled diverse positions and initiatives in an and-and logic; meanwhile the issue-driven discourse, given its focus on identifying and possibly negotiating and resolving differences, was more prone to an either-or logic. Furthermore, the partnership discourse allowed people to interact more

Table 3.2   Different ways of constructing and addressing the paradox

Level	Constructing and addressing the paradox
Single discourse	Each discourse constructs and addresses the paradox in its own specific way.
Two competing or complementary discourses	Each of the two poles of the paradox comes to be represented by one of the competing/complementary discourses.
Three or more discourses	The plurality of the available discourses constitutes divergence; now the process needs sufficient convergence to handle this plurality and keep the divergence in check.

flexibly over the course of the process, as new participants could enter it at any time without having missed out on fundamental either-or decisions. And the partnership discourse constructed collaboration as being far more action-oriented and tangible.

Through this process of interplay, which led to the discourses becoming more specified, the ways these oppositional discourses constituted the paradox continued to shift. At first, both discourses paid equable attention to both poles of the paradox. Then, the paradox was composed of two discourses, each representing one pole of the paradox. As people dismissed one of the conflicting discourses, it seemed that the paradox was resolved, but in fact it was only reconstituted. As the partnership discourse prevailed, people conceptualized convergence as networking and brokering instead of relying on a solid common ground that was to be negotiated in advance (as in the issue-driven discourse). At this point, the idea of a common framework became important, followed by questions about whether that framework would fall into place as people worked to assemble and broker the various partnership initiatives, or if the framework should be outlined on beforehand, which would again resemble the issue-driven approach. Thus, while each discourse in itself enacted a distinctive way of constructing and addressing the inevitable divergence–convergence paradox of collaboration, the interplay of the different discourses re-constituted the paradox.

Up to this point in the process, the collaborating stakeholders had already done considerable work on issue papers in the first half of the process, and had spent a whole meeting discussing the partnership versus issue-driven approach (completely ignoring the original agenda), and were desperately longing for some sort of common framework, and when they finally achieved it, this framework disappeared. Quite astonishingly, it did not appear in any of the final documents of the conference process. Apparently, since the joint development had already nurtured convergence, it was not necessary either to continue working with it during the second half of the process or to include it in the final report. Obviously, once the group developed the common framework, the significance involved in seeking convergence changed completely. From then on the work was done within the separate partnership initiatives, so the task of defining common ground was confined to each of the single groups.

At the final conference, the participants tackled the paradox in different ways: they used the passionate-transformative and normative-holistic discourses to ensure convergence *across* the individual groups, nurturing a sense of belonging among the Implementation Conference community, and the partnership and learning-sharing discourses to ensure convergence *within* the groups, by providing a concrete methodology. The divergence was supported by all remaining discourses. It became tangible as 400 participating stakeholders with different societal and geographical backgrounds assembled in the 24 final partnership initiatives launched at this event.

The demands for divergence and convergence were addressed in three ways. First, divergence came about because of the various themes, criteria, suggestions for initiatives and so on, and required a sufficient amount of convergence. Each of the discourses offered its own way of dealing with the paradox. Second, two complementary or competitive discourses each constituted one side of the paradox. Third, the paradox was constituted in the simultaneous presence of the various discourses and the need to handle them in a pragmatic way. Now, the very plurality of the available discourses constituted divergence, and the process required enough convergence to handle this potentially confusing and conflictive plurality. This was achieved through three strategies: focusing on only one or two of the discourses at a time, using discourses in a complementary manner, or dismissing certain discourses.

CONCLUSION

This chapter addressed collaboration as a fundamentally paradoxical activity from a discursive view. In the first part of the analysis, I identified five discourses of multi-actor collaboration; each enacted a distinctive way of constructing and addressing the inevitable convergence–divergence paradox of collaboration. All five tackle the challenge of securing a process that would be inclusive and open to multiple perspectives, and that could simultaneously enable focused collective action within a reasonable timeframe. In the second part of my analysis and the discussion, I showed that the paradox pervaded the entire collaborative process and became transformed within the interplay of discourses: existing at first *within* the respective discourses, it came to the fore *between* the discourses, at times between two of them and at times between the plurality of discourses, and then again crystallized *within a specific* discourse. Hence, people act to transform or 'move on' a paradox and thereby prevent the collaboration from being blocked by it (Beech et al., 2004). Instead, they explore creative ways of addressing both divergence and convergence.

The way the paradox was constructed, addressed and transformed is on the one hand affected by developments in the institutional context, and on the other hand also affects the ability of the collaborating stakeholders to remain responsive and able to act with regard to the institutional context. For example, the decision to dismiss one of the controversial discourses was strongly affected by developments within the official UN summit process, where the partnership approach was intensely promoted as an alternative to the deadlocked official negotiations. Hence, the institutional context crucially influenced the significance and the practicalities of both of the controversial discourses.

This study adds to the body of discourse analytic work which shows that the approach has much to offer for those studying organizing processes as they unfold (Hernes and Maitlis, 2010; Steyaert and Van Looy, 2010). The identification of the discourses of collaboration and their interactive use over the course of the process shed light on collaboration, as a complex and dynamic discursive accomplishment. Collaboration is messy, multifaceted and highly complex; it involves the interplay of multiple views and concerns and various interrelated tensions and contradictions in an ongoing dynamic process. Hence, multi-stakeholder collaboration raises significant managerial challenges. I suggest some important implications for organizing multi-stakeholder collaboration. First, the paradox is inevitable and must be attended to actively and managed carefully. Second, the paradox perspective provides legitimacy for each of the countervailing tendencies and for temporal discontinuities. Therefore, establishing and juggling the countervailing tendencies is the crucial task in organizing collaboration (Hardy et al., 2006). This is also why prescriptive advice on managing the paradox makes less sense, as it would deny the complexity and the situated interplay of paradox in collaboration.

Instead, my findings reflect the intricate processes of multi-stakeholder collaboration in the here-and-now interaction. Thus they allow facilitators and participants to make more conscious choices about using the different discourses that bring about specific modes of relating. Identifying the discourses that are currently in use helps to clarify what is happening in the process. This kind of attention facilitates a shift towards a different discourse if necessary by allowing participants to jointly reflect on the discursive resources in use, to bring different discourses into play, or to jointly develop new ones. Once they are sensitized to recognizing different modes of relating and ways of talking, facilitators, conveners and participants become able to play with and reflect on them: what are their effects on inclusiveness, and on achieving change? Hence, they may experiment with different ways of conceptualizing collaboration among diverse stakeholders, and discuss how to tackle emerging or long-standing conflicts. Theorizing the paradox as discursive struggle (Hardy et al., 2005) allows for an integration of diversity, not in a unifying manner, but in a way that fosters multivoicedness (Bouwen and Steyaert, 1999; Gergen and Gergen, 2010) and a lively debate among stakeholders to explore new practices and ideas in the sustainability arena (Christensen, Morsing and Thyssen, 2015). By its very nature, paradox stimulates ongoing discursive activity (Billig, Condor and Edwards, 1988; Edley, 2001, p. 204). To sum up, then, recognizing the fundamental paradox of collaboration and revealing the various discourses addressing it helps participants to make full use of their collaborative energy by increasing the transformative potential of the collaborative discourses; thus it reveals creative new ways of organizing the domain of environmental governance.

REFERENCES

Alvesson, Mats and Dan Kärreman (2000), 'Varieties of discourse: On the study of organizations through discourse analysis', *Human Relations*, **53** (9), 1125–1149.

Beech, Nic, Harry Burns, Linda de Caestecker, Robert MacIntosh and Donald MacLean (2004), 'Paradox as invitation to act in problematic change situations', *Human Relations*, **57** (10), 1313–1332.

Billig, Michael (1996), *Arguing and Thinking. A Rhetorical Approach to Social Psychology*, Cambridge: Cambridge University Press.

Billig, Michael, Susan Condor and Derek Edwards (1988), *Ideological Dilemmas: A Social Psychology of Everyday Thinking*, London: Sage.

Blumer, Herbert (1954), 'What is wrong with social theory?', *American Sociological Review*, **19** (1), 3–10.

Bouwen, René and Chris Steyaert (1999), 'From a dominant voice toward multivoiced cooperation', in David L. Cooperrider and Jane E. Dutton (eds), *Organizational Dimensions of Global Change*, London: Sage, pp. 291–319.

Bouwen, René and Tharsi Taillieu (2004), 'Multi-party collaboration as social learning for interdependence: Developing relational knowing for sustainable natural resource management', *Journal of Community & Applied Social Psychology*, **14** (3), 137–153.

Bouwen, René, Marc Craps and Enrique Santos (1999), 'Multi-party collaboration:

Building generative knowledge and developing relationships among "unequal" partners in local community projects in Ecuador', *Concepts and Transformation*, **4** (2), 133–151.

Cameron, Kim S. and Robert E. Quinn (1988), 'Organizational paradox and transformation', in Robert E. Quinn and Kim S. Cameron (eds), *Paradox and Transformation: Toward a Theory of Change in Organization and Management*, Cambridge, MA: Ballinger, pp. 1–18.

Christensen, Lars Thøger, Mette Morsing and Ole Thyssen (2015), 'Discursive closure and discursive openings in sustainability', *Management Communication Quarterly*, **29** (1), 135–144.

Clegg, Stewart R., Joao da Cunha and Miguel Pina e Cunha (2002), 'Management paradoxes: A relational view', *Human Relations*, **55** (5), 483–503.

Connelly, David R., Jing Zhang and Sue R. Faermann (2008), 'The paradoxical nature of collaboration', in Rosemary O'Leary and Lisa B. Bingham (eds), *Big Ideas in Collaborative Public Management*, Armonk, NY: M.E. Sharpe, pp. 17–35.

Edley, Nigel (2001), 'Analysing masculinity: Interpretative repertoires, ideological dilemmas and subject positions', in Margaret Wetherell, Stephanie Taylor and Simeon J. Yates (eds), *Discourse as Data: A Guide for Analysis*, London: Sage, pp. 189–228.

Gergen, Kenneth J. (1999), *An Invitation to Social Construction*, London: Sage.

Gergen, Kenneth and Mary Gergen (2010), 'Polyvocal organizing: An exploration', in Chris Steyaert and Bart Van Looy (eds), *Relational Practices, Participative Organizing*, Bingley: Emerald, pp. 261–274.

Gray, Barbara (1989), *Collaborating: Finding Common Ground for Multiparty Problems*, San Francisco, CA: Jossey Bass.

Gray, Barbara (2011), 'The complexity of multiparty negotiations: Wading into the muck', *Negotiation and Conflict Management Research*, **40** (3), 169–177.

Hardy, Cynthia, Thomas B. Lawrence and David Grant (2005), 'Discourse and collaboration: The role of conversations and collective identity', *Academy of Management Review*, **30** (1), 58–77.

Hardy, Cynthia, Thomas B. Lawrence and Nelson Phillips (2006), 'Swimming with sharks: Creating strategic change through multi-sector collaboration', *International Journal of Strategic Change Management*, **1** (1), 96–112.

Hemmati, Minu (2002), *Multi-Stakeholder Processes for Governance and Sustainability: Beyond Deadlock and Conflict*, London: Earthscan Publications.

Henttonen, Kaisa, Katja Lahikainen and Tiina Jauhiainen (2014), 'Governance mechanisms in multi-party non-profit collaboration', *Public Organization Review*, November, 1–16.

Hernes, Tor and Sally Maitlis (2010), *Process, Sensemaking, and Organizing*, Oxford: Oxford University Press.

Heydenreich, Anna-Katrin (2008), *Organising a Multi-Stakeholder Process: Creating a Paradoxical Collaborative Identity*, St. Gallen, Switzerland: University of St. Gallen.

Huxham, Chris and Nic Beech (2003), 'Contrary prescriptions: Recognizing good practice tensions in management', *Organization Studies*, **24** (1), 69–93.

Huxham, Chris and Siv Evy Vangen (2005), *Managing to Collaborate: The Theory and Practice of Collaborative Advantage*, London: Routledge.

Lewicki, Roy J., Barbara Gray and M. Elliott (2003), *Making Sense of Intractable Environmental Disputes*, Washington, DC: Island Press.

Lewis, Marianne W. (2000), 'Exploring paradox: Toward a more comprehensive guide', *Academy of Management Review*, **25** (4), 760–776.
Marshall, Catherine and Gretchen B. Rossman (1989), *Designing Qualitative Research*, Thousand Oaks, CA: Sage.
O'Leary, Rosemary and Lisa B. Bingham (2009), 'Surprising findings, paradoxes, and thoughts on the future of collaborative public management research', in Rosemary O'Leary and Lisa B. Bingham (eds), *The Collaborative Public Manager: New Ideas for the Twenty-first Century*, Washington, DC: Georgetown University Press, pp. 255–269.
Ospina, Sonia M. and Angel Saz-Carranza (2010), 'Paradox and collaboration in network management', *Administration and Society*, **42** (4), 404–440.
Phillips, Nelson and Cliff Oswick (2012), 'Organizational discourse: Domains, debates and directions', *The Academy of Management Annals*, **6** (1), 1–47.
Poole, Marshall S. and Andrew H. van de Ven (1989), 'Using paradox to build management and organization theories', *Academy of Management Review*, **14** (4), 562–578.
Potter, Jonathan and Margaret Wetherell (1987), *Discourse and Social Psychology: Beyond Attitudes and Behaviour*, London: Sage.
Potter, Jonathan and Margeret Wetherell (1994), 'Analyzing discourse', in Alan Bryman and Robert G. Burgess (eds), *Analyzing Qualitative Data*, London: Routledge, pp. 47–66.
Potter, Jonathan, Cristian Tileagă and Alexa Hepburn (2011), 'Inequality in action', *International Journal of Education and Psychology in the Community*, **1** (2), 43–60.
Putnam, Linda L., Gail T. Fairhurst and Scott Banghart (2016), 'Contradictions, dialectics, and paradoxes in organizations: A constitutive approach', *The Academy of Management Annals*, **10** (1), 65–171.
Schad, Jonathan, Marianne W. Lewis, Sebastian Raisch and Wendy K. Smith (2016), 'Paradox research in management science: Looking back to move forward', *The Academy of Management Annals*, **10** (1), 5–64.
Smith, Wendy K. and Marianne Lewis (2011), 'Toward a theory of paradox: A dynamic equilibrium model of organizing', *Academy of Management Review*, **36** (2), 381–403.
Smith, Wendy K. and Paul Tracey (2016), 'Institutional complexity and paradox theory: Complementarities of competing demands', *Strategic Organization*. Published online 4 April, doi: 10.1177/1476127016638565.
Steyaert, Chris and Bart Van Looy (2010), *Relational Practices, Participative Organizing*, Bingley: Emerald.
Tracy, Karen and Catherine Ashcraft (2001), 'Crafting policies about controversial values: How wording disputes manage a group dilemma', *Journal of Applied Communication Research*, **29** (4), 297–316.
Trist, Eric (1983), 'Referent organizations and the development of inter-organizational domains', *Human Relations*, **36** (3), 269–284.
Vangen, Siv and Chris Huxham (2012), 'The tangled web: Unraveling the principle of common goals in collaborations', *Journal of Public Administration Research and Theory*, **22** (4), 731–760.
Wetherell, Margaret (2006), 'Interpretive repertoires', in Victor R. Jupp (ed.), *The Sage Dictionary of Social Research*, London: Sage, pp. 153–155.
Wetherell, Margaret and Jonathan Potter (1988), 'Discourse analysis and the

identification of interpretative repertoires', in Charles Antaki (ed.), *Analysing Everyday Explanation*, London: Sage, pp. 168–183.

Wood, Linda A. and Rolf O. Kroger (2000), *Doing Discourse Analysis*, Thousand Oaks, CA: Sage.

Zeyen, Anica, Markus Beckmann and Stella Wolters (2014), 'Actor and institutional dynamics in the development of multi-stakeholder initiatives', *Journal of Business Ethics*, 1–20 (online first).

4. Performing participation: reassembling a new museum

Christoph Michels

INTRODUCTION

'Did someone say participate?' Sounding almost weary, this question comes from the cover of *An Atlas of Spatial Practice* published by Markus Miessen and Shumon Basar in 2006. This rhetorical question reflects the growing qualms about the general concept of participation which has been praised as a 'panacea for all the main illnesses of modern society – alienation, isolation, excessive anarchic and individualistic capitalism, social disintegration, and political indifference' (Tamir, 1998 in Amin and Thrift, 2002, p. 135). This chapter sets out to reflect upon the conceptualizations of participation and the ongoing unease with regard to its promises and inherent politics. By way of an empirical study on the participatory planning process for a new museum it presents a performative understanding of participation and suggests understanding participation as an effect of spatio-aesthetic modes of ordering which enact specific subjectivities and their respective forms of imagining the future. The conceptual shift presented in this chapter entails a move from a deliberative to an agonistic approach to democracy, stressing the importance of multiplicity and artistic modes of organizing in the performances of democratic life.

During the past two decades the concept of participation has equally been adopted in the contexts of politics (van Deth, 2014), international development (Korf, 2010), health care (Mullen, Hughes and Vincent-Jones, 2011), management (Fryer, 2011) and urban planning where participation has by 'now become the planning mainstream, central to how planning is taught and practised' (Allmendinger and Haughton, 2012, p. 2). Within the broad context of its uses participation has been conceptualized in various ways (Cornwall, 2008), but it seems fair to say that – despite their differences – most approaches address participation as a question of including a multiplicity of 'voices', 'stakeholders' or 'interest groups', giving those who are affected by decisions the opportunity to express and promote their interests and concerns in processes of decision-making (such as Parkinson, 2003). This way of conceptualizing participation is concerned with the question of how participants can (or cannot) both represent and promote their concerns in a participatory process.

In this chapter I will suggest a somewhat different conceptual route, developing Kulynych's (1997, p. 336) argument that 'it is possible, and more meaningful, to conceptualize contemporary participation as a performative rather than a representative action'. Drawing on Foucault's notion of 'resistance' as well as Butler's concept of 'performativity', Kulynych expands and redefines participation as any action that resists and potentially reconfigures 'the normalizing, regularizing, and subjectifying confines of contemporary disciplinary regimes' (p. 338). While Kulynych reflects on how her performative approach to participation may inform an understanding of deliberative democracy à la Habermas (p. 343), I will instead develop her approach in relation to the political philosophy of Chantal Mouffe, as I believe that the latter makes more space for the 'defiant creativity and disruptive diversity' (p. 345) that Kulynych sees as inherent in participatory action.

According to Mouffe (2000; 2005; 2014) democratic politics is based on the formation of multiple collective identities of different sizes and scopes, all of which rely on clearly discriminating between 'we' and 'they'. Diametrically opposed to Habermas' ideal in which people resolve such discriminations through a process of deliberation, Mouffe underlines the possibilities and positive opportunities of a democratic politics that acknowledges the irresolvable tensions between different hegemonic projects and promotes their confrontation as legitimate adversaries. Mouffe (2014, p. 151) argues that 'the agonistic confrontation, far from representing a danger for democracy, is in reality the very condition of its existence'.

This conceptual shift entails a fundamental reconfiguration of the way we understand individual and collective identities, how they are formed and how they relate to each other. While deliberative approaches to participation understand the identities of its participants (and their specific interests) as pre-given, stable and subsequently voiced or represented in participatory processes, agonistic models are interested in participation as a process of (passionate) identity formation or identification (Mouffe, 2005, pp. 25–29). Those using the latter approach believe that processes of identification can only work in the form of agonistic we/they discriminations. Thus they place the creation of differences and confrontations – and not the overcoming of them – at the centre of democratic politics. Mouffe's political theory presents a fruitful ground for Kulynych's perspective on participation, one which makes space for performing participation as a process of creative and disruptive identity formation.

I would also like to expand Kulynych's approach in a second direction, to consider the spatio-material aspects of performing participation. Kulynych (1997, p. 336) argues that a performative understanding 'widens the parameters of participation to include a host of new actors, activities, and locations for political action'. She expands potential spaces of participation beyond institutional settings, presenting housecleaning as one exemplary context for potential participation (p. 339). Almost in the same way as Cornwall (2004) does, Kesby (2007, p. 2822) calls for a 'more coherent theorisation of spaces of participation ... one that recognises that the technologies, social relations, and *arenas* of participation are inter-dependent and that the modalities and *spaces* of power and *empowerment* are entangled'. Likewise, Marres (2012) argues that 'the enactment of par-ticipation and the organization of the space-times of participation must be understood as inter-related processes' (p. 147). Along these lines, I suggest that in Kulynych's performative approach, participation can no longer be reduced to human agents but has to be seen as a process in which 'physical stuff ... is a lively participant' (Latham, McCormack, McNamara and McNeill, 2009, p. 62).

In order to explain the concept of participation as a spatio-material performance, I will draw on two interrelated research traditions in the conceptual part of this chapter. The first – which has crystallized under the label of Actor-Network Theory (ANT) and been developed from there – provides a conceptual vocabulary for addressing the role that non-human participants can play in performances of the social. Despite their extensive empirical and conceptual advances, studies using ANT remain largely silent on how socio-material relations unfold in sensual or aesthetic pro-cesses. Second, to fill this gap, I will draw on a stream of research that has been presented under the label of 'the affective turn' in the social sciences; it stresses the pre-conscious, sensual and emergent qualities of socio-spatial assemblages. Mouffe (2014, p. 157) draws on this understanding of affec-tive space and suggests that 'affects and desire play a crucial role in the con-stitution of subjectivity with the assertion that they are the moving forces of political action'. She thus proposes to 'employ this dynamic to examine the modes of transformation of political identities, seeing "affections" as the space where the discursive and the affective are articulated in specific practices' (p. 156). From a material-semiotic and affective perspective, then, participation can be understood as the performative (re)configura-tion of socio-spatial regimes that not only affect what participants can do and say but also how they feel.

In order to inform this understanding of participation empirically, in this chapter I present the participatory process for planning a new art museum in a medium-sized city in Switzerland. Drawing on Law's (1994) notion of 'modes of ordering', I describe the process as the performance of three interrelated modes of organizing human (and non-human) participants based on their distinctive ways of imagining a future museum. I present the affective dynamics of these three modes and show how they are entangled with specific material sites, performing different sensory landscapes.

Although the case and the related literature are inscribed in the context of urban planning, the insights and conceptual advances from this analysis can also contribute to the wider discourse on the politics of participation I discussed above. In particular, these insights can also contribute to reflections on the notions of worker participation (Budd, Gollan, and Wilkinson, 2010) and stakeholder dialogue (Shrivastava, 1986), as well as corporate social responsibility (Scherer and Palazzo, 2007). Therefore, they could also be understood as a response to the calls to develop understandings of organizational processes which take into account the material, affective and spatial dimensions of organizational practice (Beyes and Steyaert, 2011; Grant, Iedema, and Oswick, 2009).

The chapter is structured in the following way: having laid out my broader conceptual context in this introduction, I continue by elaborating on the conceptual framework for my case analysis. Combining the concept of 'modes of ordering' (Law, 1994) with the notion of 'affect' (Massumi, 2002), I will argue that participation can be thought of as the spatio-aesthetic co-performance of specific organizational logics and that a politics of participation necessitates experimentation with and reflection on potential modes of participation. Second, in my methods section I present a case: the process of planning for a new art museum. I researched the case as part of my doctoral research in collaboration with my two colleagues and supervisors Timon Beyes and Chris Steyaert (Michels, Beyes and Steyaert, 2014). I will describe how we gained access, what role we played in the planning process, how we gathered the empirical material, and how we structured it into three distinct modes of ordering. The analysis, then, shows how each mode of organizing the museum relies on specific sites and ways of aesthetically relating to them, how they perform participation and how they enact specific visions of a future art museum. Finally, I will discuss how each mode relies on and reproduces specific affections, reflect on the possible consequences for participatory organizing, and offer a brief conclusion.

CONCEPTUAL FRAMEWORK

In developing a performative understanding of participation I draw mainly on two research traditions and their related concepts. The first hint for rethinking participation, I take from Actor-Network Theory (ANT) and its implications (Alcadipani and Hassard, 2010; Law and Hassard, 1999). ANT aims to understand objects as vital participants in organizing 'the social' and blur the boundaries of formerly clearly demarcated actors; by doing so, its project 'is simply to extend the list and modify the shapes and figures of those assembled as participants' (Latour, 2005, p. 72). When we widen the focus, all sorts of 'non-human actors' come on stage and start to participate in shaping the social. Scallops (Callon, 2006), door-closers (Johnson, 1988), vessels (Law, 1987) and other 'non-humans' have been described as active and sometimes quite obdurate participants in the shaping of social relations. In this understanding agency is not attributed only to autonomous human actors or to essential non-human actors. Instead agency is conceptualized as an effect of socio-material practices which perform (multiple versions of) the social (Alcadipani and Hassard, 2010; Mol, 2002).

John Law (1994) elaborated this performative view of organizing by conceptualizing these socio-material practices as forming '*fairly coherent and large scale ordering patterns* in the networks of the social' (p. 107, emphasis in original). These 'modes of ordering', he says, 'speak through, act, and recursively organize the full range of social materials' (p. 109). Law describes modes of ordering as contingent (they could be otherwise), recursive (they reproduce themselves and thus have a certain autonomy), relational (they consist of specific ways of interrelating elements, not in a collection of specific elements 'themselves'), strategic (they are intentional in the effects that they produce), and more or less fragile (they can change, peter out or break down). These patterns are similar in some ways to what others have described as discourses (Foucault, 1981). But modes of ordering and what Law (1999, p. 4) calls 'semiotics of materiality' 'may be usefully distinguished from those versions of post-structuralism that attend to language and language alone'. Instead they explicitly include the performances of socio-material assemblages. Thus, an ANT-perspective and in particular the concept 'modes of ordering' allows for conceptually reframing participation as an effect of recursive performances which assemble human and non-human participants into relational networks.

While the notion 'network' is central to many ANT studies, the way that it addresses the enactment of human and non-human relations is somewhat mechanical and language-focused; thus it 'tends to limit and homogenize the character of links, the character of invariant connection, the character of possible relations, and so the character of possible entities' (Law, 1999, p. 7). Therefore just the use of ANT vocabulary makes it difficult to address the sensual or aesthetic dimensions of organizational processes (but see Hennion, 2001; 2007). By itself it does not seem to be suitable for taking account of the affects and passions that Mouffe had identified as inherent part of democratic politics. In response, to address the sensuality, the unpredictable emergence, and the preconscious unfolding inherent in the performance of participation I suggest we can inform an ANT line of conducting research through the conceptual developments of the 'affective turn' (Deleuze, 1988; Gregg and Seigworth, 2010; Massumi, 2002).

Concerning the sensuality of performing participation, Massumi's (2002) discussion of affect presents an inspiring starting point for re-thinking sensation as performance. In his work sensation is not thought of as a one-way perception of an external world through a sensing body but rather as a resonance or interference pattern between (human and non-human) bodies (Massumi, 2002, p. 14). This relational way of concep-tualizing sensation presents aesthetic experience as a way of performing specific socio-material assemblages; thus such experiences are one element in the formation of specific subjectivities. Affects are therefore not free-floating but are 'anchored in (functionally limited by) the actually existing, particular things that embody them' (Massumi, 2002, p. 35), relying on the participation of objects, architectures, smells, sounds, light and the like. This understanding of affect clearly resonates with – and in fact has been set in relation to – Actor-Network Theory (Anderson and Harrison, 2010, pp. 13–15).

Zooming in on the sensual dimensions of affects, Hickey-Moody (2013) stresses the potential of art and aesthetics for the affective unfolding of spatio-temporal assemblages and their reconfiguration. She argues that '(t)he aesthetics of everyday life choreograph connections and resist-ances to people, situations and events' (Hickey-Moody, 2013, p. 83) and that works of art are 'entities that propel the political agendas of those for whom they speak', and 'create new sensory landscapes and systems of affective relay and responsive capacity for their beholders' (p. 88). Thus she conceptualizes a way to understand the participation of humans and non-humans in the performance of spatial assemblages: consider their aesthetic capacities. Here, art and the sensual resonances between human and non-human participants are understood as 'a mode of producing subjectivity' and as 'a mode of augmenting community' (p. 87). Aesthetic sensibilities are then central for understanding how collectives and their specific sub-jectivities may be (re)assembled.

For Hickey-Moody the sensual becoming of subjectivities is intertwined with the process of (re-)imagining. She states that '(t)o feel or to sense is to imagine' (p. 82) and thus presents an understanding of imagination that relies on the sensing body and how it resonates with its environment. Taking up her understanding of aesthetics as a central dimension in the performance of participants' subjectivities, in this chapter I aim to show

how 'aesthetics can re-map affective routes', as they work with 'the body's capacity to feel, respond and imagine' (Hickey-Moody, 2013, p. 87); by doing so, aesthetics can allow new forms of participation to emerge. Thus, the first aspect of affect I consider to be relevant for the analysis is exactly this sensual capacity to become part of – or participate in – the process of forming imaginative experiences.

The second aspect of conceptualizing affect in the context of participation is the unpredictable ways it may unfold and thus its radical openness to the formation of new and unforeseeable socio-material assemblages (Massumi, 2002, pp. 8–9). Yet it is important to distinguish between the notions of 'affections' (affectio) and 'affect' (affectus) (Deleuze, 1988, p. 48). While *affections* can be thought of as modes or forms of life which constitute a specific state of affected/affecting bodies, *affects* 'refer to the passage from one state to another' (p. 49) and thus describe 'the ways mixtures or assemblages change, effecting alterations of subjectivities' (Hickey-Moody, 2013, p. 80). Referring back to the concept of modes of ordering, discussed above, I suggest we think of them as relying on the performance of specific affections and remember that these affections can be challenged and changed as their participants affect and are affected by other modes of ordering. These alterations of modes imply a modification of affections and thus a change in the participants' subjectivities. However, it is difficult, if not impossible, to predict or plan how affective dynamics unfold and what changes in subjectivity the affective unsettling of specific modes will bring about, as 'we really have no idea either what affects human bodies or minds might be capable of in a given encounter ahead of time or, indeed, more generally, what worlds human beings might be capable of building' (Thrift, 2004, pp. 62–63). The affective becoming of participation then implies experimental and playful approaches that challenge predominant modes and are fundamentally open to the emergence of new collective assemblages and their respective subjectivities.

Third, affects emerge in situations where the body responds to, or resonates with, its environment more quickly or more forcefully than the mind does. Bennett (2010 in Anderson and Harrison, 2010, p. 16) likens it to a 'push' of life, one 'which interrupts, unsettles and haunts persons, places or things'. The unfolding of affects, which is 'most directly manifested in the skin – at the surface of the body, at its interface with things' (Massumi, 2002, p. 25) might precede conscious reflection and can be understood as a precognitive and prelinguistic interaction of the body with its environment. Labanyi (2010) describes it as 'doing things', as material practices which unconsciously but nevertheless substantially impact the way we make sense of and behave in our environment. With reference to the concept of modes of ordering and their respective affections, I suggest we understand both

their stabilization and their modification in terms of more or less unconscious affective dynamics which (re)produce a number of effects, including
emotions, atmospheres, identities, places and imaginations.

For the concept of participation this turn to affect suggests that participatory processes emerge in far less rational and orderly ways than
for example the ideals of a Habermasian discourse ethics would imply.
Therefore attending to affective dynamics presents a challenge for participatory politics, as it highlights how forms of participation may emerge in
a sensual, radically open, and unconscious way. Participatory politics thus
calls not only for a playful and experimental unfolding of participation
but also for a reflexivity that relies on the experience of being subjected
to multiple modes of ordering and their respective affections. As participants experience various potential modes of participation and the tensions
between them, they can gain a form of reflexive agency that paves the way
for a sensibility about which mode they wish to participate in, and perhaps
also about making conscious decisions.

METHODOLOGY

To facilitate my empirical analysis I first present a case study of a participatory planning process concerning the question of whether a new
art museum should be built, and what kind of museum it should be. The
process was initiated in 2006 by the cultural department of a Swiss canton
and formed part of the government's strategy to make the city more attractive as a place to live, work and visit. Because the city's residents had
recently rejected two projects – a new theatre and an extension to the art
museum – in a plebiscite, the participatory planning process can be seen as
a way for the government to test the ground for its plan, and to build an alliance among experts, opinion leaders and the broader public. Therefore the
canton provided the project with a comfortable budget of CHF 500 000 and
a time span of approximately ten months. During that time the project team
organized a series of workshops with citizens, conducted expert interviews
and presented the project at public events and through the local media.

My colleague Timon Beyes and I gained access to the planning process
when the project manager invited us to co-organize the citizen workshops.
Renegotiating our roles, we became researchers who helped document
the citizen workshops and served the canton as reflection partners. The
government granted us access to all team meetings, citizen workshops and
official events and to most of the meetings of the government's steering
committee. As ethnographic researchers we participated in this project for
approximately 12 months. The fieldwork period ended in spring 2007 when

the project team presented its results and the government announced that it would withdraw from the plan for a new art museum and would instead focus on developing a new library and refurbishing the textile museum.

Apart from our participant observation (Waddington, 2004) of 12 citizen workshops and 20 team meetings we also conducted narrative interviews (Czarniawska, 2004) with nine of the more prominent players in the process and accessed another 34 transcripts of project-related interviews conducted by the project team. Furthermore we gathered and analysed a heterogeneous collection of documents, including emails, plans, newspaper articles and various leaflets and flyers (Hodder, 1994). Our initial analysis of this material included mapping (McDonald, Daniels and Harris, 2004), coding (Charmaz, 2000) and (re)reading the material in multiple iterations. However, it was only when we engaged conceptually with and searched for 'modes of ordering' that the analysis became more structured and systematic. This analytic focus allowed us to also specify the research question, asking: How did different modes of ordering (and contesting) ideas about the art museum and its future succeed or fail in engaging participants? Within this broader research question the following analysis focuses on the spaces in which each mode was performed and asks how specific architectural sites aesthetically affected the formation of the participants' identities.

My analysis of the spatio-aesthetic dimensions of the three modes of ordering was conducted as a secondary engagement with the ethnographic material and experiences. It mainly relies on my (auto)ethnographic experiences and memories of the field research. Focusing on the photographs and the auto-ethnographic vignettes taken during the field research, I reconstructed and reflected on my aesthetic experience in the performance of three different places (Humberstone, 2011), exploring 'the physically felt and barely articulable sensations that arise through embodied performances and practices within the place of fieldwork' and reporting them back by means of evocative, poetic and creative writing (Paterson, 2009, p. 785). In addition I will use three images from my field research to perform an understanding of the ethnographic field which – like the poetic use of language – makes room for (syn)aesthetic experiences and the readers' reflection on them (Pink, 2008; Steyaert, Marti, and Michels, 2012).

In reconstructing the three modes of ordering the art museum I begin by describing the tensions that became apparent during the final presentation of the results of the planning process. Instead of presenting one solution for the art museum, the government officials confronted the audience with two possibilities. First, the government could invest in a new building for the art museum, providing the city with a new cultural 'light house' and placing it firmly on the map of national and international tourism. Or the museum could stay in its current classicist building at the municipal park but gain additional exhibition space if the government removed the natural history museum currently housed in the basement of that building. While the second scenario clearly resonated with the preferences of the local art club, the canton's announcement that it would not financially support this second scenario came as something of a shock. In this latter case the canton would leave the museum project to the municipality and redirect its investments towards a new library and a new textile museum.

The tension between these two logics served as a point of departure for our further analysis of the material. It was a fairly smooth process to organize the collected documents, field notes and interview manuscripts according to the two logics – with a few exceptions. Some of the material told us about further intricacies. What stood out most obviously was a workshop conducted by a group of artists that proposed a third way of performing the museum. Thus we distinguished between a strategic mode, a classical mode and a situational mode of ordering the art museum and its future. In the next section, I introduce each mode with a short ethnographic description of a characteristic space and then describe its ordering activities and broader logic.

FINDINGS

The Strategic Mode

Passing through the train station and following the tracks outside, we reach the old train depot. Surrounded by bushes and weeds, the depot looks derelict from the outside. But upon entering we find ourselves in a bright and friendly space. The floor is covered with gravel on top of which wooden walkways seem to be floating. The ceiling is high and rests on slender concrete columns; animated light installations are suspended from above, emphasizing the spaciousness of the building and filling it with soft, warm light. From the far end of the room we hear the lively but well-tempered conversation of a group of rather elegantly dressed people, and occasional clinking of glasses. Immediately a feeling overwhelms me, evoking fragments of past experiences: highbrow culture. Gallery opening. Post-industrial lifestyle. Arty but playful. Am I dressed appropriately? Let's see who's here. (Excerpt from field notes; this and all the following quotes were translated from German.)

This vignette describes our arrival at the closing event of the government's pre-planning project. In the section that follows, I will read this event as an enactment of a set of heterogeneous relationships which combine a number of human and non-human participants in the process

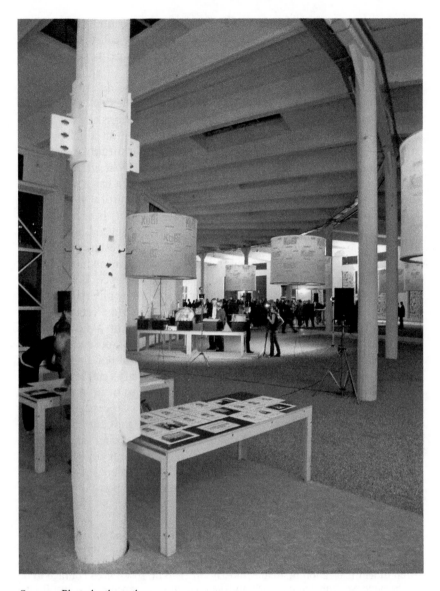

Source: Photo by the author.

Figure 4.1 Closing event at the train depot

of imagining an innovative art house next to the city's central train station. This event, I will argue, resonates with what we have called the strategic mode, which was at work throughout the pre-project period and reached far beyond this city's limits.

As a first 'participant' in the strategic mode let me describe the train depot itself. It is a relic from the 19th century when the city was booming economically and exported textile products to destinations all over Europe and the world. It is located on the city's west side, a district which had, and still has, many of the city's political and economic institutions, including the city hall, several banks, the train station, and the post office as well as trade and shopping facilities. In recent decades, the area has also attracted several young cultural institutions. In particular, a beautiful 19th-century brick warehouse, located not far from the train depot, became the new hotspot for the city's young cultural scene, housing several art galleries, artists' studios, a wine merchant and a rather exclusive restaurant. Not far from the warehouse an abandoned freight station was turned into a music club, attracting a relatively young and alternative audience. Furthermore, the depot itself had been used as an exhibition space by an internationally renowned art gallery before the government turned it into a venue for occasional cultural events. And it is right next to the depot, on a piece of waste land, that the government suggests locating the new art museum.

This kind of cultural regeneration of post-industrial buildings and city districts echoes a discourse on the entrepreneurial city (Harvey, 1989) in which culture-driven regeneration is placed at the heart of urban economic development (Hubbard and Hall, 1998; Pratt, 2009). According to Amin and Thrift (2002, p. 152), in these developments 'a tight coupling between postindustrial capitalism and urban aesthetic form is taking shape, read as necessary for the survival of the economy in general and cities in particular'. This discourse not only surfaces in tonight's presentations but also runs like a red thread through the entire planning project. For example a government strategy paper reads:

> The region's cultural landscape has to vibrate as a whole and on different levels. It has to penetrate the social and economic life. At the same time it is in need of strong icons and highlights. Convincing contents need an expressive and self-confident realization in architecture. In order to do so we need courage to do the unconventional and the will to take on additional expense. (Excerpt from a government document)

While neighbouring cities had invested in 'iconic' architecture over the last 15 years, this city government's attempts to create architectural icons had been rejected in various plebiscites. In order to build a more reliable alliance with the citizens, the government had made civic participation a central aspect of its strategy. With the old train depot and the nearby warehouse figuring as key locations for most of the citizen workshops and the presentation of their final results, the participatory process unfolded in a specific spatio-aesthetic setting, addressing its participants not only as idea generators but as co-performers of a specific way of assembling an imagination of the city and its cultural institutions and thus evoking a foretaste of the museum to come. The elaborate yet playful graphics of the documentation – including work by a local cartoonist – added to the experience of an atmosphere that implicitly made space for people to imagine a new and exciting art house, as did the fine Italian wine and food served after each workshop and the production of an inspiring video clip on one of the workshops.

To sum up, the strategic mode performs a set of relationships that connect specific spaces (the western part of the city), objects (industrial architecture, food, graphics), practices (of plebiscitary democracy, workshops, presentations), people (citizens, experts, opinion leaders, the government) and narratives (on the entrepreneurial city) into a pattern of ordering that support a new iconic building. The objects, places and bodies that participate in this mode of ordering carefully co-enact an aesthetic experience which allows people to *feel* the arrival of the new museum.

The Classical Mode

> Standing in front of the temple-like facade of the museum a feeling of sacredness overwhelms us. The building is ordered in a perfect symmetry, which extends beyond the museum's actual limits into the park. On one side of the building its longitudinal axis is continued with a lovely circular fountain and a massive steel sculpture by an internationally renowned artist; on the other side it connects over the sculptural chimney of the museum's underground archive to the central axis of the neighbouring history museum. The building's lateral axis is prolonged by the grid of the so-called museum quarter. (Excerpt from field notes)

This vignette presents a performance of the art museum which is entirely different from the strategic mode presented above. And for the moment I'm co-performing it. As at the train depot, my body falls into a specific mode – which we call classical – and makes me choose the terms 'sacredness', 'perfect symmetry' and 'internationally renowned'. While the strategic mode depended on the performance of a sentiment of excitement about the potential arrival of a new museum, the classical mode can be described as performing awe and respect for the established order of a cultural institution and its continuation. This order not only resonates with the building of the old art museum but is also reflected in the design of the surrounding urban environment, the so-called museum quarter.

Source: Photo by Daniel Giger.

Figure 4.2   In front of the art museum

Located in the eastern part of the city, this quarter also includes other classical cultural institutions which originated in the 19th and early 20th century, such as the library, the history museum, the concert hall, and the municipal garden as well as several schools. Together with rows of beautiful apartment houses and two representative villas from the same period, these institutions form a perfectly ordered symmetrical grid, evoking the city's bourgeois history.

This place is a key participant in the performance of the classical mode, the second mode at work throughout the planning process and one which, like the strategic mode, also reaches far beyond this place, this text and this body. I have heard it resonate in other places, in other texts and through other voices. The *Alte Museum* in Berlin, the *Kunsthistorische Museum* in Vienna and the National Gallery in London come to mind. In an interview a curator described the specific atmosphere of these places:

> Art has a calming effect. This has always been the museum's function. It's almost like a contemporary church . . . a place of concentration.

Another curator added:

> It makes sense that the reception of art is difficult – you only receive something from art when you use your head. That's why I appreciate the holy temples of art that produce a certain fear of entering. . . . Because, at the end of the day, not everybody has to go to the museum.

In the strategic mode, these old museums are rendered problematic as they do not evoke vibrant creativity, nor do they attract (inter)national investors or 'the creative class'. But in the classic mode these buildings become 'assets'. One of our interviewees explained that in an international contest to exhibit works by sought-after artists the classical architecture of the old museum turned out to offer a competitive advantage. Its strict order and classic decoration provides an attractive exception within a predominantly (post)modernist museum landscape.

Within this mode it is difficult to understand why the city needs a new art house. The only problem with the existing building is that it must share space with the natural history museum, leaving insufficient space to display the art club's valuable collection. A year before the canton announced that it intended to build a new art museum, the municipal museum foundation, which includes the museums of art, natural history and history, had devised its own plan with the title 'Three Museums – Three Houses'. This plan conceived of a new building for the natural history collection; thus it would have put the plebiscite's focus on 'nature' instead of 'culture', and thus was deemed to receive more support by the local population. In clear contrast to the strategic mode, the classical mode does not aim at including a wider public when it comes to decisions on the art museum. Instead the autonomy of the museum experts is of utmost importance so that the collection and exhibition of art can stay free from political influences. As a member of the art club told us, 'There is no democracy in art, it's all about knowledge, knowledge and intuition . . . absolutely. Democracy might be a laudable form of government and living, but in art democracy has no place.'

> Climbing a flight of stairs and entering through a heavy wooden door we find ourselves in the museum's entrance hall. A downward ramp leads the way to the natural history museum from where we can hear the echoing voices of children.. . . We climb the heavy staircase to the building's upper floor. Here the atmosphere is quiet. A few visitors meander through the bright, high spaces. The exhibits are abstract and sculptural. We immediately begin whispering and try to make sense of the works of art from the small captions which describe them. The always friendly guard nods in our direction. (Excerpt from field notes)

The classical mode aims at perpetuating a knowledge space that is highly specialized, recognized by international art circles and directed by independent art experts. It relates to a set of practices, buildings, artefacts and roles which in concert perform a materialized system of knowledge that dates back to the early 19th century. Among these practices are setting up and visiting highbrow exhibitions, offering pedagogical programmes, and drawing on a narrative of art connoisseurship which 'defend(s) the museum's traditional commitments to collecting, preservation, and scholarship and resist(s) the move to populist programming, building expansion, and market driven narratives' (McClellan, 2008, p. 4). Through these narratives and the design of specific spaces, this mode evokes an aesthetic experience that focuses on admiration and respect for the traditional art museum and its place in the city's cultural landscape.

In sum, the classical mode performs a pattern of relations which assembles specific spaces (the eastern part of the city), objects (the existing art museum and its exhibition spaces, the collection), practices (setting up and visiting art collections), various people (art experts, lay visitors) and narratives ('how the art world works') into a distinct performance of the museum space. Whereas the strategic mode envisaged a new architectural icon, the classical pattern of ordering aimed at reconstructing the existing building in all its grandeur. Like the strategic mode, this mode also relies upon its aesthetic performativity: its harmonious, perfectly ordered and somewhat dominant spaces and their related practices make it difficult to imagine alternatives to the classicist museum in the municipal park.

The Situational Mode

> A group of people, myself included, moves slowly through the museum quarter. Behind the concert hall, we enter a recently constructed public parking garage. Down the ramp, past the gate and the ticket machine, we arrive in the clean, bright parking area. Since it is half empty, there is lots of free space. It feels strangely inviting, reminding me of childhood adventures on our local parking lot. Moreover, walking through a parking garage is eerie when one is not looking for a car, when one is not tied into the usual parking garage constellations – occupied by shopping, the next meeting, the film just seen, etc. (Excerpt from field notes)

The performance described above is an artistic intervention into the planning process of the museum. It was initiated by a local artistic ensemble after the government asked it to conduct one of the pre-project citizen workshops. Instead of sticking to a fixed workshop location, the event unfolded as a walk through the city. Starting in the museum quarter in the east of the city, it led us through a parking garage, the central market

Source: Photo by Atelier für Sonderaufgaben.

Figure 4.3   'Warm up' in the parking garage

square, and the planning department's attic; it ended in an old warehouse
on the city's west side. This walk enacted what we have called the situational
mode of performing the art museum:

> In one of the parking spaces there is an overhead projector; we form a half-circle
> around it, taking seats on the portable folding chairs we were given earlier.
> There is an old-fashioned wooden carriage on which is mounted a sign that
> reads 'warm up'. With another carriage, folding tables are brought in and
> installed throughout the parking space . . . In changing constellations, we group
> around the tables, discussing the art museum, generating ideas and criteria.
> Occasionally, a car comes in or leaves; the drivers give us bewildered looks, or so
> it seems. (Excerpt from field notes)

This mode is characterized by the participation of rather mundane public
spaces which in contrast to the places of the other two modes do not feel
very special or exclusive. Rather, childhood memories bubble up; sensations of playful exploration and of clandestine subversion of urban space
take hold of my body. Walking into a highly functional transit space such
as a parking garage and staying there challenges the predominant logics of

its operation. Walking and sitting become practices that run counter to the place's design and the established ways of using and perceiving it. Clear tensions unfold on an aesthetic and imaginative level: What are we doing here? What will happen next? And what do other people think of this? Imagining an art museum here means literally stepping away from the two modes presented above. Questioning both predominant discourses about the museum and the predominant uses of public spaces, this mode performs art in an almost situationist way, provoking 'moments of disruption in everyday life . . . in which the apparent homogeneity of the spectacle-city (is) fractured to reveal the richness of possibilities offered by movement through the modern city' (McDonough, 1996, p. 63). In other words, the situational mode reflects on the relationships between art, the city and its inhabitants and plays with the possibilities of reassembling them in new ways. Thus it allows for 'the organization of another meaningful ensemble which confers on each element its new scope and effect' (Debord, cited in Andreotti, 1996, p. 28). As one of the artists explained, the intervention is based on a sort of strategy:

> [The strategy] takes the resources, jumbles them and creates something that does not exist. It's about the immediate creativity in everyday life, about the shifting of existing conditions. It reassembles the given and in that way creates a certain form, so that something emerges that was not part of the world until then.

This is achieved by reconnecting given elements into new relationships and thus reframing the situation:

> The next stop is the city's central marketplace. Underneath the large roof of the central bus stop, we find flip charts and an illuminated sign that reads 'taking the pulse' – it's duct-taped to the ticket machine. A few chairs are arranged in the form of a little auditorium. Equipped with writing pads and questionnaires the participants set off to interview pedestrians. The questions circle around the popularity of the art museum and people's wishes and visions for its future. After interviewing a couple of people, the participants return to the bus stop and report their findings. Curious pedestrians stop for a while and observe the proceedings. Quickly sketched diagrams summarize the findings, which are briefly discussed before the group moves on. (Excerpt from field notes)

By setting up a temporary research centre labelled 'taking the pulse', where people take on the roles of journalists, report back, draw charts, and use questionnaires and flip charts, the organizers temporarily reframed the space around the bus stop: it feels like a combination of a clinic and a research centre. However, the staging is humorous and playful and can be described with the situationist term 'détournement'; that is, it consists of 'the creative appropriation and reorganization of pre-existing elements' and implies 'a process of de-contextualization and re-contextualization' (Andreotti 1996, pp. 27–28). The bus stop is simultaneously de- and recontextualized through the staging of 'strange', collage-like narratives. This mode of ordering the art museum differs from the other two modes in that it aims not to stabilize a lasting (new) order but to spontaneously reconfigure the present.

To sum up, the situational mode can be described as reassembling urban spaces (parking garages, bus stops, attics), their inhabitants and users (pedestrians, workshop participants, artists), imaginative narratives (pulse taking, surveying), and simple technical devices (folding chairs, duct tape, projectors) through practices of enacting new situations (walking and sitting in strange places, doing research, entering otherwise inaccessible places). Art serves as a vehicle for making these interventions, and the museum is dispersed, potentially present in multiple urban spaces. The participant is welcomed as an engaged accomplice, if not a creative contestant, and the temporary character of the practices and their material minimalism leaves open the question of what may happen next. This mode gathers its imaginative force mainly by way of aesthetic performances. By playfully bringing together what is usually kept apart it produces tensions and creates openings for multiple new ways of imagining the art museum.

DISCUSSION

Reframing participation as performance shifts the research focus away from mechanisms for representing participants' interests and towards the question of how participants co-enact modes of ordering and their specific aesthetics. In the analysis I described three modes of ordering the art museum and how they enact different ways of imagining its future. Each mode depends on and reproduces different forms of aesthetic experiences and thus enacts different subjectivities. In this sense, the city was conceived of 'as a kind of force-field of passions that associate and pulse bodies in particular ways' (Amin and Thrift, 2002, p. 84). By showing how the three modes involve (and evolve from) distinct spaces and how their aesthetics participate as people imagine the future museum, I reframed participation as spatio-aesthetic performance. These performances rely on and work through the unfolding of specific affections. While the strategic mode relies on enacting excitement about a new building, the classical mode performs awe and admiration for the history of the existing institution. The situational mode can be described as unfolding through enjoyment and humour. These affections or bodily states are essential to the performance of each mode of ordering the art museum.

However, these affections differ in important ways when we consider how they affect the performance of subjectivities in the museum context. Each mode thus presents a different form of affective politics. In the classical mode the affections of awe and admiration sustain an already established way of relating to the art museum and thus inhibit other forms from participating in its performance. The classicist museum building is a key site for the performance of these affections. Symmetrically formed and expertly qualified, the existing museum building (and its related practices) allow for very little imagination and render the identities of the participating actors mostly as passive and receiving, leaving the work of imagination to only a select number of experts.

In contrast, the affections of the strategic mode are directed towards imagining a new – although predefined – version of the museum and thus foster a specific form of participation. It assembles a set of carefully chosen places, meticulously designed artefacts and a selected number of people into one vision for a new art museum. By presenting a number of aesthetic references it establishes a longing to perform a logic which has been already established elsewhere. In drawing comparisons to other cities and their cultural institutions, this mode renders problematic the current situation of the museum and the identities of its participants with respect to their economic sensibility; it also enacts them as outdated and even boring. Simultaneously the strategic mode promises new and exciting identities for its participants as they are invited to join the (potentially successful) competition against other performances of this very same logic.

Finally the affective dynamic of the situational mode stimulates the emergence of previously unimagined forms of performing the art museum. Instead of being inscribed in an established agenda where aesthetics are produced to satisfy instrumental needs, the situational mode invites its participants to explore their sensual and imaginative capacities. It continuously disturbs or interrupts emerging configurations and in doing so keeps participants and their imaginations alive, relying on the principle that 'actually existing, structured things live in and through that which escapes them' (Massumi, 2002, p. 35).

The three modes create several tensions that go beyond a discursive debate about the future of the art museum. Instead they are concerned with the aesthetic performance of visions for a future art museum and its respective subjectivities. As I described above, the performance of specific spaces and the affections through which they are experienced contribute to the emergence of specific collectives, subjectivities and imaginings. These performances are in agonistic tension with each other as they not only contest the identities of the participating citizens but also challenge (or reaffirm) those of other actors such as the museum directors, the art club, the artists and the cantonal government. Finally the modes create tensions with several non-human actors, as they organize various sites around the city, along with financial resources, the art collection and other elements in distinct ways, assigning them different roles in their different versions of the museum.

In terms of Mouffe's agonistic politics the three modes can be understood as conflicting hegemonic projects and their specific affections as co-constituting specific versions of collective identities (Mouffe, 2014). This reading redirects the focus of participatory politics from the moment of decision-making towards the affective formation of subjectivities and individuals' imaginations. Yet I would argue that as people form visions or imaginations they prepare to articulate their decisions, making this an integral part of the decision-making process. The empirical analysis of the pre-project for a new art museum served as an example of how we can understand the formation of imaginations as a case of agonistic politics and an opportunity to realize democratic potential in a Mouffian sense. Therefore I propose that we explicitly extend Mouffe's concept of agonistic struggle to include the struggle over the unfolding of imaginations through spatio-aesthetic performances of conflicting (hegemonic) projects and their specific affections. Thus, we can see participating in the socio-aesthetic performance of specific spaces as one potential way of taking part in the agonistic struggles of a democratic society.

With regard to the potential outcomes of socio-aesthetic performances my analysis identified important differences between the three modes of ordering the art museum. While both the classical and the strategic mode orchestrated the participants' visions into rather fixed and pre-defined outcomes, the situational mode was far more experimental and open-ended, leading participants to find new ways to imagine the future museum. Although these imaginations remained minor compared to those of the classical and strategic mode and although they never came close to influencing formal politics, we must see them as radical interventions into the imaginative landscape around the art museum and its future conceptions. The strength of such imaginative in(ter)ventions then lies not so much in presenting elaborate alternatives but in partially prising open the imaginative gridlock of predominant modes of ordering.

As I showed in this auto-ethnographic analysis, bodies can participate in various modes of ordering and can be subject to more than one way of sensually experiencing the world. By moving between various and conflicting modes of ordering we can not only gain a sensibility for potential ways of performing participation but may also become aware of their inherent politics. Experiencing the tensions between conflicting modes of ordering allows for what we can call 'sensual reflexivity' with regard to one's co-performance through participation. In this sense a performative understanding of participation cannot replace participatory decision-making but rather should be understood as an extension of it. A performative approach to participation thus calls for an expanded understanding of the political that goes beyond the articulation of voices, opinions and arguments. Instead it directs the focus to processes of agonistic struggle that concern the spatio-aesthetic performance of conflicting imaginations and their specific subjectivities.

CONCLUSION

To conclude I would like to spell out three aspects of my analysis that may inform a performative understanding of participation. First, I suggested that we understand participation as an effect of spatio-aesthetic performances which enact specific subjectivities and their respective imaginations. This implies that every form of participation always adheres to and propels a specific organizational logic which unfolds through its spatial and aesthetic performance. Participation must therefore not be restricted to participatory processes in a formal sense, but can also be understood as unfolding through the practices of everyday life. Our participation in specific modes not only affects who we are but also what we (can) imagine and how we articulate these imaginations in the form of 'decisions'.

Second, stepping out of a specific mode of ordering by spatially and aesthetically venturing into other performances may allow for a form of reflexive agency that relies on people's experience of multiple potential forms of participation. This requires the co-existence and accessibility of multiple and conflicting modes of performing participation and thus calls for democratic societies, communities or organizations that allow for and appreciate the performance of inconsistencies and conflicts. Finally, I would like to stress the potential of artistic modes of ordering as a way to experiment with participants' affective capacities and thus allow for the sensual emergence of new and inspiring forms of performing participation and their related imaginations.

REFERENCES

Alcadipani, Rafael and John Hassard (2010), 'Actor-network theory, organizations and critique: Towards a politics of organizing', *Organization*, **17** (4), 419–435.
Allmendinger, Phil and Graham Haughton (2012), 'Post-political spatial planning

in England: A crisis of consensus?', *Transactions of the Institute of British Geographers*, **37** (1), 89–103.

Amin, Ash and Nigel Thrift (2002), *Cities: Reimagining the Urban*, Cambridge: Polity Press.

Anderson, Ben and Paul Harrison (2010), *Taking-Place: Non-Representational Theories and Geography*, Farnham: Ashgate Publishing.

Andreotti, Libero (1996). 'The urban politics of the internationale situationniste', in Libero Andreotti and Xavier Costa (eds), *Situationists: Art, Politics, Urbanism*, Barcelona: ACTAR, pp. 11–35.

Beyes, Timon and Chris Steyaert (2011), 'Spacing organization: Non-representational theory and performing organizational space', *Organization*, **19** (1), 45–61.

Budd, John W., Paul J. Gollan and Adrian Wilkinson (2010), 'New approaches to employee voice and participation in organizations', *Human Relations*, **63** (3), 303–310.

Callon, Michel (2006), 'Einige Elemente einer Soziologie der Übersetzung: Die Domestikation der Kammmuscheln und der Fischer der St. Brieuc-Bucht', in Andréa Bellinger and David Krieger (eds), *ANThology*, Bielefeld: Transcript, pp. 175–194.

Charmaz, Kathy (2000), 'Grounded theory: Objectivist and constructivist methods', in Norman K. Denzin and Yvonna S. Lincoln (eds), *Handbook of Qualitative Research*, vol. 2, Thousand Oaks, CA: Sage, pp. 509–537.

Cornwall, Andrea (2004), 'Spaces for transformation? Reflections on issues of power and difference in participation in development', in Samuel Hickey and Giles Mohan (eds), *Participation: From Tyranny to Transformation*, London: Zed Books, pp. 75–91.

Cornwall, Andrea (2008), 'Unpacking "participation": Models, meanings and practices', *Community Development Journal*, **43** (3), 269–283.

Czarniawska, Barbara (2004), *Narratives in Social Science Research*, London: Sage.

Deleuze, Gilles (1988), *Spinoza: Practical Philosophy*, San Francisco, CA: City Lights Books.

Foucault, Michel (1981), *Archäologie des Wissens*, Frankfurt a.M.: Suhrkamp.

Fryer, Mick (2011), 'Facilitative leadership: Drawing on Jürgen Habermas' model of ideal speech to propose a less impositional way to lead', *Organization*, **19** (1), 25–43.

Grant, David, Rick Iedema and Cliff Oswick (2009), 'Discourse and critical management studies', in Mats Alvesson, Todd Bridgman and Hugh Willmott (eds), *The Oxford Handbook of Critical Management Studies*, Oxford: Oxford University Press, pp. 213–231.

Gregg, Melissa and Gregory J. Seigworth (eds) (2010), *The Affect Theory Reader*, Durham, NC: Duke University Press Books.

Harvey, David (1989), 'From managerialism to entrepreneurialism: The transformation in urban governance in late capitalism', *Geografiska Annaler. Series B. Human Geography*, **71** (1), 3–17.

Hennion, Antoine (2001), 'Music lovers. Taste as performance', *Theory, Culture & Society*, **18** (5), 1–22.

Hennion, Antoine (2007), 'Those things that hold us together: Taste and sociology', *Cultural Sociology*, **1** (1), 97–114.

Hickey-Moody, Anna (2013), 'Affect as method: Feelings, aesthetics and affective pedagogy', in Rebecca Coleman and Jessica Ringrose (eds), *Deleuze and Research Methodologies*, Edinburgh: Edinburgh University Press, pp. 79–95.

Hodder, Ian (1994), 'The interpretation of documents and material culture', in Norman K. Denzin and Yvonna Lincoln (eds), *Handbook of Qualitative Research*, Thousand Oaks: Sage, pp. 393–402.

Hubbard, Phil and Tim Hall (1998), 'The entrepreneurial city and the "new urban politics"', in Tim Hall and Phil Hubbard (eds), *The Entrepreneurial City: Geographies of Politics, Regime and Representation*, Chichester: John Wiley, pp. 1–30.

Humberstone, Barbara (2011), 'Embodiment and social and environmental action in nature-based sport: Spiritual spaces', *Leisure Studies*, **30** (4), 495–512.

Johnson, Jim (1988), 'Mixing humans and nonhumans together: The sociology of a door-closer', *Social Problems*, **35** (3), 298–310.

Kesby, Mike (2007), 'Spatialising participatory approaches: The contribution of geography to a mature debate', *Environment and Planning A*, **39** (12), 2813–2831.

Korf, Benedikt (2010), 'The geography of participation', *Third World Quarterly*, **31** (5), 709–720.

Kulynych, Jessica (1997), 'Performing politics: Foucault, Habermas, and postmodern participation', *Polity*, **30** (2), 315–346.

Labanyi, Jo (2010), 'Doing things: Emotion, affect, and materiality', *Journal of Spanish Cultural Studies*, **11** (3–4), 223–233.

Latham, Alan, Derek McCormack, Kim McNamara and Donald McNeill (2009), *Key Concepts in Urban Geography*, Thousand Oaks, CA: Sage.

Latour, Bruno (2005), *Reassembling the Social. An Introduction to Actor-Network-Theory*, Oxford: Oxford University Press.

Law, John (1987), 'Technology and heterogeneous engineering: The case of the Portuguese expansion', in Wiebe E. Bijker, Thomas P. Hughes and Trevor Pinch (eds), *The Social Construction of Technological Systems. New Directions in the Sociology and History of Technology*, Cambridge, MA: MIT Press, pp. 111–134.

Law, John (1994), *Organizing Modernity*, Oxford: Blackwell.

Law, John (1999), 'After ANT: Complexity, naming and topology', in John Law and John Hassard (eds), *Actor Network Theory and After*, Oxford: Blackwell, pp. 1–14.

Law, John and John Hassard (1999), *Actor Network Theory and After*, Oxford: Blackwell.

Marres, Noortje (2012), *Material Participation Technology, the Environment and Everyday Publics*, Basingstoke: Palgrave Macmillan.

Massumi, Brian (2002), *Parables for the Virtual: Movement, Affect, Sensation*, Durham, NC: Duke University Press.

McClellan, Andrew (2008), *The Art Museum: From Boulleé to Bilbao*, Berkeley, CA: University of California Press.

McDonald, Seonaidh, Kevin Daniels and Clair Harris (2004), 'Cognitive mapping in organization research', in Catherine Cassell and Gillian Symon (eds), *Essential Guide to Qualitative Methods in Organizational Research*, London: Sage, pp. 73–85.

McDonough, Thomas (1996), 'The dérive and situationist Paris', in Libero Andreotti and Xavier Costa (eds), *Situationists Art, Politics, Urbanism*, Barcelona: ACTAR, pp. 54–72.

Michels, Christoph, Timon Beyes and Chris Steyaert (2014), 'Another new museum? Imagining the space of art in the creative city', *Scandinavian Journal of Public Administration*, **18** (3), 9–28.

Miessen, Markus and Basar, Shumon (eds) (2006), *Did Someone Say Participate? An Atlas of Spatial Practice*, Frankfurt a. M.: Revolver.

Mol, Annemarie (2002), *The Body Multiple: Ontology in Medical Practice*, Durham, NC: Duke University Press.

Mouffe, Chantal (2000), 'Deliberative democracy or agonistic pluralism', *Reihe Politikwissenschaft*, (72).

Mouffe, Chantal (2005), *On the Political*, Abingdon: Routledge.

Mouffe, Chantal (2014), 'By way of a postscript', *Parallax*, **20** (2), 149–157.

Mullen, Caroline, David Hughes and Peter Vincent-Jones (2011), 'The democratic potential of public participation: Healthcare governance in England', *Social & Legal Studies*, **20** (1), 21–38.

Parkinson, John (2003), 'Legitimacy problems in deliberative democracy', *Political Studies*, **51** (1), 180–196.

Paterson, Mark (2009), 'Haptic geographies: Ethnography, haptic knowledges and sensuous dispositions', *Progress in Human Geography*, **33** (6), 766–788.

Pink, Sarah (2008), 'Mobilising visual ethnography: Making routes, making place and making images', *Forum Qualitative Sozialforschung / Forum: Qualitative Social Research*, **9** (3), 1–17.

Pratt, Andy C. (2009), 'Urban regeneration: From the arts "feel good" factor to the cultural economy: A case study of Hoxton, London', *Urban Studies*, **46** (5–6), 1041–1061.

Scherer, Andreas and Guido Palazzo (2007), 'Toward a political conception of corporate responsibility: Business and society seen from a Habermasian perspective', *Academy of Management Review*, **32** (4), 1096–1120.

Shrivastava, Paul (1986), 'Is strategic management ideological?', *Journal of Management*, **12** (3), 363–377.

Steyaert, Chris, Laurent Marti and Christoph Michels (2012), 'Multiplicity and reflexivity in organizational research: Towards a performative approach to the visual', *Qualitative Research in Organizations and Management*, **7** (1), 34–53.

Thrift, Nigel (2004), 'Intensities of feeling: Towards a spatial politics of affect', *Geografiska Annaler. Series B. Human Geography*, **86** (1), 57–78.

van Deth, Jan W. (2014), 'A conceptual map of political participation', *Acta Politica*, **49** (3), 349–367.

Waddington, David (2004), 'Participant observation', in Catherine Cassell and Gillian Symon (eds), *Essential Guide to Qualitative Methods in Organizational Research*, London: Sage, pp. 154–164.

5. Manoeuvring acts: inclusion and exclusion in a women's sports club

Julia C. Nentwich and Anja Ostendorp

INTRODUCTION

Associations of all types are said to play a major role in developing 'social glue' and democratic engagement (Braun and Nobis, 2011), as well as integration and inclusion (Freitag, 2004). As in many other places, sports clubs and associations in Switzerland are part of a long-standing tradition; even today 25 per cent of Swiss citizens and 20 per cent of non-Swiss residents are active members in a sports association (Lamprecht, Fischer and Stamm, 2012, p. 79). However, while rates of membership in sport associations doubled between 1968 and 1988, this boom came to an end in the 1990s (Lamprecht et al., 2012, p. 76). In the following years, demographic change has resulted in a decrease in the percentage of members. Although the framing of these changes as leading to a 'death of the association' (*Vereinssterben*) has not turned out to be accurate as membership rates have increased since then, sports associations see the recruitment of new and especially active members as an important issue to address. In particular, attracting members from different social groups is seen as crucial (Lamprecht et al., 2012). For instance, two thirds of the active members are men (Lamprecht et al., 2012, p. 81) and among non-Swiss members the percentages are even higher. In fact, the integrative function of sports associations cannot be taken for granted but is continuously in the making.

Most scholars writing on how to foster inclusion in a society through membership in sports associations have approached the question from a social identity perspective. Here, inclusion is closely connected to the creation of in- and out-groups based on general categories of social identity such as race, gender or nationality (Mor Barak, Cherin and Berkman, 1998, p. 67). While inclusion means making it possible for members of other social identity groups to participate in the in-group activities and thereby become members of that group, exclusion is explained as a matter of categorizing non-members as belonging to the out-group. Thus the relationship between inclusion and exclusion is paradoxical, as creating a strong in-group also reinforces differences between the in-group and the out-group. In that sense, membership in sports associations might also contribute to making the in-group more exclusive; hence it would foster exclusion alongside inclusion.

While inclusion is seen as positive, exclusion is seen as violating basic enlightenment ideals that lie at the heart of western liberal societies: rationality, fairness and equal opportunities (Wetherell and Potter, 1992). As facilitating a strong in-group also results in emphasizing the out-group, any practice of exclusion needs legitimacy. Hence the need for what we have termed 'manoeuvring acts': a well-orchestrated interplay between creating legitimacy for positive in-group and negative out-group positions.

Our research question aims at exactly this paradoxical relationship between the ideal of inclusion generally attributed to sports associations and the legitimacy of exclusion that is often practised at the very same time. From the perspective of discursive psychology, neither inclusion nor exclusion refer to static states, though it is easily assumed in the literature on social identity and organizational inclusion (Hogg and Terry, 2000; Mor Barak, Cherin and Berkman, 1998; Nkomo and Stewart, 2006). As we will show in this chapter, both the in-group and the out-group, as well as the legitimacy of exclusion resulting from this dichotomy, are negotiated through talk.

For investigating *how* this negotiating is done, we develop the concept of manoeuvring acts. With this concept we pull together findings from two distinctive traditions in discursive psychology. First, the tradition of analysing discursive meaning making as 'interpretative repertoires' (Potter and Wetherell, 1989) and second, the different 'rhetorical strategies' (Billig, 1996; Condor, Figgou, Abell, Gibson and Stevenson, 2006; van Dijk, 1992) that are involved in creating the legitimacy of talk. As we will show in greater detail, it is especially the manoeuvring acts of shifting between interpretative repertoires and drawing on distinctive rhetorical strategies that brings specific consequences of inclusion and exclusion to the foreground.

In this chapter, we first sketch out this discourse psychological understanding of inclusion and exclusion as manoeuvring acts, thereby developing the perspective of the interplay between the concepts of interpretative repertoires and rhetorical strategies. Second, we present an in-depth analysis of a group discussion with members of a women's sports club in a medium-sized city in Switzerland which illustrates this interplay. Applying discursive psychology's perspective on inclusion and exclusion, we theorize inclusion and exclusion as effects of defining both the in- and the out-group as mutually exclusive in manoeuvring acts.

INCLUSION AND EXCLUSION AS MANOEUVRING ACTS

The notion of inclusion has become an increasingly important concept for organizing in the 21st-century's globalized companies, communities and societies, and it has had a major impact on recent developments in the field of organizational diversity studies (Feldman and Khademian, 2007; Nentwich, 2006; Özbilgin, 2009; Roberson, 2006). Inclusion mainly refocuses the objective of diversity initiatives, from problematizing 'the Other' to becoming an issue of concern to everyone (Ostendorp and Steyaert, 2009). Organizational participation – that is, a person's ability to contribute fully and effectively to an organization (Mor Barak, Cherin and Berkman, 1998) – is seen as an important theme both for overcoming barriers to inclusion and for dealing with the subtle and blatant practices of exclusion (Miller and Katz, 1995, 2002; Wilson, 2000).

In this study we tackle the issue of inclusion and exclusion within a discourse psychological framing in an attempt to re-address the usual conceptualizations in social identity theory. Analysing the discursive work done in everyday talk, we understand the organization of inclusion and exclusion as distinctive discursive and hence communicative and relational acts (Wetherell and Potter, 1992). Although social identity theory's notion of 'salience' already emphasizes the importance of situated acts of interpretation – that means highlighting something as important in a certain context and bringing it to the foreground – a discourse psychological understanding puts greater emphasis on the situational negotiation or on the question how salience is actually enabled and established as taken-for-granted in a specific situation. Therefore, we mainly focus our analysis on the question how the differences between 'us' and 'them' – or in-group and out-group identities – are constructed as well as legitimized through discourse.

Two distinctive concepts stemming from discursive psychology, and the specific ways they are arranged, have guided our analysis of manoeuvring acts. These are interpretative repertoires and rhetorical strategies. First, we draw upon the notion of *interpretative repertoire* (Potter and Wetherell, 1987) reframing Foucault's notion of discourse for the more flexible, fluid and shifting mundane practices of everyday talk. Central for our analysis is the interpretative repertoire's 'concept of consistency and variability' (Gilbert and Mulkay, 1984; Ostendorp, 2009; van den Berg, 2004): assuming that different and often very contradictory repertoires are used as a vital resource for sensemaking. Although repertoires are consistent within themselves, they often contain contradictory assumptions. For instance, when talking about inclusion and exclusion, speakers shift between different interpretative repertoires (Nentwich and Ostendorp,

2012), thereby negotiating and balancing contradictory consequences (van den Berg, 2004). Hence, from this perspective, both inclusion and exclusion are available concepts in everyday, commonsense talk, and participants are *shifting* from one to the other.

This shifting between repertoires and the way it camouflages and stabilizes exclusion or inclusion in everyday talk can be depicted as a *rhetorical strategy* (Condor et al., 2006; van Dijk, 1992). Rhetorical strategies are further used to stabilize the variability of repertoires (van den Berg, 2004) and thereby create legitimacy for both the argument and the speaker (Nentwich and Ostendorp, 2012). Rhetorical strategies are especially needed when an interpretative repertoire is violating basic assumptions such as rationality, fairness and equal opportunities.

For our analysis of rhetorical strategies, we mainly draw on the attempt by Augoustinos and Every (2007) to integrate recent studies and theoretical perspectives for developing an inventory of such strategies, but we also add some more strategies that have not been covered in their article and turned out to be relevant for the analysis of our material. Table 5.1 provides an overview of strategies relevant to our particular study, which will be described in further detail in the following.

The first strategy is positioning the speaker and its in-group as 'positive' and the Other as 'negative' (van Dijk, 1992, 1993). Here, speakers use

Table 5.1   Rhetorical strategies

Rhetorical strategy	Example
Categorization and generalization	Speaker builds general categories and labels individuals as members of groups with stereotyped attributes.
Particularization	Speaker labels specific members of a group as exceptional for their group.
Camouflaging racism/ sexism/ageism. . .	Speaker provides explanations for the negative perception of a specific group, other than race, sex, or age.
Disclaiming	Speaker denies prejudice by distancing: 'I am not racist, but. . .'
Calling a spade a spade	Speaker emphasizes a close and intimate relationship between speakers where problems can be named openly: 'To be honest. . .'
Creating facticity	Speaker emphasizes the objectivity and facticity of the utterance by citing something as 'first-hand experience' or validated by an 'expert', often using reported speech.

very general social identity *categories* to label individuals as members of the group of 'foreigners' or of other groups such as 'the Yugoslavs' (LeCouteur and Augoustinos, 2001). As a consequence, they attribute stereotyped and over-generalized characteristics. In a similar vein, they create distinctive social identity groups of 'the good' and 'the bad' foreigner. This distinction also serves as a discursive manoeuvre devaluing a specific group, delegitimizing their possible claims and thereby legitimizing their exclusion. Through its 'splitting function' (Augoustinos and Every, 2007, p. 131) it also sidelines 'any examination from the dominant group's history and practices' (p. 132) and thereby distances the speaker. This rhetorical strategy of *generalization* is often accompanied by another strategy, that of *particularization* (Billig, 1996). Naming particular out-group members as exceptional for their identity group softens the impression that one is bluntly stereotyping an out-group.

Next, speakers can *camouflage* their negative presentations of the out-group as being not about racism, sexism or any other generalized attribution, but instead about something else (Augoustinos and Every, 2007, p. 133). For instance, they may explain negative perceptions about a specific group on other grounds, especially when discourses around nationality, culture and belonging are creating strong notions of 'us' and 'them'. For instance, Potter and Wetherell (1989) have depicted a repertoire of 'togetherness' in which speakers emphasize the commonalities shared by the in-group. By refocusing the issue around the topics of nationality and culture and emphasizing the similarity of the in-group, the speaker can be more subtle in 'Othering' the out-group. Furthermore, speakers can deny prejudice by making use of '*disclaimers*' (Condor et al., 2006). For instance, a speaker may make an opening statement such as 'I am not racist, but . . .' (Bonilla-Silva and Forman, 2000), and follow it with a pejorative utterance about the general characteristics of a certain group of people. Such statements are interpreted as disclaimers, and they allow the speaker to utter a statement that is racist, sexist or otherwise discriminatory, but without being depicted as a racist.

The strategy of '*calling a spade a spade*' (Verkuyten, de Jong and Masson, 1994, p. 290) works in a similar direction. For instance, by opening a sentence with the phrase 'to be honest', the speaker can utter a potentially discriminatory explanation without it being depicted as bluntly discriminatory. By emphasizing their close and intimate relationship with the others in the conversation, speakers can name problems that would be kept unspoken in a more general public. These latter two strategies – *disclaiming and calling a spade a spade* – allow speakers to make blunt, discriminatory utterances and deny the subject position that comes with doing so.

Another strategy is to create *facticity*. Here, for instance, the speaker labels a narrated story as a 'first-hand experience' (van Dijk, 1992), or positions someone in the group as an 'expert', or uses reported speech and vivid explanations (Edwards and Potter, 1992). *Creating facticity* 'is a discursive tool that helps build the facticity of an account or version of an event, grounding that account in the external world rather than in the psychology or mind of the speaker' (Augoustinos and Every, 2007, p. 128, citing Edwards, 2003). Here the speaker legitimizes the negative characteristics ascribed to the out-group as reasonable, objective facts and hence justifiable reactions.

Altogether, this research in discursive psychology suggests that speakers orchestrate the variety of interpretative repertoires and the various rhetorical strategies in a way that camouflages exclusion within the broader discourse of liberal values (Nentwich and Ostendorp, 2012). They 'perform social actions such as blaming, justifying, rationalizing, and constructing particular identities for speakers and those who are positioned as other' (Augoustinos and Every, 2007, p. 125). Furthermore, and that is our point in this chapter, the various strategies and repertoires also interact and contribute to the more complex moves that we call 'discursive manoeuvring'. Given this conceptual background, the question for our empirical analysis is this: *How is the co-existence of exclusion and inclusion enabled in manoeuvring acts?* Our analysis shows how speakers use specific interpretative repertoires and rhetorical strategies in discursive manoeuvres that result in specific effects of inclusion and exclusion.

METHODOLOGY

The analysis we present here is part of a larger research project investigating the discursive constructions of integration in neighbourhood talk (Nentwich and Ostendorp, 2012). Using the criteria for theoretical sampling (Glaser and Strauss, 1967) we conducted 19 group discussions and 16 individual interviews with actors in the neighbourhoods and ten problem-centred interviews (Witzel, 2000) with integration agents in three different neighbourhoods of a medium-sized city in the German-speaking part of Switzerland.

We worked with a research assistant to organize and facilitate the 19 group discussions (Steyaert and Bouwen, 2004) that are of closer interest in this chapter. We intended the discussions to be as close as possible to everyday talk, but also to allow opportunities to discuss specific topics and to initiate controversial topics. Choosing mostly 'natural' groups (Korobov and Bamberg, 2004), we mainly followed the idea of having the participants develop their own narratives without too much interference from us. Based on a mind map displaying possible topics such as everyday life, migration, gender, generations, and so on, we introduced the groups to our research study. We introduced the objective of the study with a short narrative about what we were interested in: how things are being done and organized in this neighbourhood, what forms of social gatherings and events are relevant and what kind of interactions people perceive as either 'highlights' or 'challenges'. Following this general introduction, we opened the group discussion with a very general question: 'You live in this neighbourhood. Could you please tell us something about what it's like to live here?'

Each group discussion lasted for about 90 minutes with a minimum of three and a maximum of eleven persons participating. We were able to involve representatives from local sports clubs, like the one we analyse in depth in this chapter. Other discussions included people involved in youth groups, schools, institutions caring for the disabled and elderly, and other actors in the everyday life of the three neighbourhoods, such as janitors, policemen, priests, innkeepers, and shop owners, as well as informal groups of neighbours and a regulars table that gathered weekly in the local pub.

The analysis was done in two major steps. First, we identified interpretative repertoires and rhetorical strategies throughout the full sample. Second, we conducted an in-depth analysis of the interplays between interpretative repertoires and rhetorical strategies in the group discussion facilitated with a women's sports association. We began analysing the data by first transcribing all the discussions. The analysis was performed with the original transcript in German while the translation presented later in this chapter aims at capturing the basic elements of the manoeuvring shown in the German original. Transcribing and listening to the recorded material again and again is an integral part of the analysis and initially guided our attention and sensitized us to particular topics. Second, we used a software program for qualitative data analysis, ATLAS/ti (Kelle, 2000); it enabled us to categorize and code the material, and to reconnect with and retrieve certain elements of the texts.

For our first focus of identifying the interpretative repertoires and rhetorical strategies throughout all the group discussions (Antaki, Billig, Edwards and Potter, 2007; Potter, 2003; Potter and Wetherell, 1987), we both coded the material for the basic accounts that participants drew upon. In a first step, we made use of in-vivo codes that we compared in several discussions; we then analysed their respective effects within the text. Constantly comparing accounts and effects, we were able to group several accounts to form one distinctive interpretative repertoire (IR). Overall we identified three IRs: (1) *harmony with like-minded people*,

emphasizing the good established relationships and support in the neighbourhood; (2) *open-minded cosmopolitanism*, drawing on liberal arguments
to emphasize openness and interest in 'the Other'; and (3) the problematic
Other, attributing problematic aspects in the neighbourhood to persons or
groups depicted as 'the Other'.

To identify rhetorical strategies we first coded the material according
to the strategies described in Table 5.1. While we had started the analysis
with the overview on rhetorical strategies from Condor et al. (2006), we
also came across several other strategies not covered in their overview. For
instance, the strategies of 'calling a spade a spade' and 'particularization'
were strategies that we searched for and found in the literature after we had
identified them in our material.

In a second reading of the material we focused on the manoeuvring
acts, that is the interplay of repertoires and rhetorical strategies and
how they affect the specific way that people construct living together
as either including or excluding other individuals or groups (Potter and
Wetherell, 1987, p. 149; Wood and Kroger, 2000, p. 95). For this analysis,
we went through the material again and analysed for the three interpretative repertoires how each one allows for a specific understanding of
'living together'. Subsequently, we analysed how this understanding was
legitimated by making use of specific rhetorical strategies. The analysis
we discuss further in this chapter stems from this in-depth analysis of
manoeuvring acts.

RESULTS

For the analysis presented here we chose to focus in depth on the group discussion with members of the women's sports association. The 11 women
who participated were deeply engaged and drew on a wide range of topics.
Hence the discussion served as a vivid illustration of ways that speakers use
discursive manoeuvring to produce both inclusion and exclusion.

The women's sports association is located in a neighbourhood where
associations are said to play a major role in social life; hence they perform
integrative functions. However, the social life within the association seems
to be rather static, as all the women introduced themselves as having been a
member for at least 20, if not 30, years. They come together once a week to
practise gymnastics and then go out for drinks in a nearby pub. Their discussion with us evolved around four topics, all of which tackled issues of
inclusion and exclusion. The first was being an in-group of women of one
generation who regret the lack of younger women members. The second
was being a women-only association and purposely excluding men. The

third was identifying being new in the neighbourhood as a critical issue for inclusion and, fourth, slowly recognizing and then reflecting on the fact that they are a Swiss-only club. Hence, they discussed issues of exclusion in relation to a total of four different social identity groups, based on generations, gender, time in the neighbourhood, and nationality.

Challenging Harmony: Constructing the Other as Responsible

An important topic, and not only in this discussion, is the strong comradeship these women experience both in the association and the neighbourhood. Drawing mainly on the repertoire of *harmony with like-minded people*, they describe the social life in the neighbourhood and especially the sports association as something very positive and idyllic, taking place within an in-group of people who feel they have been living there forever (Potter and Wetherell, 1989). Strong company, comradeship, cooperation, engagement and sociability are important elements. However, harmony also gets contested, jeopardizing both the harmony and the speaker drawing upon this repertoire. It is here that rhetorical strategies become especially important. Therefore, the analysis we present specifically focuses on the question of how the *harmony repertoire* is contested and stabilized and how the manoeuvring shown in this specific group discussion results in different consequences for inclusion and exclusion. In what follows, we analyse the four vignettes from the group discussion in which speakers contested the *harmony repertoire*. All names are pseudonyms.

Vignette One: Generations

Author: To start off, a general question to you: How does your women's sports association work?

Andrea: Well, I'd say that our sports association works quite well. We have a very good president, who organizes and coordinates the technical side of things. In my opinion, it runs very well.

Emma: We also have good camaraderie. To me, this is very important in an association. Here you find support when you need it. Isn't that the reason you join an association? I find this a bit disappointing with the young people: 'Being a member of an association? No, heaven forbid. That means I have to go every Monday or Tuesday'. That's such a pity. They don't realize that in an association, you can get help when you need it or something happens. You always have friends and I find that wonderful.

Anna: Yes, I think the best proof is that so many of us came today, isn't it? That when one of us has or needs something, then we can be there, if possible.

Bea: Yes, I feel the same as you do, Emma. I have a feeling that young people don't necessarily want this. It's a pity that this is vanishing a bit, getting lost a bit somehow.

Emma [simultaneously]: Mmh, mmh.

Doris [simultaneously]: Yes, this only becomes important to them later.

Andrea: But it's like that in all associations.

Bea: Yes, it's a bit like this everywhere, isn't it? That's exactly why it's a pity, because the friendships and the comradeship here in the association are something so special. (Lines 77–103)

In this first vignette, several speakers put forward the interpretative repertoire of *harmony with like-minded people* in order to define the elements they see as important for the association, including camaraderie and mutual support. Soon it is challenged by the narrative about younger women who are not willing to join. The association's inability to attract younger women is depicted as a problem for the future of their community and thereby challenges the idea of the association running well: obviously it is not running well enough. In order to defend harmony, a shift between repertoires takes place towards *the Other as problematic*. This repertoire depicts living together and social life encountering 'the Other' in general as inherently problematic. The women perceive people who do not belong to the defined in-group as somehow 'different' or 'strange' and they see these differences as basically negative.

Shifting from *harmony* to the *problematic Other*, these women produce the in-group of older women and the out-group of younger women in two steps. First, they depict the category of 'the young people' and refer to it as 'they'. While they position young women as 'the Other', they then attach several generalized attributes. For instance, they attribute their not participating in association activities as exclusively due to their own lack of motivation for scheduling and fixing a certain time of the week for activities, and they then ascribe other attributes to 'them' as belonging to a different generation.

While the first repertoire constructs the in-group as unproblematic and in harmony, problems arise when a new generation is growing into the association. The conflict is a direct result of the clear line drawn between the in- and the out-group, the older and the younger generations. At the same time they also attribute responsibility: they depict the in-group as living in harmony, but make the out-group fully responsible for their failure to integrate into the organization. Referring to the lack of young women in associations as a general trend, the speakers position themselves as victims of their times. There is nothing much to do about this – and everything might just stay the same. By this act of manoeuvring from one repertoire to the other, they keep intact the harmony within the in-group and neutralize any possible critique.

They discuss gender issues in a similar vein and rather briefly. The sports club has traditionally been gender segregated; men (many of them these women's husbands) have their groups within the same association. Although some joint activities are part of the tradition, these women would simply not welcome a full integration of the groups. By emphasizing the different ways that men and women engage in gymnastics they legitimate their choice. It is sufficient here to legitimate exclusion with 'maybe' and to emphasize the positive aspects of gender-segregated groups.

Vignette Two: Gender

Bea: Well yes, and as a woman you may also enjoy it [being with women only] every now and then [laughs].

Gertrud: Yes.

Bea: Well, I think that also in the girls' club, even the girls enjoy being among themselves in the girls' club, because, at school, they are always together with the boys, they have to be. Recently, they have all been complaining that they have to play football so often . . . [laughter].

Bea: Exactly, and that's what they are sometimes a bit fed up with . . . and then you can really do something that the girls like and that is only for them. That is similar to us women, isn't it? [laughs].

Anna: Yes, of course.

Bea: And of course it is a different kind of gymnastics . . .

Anna   [together with Bea]: Yes indeed. Women do different gymnastics than men . . . (Lines 750–764)

By emphasizing the differences between women and men and their sports activities, these women construct two groups. However, they do this not by devaluing the out-group but rather by putting both groups on equal terms. They stress equality between groups by emphasizing that they are actually married to the men they mention. Arguing for a women-only activity once a weak 'softens the blow' and legitimates their call for segregation:

Gudrun [simultaneously]: But somehow I don't want my husband here in our club. . . . He is also a member of an association, and I am too, but, well, this is not something that I need.

Andrea   [together with Gudrun]: No, I don't think we are talking about a mixed
club. You know, instead we mean to have joint activities, just to do something together once. It's not that we want to do gymnastics together on a
regular basis, that's not what I want. Otherwise we could just as well go to
a mixed group. (Lines 766–773)

While the women perceive the mono-generational situation as
problematic, they do not see gender segregation as a problem, but rather
as a positive feature of their group. Thus they produce its legitimacy as
self-evident.

Challenging Harmony: Making Exclusion (In)visible

As the discussion moves on, the topic shifts to the association's function
as a force for integration in the neighbourhood. Framing it as a question and thereby challenging the normative assumptions of the *harmony
repertoire*, one woman utters a concern about how they could include
others – and thus introduces the interpretative repertoire of *open-minded
cosmopolitanism*. Openness, curiosity, diversity, self-reflection and toler-
ance are important elements of this repertoire. Differences in cultures
and perspectives are emphasized as positive, vital and important for the
neighbourhood. In contrast to the *harmony repertoire*, what characterizes
this in-group is not sameness but diversity. Living together is understood
here as '*open togetherness*' (Group discussion 10: 72) that is actively shaped
by the people living in the neighbourhood. These women emphasize that
interacting with others on a daily basis, in the supermarket or on the street,
is important for feeling at home in this neighbourhood. However, they
dismiss as unrealistic the idea of simply joining an association as a way to
get to know people. In contrast to their talk about generations, in which
they held potential newcomers responsible for being included, in this discussion they depict meeting others as possible only for those who already
know someone.

Vignette Three: Newcomers

Andrea   [cuts in]: No, in our neighbourhood, we meet quite often.

Gertrud   [simultaneously]: Really?

Andrea: Yes, you wave through the window and have a quick chat before you go
home. Well, I can't say that I have no contact with people in the neighbourhood, absolutely [emphasized] not.

Gertrud   [simultaneously]: Yes, yes, yes.

Anna: But where do you meet one another?

Andrea: Well, outside on the street, and also, well not that I stand out in front of my house but when I come and go, I always see someone. Or sometimes when I air the place out in the morning, then I see someone and we have a quick chat. And just a while ago a neighbour called to ask if I have a litre of milk. Of course I had a litre of milk for her . . .

Gertrud: Okay, when I walk home I also meet people, but I mean old friends, not new faces . . . It's about how one can meet new people, or how I can get to know someone I don't know . . .

Andrea: Yes, exactly, it's incredibly hard to meet people when you are new, especially when the neighbourhood is already established and you are newly arrived and not sure how to forge a connection. (Lines 656–679)

Bringing in the idea of meeting new people, Gertrud's comment enables the group to reflect for a moment. The harmony they describe in this vignette is only about meeting neighbours they already know, not new people. Andrea then depicts meeting people as 'incredibly hard' for newcomers, thereby emphasizing a tension that leads to an atmosphere of helplessness in the following exchange.

Andrea: No, I really don't know how one does that in [our neighbourhood], I really don't.

Doris: You have to chat a little bit and say, 'Hello, the weather today is . . .'

Elsbeth   [simultaneously]: Well, the neighbourhood association has a homepage and you can find the address on there, if you want to. Sometimes people are too passive. There are many people who simply wait for someone else to come and involve them.

Several voices [simultaneously]: Yes.

Gertrud   [simultaneously]: They don't want that either.

Erika   [cuts in]: Yes, and I think that before . . .

Elsbeth   [cuts in]: And here people say, in defence, that no one has come to them to involve them. I experience that more and more. (Lines 682–694)

Dismantling the harmony as a harmony between people who have known each other for a long time, the women have to confess that they don't know how they could get into contact with others in their neighbourhood if they were newcomers. They suggest talking to people and saying

'Grüezi' ('hello') when meeting people on the street, or making use of the homepage of the neighbourhood organization, as ways of making contact. Here, the discussion shifts back to the repertoire of *the Other as problematic*, as they reframe the issue of making contact as the responsibility of newcomers.

Referring to those new to the neighbourhood as the out-group, as 'they', they position them as a category of people who would not act proactively but would wait until they are approached by those in the in-group, or else as simply not interested in being included. These women draw again on the repertoire of the *problematic Other* to depict 'them' who are responsible and not willing or capable of coping. As a consequence, they silence the intentions of the *cosmopolitanism repertoire*, such as including others and actively making contact; hence they counteract the possible effect of fostering inclusion.

Harmony in Trouble: Producing Legitimacy for Exclusion

As excluding others means violating both the norm of cosmopolitanism and the assumed harmony within the in-group, several rhetorical strategies become necessary as soon as this repertoire comes into play. An interesting exception from the general discursive pattern here is Gertrud's short critical reflection on the in-group's practices of relationship, in which she elaborates an idea about inclusion on the basis of everyday contacts. However, she is harshly interrupted by another woman who blames foreigners for speaking only Turkish and not being able to speak German. She interprets not knowing German as unwillingness to participate in the social life in Switzerland. This act of categorizing opens the group to the interpretative repertoire of *the problematic Other* and blunt racism.

Vignette Four: Nationality

Gertrud   [cuts in]: It would interest me to know who in our circle has contact with Turks or [former] Yugoslavs in the neighbourhood in the same way that we Swiss have contact with one another. Does anyone have that? So, it starts with social contact and I, uh, don't want to say that we don't allow them into our circles, but because there is so little contact that's why they don't come. If you'd socialize with them like you do with Swiss couples, then maybe one could encourage them to come to an association. But I don't have that, that's why I'm wondering who of us has that with, uh, a foreigner, no matter what kind of social contact in which you do something on Sunday together or you go walking together, because that's when one gets into a conversation and so one can discuss these things . . .

Gudrun   [cuts in]: Well having a conversation; they can't speak German and they only speak Turkish. That's so [unintelligible] and Turks have no interest in learning German, that is . . .

Several voices   [simultaneously]: [unintelligible]

Andrea   [cuts in]: Yes, they are always with their own kind, aren't they.

Doris   [simultaneously]: They don't come to sports anyway.

Elsbeth: Many live like a clan.

Andrea: Yes, that's true.

Anna: You hardly see one alone [unintelligible], it's mostly groups, also the women . . .

Emma   [cuts in]: Yes, women, men and children.

Anna: In any case, I'd just like to say that we are, of course, not standing in the way of any woman coming to gymnastics, no matter where she comes from or what her religion is. We are just women so we can guarantee 100 per cent that nothing can happen here, so [unintelligible] . . .

Heidi   [cuts in]: It's not because of us.

[laughter]

Emma: So this raises the question, what is it then?

Heidi   [cuts in]: Something could happen or occur . . .

Gertrud   [cuts in]: But they don't even socialize, do they?

Heidi   [cuts in]: [unintelligible] exactly because of that, it's quite difficult.

Several voices   [simultaneously]: [unintelligible]

Emma: Well, I think I have never seen them.

Gertrud: No?

Emma: No, they wear a headscarf and they are definitely not coming to gymnastics. (Lines 950–989)

In this sequence the speakers establish a strong out-group of 'Turks', and eventually also of 'people from former Yugoslavia'. It is 'them' who speak a different language and do not want to learn German. It is 'them' who socialize only with members of their group and are not interested in coming to sports classes. It is 'them' who do not want to socialize with the members of the in-group. On the other hand, the in-group is depicted as not responsible for the obvious separation of sports activities into the category of different nationalities identified in this excerpt. The speakers use the rhetorical strategy of *generalization* here; it legitimizes the bluntly uttered negative and racist stereotypes towards what they depict as the generalized group of 'Turks' as the out-group.

In the following passages, we see the women use several rhetorical strategies in a highly intense exchange. First, the rhetorical strategy of particularization enforces their categorizing of what they later depict in the discussion as the difference between 'Europeans' and non-Europeans along a line of similarities and dissimilarities. They depict specific subgroups or individuals as exceptional members of their group:

Andrea: But they don't want to. You know, the Italians or the Spanish were different. When they arrived here, they sought contact and they made connections and compared to the others, these are simply . . .

Bea [cuts in]: Of course, they are already second or third generation and of course that is totally different.

Andrea [simultaneously]: Yes, and they are not foreigners. Let's be honest, Italians are not foreigners anymore, really if you think about it. There are a lot of them down there where you live . . . [unintelligible]. (Lines 990–997)

Here, the neighbours whose nationalities are Turkish or former Yugoslav are categorized as different and more problematic compared to those who are Italian or Spanish. This generalization of attributes is enforced with the rhetorical strategy of *creating facticity*. Using the phrase 'of course', Bea emphasizes how natural the category is, and then explains it as a historical fact. In the ongoing discussion, Andrea even underlines this assumption by using the strategy of *calling a spade a spade*: With her appeal to the other women to 'be honest' and to 'really think about it', she urges them to agree that they can all recognize the differences between different categories of foreigners if they will only focus on the real facts. Both she and Gertrud use the *particularizing strategy*, and then she moves into her own manoeuvre of *particularization*. Here Marina, a woman of Italian origin, is depicted as an exceptional case of a foreigner who was successfully included, along with some 'Yugoslavs' that Andrea calls 'great'.

Gertrud [cuts in]: Marina also joined us once. She is also an Italian, and both her boys played football. We saw one another at the football matches and so we got to know one another and because of that she came for a while . . .

Andrea: Of course we also had, uh, barbecue parties, you know, and then everyone came, foreigners and Swiss. Back then it was the Italians or a few Yugoslavs, in this sense. Well, I know some great Yugoslavs, I have nothing against them.

Andrea: No, but they don't want to at all.

Emma: They have a completely different mentality.

Heidi: Well, I don't have any trouble with anyone. (Lines 1001–1032)

Using the rhetorical strategy of *disclaiming*, Andrea is able to shift from a positive account of people from former Yugoslavia to another act of *generalization* and *out-group construction*; she also opens a door for Emma to add to it. Although she has nothing against them (*disclaiming*), she depicts them as passive ('they don't want to at all') and 'completely different'. Heidi closes the sequence by distancing herself from the discussion, emphasizing that she has no 'trouble with anyone'.

As a consequence of this discursive manoeuvring, the women interrupt their reflection on exclusion that started this sequence, and they silence the emerging impulse to focus on themselves and their own contribution. They blame 'them', the out-group, for not learning the language, not making contact, or no longer coming to training sessions. These moves balance the dilemma of *open-minded cosmopolitanism* and the *problematic Other* with the help of a whole series of rhetorical strategies. While they highlight the importance of inclusion, they generalize about the needs of 'foreign women'. As a consequence, they both rationalize and legitimize exclusion.

What is at stake here is not so much the impression that individual speakers are giving of themselves, but the legitimacy of the *harmony repertoire* and hence the in-group. The more the *cosmopolitanism repertoire* enters the conversation, the more we see the excluding consequences of the *harmony repertoire*. As they attribute non-willingness to integrate to the generalized Other, it becomes more than simply an 'Othering' technique; it also keeps them from reflecting on the exclusion that results from the *harmony repertoire*.

DISCUSSION

In the in-depth analysis of the group discussion with members of the women's sports association, we set out to analyse the interplay between three interpretative repertoires and several rhetorical strategies as manoeuvring acts. We thereby suggested an alternative perspective on the relevance that in- and out-groups have for inclusion. Not taking the social identity categories and their salience as important as such, our focus was rather on the analysis of the manoeuvring acts that creates both the relevance of the category and its effect. This perspective emphasizes the paradoxical effects of in- and out-group creation: fostering exclusion while talking about inclusion. With our empirical analysis we set out to further explore how this paradoxical effect is created.

Throughout all four vignettes, the issue at stake was how these women constructed in- and out-groups and how they generalized the groups' attributes. Through the process the women strengthened the in-group identity of their sports club as a homogeneous group with common interests, and depicted members of all other groups (men, younger women, newcomers, people of other nationalities) as not fitting in. In this way, they reassured themselves about the harmony of the in-group and neutralized any critique by constructing the other as not only problematic, but also responsible for their own exclusion.

In fact, we noticed that two themes – harmony with like-minded people and the emphasis on the strong comradeship experienced in the in-group – were important throughout the discussion in both the sports club and in other group discussions. Only when something in the discussion threatened to jeopardize this harmony and its excluding effects did further rhetorical strategies seem necessary to legitimize exclusion.

By making use of rhetorical strategies and shifting between the three interpretative repertoires of *harmony with like-minded people, open minded cosmopolitanism* and *the problematic Other*, these women practised exclusion in several legitimate ways. However, they did this differently throughout the vignettes. When the issue was gender and excluding men from the weekly gymnastics practices, they produced the legitimacy in a quite straightforward way. When they tackled generational issues they had to shift between the repertoires of *harmony* and *the problematic Other*. To legitimize the absence of younger women, the discussants drew on the repertoire of *the problematic Other* to depict the out-group as problematic and thus preserve the in-group's harmony. When they discussed the issue of newcomers in the neighbourhood, *the cosmopolitanism repertoire* became important and posed a real challenge to the exclusion they practise. However, they quickly disabled it by using the rhetorical strategies of *creating facticity* and *calling a spade a spade*; they were then able to rationalize and thereby legitimize exclusion.

When they talked about newcomers in the neighbourhood, the issues at stake were self-reflexivity and creating understanding about the problematic situation of newcomers. However, they turned to other successful manoeuvres: they categorized and generalized and also shifted towards the repertoire of *the Other as problematic*. These manoeuvres allowed them to silence and de-legitimize the *cosmopolitanism repertoire's* intentions of integration, communication and making contact. Here, balancing the repertoires of *cosmopolitanism* and *problematic Otherness* enabled them to neutralize the critique put forward and it resulted in several moves in which speakers positioned themselves as belonging to either the in- or the out-group.

Furthermore, we noticed that the majority of rhetorical strategies were relevant mostly when it came to issues of nationality and ethnicity, and were less important when they were talking about gender or generational issues. From van Dijk's (1992) perspective, this can be interpreted as evidence for the strong anti-discriminatory norms that are at work in liberal societies. While excluding newcomers and people of other nationalities or ethnicities seems to be depicted as going against these norms, discrimination based on gender and generational difference seems to be legitimate in this specific context. A possible explanation for this difference is that distinctions about both gender and generation apply to persons who are part of the women's social networks, whether husbands or daughters. They are not excluding them from the neighbourhood community, but from the specific activity in the sports club. However, a different issue is at stake when they are talking about newcomers and other nationalities; now the issue is inclusion in the wider neighbourhood and hence exclusion has far-reaching consequences.

The overall pattern of the exclusion we saw practised throughout the group discussion also resulted in severe consequences for the possible practice of inclusion. Throughout large portions of the discussion, participants negotiated responsibility: they positioned themselves as being the 'innocent' Swiss living in harmony, or challenged that position with the assumption that they were responsible for change. Shifting between repertoires goes very well together with the construction of binary categories of 'us' as the good guys and 'them' as the bad. While the *Other as problematic* repertoire proved to legitimate the exclusion resulting from the *harmony repertoire*, the *cosmopolitism repertoire* posed a severe danger. Balancing this tension, the discussion shows that it is rather the legitimacy of the *harmony repertoire* that is at stake and not so much the impression management of the individual speakers. Indeed, face keeping strategies such as denying racism are only salient when the *harmony repertoire* is contested. Producing the legitimacy of the *harmony repertoire*, the in-group is reassured and defended against critiques and possible changes. As a consequence, the out-group is not only excluded but also held responsible for their own exclusion.

CONCLUSION

With a discourse psychological perspective on in- and out-group construction we took the question of how differences between 'us' and 'them' – or in-group and out-group identities – are constructed as a starting point. With our specific perspective on the *discursive manoeuvring* that bridges both the effects of shifting between repertoires and rhetorical strategies, we were able to document how the depicted coexistence of inclusion and exclusion is made possible. The analysis shows how the excluding effects of this manoeuvring are legitimated and hence made possible within the broader discourse of liberal societies.

The analysis shows that the exclusion of 'the Other' does not so much result from any one specific rhetorical strategy, but from the discursive manoeuvring that aims at protecting the *harmony repertoire* as a prominent resource. Thus, using disclaimers and shifting between the three available interpretative repertoires proved to be an unpleasant necessity in order to preserve the positive definition of the in-group. Hence, a strong in-group identity does not only have consequences for the exclusion practised but also camouflages this exclusion as legitimate at the very same time. It strikes us as crucial that future research as well as intervention programmes aiming at inclusion further explore these paradoxical effects.

REFERENCES

Antaki, Charles, Michael Billig, Derek Edwards and Jonathan Potter (2007), 'Discourse analysis means doing analysis: A critique of six analytic shortcomings', in Jonathan Potter (ed.), *Discourse and Psychology*, London: Sage, pp. 332–349.

Augoustinos, Martha and Danielle Every (2007), 'The language of "race" and "prejudice". A discourse of denial, reason, and liberal-practical politics', *Journal of Language and Social Psychology*, **26** (2), 123–141.

Billig, Michael (1996), *Arguing and Thinking. A Rhetorical Approach to Social Psychology*, Cambridge: Cambridge University Press.

Bonilla-Silva, Eduardo and Tyrone A. Forman (2000), '"I am not a racist but . . .": Mapping white college students' racial ideology in the USA', *Discourse & Society*, **11** (1), 50–85.

Braun, Sebastian and Tina Nobis (2011), *Migration, Integration und Sport: Zivilgesellschaft vor Ort*, Wiesbaden: VS Verlag.

Condor, Susan, Lia Figgou, Jackie Abell, Stephen Gibson and Clifford Stevenson (2006), '"They're not racist . . .": Prejudice denial, mitigation and suppression in dialogue', *British Journal of Social Psychology*, **45** (3), 441–462.

Edwards, Derek and Jonathan Potter (1992), *Discursive Psychology*, London: Sage.

Feldman, Martha S. and Anne M. Khademian (2007), 'The role of the public manager in inclusion: Creating communities of participation', *Governance: An International Journal of Policy, Administration, and Institutions*, **20** (2), 305–324.

Freitag, Markus (2004), 'Swiss worlds of social capital. Swiss regions and cantons in comparative perspective', *Swiss Political Science Review*, **10** (2), 87–118.

Gilbert, G. Nigel and Michael Mulkay (1984), *Opening Pandora's Box: A Sociological Analysis of Scientist's Discourses*, Cambridge: Cambridge University Press.

Glaser, Barney G. and Anselm L. Strauss (1967), *The Discovery of Grounded Theory: Strategies for Qualitative Research*, Chicago, IL: Aldine Publishing.

Hogg, Michael A. and Deborah J. Terry (2000), 'Social identity and self-categorization processes in organizational contexts', *Academy of Management Review*, **25** (1), 121–140.

Kelle, Udo (2000), 'Computergestützte Analyse qualitativer Daten', in Uwe Flick, Erich Kardorff, Ines Steinke (eds), *Qualitative Sozialforschung. Ein Handbuch*, Reinbek: Rowohlt, pp. 485–501.

Korobov, Neill and Michael Bamberg (2004), 'Positioning a "mature" self in interactive practices: How adolescent males negotiate "physical attraction" in group talk', *British Journal of Developmental Psychology*, **22** (4), 471–492.

Lamprecht, Markus, Adrian Fischer and Hanspeter Stamm (2012), *Die Schweizer Sportvereine. Strukturen, Leistungen, Herausforderung*, Zürich: Seismo.

LeCouteur, Amanda and Martha Augoustinos (2001), 'The language of prejudice and racism', in Martha Augoustinos and Katherine J. Reynolds (eds), *Understanding Prejudice, Racism, and Social Conflict*, London: Sage, pp. 215–230.

Miller, Frederick A. and Judith H. Katz (1995), 'Cultural diversity as a developmental process: The path from monocultural club to inclusive organization', in J. William Pfeiffer (ed.), *The 1995 Annua (Vol 2): Consulting*, San Diego, CA: Pfeiffer and Company, pp. 267–281.

Miller, Frederick A. and Judith H. Katz (2002), *The Inclusion Breakthrough: Unleashing the Real Power of Diversity*, San Francisco, CA: Berrett-Koehler Publishers.

Mor Barak, Michàl E., David A. Cherin and Sherry Berkman (1998), 'Organizational and personal dimensions in diversity climate – ethic and gender differences in employee perceptions', *Journal of Applied Behavioural Science*, **34** (1), 82–104.

Nentwich, Julia C. (2006), 'Changing gender: The discursive construction of equal opportunities', *Gender, Work & Organization*, **13** (6), 499–521.

Nentwich, Julia C. and Anja Ostendorp (2012), 'Weltoffenheit unter Gleichgesinnten. Widersprüchlicher Ein- und Ausschluss als diskursive Alltagspraxis', *Swiss Journal of Psychology*, **71** (4), 175–185.

Nkomo, Stella. M. and Marcus M. Stewart (2006), 'Diverse identities in organizations', in Stewart R. Clegg, Cynthia Hardy, Tom Lawrence and Walter R. Nord (eds), *The Sage Handbook of Organization Studies* (Second Edition), London: Sage Publications, pp. 520–541.

Ostendorp, Anja (2009), 'Konsistenz und Variabilität beim Reden über "Diversity". Eine empirische Untersuchung diskursiver Spielräume in Organisationen' (66 paragraphs), *Forum Qualitative Sozialforschung/Forum: Qualitative Social Research*, **10** (2), Art. 1.

Ostendorp, Anja and Chris Steyaert (2009), 'How different can differences be(come)?: Interpretative repertoires of diversity concepts in Swiss-based organizations', *Scandinavian Journal of Management*, **25** (4), 374–384.

Özbilgin, Mustafa F. (2009), *Equality, Diversity and Inclusion at Work: A Research*

Companion, Cheltenham, UK and Northampton, MA, USA: Edward Elgar Publishing.

Potter, Jonathan (2003), 'Discursive psychology: Between method and paradigm', *Discourse and Society*, **14** (6), 783–794.

Potter, Jonathan and Margaret Wetherell (1987), *Discourse and Social Psychology: Beyond Attitudes and Behaviour*, London: Sage.

Potter, Jonathan and Margaret Wetherell (1989), 'Fragmented ideologies: Accounts of educational failure and positive discrimination', *Text: Interdisciplinary Journal for the Study of Discourse*, **9** (2), 175–190.

Roberson, Quinetta M. (2006), 'Disentangling the meanings of diversity and inclusion in organizations', *Group & Organization Management*, **31** (2), 212–236.

Steyaert, Chris and René Bouwen (2004), 'Group methods of organizational analysis', in Catherine Cassell and Gillian Symon (eds), *Essential Guide to Qualitative Methods in Organizational Research*, London: Sage, pp. 140–153.

van den Berg, Harry (2004), 'Contradictions in interview discourse', in Harry van den Berg, Margaret Wetherell and Hanneke Houtkoop-Steenstra (eds), *Analyzing Race Talk. Multidisciplinary Perspectives on the Research Interview*, Cambridge: Cambridge University Press, pp. 119–137.

van Dijk, Teun (1992), 'Discourse and the denial of racism', *Discourse & Society*, **3** (1), 87–118.

van Dijk, Teun (1993), *Elite Discourse and Racism*, London: Sage.

Verkuyten, Maykel, Wiebe de Jong and Kees Masson (1994), 'Racial discourse, attitude and rhetorical manoeuvres: Race talk in the Netherlands', *Journal of Language and Social Psychology*, **13** (3), 278–298.

Wetherell, Margaret and Jonathan Potter (1992), *Mapping the Language of Racism. Discourse and the Legitimation of Exploitation*, London: Sage.

Wilson, Elisabeth (2000), 'Inclusion, exclusion and ambiguity. The role of organisational culture', *Personnel Review*, **29** (3), 274–303.

Witzel, Andreas (2000), 'Das problemzentrierte Interview', *Forum Qualitative Sozialforschung/Forum: Qualitative Social Research*, **1** (1), Art. 22.

Wood, Linda A. and Rolf O. Kroger (2000), *Doing Discourse Analysis. Methods for Studying Action in Talk and Text*, Thousand Oaks, CA: Sage.

PART III

Resistance and change

6. Probing the power of entrepreneurship discourse: an immanent critique

Pascal Dey

[E]ntrepreneurship . . . has stained nearly every aspect of public life.
(Jones and Spicer, 2006, p. 179)

INTRODUCTION

The discourse of entrepreneurship became a pervasive force of social imagination during the 1980s (Cohen and Musson, 2000). Whilst at first used mainly to denote economic phenomena such as growth, wealth creation and prosperity (Drucker, 1985), 'enterprise' and 'entrepreneurship' today are connected to a myriad of non-economic activities, phenomena and values. For instance, entrepreneurship is related to issues as diverse as urban space, street markets, public bureaucracies and society at large. Of late, the discourse of entrepreneurship has been used as an explanatory link between market mechanisms and some of today's most wicked problems such as abject poverty. Examples can be found in an influential UN report entitled *Unleashing Entrepreneurship: Making Business Work for the Poor* (United Nations, 2004); in it, then Secretary-General Kofi Annan identifies entrepreneurship as the key mechanism for leveraging the private sector in developing nations. Annan thus promotes the view that entrepreneurship will bring market-driven solutions to the sphere of poverty alleviation.

More recently, this 'entrepreneurship-against-poverty' argument has been reiterated through so-called 'bottom of the pyramid' approaches (Brugmann, 2005), which tout the possibility of 'eradicating poverty through profits', to quote the subtitle of Prahalad's (2004) influential *The Fortune at the Bottom of the Pyramid*. Entrepreneurship's flexibility is further epitomized in how it has come to reshape not only the subjectivity of firm employees (Pongratz and Voß, 2003) but also of artists (Loacker,

2013), academics (Hatcher, 2001), parents (Eleff and Trethewey, 2006) and clerks (du Gay, 2004) according to the image of the 'enterprising self' (Bröckling, 2002). On the face of it, these tentative examples seem to indicate that 'entrepreneurship today can be almost anything' (Jones and Spicer, 2009, p. 1).

However, although there is no way around conceding that entrepreneurship is a polymorphous signifier without stable meaning, a relatively stable feature of the discourse of enterprise nevertheless is that it endows the various aspects of social, cultural, public and community life to which it gets related with a positive evaluative accent (Weiskopf and Steyaert, 2009). We can hence speak of a purified discourse which effectively hides entrepreneurship's dark sides, predicaments and flaws. It is this purification, however, which ultimately explains why entrepreneurship is univocally regarded as a 'good thing that needs to be wholeheartedly encouraged' (Spicer, 2012, p. 151).

And yet, to translate the orthodoxy of entrepreneurship into a material reality is anything but straightforward. Making entrepreneurship relevant for people's everyday lives presupposes that it discursively affects their habitual way of thinking, acting and talking. That is to say: the discourse of entrepreneurship successfully turns individuals into entrepreneurial subjects only if people get to accept the enterprising self as their 'true nature' (Dey, 2014; Dey and Steyaert, 2016). Interestingly enough, the power of entrepreneurship discourse often seems rather limited as people are reluctant to embrace it uncritically. For instance, Storey, Salaman and Platman (2005), who looked at how the discourse of entrepreneurship has been used to justify changes in the creative industry, were able to show that freelance workers did not endorse the entrepreneurship discourse in a blindfolded manner. Whilst generally very positive about the core features of this discourse, employees evaluated and appropriated entrepreneurship's value according to their own interests; this in turn created 'variety, complexity and in some cases, paradox' (p. 1050). These insights, together with those of similar studies (Cohen and Musson, 2000; Essers and Benschop, 2007; Loacker, 2013), support the conclusion that any inquiry which aims to understand the power of the discourse of entrepreneurship needs to account for how this discourse is received at the local level.

Expanding on these findings, in this chapter I ask how individuals targeted by the discourse of entrepreneurship either identify with or resist it. This question is investigated in the realm of development aid, a context in which discussions of entrepreneurship and business savvy have acquired increasing prominence over the last decades. Rendering non-governmental organizations (NGOs) the focal attention of this chapter seems timely in view of how these organizations have stirred controversy with regard to their effectiveness and legitimacy (notably in the realm of development aid), which was followed by suggestions to align them more closely with the principles and values of the private sector. Further, investigating the extent to which the normative desideratum of 'entrepreneurship' is received by development NGO practitioners bears critical currency in the way it exposes possible limits and dangers associated with this discourse (Ainsworth and Hardy, 2008). However, unlike forms of critique which aspire to challenge the discourse of entrepreneurship from a position of exteriority, for example from the transcendental vantage point of moral philosophy, the present critique is conducted from within the coordinates of the entrepreneurship discourse. Framing it as an 'immanent critique' (from Latin *immanere*, 'to dwell in, remain in'), I subject the discourse of entrepreneurship to critical scrutiny not via universal judgment of 'good' and 'bad' but by attending to the viewpoints of those being addressed or 'hailed' as entrepreneurs.

Thus, the primary objective of the ensuing 'immanent critique' is to disclose the situated agency of development NGO practitioners. Put succinctly, 'situated agency' suggests that even though practitioners might not be able to fully escape the influence of entrepreneurship discourse, they might nevertheless find different ways to resist the discourse (Foucault, 1997a). Therefore I am particularly interested in how practitioners' situated agency gets played out through acts of discursive resistance. My analysis tries to disclose how NGO practitioners use language to displace, negotiate, reconstruct or create alternatives to the discourse of entrepreneurship. Evidently, 'discursive resistance' is a situated and relational activity (Steyaert and Van Looy, 2010) which entails the disruption of the unanimity and authority of the dominant discourse. Involving a refusal to simply endorse entrepreneurship as the object towards which desire must flow, discursive resistance appeals to the transgressive potential of language epitomized in how ordinary conversations and utterances loosen the grip of powerful discourses (Foucault, 1997b).

Against this backdrop, I draw on interviews with practitioners from 12 Swiss non-governmental organizations to probe the extent to which the discourse of entrepreneurship, and its foundational repertoires of 'results-based management', 'inputs', 'outcomes', 'indicators' and 'internal and external accounting', are or are not resisted through language. Using the micro-discursive analysis developed by Potter and Wetherell (1987) to gain a clearer understanding of NGO practitioners' interpretations of their everyday (working) life, the study, by remaining attentive to practitioners' own accounts, puts into perspective the sweeping pretention that all development aid NGOs have become subservient to an economic rationality. In this way, the investigation demonstrates how micro-discursive approaches permit us to pinpoint language's inherently critical capacity to create socially pertinent meaning that resists dominant discourse.

The chapter is structured as follows. The next section offers a brief elaboration of the NGO sector, including the increasingly important role the discourse of entrepreneurship plays therein. This is followed, second, by a discussion of the micro-discourse analysis' methodology and, third, by the presentation of the findings. Finally, I discuss the results and offer some concluding remarks.

FROM DEVELOPMENT NGOs TO SOCIAL ENTERPRISES

Developmental non-governmental organizations (development NGOs) are deemed an exciting field of inquiry precisely because their raison d'être has been fundamentally called into question over the past decades. Defenders and proponents usually regard NGOs as prolific actors in the domain of development aid, where they inter alia provide essential services to the most vulnerable people on the planet. However, this only represents the more rose-tinted side of the story. Put briefly, after having been ushered into existence in the post-World War II era, development NGOs have been interrogated with regard to their actual effectiveness and legitimacy. Since the 1960s there has been widespread concern that NGOs were not able, or insufficiently able, to measure up to the (high) expectations bestowed upon them. While the issues of concern vary, the more widespread critiques are the following: despite the best of intent, development NGOs lack proper understanding of the causes of the problems they seek to solve (Shivji, 2007); they have become too closely aligned with the agendas of those in power and too far removed from the powerless (Banks and Hulme, 2012); NGOs have an appallingly low aid effectiveness record (ISG, 2008); the rise of corporate-NGO partnerships risks compromising the autonomy of the latter (Baur and Schmitz, 2012); and, at worst, this creates a situation where NGOs become co-opted by the hegemonic neoliberal capitalist project (Katz, 2006).

Interestingly enough, though the debate on development NGOs has now been pursued for more than half a century, and harbours different theoretical orientations such as populist thought, neo-Marxism, and anti-imperialist and post-colonial theory (Dey, 2007), the critique has increasingly shifted towards the orthodoxy of entrepreneurship. Noteworthy in this regard is William Easterly's (2006) seminal *The White Man's Burden* which contends that development continues to fail precisely because of a lack of what the author calls 'searchers': people who find ways to get things done, who firmly concentrate on the problems to be solved and who are keen to use feedback from those whom they try to serve to fully understand the problem. Playing off searchers against the 'planner' approach, characteristic of the typical centralized and bureaucratic development approach, the implications of Easterly's message are straightforward: given that the approach of the searcher, an obvious analogy for 'entrepreneur', has proven effective in Western democracies, then the NGOs worth thinking of are precisely those that experiment with ideas, that constantly innovate without fear of failure and that rely on competition and consumer feedback to figure out what works.

Easterly is not alone in this assessment. Among others, economist Paul Collier – who is probably best known for his epic treatise on poverty *The Bottom Billion* (Collier, 2007) – shares many of Easterly's concerns. With over US$2 trillion spent on development aid since the 1950s with ostensibly little effect, Collier (2013) in a recent speech developed the point that it is the lack of effective organizations that explains why many people earn as little as US$2 per day. Equating the failure of development aid with the ineffectiveness of the organizations working therein, the solution Collier puts forward hardly comes as a surprise: what development aid organizations need, first and foremost, is a new, more entrepreneurial philosophy. There are a variety of reasons for this, including the belief that incorporating entrepreneurial practices into development endeavours leads to innovation, that is, smarter solutions in poverty alleviation.

Evidently, these ideas go way back to management bestsellers such as Peters and Waterman's (1982) *In Search of Excellence* which identifies the problem of business in their overly bureaucratic and centralized way of organizing. The solution to such inefficiencies is to be found in what du Gay (2004) calls the process of 'enterprising up': individuals, groups and organizations are made 'fit' and 'lean' by instilling economic thinking and by unleashing an entrepreneurial spark. The utility and indeed the necessity of enterprise are implicated in the ever-growing number of development NGOs which are increasingly dependent on a limited donor base. The argument goes that competition over funds literally pushes NGOs towards more entrepreneurial conduct as this allows them to become self-sufficient. Though it remains to be seen whether entrepreneurship will eventually engender the anticipated results, the fact of the matter is that entrepreneurship has already been established as the moral high ground offering development NGOs direction in their quest for effectiveness and survival.

What bears emphasizing here is that entrepreneurship gets related to development NGOs in two different ways. On the one hand, entrepreneurship gets construed as a product or outcome of development NGOs. The basic thinking thus is that entrepreneurship has the greatest leverage in eradicating poverty. Micro-credit programmes epitomize, in an emblematic fashion, the hope that the promotion of entrepreneurship in rural areas and deprived urban areas will leverage stagnating economies in Third World countries, a point which is increasingly dismantled as one of the great myths of poverty eradication (Onyuma and Shem, 2005). On the other hand, entrepreneurship gets directly connected with the modus operandi of development NGOs, thus forming a *terminus technicus* that envisions a new, ostensibly more progressive kind of development organization (if compared with 'traditional' NGOs) whose practice is informed by the logic of the private sector. The blueprint for such a new model of development NGOs is often referred to as 'social entrepreneurship', which is seen as an effective response to the notorious inability of both the market and the state to solve intricate social and ecological problems (Nicholls, 2006).

Social entrepreneurship envisions the ideal development organization as a combination of market efficiency, business savvy and financial self-sufficiency as requisite ingredients for accomplishing social ends (Chand, 2009). While social enterprises retain many of the positive features related to entrepreneurship such as innovation, performance and a heroic outlook (Dey and Steyaert, 2010), it adds to it an almost evangelical belief that social and economic objectives can be combined in such a way that it produces largely positive, win–win situations (Hervieux, Gedajlovic and Turcotte, 2010; for a worthwhile critique compare with Berglund and Schwartz, 2013).

Turning to the Swiss context in which the present study took place, it can be said that social entrepreneurship – quite in contrast to countries such as the United Kingdom and the United States (Nicholls, 2010) – has only just started to infiltrate the public agenda. Though it lags behind most other European countries in terms of government support, signs of change can be found in recent feasibility studies commissioned by the Federal Government and aimed at probing the utility of the concept in the domain of work integration. Also, of late government authorities have started to discuss the value of a specific legal form for social enterprises, and the establishment of capital banks tailored to social enterprises' specific financial needs.

The idea of social entrepreneurship has also gained increasing institutional support from the private and voluntary sector. Social entrepreneurship has received support, in the form of money, knowledge and legitimacy, from representatives of the banking sector such as Credit Suisse, foundations such as Avina and Schwab, a mounting number of globally operating fellowship programmes (such as Ashoka), start-up incubators (such as the Impact Hub), strategy consultancies and law firms, as well as a few academic programmes.

Interestingly enough, while social entrepreneurship in Switzerland has not experienced the hype that has been seen as in other parts of the world, social entrepreneurship nevertheless appears to be firmly established in practice. This is what is suggested by a recent overview of the state of social entrepreneurship in Switzerland (Gonin and Gachet, 2014) as well as by the results of the Global Enterprise Monitor (GEM) which in 2009 attested that Switzerland had the second highest nascent social entrepreneurship activity (topped only by the USA; Bosma and Levie, 2010). What the report does not reveal, but what is put at centre stage in the ensuing micro-discourse analysis, is the extent to which NGO practitioners emulate the discourse of entrepreneurship which demands attributes like flexibility, risk-taking, perseverance, innovation, and so on, from people who might have hitherto not been deemed, by ruling standards, to be social entrepreneurs.

METHODOLOGY

Potter and Wetherell's Micro-discourse Analysis

Informed by an interpretive perspective, the primary aim of the empirical study (Dey, 2007) was to gain an understanding of the power of the discourse of entrepreneurship in development NGOs. Studying discourse's power on the level of how it shapes (or not) individuals in determinate ways, such a focus, as discussed above, opens up an opportunity to gain an embedded understanding of practitioners' situated agency by looking at the contingent choices they make to either endorse or resist the discourse of entrepreneurship. Accordingly, language offers a fitting entry point for studying the extent to which the discourse of entrepreneurship has actually permeated the realm of development aid by affecting practitioners' way of thinking as well as their sense of self.

The analysis of interpretative repertoires (Potter and Wetherell, 1987; Wetherell and Potter, 1988) is particularly pertinent for the task at hand. Of note here is that Potter and Wetherell talk of 'interpretative repertoire' instead of 'discourse' to distinguish their micro-discursive approach from Foucauldian-inspired macro-analysis which conceives of discourse as a regulated system of statements that is relatively independent from specific, local conversations. In concrete terms, informed by ethnomethodology and speech act theory as well as semiology, Potter and Wetherell (1987) put forward a micro-discourse analysis which investigates interpretative repertoires as the linguistic resources which people invoke to constitute their realities and identities. Stressing the constitutive role of language, the analysis of interpretative repertoires takes as its level of analysis the 'range of linguistic resources that can be drawn upon and utilized in the course of everyday social interaction' (Edley, 2001, p. 198).

Transposed to the present study, the analysis of interpretative repertoires offers a window for looking at whether and how practitioners adopt and reproduce or resist and transgress the discourse of entrepreneurship. My initial assumption was that the ubiquitous imperatives to become leaner, and more business-like and enterprising would in one way or another be reflected in NGO practitioners' accounts of themselves and their work. Conversely, I was also anticipating the possibility that practitioners – within existing limits – would remain situated agents who are able to produce their own socially pertinent meanings. Thus one strength of Potter and Wetherell's analysis of interpretative repertoires is precisely that it offers in-depth insights into how complex, often interwoven processes of affirmation and resistance of the discourse of entrepreneurship are played out at the level of colloquial language. In this way, the analysis of interpretative repertoires captures resistance as a complex language-based process of constant 'adaptation, subversion and reinscription of dominant discourse' (Thomas and Davies, 2005, p. 687).

The question of identity, or what Potter and Wetherell refer to as subject position, is of crucial importance in the present context because the way any given NGO practitioner can think of herself/himself as a person depends upon the interpretative (linguistic) conventions offered to her/him by discourse at a particular point in time. Interpretative repertoires, which offer a basic lexicon of terms for making sense of 'actions and events' (Potter and Wetherell, 1987, p. 187), simultaneously form the corpus of common sense upon which individuals craft a sense of who they are. As Taylor (2005, p. 96) mentions, a subject position is 'a temporary identity which is conferred on or taken up by a speaker and which becomes both who she or he is seen to be by others, and the perspective from which she or he sees the world'. Hence, while the discourse of entrepreneurship seeks to transform NGO practitioners on the level of their being, a key purpose of the present inquiry is to shed light on practitioners' discursive identities or, more precisely, the subject positions rendered available to them by specific ways of talking (Edley, 2001).

Description of Sample

To achieve these aims, I approached around 30 Swiss-based NGOs, asking them whether they would be willing to participate in an interview-based study dealing with the everyday practices and reality of development aid organizations. This resulted in a sample of 12 NGOs. To ensure an adequate amount of variability in practitioners' stories, the investigation included a maximum of three participants per organization, which eventually led to a sample of 30 practitioners. All interviews were carried out in the period from early 2003 to late 2004. All organizations were accredited by ZEWO, an independent foundation which provides a seal of approval for Swiss-based voluntary organizations. The organizations' field of activity was international development aid (including relief work, ecological, economic or sustainable development, human rights, migration, or medical or educational support) in countries in the southern hemisphere. A few organizations, particularly the larger ones, also offered their services in Switzerland. The sample mainly consisted of small and medium-sized organizations, with only two organizations employing more than a hundred people, including both paid staff and volunteers. In total, 14 women and 16 men took part in the study. The study included people from different hierarchical levels: office administrators, project administrators and assistants, heads of projects, and volunteers, as well as directors, managers and founders.

Data Collection and Analysis

Interviews – with one exception – took place at the offices of the respective development NGOs. The interviews were usually initiated by a welcoming remark and a brief outline of the objective of the research project. After that, practitioners were invited to give their account of what they were doing on a day-to-day basis. I tried to step back as much as possible during the interview process, giving maximum space to practitioners' own stories. I became active as an interlocutor during the conversations mainly to keep practitioners' stories going and to make sure that they remained within the broader boundaries of my research project. Interviews lasted between one and two hours, and were guided by a semi-structured interview script. The focus of those questions, which were not shared with practitioners prior to the interviews, was to establish a 'field of visibility' with regard to NGOs' main activities, purposes, crucial challenges and success factors. All interviews were digitally recorded and transcribed.

After a failed attempt at using ATLAS.ti (which proved unhelpful in identifying patterns of meaning between individual interviews), I decided to carry out the analysis on a paper-and-pencil basis, which essentially entailed the following steps. The first analytic step was an iterative reading of the printed transcripts; I marked frequently used words and took notes on recurring topics. This step was descriptive in nature and geared primarily towards getting acquainted with the linguistic corpus (individual concepts) mobilized during the interviews. In the second analytic step I aggregated individual utterances and sentences on the level of interpretative repertoires, thus identifying 'relatively internally consistent, bounded language units' (Wetherell and Potter, 1988, p.171) that constitute a particular understanding of development aid. In the third and related analytic step I further specified the interpretative repertoires with regard to their respective focus (what is the main emphasis of the discursive account?), their protagonist (what are the main actors of the discursive account?) and subject position (what 'location' of the self does the discursive account produce?). From this information, I extracted three interpretative repertoires (described below) which together offer a tentative understanding of the situated agency of NGO practitioners based on the extent to which the interpretative repertoires they summon either affirm or resist its invocation.

RESULTS

The three interpretative repertoires are shown in Table 6.1. The excerpts used to illustrate the repertoires have been translated from the (Swiss) German transcripts.

Table 6.1   Results from the analysis of interpretative repertoires

	Benevolence repertoire: 'Being among equals'	Professionalism repertoire: 'Doing the small things right'	Enterprising repertoire: 'Enduring hardship to become free'
Core terms	'helping', 'supporting' or 'identification'	'liability', 'reasonableness' or 'sincerity'	'innovativeness', 'perseverance' or 'endurance'
Addressee	Beneficiaries	Donors	Practitioners
Subject position	Ideal-type helper 'supportive, upright and non-dominant'	Down-to-earth professional	Autonomous and risk-taking self-starter
Emphasis	Being close to the field, equality and pragmatism	Being close to donors, efficiency of administrative practices	Innovativeness, hard work, being different

Benevolence Repertoire: 'Being Among Equals'

The first repertoire, called 'benevolence', strongly and at times exclusively associates development aid work with the organization's stated purpose.

Making frequent use of terms such as 'helping', 'supporting' or 'identification', the benevolence repertoire portrays development NGOs as being chiefly concerned with the well-being of beneficiaries. Practitioners who mobilize the benevolence repertoire use it to delineate the work of development NGOs as 'useful' and 'much needed'. The analysis revealed that the benevolence repertoire's positive evaluative accent largely derives from lauding the importance of human relations:

> and that's why it probably worked out in my case . . . because the factor 'man' was pivotal, that is, the connection with human fate . . . (Interview partner 1)

It must be noted that the category 'man' for the most part encompasses the perspective of beneficiaries, of their relationship with NGO practitioners.

The benevolence repertoire conveys detailed and normative descriptions about how beneficiaries should be treated by practitioners or by the NGO more generally. While the relative emphasis of the different accounts varied considerably, practitioners relying on the benevolence repertoire usually used words such as 'sensitive', 'understanding', 'commitment' and 'empathy' to delineate the proper mindset of NGO practitioners:

> We decided to make those children in [name of country] our target group, that's when we began to commit and identify ourselves. (Interview partner 7)

Moreover, the benevolence repertoire uses terms such as 'partnership', 'cooperation' and 'trust' to pinpoint the relational side of development aid work, which is usually depicted as something which requires time, patience and dedication. At the base of the benevolence repertoire is the conviction that beneficiaries can be 'empowered' or 'emancipated'. The support offered by the NGO is mostly seen as temporary, as many accounts stress the principle of 'help for self-help'. The sense of fulfilment associated with development aid work derives from accounts which delineate encounters with beneficiaries as sites of mutual 'learning' and 'growth':

> we then went over to [name of region] . . . I then realized that we could start an exchange . . . meaning that we could learn from each other. (Interview partner 11)

It is hence by acknowledging that the helper and the help recipient both benefit from the encounters that the benevolence repertoire gets to defy a hierarchical pedagogy of help.

Though development NGOs are associated with terms such as 'emancipation', it is conspicuous that the benevolence repertoire retains a decisively pragmatic spirit. Instead of using, for instance, political slogans to justify their accounts, practitioners using the benevolence repertoire engender a pragmatic vision of development NGOs by providing detailed descriptions of concrete projects. Such elaborate reports of projects on the one hand stress the everydayness of development aid. On the other hand, they discursively legitimate the speaker by purporting that she/he is 'in touch with' or 'close to' the field. Being close with beneficiaries forms a rhetorical trope for justifying that what the organization or practitioners do is grounded in concrete experiences and knowledge.

A last, and important, point which is characteristic of the benevolence repertoire is that it emphasizes 'equality' between NGO practitioners and beneficiaries: 'for instance . . . our approach in development work is based on the premise that one is among equals . . .' (Interview partner 23). The notion of 'equality' and 'equals' is employed to delineate the work of development NGOs as non-oppressive. Furthermore, it is by positioning normative ideals such as equality and sameness as a proxy for justice that the benevolence repertoire works to rule out possibilities of control, patronage or unequal relations of power at large.

Concerning the subject position implied in the benevolence repertoire, it follows from the analysis that the ideal-type helper is constructed as supportive, upright and non-dominant. The point to note here is that the benevolence repertoire does not engender images of self-sacrifice, which has been identified elsewhere as an inherent part of social work (Dempsey and Sanders, 2010). Though stressing activities such as 'supporting' or 'helping', the helper is usually not construed as a person who subordinates her/his own interests to those of beneficiaries. Instead, working with beneficiaries is portrayed as an activity that is equally fulfilling for the helper and the help recipient. Helpers are assumed to understand that 'equality' forms a higher good which has to be constantly worked on and protected. Helpers thus simultaneously treat 'equality' as a pre-condition of successful development aid work and as an end in itself. It is this latter aspect which renders the helper a subject for whom the journey (and not necessarily the journey's outcome) forms the reward. Though a genuine interest in beneficiaries is one of their key characteristics, helpers are not naïve idealists chasing high-flying dreams. Instead of 'thinking big' and envisioning development aid as necessarily leading to landslide changes, the helper is someone who remains in the 'here and now', thus focusing on the challenges associated with NGOs' mundane practices.

Professionalism Repertoire: 'Doing the Small Things Right'

Practitioners who enact the professionalism repertoire get to emphasize the crucial importance of donors and the role of administrative practices. At base, the professionalism repertoire construes development NGOs as being largely about 'good management'. However, professionalism exceeds the sort of 'entrepreneurial new wave management' discussed by du Gay (2000). In concrete terms, the professionalism repertoire is underpinned by terms such as 'liability', 'reasonableness', and 'sincerity' in praising the ethos of bureaucracy. With development NGOs conceived of as a bundle of well-coordinated yet divisible administrative practices, the yardstick of good management is 'doing one's job right', that is, focusing on one's immediate task without necessarily taking into account the 'big picture':

> the only thing which he [the director] asks me about is when he wants to make payments and that's when I can say yes or no . . . other than that I don't influence the decisions of the organization . . . (Interview partner 14)

On the face of it, stressing the view that the success of development NGOs is a matter of clearly defined roles and responsibilities, the professionalism repertoire gets to connect practitioners' liabilities to their immediate realm of specialization. That is, responsibilities and duties are defined and thus limited by the role, position or function a given individual holds within the organization. While this might be taken as an indication that professionals are people who are disinterested and who have no virtues, it should be noted that the professionalism repertoire does in fact speak about values. Yet, in contrast to the benevolence repertoire which is based on a strong moral foundation (read 'equality'), the professionalism repertoire mainly envisions values in relation to efficiency. In doing so, it promotes the idea that good things become possible only if each and every member of the organization fulfils her/his personal duties in the best possible way, that is, efficiently.

What is of particular interest here is that efficiency functions as a dividing practice that distinguishes between admissible and inadmissible development NGOs, legitimate development NGOs obviously being those who are efficient: 'what distinguishes us from others is our efficiency . . .' (Interview partner 9). On the other hand, a sense of legitimacy is also built by associating efficiency with the broader responsibility of development NGOs. Hence, legitimate development NGOs are not just those who are efficient but also those which measure their efficiency and which transparently communicate their performance to their donors (read accountability). Essentially, where the benevolence repertoire positions 'being close to beneficiaries' as both a moral imperative and a source of fulfilment, the professionalism repertoire construes the ethos of development NGOs in relation to 'being close to donors'. Relations with donors are thus positioned in a business-case logic, meaning that practices of transparency and accountability are evaluated according to whether or not they improve the NGO's reputation and, ultimately, whether they secure donors' financial support.

The professionalism repertoire's subject position construes NGO practitioners as down-to-earth professionals who pursue their work in a calm and logical manner. Professionals are construed as prudent problem-solvers who rely on their expertise and knowledge. Practitioners who make use of this repertoire clearly do not radiate the sense of excitement one finds in the subject position of the ideal-type helper. Yet, this does not mean that professionals are not committed to their work. Rather, professionals convey a work ethos that construes responsibility in relation with expertise and efficiency. As a result, professionals act responsibly if they efficiently carry out their work in their respective field of specialization, thus explicitly not assuming responsibility beyond their designated institutional role. Professionals are deeply moral subjects to the extent that they accept that the success of development NGOs depends on the contribution of each and every individual and, consequently, that people must at all times remain reliable, transparent and efficient.

Enterprising Repertoire: 'Enduring Hardship to Become Free'

The third repertoire, coined 'enterprising', is clearly less palpable in practitioners' accounts. In fact, I only identified the enterprising repertoire in accounts uttered by founders of development NGOs. In contrast to the benevolence repertoire which focuses on beneficiaries, or the professionalism repertoire which focuses on donors, the enterprising repertoire puts the perspective of NGO practitioners on centre stage. Apart from construing development aid work as being based on individual attributes such as 'innovativeness', 'perseverance' or 'endurance', the enterprising repertoire also stresses relational practices such as 'collaborating' and 'dialogue':

> it would not have been possible to start [name of the organization] without . . . without leading discussions . . . without people with whom I was able to have discussions and whom I could ask things. (Interview partner 19)

This clearly contradicts the idea that the competition over scarce financial resources has delimited the likelihood of dialogue and cooperation among development NGOs.

A further point to be mentioned is that at first sight the enterprising repertoire seems to create a good fit with the benevolence repertoire as both employ attributes such as 'involvement', 'commitment' and 'passion'. However, there are subtleties which clearly distinguish the two repertoires. In contrast to the benevolence repertoire which relates the affective qualities of development aid work with the beneficiaries and, by doing so, depicts them as ends in themselves, the enterprising repertoire uses those qualities in a more instrumental way. That is, practitioners who enact the enterprising repertoire suggest that affective qualities such as passion are necessary to endure the 'hardship' related with development aid work.

The notion of 'hardship' is thus endowed with two distinct meanings. On the one hand, individual 'hardship' is exemplified through the daily hassles and obstacles of everyday life, and thus denoted as an inevitable 'side effect' in the pursuit of the organization's mission. On the other hand, and more poetically, 'hardship' gets conceived of as a rite of passage in the quest towards being free: while development aid work is conceived of as offering individuals an autonomous and free style of existence, it is through 'hardship' that the person's transformation materializes:

> of course we earn less than others but that doesn't bother me much . . . all that counts today is that I'm free to do what I please. (Interview partner 2)

A last point worth noting concerns the enterprising repertoire's emphasis on 'being small' and 'being innovative'. Juxtaposing small and big organizations, the enterprising repertoire gets to defy bureaucratic organizations based on the argument that they are not innovative. Innovativeness is thus located within an economic logic as small organizations are delineated as compensating for their relative lack of financial resources by being innovative:

> there are a lot of good . . . organizations which do not need that much money because they largely depend on people's innovativeness. . . . (Interview partner 30)

A striking aspect of the enterprising repertoire is that it produces its subject position (read the entrepreneur) without actually using the term 'entrepreneur' or 'enterprising'. Though clearly surprising, this is not a general paradox because the enterprising repertoire does produce the subject position of the entrepreneur based on attributes which are seen as typical of entrepreneurs. That is, interweaving attributes such as 'self-made', 'persevering' and 'risk-taking', the entrepreneur is discursively produced as someone who approaches work in an enterprising fashion. At this juncture, I should mention that attributes such as 'risk-taking', which is commonly seen as a characteristic aspect of the entrepreneur's innate personality, are discursively created as contingent behaviours. More precisely, the analysis showed that 'risk-taking' is construed as a behaviour which is made necessary due to the NGO sector's 'open' or 'insecure' prospects. Construing 'risk-taking' as a necessary consequence in the face of an uncertain environment rather than an innate quality of the person clearly challenges the idea of possessive individualism which sees the social entrepreneur as a free agent who owns herself/himself completely.

Furthermore, the entrepreneur is not delineated as a larger-than-life figure but as a hard-working, at times creative, person and, most importantly, as someone who wants to be autonomous and free. At heart, the sense of enjoyment associated with the prospect of becoming an entrepreneur is intimately conjoined with the desire to lead a more autonomous life. Though representing entrepreneurs as people who 'go against the grain', the enterprising repertoire does not invoke the image of the isolated maverick which is commonplace in popular renditions of entrepreneurship. Instead, it produces a logic which sees 'being different' as the entrepreneur's primary drive to become free in the first place.

DISCUSSION

The starting point of this contribution has been that the discourse of entrepreneurship has permeated the field of development aid while increasingly demanding that NGO practitioners should think and act more like their entrepreneurial counterparts from the business world. A key insight that can be gleaned from the analysis is that although NGO practitioners might have increasingly become the object of a kind of knowledge that seeks to render development aid more enterprising, they are not determined by it, since they retain the possibility of producing their own pertinent meanings (Fiske, 1989).

But saying that the discourse of entrepreneurship is not deterministic or 'muscular' (Alvesson and Kärreman, 2000) because practitioners are variously able to resist it is not to say that NGO practitioners are autonomous in deciding who they want to be. Hence, rather than standing in a position exterior to the discourse of entrepreneurship, our results sensitize us about the situated agency of practitioners by highlighting how they try to resist the ubiquitous call to enterprise up by immersing themselves in complex struggles over meaning (Putnam, Grant, Michelson and Cutcher, 2005).

To deepen our understanding of the power of the discourse of entrepreneurship, including its very limit, one should note that participants in my study rarely resisted the discourse of entrepreneurship head-on, as they did in the Parkinson and Howorth (2008) study where reservations against and dislike of social entrepreneurship formed the core of practitioners' talk. Perceiving the term 'entrepreneurship' as too closely associated with the world of business, practitioners in that study framed the concept in negative terms, inter alia describing it as 'dirty', 'ruthless', 'ogres', 'exploiting the black economy', 'wealth and empire building' and 'treating people as second class' (Parkinson and Howorth, 2008, pp. 300–301). From my own analysis, such oppositional forms of discursive resistance are most likely if participants are explicitly asked for their opinion on a contested subject (Dey and Teasdale, 2013). If instead participants were simply invited to offer an account of their everyday work, and thus given the opportunity to sketch their experiences in their own words, this mostly resulted in more subtle forms of resistance which were less based on overt antagonism than on either the introduction of alternative repertoires or on the appropriation of the discourse of entrepreneurship.

The first form of resistance occurs in the benevolence repertoire, which is reminiscent of traditional notions of development aid that stress issues such as equality, non-dominance and support. While the benevolence repertoire embodies precisely the kind of rationality which the discourse of entrepreneurship portrays as outdated (since it is ineffective), we can understand that enacting this repertoire forms a cunning attempt at re-inheriting the kind of values and subject positions which have 'gone missing' in the wake of the 'enterprising up' of development aid. As speakers establish a connection with the aborted past of development aid by touching on the importance of values such as equality, togetherness and unconditionality, they in turn get to disrupt the coherence and authority of the discourse of entrepreneurship by demonstrating that the entrepreneurial revolution of development aid is anything but inevitable.

Similar things can be said about the professionalism repertoire. Although its focus on accountability and efficiency seems to put the professionalism repertoire squarely on par with the discourse of entrepreneurship, the professionalism repertoire nevertheless resists the anti-bureaucratic ethos which characterizes the discourse of entrepreneurship. Resistance becomes palpable in how the professionalism repertoire reconciles the virtues of bureaucratic organizing with the idea of effective development aid, thus placing on centre stage a form of organizing which, according to the discourse of entrepreneurship, has long since lost its right to exist. Just like the benevolence repertoire, the professionalism repertoire makes the case for the continuing importance of the past. Invigorating the virtues of bureaucracy entails a political thrust in the way it prevents the discourse of entrepreneurship from fully encroaching upon the meaning of development aid. Both the benevolence and professionalism repertoires support the conclusion that the ostensible marginalization of the social being proclaimed by critics of the discourse of entrepreneurship might be overestimated as practitioners keep resisting its power by invoking alternative repertoires (Froggett and Chamberlayne, 2004; Parkinson and Howorth, 2008; Seanor and Baines, 2013).

The second form of resistance is based on appropriating the meaning of the discourse of entrepreneurship and can be observed most clearly in the enterprising repertoire. A pervasive feature of the enterprising repertoire is that it entails intermittent moments of reproduction and resistance (Thomas and Davies, 2005). Indeed, a cursory glance at the enterprising repertoire seems to suggest that practitioners' talk is firmly co-opted by the discourse of entrepreneurship, as it reproduces issues such as innovativeness, perseverance and an anti-bureaucratic stance, said to be essential characteristics of entrepreneurship.

However, such an appraisal is misleading to the extent that it fails to acknowledge that the enterprising repertoire is not a mimetic reproduction of the discourse of entrepreneurship, because it includes various, if elusive, modifications. As already mentioned, the enterprising repertoire lacks the sort of pomp and utopianism radiated by the discourse of entrepreneurship. Further, an important aberration of the enterprising repertoire is that it values being small, whereas the discourse of entrepreneurship emphasizes the need to 'go big', to scale up and hence to reach as many beneficiaries as possible (Alvord, Brown and Letts, 2004).

Probably an even more noteworthy sign of appropriation can be detected in the reasons the enterprising repertoire offers as to why people get involved in an entrepreneurial career or venture. Unlike the discourse of entrepreneurship which conceives of entrepreneurship as an innate attribute of the individual which is triggered by the desire to offer solutions to difficult problems, in the enterprising repertoire the individual's desire to have a lasting effect on the world is of secondary importance. Rather than trying to save the world on a shoestring, as it were, the enterprising repertoire tells a story of personal transformation where the individual embarks on a journey which leaves him/her changed. Development aid thus represents the context in which a transformation of the self is deemed possible. This is important not only because it counteracts the spectacular undertone of the discourse of entrepreneurship (Dempsey and Sanders, 2010) but also because it shows that in the enterprising repertoire the primary purpose of becoming an entrepreneur is to become free. The entrepreneur in this repertoire is an individual who 'sacrifices' a normal life for a lifestyle which offers freedom and individual self-fulfilment.

Cursory though these illustrations have been, they alert us to how NGO practitioners, as they use language to give an account of themselves and their work, manage to resist the discourse of entrepreneurship in important ways. Both forms of discursive resistance just discussed stand in obvious contrast to the etymological meaning of 'resistance' (from Latin *resistere* 'to make a stand against') as oppositional practice. The analysis of practitioners' interpretative repertoires has confirmed that resistance entails a strong creative element, as they constantly make choices between competing meanings while accounting for their choices by negotiating 'their own understanding within their own particular worlds' (Cohen and

Musson, 2000, p. 44). By implication, the force of both forms of resistance results from how they play with the possibilities offered by the ambivalence entailed by the discourse of entrepreneurship. Such a view evidently contradicts interpretations which see the discourse of entrepreneurship as capable of completely positioning individuals in terms of their being and, by implication, making them governable (Carmel and Harlock, 2008).

This said, I must immediately reiterate that the sort of resistance my micro-discursive analysis was able to disclose entails a situated agency, not an absolute one. NGO practitioners' choices are not entirely free (read 'anything goes') as they are restricted to choosing among or appropriating discourses which are already socially legitimated (Dart, 2004). Therefore, although it may be true that NGO practitioners cannot remove themselves completely from the influences of the discourse of entrepreneurship, what they can do is appropriate existing discourses or introduce alternative ones in a way that develops creative opportunities for venturing beyond the dominant discourse.

CONCLUSION

A crucial contention I have made in this chapter is that any understanding of the power of the discourse of entrepreneurship would be incomplete without taking into account the perspective of those who are usually seen as mere objects of this discourse (Parkinson and Howorth, 2008). Exemplified through the usage of Potter and Wetherell's methodology, this analysis of practitioners' language use has helped us rebuild a sense of agency back into our understanding of the discourse of entrepreneurship (Jones and Spicer, 2009) by hinting at how people resist it in largely creative ways.

Micro-discourse analytic methods, such as the one developed by Potter and Wetherell, offer important means for enhancing our understanding of the subtlety and creativity of resistance, and thus render visible how resistance unfolds around struggles around meaning (Putnam et al., 2005). Importantly, micro-discourse analyses derive their force as an instrument of critical analysis from unveiling aspects of social reality which are marginalized or rendered unimaginable by dominant discourse. Bringing into play that which is 'excluded, ignored or repressed' in the dominant discourse of entrepreneurship (Froggett and Chamberlayne, 2004, p. 71), micro-discourse analysis can operate as a means of immanent critique whose primary function is to probe the disjuncture between what is strategically defined and what might become possible but is yet only a transient possibility embodied in the local use of language. As immanent critique, micro-discourse analysis is able to root out precisely those alternatives 'which are often in conflict with the wave of euphoria and optimism that is driving current theoretical development in the field of social enterprise and entrepreneurship' (Bull, 2008, p. 272). Where the critical function of micro-discourse analysis is to denaturalize dominant discourses by dissolving their apparent authority and inevitability into contingent knowledge, the attribute 'immanent' further indicates that no erudition is needed to clarify what is best for the people concerned. Indeed, what micro-discourse analysis brings to the forefront is that the potential for resistance and, by implication, change, is always already part of people's everyday existence.

To conclude, there is no reason to romanticize micro-discourse analysis since one never knows whether the immanent potential to which such analyses point will ever prevail or whether people's resistance will ultimately remain without broader effect. Given that we cannot know what will happen, I believe that micro-discourse analysis merits further attention as it offers the means for investigating when and where resistance is disruptive, that is, when and where local discursive resistance of the kind discussed in this chapter will translate into transversal, more coordinated and orchestrated forms of resistance (Marchart, 2003). Hence, will the discourse of entrepreneurship ever make development aid subservient to economic and managerial thinking? We do not know. What we do know is that micro-discourse analysis can help us address this question by offering the tools to document the minutiae of the power of the discourse of entrepreneurship, including ways this power might be subverted and changed over time.

REFERENCES

Ainsworth, Susanne and Cynthia Hardy (2008), 'The enterprising self: An unsuitable job for an older worker', *Organization*, **15** (3), 389–405.

Alvesson, Mats and Dan Kärreman (2000), 'Varieties of discourse: On the study of organizations through discourse analysis', *Human Relations*, **53** (9), 1125–1149.

Alvord, Sarah H., L. David Brown and Christine W. Letts (2004), 'Social entrepreneurship and societal transformation: An exploratory study', *The Journal of Applied Behavioral Science*, **40** (3), 260–282.

Banks, Nicola and David Hulme (2012), 'The role of NGOs and civil society in development and poverty reduction', accessed 7 September 2013 at www.bwpi.manchester.ac.uk/resources/Working-Papers/bwpi-wp-17112.pdf.

Baur, Dorothea and Hans Peter Schmitz (2012), 'Corporations and NGOs: When accountability leads to co-optation', *Journal of Business Ethics*, **106** (1), 9–21.

Berglund, Karin and Brigitta Schwartz (2013), 'Holding on to the anomaly of social entrepreneurship: Dilemmas in starting up and running a fair-trade enterprise', *Journal of Social Entrepreneurship*, **4** (3), 237–255.

Bosma, Niels and Jonathan Levie (2010), 'Global entrepreneurship monitor: 2009 Executive Report', accessed 23 July 2013 at www.gemconsortium.org/docs/download/666.

Bröckling, Ulrich (2002), 'Das unternehmerische Selbst und seine Geschlechter. Gender-Konstruktionen in Erfolgsratgebern', *Leviathan*, **48**, 175–194.

Brugmann, Jeb (2005), 'All paths lead to BOP', *Alliance*, **10**, 1 September.

Bull, Michael (2008), 'Challenging tensions: Critical, theoretical and empirical perspectives on social enterprise', *International Journal of Entrepreneurial Behaviour & Research*, **14** (5), 268–275.

Carmel, Emma and Jenny Harlock (2008), 'Instituting the "third sector" as a governable terrain: Partnership, performance and procurement in the UK', *Policy and Politics*, **36** (2), 155–171.

Chand, Vijaya Sherry (2009), 'Beyond nongovernmental development action into social entrepreneurship', *Journal of Entrepreneurship*, **18** (2), 139–166.

Cohen, Laurie and Gill Musson (2000), 'Entrepreneurial identities: Reflections from two case studies', *Organization*, **7** (1), 31–48.

Collier, Paul (2007), *The Bottom Billion: Why the Poorest Countries are Failing and What can be Done About It*, Oxford: Oxford University Press.

Collier, Paul (2013), 'Social enterprise and aid: Pump-priming the missing effective organizations', Keynote presented at Locating Social Entrepreneurship in the Global South: Innovations in Development Aid Conference, Washington, DC, 12 March.

Dart, Raymond (2004), 'The legitimacy of social enterprise', *Non-profit Management & Leadership*, **14** (4), 411–424.

Dempsey, Sarah E. and Matthew L. Sanders (2010), 'Meaningful work? Nonprofit marketisation and work/life balance in popular autobiographies of social entrepreneurship', *Organization*, **17** (4), 437–459.

Dey, Pascal (2007), *On the Name of Social Entrepreneurship: Business School Teaching, Research, and Development Aid*, unpublished doctoral dissertation, Basel, Switzerland: University of Basel.

Dey, Pascal (2014), 'Governing the social through "social entrepreneurship": A Foucauldian view of the "art of governing in advanced liberalism"', in Heather Douglas and Suzanne Grant (eds), *Social Innovation and Social Entrepreneurship: Context and Theories*, Melbourne: Tilde University Press, pp. 55–72.

Dey, Pascal and Chris Steyaert (2010), 'The politics of narrating social entrepreneurship', *Journal of Enterprising Communities*, **4** (1), 85–108.

Dey, Pascal and Chris Steyaert (2016), 'Rethinking the space of ethics in social entrepreneurship: Power, subjectivity, and practices of concrete freedom', *Journal of Business Ethics*, **133** (4), 627–641.

Dey, Pascal and Simon Teasdale (2013), '"Social enterprise" and dis/identification: The politics of identity work in the UK third sector', *Administrative Theory and Praxis*, **35** (2), 249–271.

Drucker, Peter (1985), *Innovation and Entrepreneurship*, London: Sage.

Easterly, William (2006), *The White Man's Burden: Why the West's Efforts to Aid the Rest have done so much Ill and so little Good*, New York: Penguin Press.

Edley, Nigel (2001), 'Analysing masculinity: Interpretative repertoires, ideological dilemmas and subject positions', in Margaret Wetherell, Stephanie Taylor and Simeon J. Yates (eds), *Discourse as Data: A Guide for Analysis*, London: Open University Press & Sage, pp. 189–228.

Eleff, Leanne Ralya and Angela Trethewey (2006), 'The enterprising parent: A critical examination of parenting, consumption and identity', *Journal of the Association for Research on Mothering*, **8** (1–2), 242–251.

Essers, Caroline and Yvonne Benschop (2007), 'Enterprising identities: Female entrepreneurs of Moroccan or Turkish origin in the Netherlands', *Organization Studies*, **28** (1), 49–69.

Fiske, John (1989), *Reading the Popular*, New York: Routledge.

Foucault, Michel (1997a), 'Sex, power and the politics of identity', in Paul Rabinow (ed.), *Ethics: Subjectivity and Truth*, New York: The New York Press, pp. 163–173.

Foucault, Michel (1997b), 'What is critique?', in Paul Rabinow (ed.), *The Essential Works of Michel Foucault, Vol. 1: Ethics, Subjectivity and Truth*, New York: The New Press, pp. 263–278.

Froggett, Lynn and Prue Chamberlayne (2004), 'Narratives of social enterprise: From biography to practice and policy critique', *Qualitative Social Work*, **3** (1), 61–77.

du Gay, Paul (2000), *In Praise of Bureaucracy: Weber, Organization, Ethics*, London: Sage.

du Gay, Paul (2004), 'Against "Enterprise" (but not against "enterprise", for that would make no sense)', *Organization*, **11** (1), 37–57.

Gonin, Michaël and Nicolas Gachet (2014), 'Social enterprise models in Switzerland: An overview of existing streams, practices, and institutional structures', working paper presented at the ICSEM project, Lausanne, Switzerland, July.

Hatcher, Caroline (2001), 'The enterprising academic: Transforming the master', *Electronic Journal of Radical Organizational Theory*, accessed 2 August 2015 at www.mngt.waikato.ac.nz/ejrot/. . ./Hatcher.pdf.

Hervieux, Chantal, Eric Gedajlovic and Marie-France B. Turcotte (2010), 'The legitimization of social entrepreneurship', *Journal of Enterprising Communities*, **4** (1), 37–67.

ISG (2008), *CSO parallel process to the Ghana High Level Forum Network*, accessed 16 March 2006 at http://www.whiteband.org/resources/issues/aid/index_html/the-aid-effectivenessdebate/a-critical-approach-to-the-aid-effectiveness-agenda.

Jones, Campbell and André Spicer (2006), 'Outline of a genealogy of the value of the entrepreneur', in Guido Erreygers and Geert Jacobs (eds), *Language, Communication and the Economy*, Amsterdam: John Benjamins Publishing, pp. 179–197.

Jones, Campbell and André Spicer (2009), *Unmasking the Entrepreneur*, Cheltenham, UK and Northampton, MA, USA: Edward Elgar Publishing.

Katz, Hagai (2006), 'Gramsci, hegemony, and global civil society networks', *Voluntas*, **17** (4), 333–348.

Loacker, Bernadette (2013), 'Becoming "culturpreneur": How the "neoliberal regime of truth" affects and redefines artistic subject positions', *Culture and Organization*, **19** (2), 124–145.

Marchart, Oliver (2003), 'Bridging in micro-macro-gap: Is there such a thing as post-subcultural politics?', in David Muggleton and Rupert Weinzierl (eds), *The Post-subcultures Reader*, New York: Berg, pp. 83–97.

Nicholls, Alex (2006), *Social Entrepreneurship: New Paradigms of Sustainable Social Change*, Oxford: Oxford University Press.

Nicholls, Alex (2010), 'The legitimacy of social entrepreneurship: Reflexive isomorphism in a pre-paradigmatic field', *Entrepreneurship Theory and Practice*, **34** (4), 611–633.

Onyuma, Samuel O. and Alfred O. Shem (2005), 'Myths of microfinance as a panacea for poverty eradication and women empowerment', *Savings and Development*, **29** (2), 199–222.

Parkinson, Caroline and Carole Howorth (2008), 'The language of social entrepreneurs', *Entrepreneurship & Regional Development*, **20** (3), 285–309.

Peters, Tom and Robert H. Waterman (1982), *In Search of Excellence: Lessons from America's Best-Run Companies*, New York: Harper & Row.

Pongratz, Hans J. and Günter G. Voß (2003), *Arbeitskraftunternehmer: Erwerbsorientierungen in entgrenzten Arbeitsformen*, Berlin: edition sigma.

Potter, Jonathan and Margaret Wetherell (1987), *Discourse and Social Psychology: Beyond Attitudes and Behaviour*, London: Sage.

Prahalad, C.K. (2004), *The Fortune at the Bottom of the Pyramid: Eradicating Poverty through Profits*, Upper Saddle River, NJ: The Free Press.

Putnam, Linda L., David Grant, Grant Michelson and Leanne Cutcher (2005), 'Discourse and resistance: Targets, practices, and consequences', *Management Communication Quarterly*, **19** (1), 5–18.

Seanor, Pam and Sue Baines (2013), 'Narratives of transition from social to enterprise: You can't get there from here!', *Journal of Entrepreneurial Behavior & Research*, **19** (3), 324–343.

Shivji, Issa G. (2007), *Silences in NGO Discourse: The Role and Future of NGOs in Africa*, Oxford: Fahamu.

Spicer, André (2012), 'Critical theories of entrepreneurship', in Kevin Mole and Monder Ram (eds), *Perspectives in Entrepreneurship: A Critical Approach*, Basingstoke: Palgrave Macmillan, pp. 149–160.

Steyaert, Chris and Bart Van Looy (eds) (2010), *Relational Practices, Participative Organizing. Advanced Series in Management Vol. 7*, Bingley: Emerald.

Storey, John, Graeme Salaman and Kerry Platman (2005), 'Living with enterprise in an enterprise economy: Freelance and contract workers in the media', *Human Relations*, **58** (8), 1033–1054.

Taylor, Stephanie (2005), 'Narrative as construction and discursive resource', *Narrative Inquiry*, **16** (1), 94–102.

Thomas, Robyn and Annette Davies (2005), 'Theorizing the micro-politics of resistance: New public management and managerial identities in the UK public services', *Organization Studies*, **26** (5), 683–706.

United Nations (2004), *Unleashing entrepreneurship: Making business work for the poor*, accessed 2 July 2006 at web.undp.org/cpsd/documents/report/english/fullreport.pdf.

Weiskopf, Richard and Chris Steyaert (2009), 'Metamorphoses in entrepreneurship studies: Towards an affirmative politics of entrepreneuring', in Daniel Hjorth and Chris Steyaert (eds), *The Politics and Aesthetics of Entrepreneurship. A Fourth Movements in Entrepreneurship Book*, Cheltenham, UK and Northampton, MA, USA: Edward Elgar Publishing, pp. 183–201.

Wetherell, Margaret and Jonathan Potter (1988), 'Discourse analysis and the identification of interpretative repertoires', in Charles Antaki (ed.), *Analysing Everyday Explanation: A Casebook of Methods*, Newbury Park, CA: Sage, pp. 168–183.

7. Part-time work as resistance: the rhetorical interplay between argument and counter-argument

Patrizia Hoyer and Julia C. Nentwich

INTRODUCTION

The notions of control and resistance are increasingly being reassessed, with concepts of discourse and rhetoric taking centre stage. This development is based on the assumption that organizational control is no longer achieved through coercion, but rather through processes of discursive normalization (Meriläinen, Tienari, Thomas and Davies, 2004), that is through ways of differentiating, homogenizing or excluding (Collinson, 2003). In that view, dominant organizational discourses are considered to be productive as they construct an image of the 'ideal worker' (Benschop and Dooreward, 1998; Tienari, Quack and Theobald, 2002) whose attitudes, values and thoughts are aligned with organizational goals. At the same time, dominant discourses may marginalize those workers who do not perform within the boundaries of a given norm by constructing them as 'problematic' or 'inferior' (Fournier, 1998).

While many studies have framed discourse as a potential site of 'idealization' and 'marginalization' (Alvesson and Willmott, 2002; Kärreman and Alvesson, 2004; Meriläinen et al., 2004), discourse can also become a source from which to fashion alternative realities and thus a site from which to resist normalization (Burr, 2003; Fleming and Spicer, 2003; Kärreman and Alvesson, 2009; Kärreman and Spicer, 2009). This chapter will particularly look at how people can use 'rhetorical strategies' (Suddaby and Greenwood, 2005) to resist dominant discourses that have potentially normalizing effects. To investigate this question, we conducted a micro-discursive analysis on the rhetorical interplay between arguments that construct a dominant discourse and counter-arguments that contest exactly these arguments, thereby legitimizing alternative constructions of reality.

We illustrate this rhetorical interplay between arguments and counter-arguments by drawing on an ongoing debate in organizations around work-time arrangements. As dominant organizational discourses link the amount of time spent at work with concepts of commitment and professionalism, full-time work is constructed as the standard practice, while working part-time is depicted as a violation of this standard; this leaves part-timers in subordinate and marginalized positions in the way they are deployed and managed in organizations (Dick and Hyde, 2006).

After providing a brief literature review that problematizes the discursive construction of working time and the resulting marginalization of part-time workers, we frame resistance as a matter of rhetorical moves towards undermining and altering the dominant discourse of full-time work arrangements. In the methods section we provide a detailed description of how we conducted the rhetorical analysis and in the results section we lay out four different 'rhetorical strategies' (interplays of argument and counter-argument) whose effects we then discuss: How do they allow their users to resist the full-time discourse and construct part-time work as a valid alternative to this norm? We observed that the two rhetorical strategies in which counter-arguments addressed arguments by challenging or changing their underlying assumptions were more successful in contesting the dominant discourse than the two strategies in which the counter-arguments simply tried to invalidate arguments or claimed their opposite without questioning the argumentative base of their underlying assumptions.

By taking this rhetorical perspective on resistance, we aspire to contribute to a micro-discursive understanding of how organizational logics may gradually shift over time as the dominant discourses that shape these logics are persistently undermined and altered in small rhetorical moves.

THE EVERYDAY MARGINALIZATION OF PART-TIME WORKERS

As professional roles have historically been undertaken on a permanent full-time basis, part-time work has traditionally been associated with poorly paid, low-status positions that offer little job security and virtually no opportunities for professional development and career advancement (Lawrence and Corwin, 2003). However, as both workers and employers demand more flexibility in both the patterns and hours of their work schedules so they can better accommodate work and personal life demands, a steadily increasing number of organizations are allowing for part-time work by implementing flexible working policies. And as research suggests, part-time arrangements benefit not only the workers (Dick and Hyde, 2006), but also the organizations that offer them (Lawrence and

Corwin, 2003). Hence, the myth of a lifelong full-time career with a single employer is gradually becoming an anachronistic model of the way that individuals interact with organizations.

Despite this steady shift towards part-time work and the optimistic positioning of part-timers in professional roles with good compensation and retention packages, the marginalization and occupational downgrading of part-time work is still widely accepted. Both part-timers and their full-time colleagues see this marginalization as a legitimate and inevitable response to working reduced hours. Hence, within the systems and structures created for full-time employees, part-time workers continue to be constructed as presenting problems for managers with regards to issues of communication, supervision and accountability. Most detrimental to the image of the part-timer is the continuing notion that people working part-time are less committed to their paid employment. While full-timers are associated with a willingness and ability to work long hours, providing evidence that they have set their time priorities in line with their professional career aspirations, part-time workers are perceived as prioritizing non-work commitments and as being less career focused. Thus, part-time workers are often given assignments and roles that are compatible with their reduced hours, but not with their professional capabilities (Dick and Hyde, 2006).

Since the shift towards more flexible work-time schedules in organizations has not achieved a more legitimate positioning of part-timers in the professional context, we take the view that the marginalization of part-timers cannot be changed as long as dominant organizational discourses construct full-time work as the norm and part-time work as a violation of this norm. How, then, can the full-time discourse be resisted rhetorically, in order to eventually shift organizational logics around work-time arrangements? In the following section we suggest a micro-discursive investigation of resistance through rhetorical analysis.

RESISTANCE AS A MATTER OF MICRO-DISCURSIVE MOVES

While most research on organizational control has focused on how employee behaviour is shaped through dominant discourses that have normalizing effects, some researchers have also considered ways to discursively resist this normalization (Burr, 2003; Fleming and Spicer, 2003; Kärreman and Alvesson, 2009; Kärreman and Spicer, 2009). These notions of discursive control and resistance can be related back to and situated within the writings of Michel Foucault (1977), who in the 1970s introduced a processual understanding of power in organizations. Interested in the practice rather than the essence of power, he examined how it is circulated and how it functions in a productive way. In his discursive framework Foucault treated the 'mind' as a surface where power is inscribed and discourse as the tool for controlling ideas and behaviour; he claimed that the notions of control and resistance are inextricably linked as two sides of the same coin (Burr, 2003).

In particular, Foucault (1976) saw resistance as a tactical reversal: even though power always triggers resistance, it cannot succeed as it 'is never in a position of exteriority in relation to power' (p. 95). From this viewpoint, resistance – rather than being a disruptive force – actually strengthens or reproduces the power regime that it tries to confront. On a different note, in his essay 'The Subject and Power' (1982) as well as in his later writings on governmentality and the ethic of care for the self, Foucault (1988, 1991) argues that power necessarily entails the capacity for 'positive' and 'productive' resistance, as power – in contrast to violence – can only be exercised over free subjects: agents who have a real choice to behave in a variety of ways (Bevir, 1999).

These different ideas on resistance have been taken up by various camps of researchers, some more optimistic than others (Mumby, 2005). For example critical voices have followed up Foucault's idea that resistance only exists as part of the discourse it seeks to confront, and that it may therefore be less effective or even self-defeating (for example, Fleming and Spicer, 2003). Since dominant discourses may form the kind of employee the company desires – one who is less recalcitrant and more productive – resistance to discursive normalization has often been framed as very difficult. Through notions such as the 'enterprising self' (du Gay, 1996) workers become inscribed in power relations which make them 'the principle of [their] own subjection' (Foucault, 1977, p. 203) as their sense of meaning is determined by their participation in dominant discourses. Through that process the locus of control has shifted from the outside of the workers to their inside (Kärreman and Alvesson, 2004), thereby making resistance appear almost impossible.

Others have maintained that it is exactly this link between discursive control and resistance – the fact that discourse contains its antithesis – that opens up space for agency. Researchers from this side argue that even though individuals may be constrained to some extent by the dominant discourses available to them in a given context, we must not underestimate the creative capacity to resist and subvert discourses and prescribed identities. For example Hyde (2008) explored the identities of female part-time police officers and noted that the same techniques that generate discourses and their potentially normalizing effects (in this case the construction of the police profession as calling for male employees and full-time engagement) are also deemed to generate resistance. In this view marginalized and repressed discourses offer an opening through which resistance becomes possible; they become available as a source from which to fashion alternative realities.

This does not imply, though, that change is a matter of easily talking oneself out of oppressive social relations or damaging identity constructions (Burr, 2003). A first step would be to recognize the discourses that are currently leading to marginalization in order to work towards discursive positions that appear more appropriate and are less personally damaging (Burr, 2003). In a study looking at the marginalized position of part-timers and especially the problematic use of the part-time category for men, Smithson (2005) maintains that discourses may become a site of resistance where identities are produced and transformed – not along a traditional list of characteristics, but in creative and unpredictable ways.

Though a vigorous debate continues around this question of whether or not people can successfully resist discursive normalization, researchers have shifted their focus towards more micro-discursive investigations of how – rather than if – resistance may be possible within this framework. Such studies, for example, take an interest in how 'rhetorical strategies' (Suddaby and Greenwood, 2005) – deliberately using persuasive language to undermine or reify particular reality constructions – can achieve this goal. Though rhetorical strategies may not mark a radical emancipation from dominant discourses, they may be able to gradually shift organizational logics by continuously engaging with and tweaking the boundaries of these dominant discourses.

Using this kind of micro-discursive approach to investigating resistance, in the following sections we delineate a framework for rhetorical analysis. We then use that framework to analyse the ways that rhetorical strategies can be used to help undermine and alter the dominant full-time discourse that marginalizes part-time workers.

ZOOMING IN ON THE MICRO-DISCURSIVE MECHANISMS OF RESISTANCE

Phillips and Hardy (2002) frame rhetorical analysis, like the investigation of rhetorical strategies undertaken by Suddaby and Greenwood (2005), as a form of social linguistic discourse analysis that focuses on the strategies of argumentation that can be used to construct certain versions of reality and undermine others. With a focus on resistance, the rhetorical analysis we suggest here might share similarities with some approaches based on Foucauldian notions of discourse that try to detect how unequal power relations are constituted and resisted through discourse. While a Foucauldian discourse analysis assumes that idealizing and marginalizing effects are inherent within dominant discourses per se, a rhetorical investigation takes a micro-discursive approach to analyse exactly how people create or resist certain phenomena rhetorically in order to constitute or undermine certain versions of reality.

More concretely, in this chapter we adopt a rhetorical perspective on control-resistance dynamics that has been inspired by the work of Symon (2000, 2005, 2008) who has looked particularly at rhetorical strategies applied to promote and resist technological change in a UK public sector firm. Following Symon's approach, we will also draw on the work of Billig (1996, 1998) and Potter (1996) to make two points about rhetoric: it is (a) dialogically constructed in the interplay between arguments and counter-arguments, and (b) applied to make certain versions of reality persuasive by either drawing on defensive (reifying) or offensive (ironizing) rhetoric. To add a third element to the specific rhetorical framework we suggest here, we also draw on the work of Bamberg and Andrews (2004) who maintain that rhetorical strategies have stronger effects in terms of resistance when counter-arguments target the underlying assumptions of arguments. In the following paragraphs we elaborate on these three elements within our rhetorical framework.

Starting with the work of Billig (1998), we take the view that rhetoric – just like language itself – is dialogical. Billig, who himself took inspiration from the works of Bakhtin (1981, 1986) maintained that by studying the micro-processes of talk, we can observe how human thinking is rhetorically accomplished and contested in argument; this led him to the conclusion that 'human thinking is inherently dialogical' (Billig, 1998, p. 200). In that view, any topic can be opened up either for public debate or for internal debates of solitary thought. By taking up this dialogical notion of rhetoric in our analytical framework, we assume that certain arguments on an issue always carry the possibility of counter-arguments and a space for exercising rhetorical ingenuity.

Symon (2008) noted that to legitimize particular arguments, rhetoricians may in fact draw on dominant discourses (such as the discourse about full-time work) that prevail in the context of a given organization or society more generally. Only by taking note of this 'argumentative context' can one understand a particular argument in terms of what is being argued against, in this case the notion that part-time work is a valid alternative to full-time work. This argumentative context might not always mark an explicitly public debate, but as Billig states, rhetoric is often concerned with issues that are controversial and that are therefore open to debate such as those surrounding part-time work.

Setting out to justify one position and to destabilize the other, the arguments and counter-arguments in any dialogue have to constantly anticipate potential criticism. Therefore, individuals involved in rhetoric not only have to be acquainted with the range of existing arguments on a given controversy; they also need to arm themselves with counter-arguments. Thus, the rhetorical interplay between argument and counter-argument holds the potential for continuous reinvention: 'the creation of particular arguments allows the possibility of new (counter-)arguments, which, in turn, introduces further arguments and so on' (Symon, 2005, p. 1661).

Second, drawing on the work of Potter (1996), in our rhetorical framework we explore how certain discursive constructions are made persuasive; that is, how are they rhetorically enforced to constitute reality? To answer this, Potter identifies two particular forms of rhetorical talk. One is 'reifying': trying to convince others that accounts are facts. The second is 'ironizing': exposing those 'facts' as a social construction. In this view, individuals may be seeking to convince an audience that a particular social construction is true (and *not* a social construction) by drawing on 'defensive rhetoric' that aims to protect its own accounts; that is, they are 'reifying'. Simultaneously they may be seeking to expose other accounts as social constructions (or as not being true) by engaging in 'offensive rhetoric' that is targeted towards undermining alternative accounts; that is, they are 'ironizing'. Identifying how constructions of 'the real' are made persuasive will become an important part of our rhetorical analysis.

And finally, to better understand the potential effects of resistance through a rhetorical lens, we draw on the work of Bamberg and Andrews (2004) who claim that even when speakers are producing counter-arguments, they may not 'totally step outside the dominating framework of the master narrative, but . . . remain somewhat complicit and work with components and parts of the existent frame "from within"' (Bamberg and Andrews, 2004, p. 363). As they are based on the very same logic and assumptions as the arguments they try to oppose, counter-arguments of this type might have only minor effects in terms of resistance. In contrast, counter-arguments that fundamentally contest the underlying assumptions of arguments and try to invent new realities can be seen as an ongoing rhetorical achievement in terms of resisting the norm. And this, according to Symon (2008), is also what makes rhetoric so creative: through rhetoric, people can rework the underlying assumptions of (counter-)arguments to construct new organizational realities. Understanding how alternative viewpoints are constructed and presented makes it possible to engage with and to counter these arguments more effectively (Symon, 2000). It is this rhetorical creativity which then allows people to develop 'micro-emancipatory' moves (Alvesson and Willmott, 2002).

In the methods section, after providing some information on the research setting, we will lay out more precisely how we applied a rhetorical analysis to the debate around part-time work along the three dimensions delineated in this section.

METHODOLOGY

To explore how part-time work was either constructed as a violation of the norm of full-time work (argument) or else as a legitimate alternative to this norm (counter-argument), 21 interviews were conducted with employees of a science and engineering research institute in Switzerland (Nentwich, 2004). We deliberately chose that organization because it has a positive stance towards part-time work overall, and quite a high proportion of both male and female part-time employees (28 per cent). This can be considered a special setting; in Switzerland science and engineering research is still quite a male-dominated field, whereas part-time work is strongly considered to be a female practice (Strub, 2003; Swiss Federal Statistical Office, 2003).

To investigate our subject, the second author of this chapter interviewed 12 people working part-time and 9 working full-time, in both employee (11) and management (10) positions. Their ages ranged from 35 to 45; of the total of 21 interviewees, 10 were male and 11 female, and 13 were parents. Full-time work was defined as working 90 per cent or more of the Swiss standard of 42 hours, while part-time work was defined as any work-time arrangement below 90 per cent. All the interviews, which lasted between 30 and 90 minutes and were audio recorded, were conducted over a period of 3 months in 2002.

During the interviews, a flexible interview guide integrated very specific questions with more narrative elements as suggested by Witzel's (1996, 2000) problem-centred interview approach. The opening question was kept very broad: interviewees were asked to explain how they came to work for the institute in their particular position. Addressing interviewees' organizational positions evoked explanations about being in that given position, and also allowed them to raise related topics, including part-time work, and family and other commitments as well as equal opportunity issues.

For the data analysis, all 21 interviews were fully transcribed and then organized electronically using Atlas.ti. After coding the interviews along various themes around work-time arrangements, we developed three analytical questions in line with our rhetorical framework and directed them to the interview texts to further refine our analysis:

1. How/through what rhetorical strategies did counter-arguments contest arguments to eventually undermine and alter the dominant discourse on full-time work?
2. How were arguments and counter-arguments made rhetorically persuasive, either through defensive rhetorical moves to reify their own account or offensive rhetorical moves to ironize the anticipated or implicit (counter-)arguments of others?
3. What were the effects of rhetorical strategies in terms of resisting the dominant full-time discourse and of constructing part-time work as a legitimate alternative to this norm?

In line with the conceptual framework delineated above, these questions allowed us to identify the various rhetorical strategies, that is the different rhetorical interplays through which counter-arguments dialogically addressed arguments for resisting the dominant discourse of full-time work (Billig, 1996). Then, we looked at the micro-discursive rhetorical moves that speakers used to make their arguments and counter-arguments persuasive, by either reifying one version of reality or ironizing another (Potter, 1996). Finally, we looked at the effects of the rhetorical strategies in terms of resisting the dominant discourse of full-time work by constructing part-time work as a legitimate alterative to this norm. Here, we paid special attention to whether or not counter-arguments questioned the underlying assumptions of arguments (Bamberg and Andrews, 2004).

RESULTS

Through our analysis we identified four rhetorical strategies through which speakers used counter-arguments to interact with arguments, in order to resist the dominant discourse that constructs full-time work as the norm and part-time work as a violation of this norm. These strategies were (1) invalidating arguments, (2) claiming the opposite, (3) challenging basic assumptions, and (4) changing basic assumptions. We observed that each of these strategies, which often relied predominantly on either a defensive or an offensive rhetoric, had a different effect in resisting the discourse of full-time work, depending on whether or not the underlying assumptions of the arguments were questioned in the counter-arguments.

Invalidating Arguments

In the first rhetorical strategy, counter-arguments aimed at 'invalidating arguments' by making claims that directly questioned these arguments and by providing examples that contested the marginalizing reality constructions around part-timers. This rhetorical interplay is illustrated in the following discussion around whether or not part-time workers could potentially hold management positions:

> I would say from the level of department head onwards, where they are responsible for 10 to 30 people, that doesn't work if they are not there 100 per cent. . . . They have to be approachable, they have to be available, they have responsibilities both internal and external. And at some point they run out of appointments if they are only around four days or three. It just doesn't work out. (Interview 13)

Here the argument that part-timers are not suitable for highly responsible positions is based on the notion that these positions require the employee to be present in the office 100 per cent of the time. The underlying assumption for this argument is a constructed link between the concepts of being present and carrying responsibility that the speaker supports by drawing on notions of approachability and availability. He then makes the claim persuasive by using offensive rhetoric to undermine/ironize the idea that managers could work part-time and thus maintains that 'it just doesn't work like that', pointing out potential problems like a lack of time for appointments.

To invalidate this argument that part-timers are not suitable for positions higher up in the organizational hierarchy, other interviewees, also using a form of offensive rhetoric, formulated reasons why the given argument could be considered inaccurate or irrelevant. For instance, they invalidated arguments by drawing attention to their prejudiced nature or even by rejecting them as nonsense, thereby ironizing the opposite position. More concretely, in the following extract the interviewee clearly objects to the argument that managers must be present all the time:

> People generally say that superiors should preferably be there all the time. Whereas, if you look more closely, superiors are around the office less than others, right? That's how it is. (Interview 7)

Analysing the dialogical nature of this rhetorical interplay, we notice that the opposing party is actually not present in the interview setting, but is still represented in the statement about what 'people generally say'. Thus, we see that this counter-argument is clearly targeted towards the (earlier shown) argument 'that superiors should preferably be there all the time'. The speaker offensively discounts this claim with an alternative reality construction: that superiors, just like part-timers, are actually not in the office all that much. Also in this rhetorical construction the speaker uses fragments – 'whereas, if you look more closely' and 'that's how it (really) is' – to defensively reify the alternative construction and make it persuasive. However, when we look at the assumption on which this counter-argument operates it becomes obvious that the speaker has actually not questioned the link constructed in the argument, that between being present and carrying responsibility. Since the dimensions of being present and carrying responsibility are still the ones drawn upon to invalidate the argument, we can see that, in this strategy, the rhetorical creativity for constructing an alternative account is rather limited.

A similar rhetorical interplay can be observed in the discussion around whether or not part-time work causes problems:

> Oh well, one problem would be, if maybe I did less than 80 per cent . . . Then you lose the plot and a certain rhythm, or the planning goes wrong, no, that doesn't work. (Interview 19)

In this argument the speaker assembles a list of potential problems with working less than 80 per cent; that list constructs part-time work as problematic for the individual (as she rules out the option for herself), but also for the organization if things 'go wrong'. The underlying assumption here is that part-time work creates disadvantages for the organizations that offer it. Even though the interviewee's claims remain hypothetical, by stating so firmly that 'that doesn't work' she offensively objects to the viability of part-time models and reifies her concerns as actual facts. A second interviewee counters this very argument: 'When I'm not there, well, nothing ever happened just because I wasn't there' (Interview 2).

Asserting that nothing ever happened 'just' because she was not in the office implies that other people might argue exactly that; thus she draws attention to the dialogical nature of her claim. But since she can provide evidence that nothing ever 'went wrong' in her absence, she offensively ironizes and thereby invalidates the argument that part-time work is problematic. Again, this counter-argument operates on the basis of the same assumption as the argument: that part-time work creates disadvantages for organizations that offer it. Even though the speaker invalidates the argument on the surface by refusing to give in to this reality construction, the underlying assumption at the heart of the construction remains intact.

Thus, we consider that this rhetorical strategy of invalidating arguments has only minor effects in terms of either resisting the dominant discourse on full-time work or constructing part-time work as a legitimate alternative. Even though the counter-arguments were directed towards ironizing the reality constructions made in the arguments, especially by drawing on offensive rhetoric, they did not challenge the underlying assumptions around which these arguments were constructed. By continuing to argue along the same lines – focusing on the assumed link between being present and carrying responsibility, or the assumption that part-time work does or does not create disadvantages for organizations – the speakers did not make any substantial emancipatory move that might seriously shift the organizational logics around work-time arrangements.

Claiming the Opposite

In the second rhetorical strategy for resisting the dominant full-time discourse, speakers' counter-arguments aimed to undermine arguments by claiming the opposite. For example, in the following rhetorical interplay, part-time workers are constructed as being either less or more committed to their work than full-timers:

> Well, the problem also is that, I think, most people who work 30 per cent, they are emotionally somewhere else. . . . Indeed, I have the feeling, well, people who work so little, they are usually at a different place emotionally and then there is also a lack of commitment. (Interview 9)

Here the underlying assumption is an unambiguous link between working time and commitment, while commitment is defined as prioritizing work over non-work. Within the boundaries of that argument, part-time workers who do not spend 42 hours a week at the workplace are regarded as distracted from their work commitments by other engagements. Hence, this argument marginalizes part-timers as the inferior, uncommitted and low-performing other, thereby strengthening the norm that is constructed in the dominant full-time discourse.

In clear conflict to this argument, another interviewee claimed the exact opposite: that part-timers are more committed to their work, as they actually work more hours than they are paid for. This argument constructs part-timers as an organizational benefit rather than a burden:

> I think, for the employer it is beneficial to have part-timers – to have people working part-time, when you just look at the financials. Because they actually work harder for the money they get paid. And one could very well say that someone who maybe de facto works 90 per cent gets 80 per cent pay. (Interview 7)

To reify this opposite reality claim and to undermine the argument that part-timers work less, the interviewee uses defensive rhetoric, referring to the supposedly hard facts of 'financials' to claim the opposite. Moreover, he ironizes the counter-position, with offensive rhetoric, using the words 'actually' and 'de facto' to state what part-time work looks like in organizations. Though these rhetorical moves help to strengthen his counter-argument, the assumption that a link exists between working time and commitment remains unquestioned, hence weakening the potential effects of this rhetorical resistance strategy.

Another rhetorical interplay between arguments and counter-arguments on part-time work focused on the boundaries between private life and working life. While those using arguments in favour of full-time work constructed these areas of life as having clear boundaries between them, those using counter-arguments claimed exactly the opposite:

> And of course we have tried to find a solution so that he would be able to reduce maybe by one day, but that was unfortunately not possible. If you're in the sales force it's simply impossible . . . If something should happen somewhere . . . then he has to be on the spot, then he can't say, today I'm looking after my kid, I'll get back to you on Monday [laughs]. (Interview 4)

Here the interviewee tries to make her argument rhetorically persuasive by drawing on both defensive (reifying) and offensive (ironizing) rhetoric. She defensively claims that, despite all efforts, it was 'simply impossible' to find a part-time solution for someone working in the sales force (thereby reifying this 'impossibility'); the word 'unfortunately' frames this failed effort as not being a matter of lacking goodwill (which might be the anticipated counter-argument), but rather as an inevitable constraint of that position. This argument is based on the assumption that private life and working life are two distinct spheres that are not to be mixed with one another. By laughing at her own statement at the end, the interviewee, through offensive rhetoric, ironizes the potential to successfully accommodate the demands of private life (for example, child care) with professional work commitments by positioning this combination as ridiculously impractical.

In stark contrast to that argument, the following counter-argument simply blows away this separation between the private and the working sphere by drawing attention to the blurred boundaries between these two life areas:

> I'm always reachable on my mobile to give short-notice replies on how to proceed if something happens in the lab that day that maybe was not planned. (Interview 1)

Introducing the concepts of 'flexibility' and 'working from home', this counter-argument, in a dialogical response, manages to claim the opposite of what the argument maintained: that it is not a problem to be absent from the office, as even short-notice, unforeseen events can be managed while one is in the private sphere. This counter-argument, however, fails to question the assumption that workers may operate in two distinct spheres of life.

Hence, we also hold that this second rhetorical strategy, of claiming the opposite, is only slightly effective in resisting the dominant discourse of full-time work. In all the various offensive rhetorical moves to oppose the reality constructions of arguments, and the defensive rhetorical moves to legitimate opposite claims, the counter-arguments merely tackled the arguments on their argumentative surface and did not question the basic assumptions: that working time and commitment are linked unambiguously, and that private life and working life are two distinct spheres of life. Thus the speakers using this strategy simply preserved the very pillars on which the dominant arguments are built.

Challenging Basic Assumptions

In the third rhetorical strategy, speakers dispute arguments using counter-arguments that challenge those arguments' basic assumptions. The following example, in which a speaker discusses the notion of performance, demonstrates this rhetorical interplay between arguments and counter-arguments:

> People would assume that if I wanted to work let's say 80 per cent, that I would only accomplish an 80 per cent result [laughs]. That's what I believe would happen. (Interview 16)

Here the underlying assumption of the argument is that the time spent in the office is a reliable indicator of performance. Again we see clearly that the interviewee's perception of reality and his behaviour are guided by the argumentative context, that is by what people would assume about him and his work and what he believes would happen as a consequence of working less than full time: his work would be degraded, and that might then lead to an undesirable marginalization. He (defensively) reifies this reality construction and makes it persuasive by nervously laughing at his own claim to reveal his discomfort at merely thinking of a part-time model and its consequences. To counter this view, another interviewee made this statement about the issue of performance:

> It's not a matter of being present if you ask me. It's more a question of how you make use of that working time. It's no use if someone sits here for 42 hours and is just hanging around chatting. (Interview 19)

With the words 'if you ask me', the interviewee projects herself into the middle of a rhetorical interplay in which the most suitable approach to measuring performance is open to debate. While her argument also contains elements of the invalidation strategy ('it's not a matter of being present/of sitting around for 42 hours'), what is particularly noteworthy is her statement of what does matter: 'how you make use of that working time'. This statement defensively ('it's more a question of') introduces a new understanding which challenges the basic assumption that time spent in the office is a reliable indicator of performance.

Another counter-argument challenges the underlying assumption that long hours can be equated with good performance. This one does so by focusing attention on the notion of leadership qualities:

> Leadership is not just a matter of being present, but a matter – taking respon-sibility and whatever, well – all that it involves, I mean, also a feeling for the people, isn't it?! (Interview 10)

This speaker re-introduces two other elements of management, not men-tioned earlier: taking responsibility and having 'a feeling for the people'. Thus she creates a strong counterpoint that uncouples the link between working time and performance. She also uses a defensive rhetorical move, one that pulls the audience in to take a position in the dialogical debate, by asking 'isn't it?!' Thus she seeks to reify her claim as a widely accepted fact, and thereby makes the alternative reality construction persuasive.

We argue that this rhetorical strategy, of challenging basic assump-tions, can be considered successful. Mostly through the defensive rhetoric of producing and reifying alternative claims, it challenges the dominant discourse about full-time work, by helping to legitimize part-time work as a valid alternative. It departs from the assumption on which the earlier arguments were based: that time spent in the office is a reliable indicator of performance. Instead, it challenges this assumption, suggesting that the issue is how the time is used and that better indicators of performance can be found. Because of these elements, this rhetorical strategy can be said to creatively tweak the boundaries of the dominant full-time discourse that marginalizes part-time workers.

Changing Basic Assumptions

In the fourth rhetorical strategy, speakers use counter-arguments not only to challenge, but even to change, the basic assumptions underlying the arguments about full-time work. This becomes obvious in the following interplay between an argument and a counter-argument on the issue of whether or not a task can be divided between workers:

> Book-keeping . . . one can easily start that part-time. Because most of the time 200 invoices, standardized tasks: that can be distributed. It doesn't matter now who does what . . . it doesn't matter whether this or that person logs the 100 invoices. And there I think that is a good area for, I would say not so

demanding work. It's a lot of routine work that can be accomplished very well on the basis of part-time models. (Interview 18)

The assumption underlying this argument is that job demands are fixed and unchangeable, and that people can use those demands to assess whether or not a job can be divided and is thus appropriate for part-time work. The argument here is that only the less demanding jobs can be divided and thus accomplished by part-time employees. In terms of rhetorical moves, the speaker defensively reifies this point through repetition: by stating twice that in these low-skill jobs 'it doesn't matter' who does what. This also implies, of course, that in other positions that carry more responsibility, it would actually matter.

If the demands of various jobs are seen as being fixed and inflexible, which would determine whether part-time arrangements are possible, how can the underlying assumptions be changed? Doing so requires deconstructing this link and replacing it with a different notion: that part-time work is always possible and that job demands can be organized in such a way that all tasks, including management tasks, can be divided. The following speaker did just that:

Well I think, when a firm or a department is well organized, then someone can also be in a management position here or work part-time as supervisor and that can work just as well. Well it is, I think, at the end of the day it is a matter of organizing. (Interview 3)

Through maintaining that 'that can work just as well', and implying a dialogical counter-position, in this defensive rhetorical move the interviewee explicitly seeks to reify an alternative construction of reality. Because she changes the underlying assumptions of the argument, suddenly something different is at stake: the taken-for-granted way that work is organized. In this context, part-time work is only seen as a disadvantage to the organization if it fails to change the practices through which work is organized within the dominant logic of full-time work.

In a similar fashion, the following argument assuming that tasks are assigned to specific persons was opposed by promoting an alternative assumption: that tasks are assigned to functions and not so much to individual people. While a person cannot be divided, in the alternative assumption a function may very well be shared by part-timers, thus opening up space for an alternative model of organizing:

Well, I think for a management position it is appropriate to have one person as a contact point or who passes on certain things, instead of having two people doing the job. Well, I couldn't imagine it that way, no. (Interview 14)

This argument, which is built on the assumption that important tasks are assigned to important and irreplaceable people, makes it virtually impossible to imagine transferring management responsibilities to anyone else. By rhetorically framing it as inappropriate, and by being unable to imagine part-timers in a responsible management position, the interviewee offensively ironizes the option of part-time workers holding responsible positions.

To oppose that view, another speaker gives the example of a hospital situation where qualified personnel must be present, but much of the work cannot be predicted; the solution is for doctors and nurses to react flexibly to the daily demands. The alternative assumption here is that in a hospital tasks are assigned to functions with clearly established routines for transferring knowledge between people on different shifts:

> In the hospitals it has to work as well. The doctors are not around 24 hours a day, 7 days a week. So they have to pass the work on as well. (Interview 17)

The claim that 'in the hospital it has to work as well' objects to the implied argument that 'it cannot work'. In this interview excerpt, part-time work is enacted as a critique of the way work is organized when full-time availability is taken for granted. In fact, when a speaker reifies this alternative model for organizing tasks and thus for arranging working time and responsibilities, the possibility of part-time work becomes the new taken-for-granted assumption.

In that sense, this fourth rhetorical strategy – in which counter-arguments set out to change the basic assumptions that underlie arguments – may be the most promising for resisting the dominant discourse of full-time work. By reinventing the argumentative base, mainly through defensive rhetoric that helps to construct counter-realities, the creative rhetorical moves in this strategy show the potential to substantially shift organizational logics around part-time work in the long run.

DISCUSSION

Driven by our interest in exploring *how dominant discourses can be resisted through rhetorical strategies*, our rhetorical analysis has focused on three aspects in order to shed more light on the micro-discursive mechanisms through which speakers construct and contest the discourse about full-time work that marginalizes part-time workers. First of all, by taking a rhetorical perspective, we observed that a norm such as full-time work, which entails the marginalization of part-time work, is discursively constructed within an argumentative context that is within an interplay of word and counter word (Billig, 1996). Even though all the interviews were conducted individually, we noticed that as speakers made various argumentative moves to strengthen their own claims, they often implicitly, and even explicitly, addressed a counter-position of 'what others would argue'. Hence, our analysis supported the view that rhetoric is dialogical as it unfolds in the interplay between arguments and counter-arguments, in this case those put forth by opponents and proponents of new and more flexible work-time arrangements. We illustrated a range of such interplays on the issue of part-time work that revolved around questions of being present, responsibility, commitment, organizational disadvantages, the separation of work and private life, performance measurement, and the divisibility of tasks and functions. Together these rhetorical moves show that part-time work is indeed a controversial and highly debated issue and that organizational logics around work-time arrangements are constantly negotiated through argument and counter-argument.

Second, rather than assuming that some discourses and reality constructions are dominant per se, and that resistance is either inherent to a counter-discourse or not, our micro-discursive analysis has investigated the 'how': How were certain reality constructions reified and made rhetorically persuasive and how were other arguments ironized in an equally convincing way (Potter, 1996)? By focusing on these small rhetorical nuances, we have aimed to shed more light on the defensive rhetorical moves ('that's how it is'; 'it's simply impossible'; 'isn't it?!') as well as the offensive rhetorical moves ('I couldn't imagine it that way'; 'it just doesn't work out') that speakers used to strengthen and undermine certain reality constructions. We observed that in order to invalidate and oppose arguments, interviewees mainly drew on offensive rhetoric to undermine the given argument; when they were claiming an opposite reality construction, or challenging or changing the underlying assumption of an argument, they predominantly drew on defensive rhetoric to stabilize and reify their counter-constructions in which part-time work became a valid alternative to the norm. By zooming in on these rhetorical nuances, we have tried to show that resistance is not necessarily a matter of grand opposition, but rather an achievement of small rhetorical moves that can only be detected by paying attention to these micro-discursive dynamics.

And finally, by examining how rhetorical strategies are effective in resisting the dominant discourse of full-time work and in constructing part-time work as a valid alternative, we placed a special focus on whether or not counter-arguments addressed the different underlying assumptions of arguments that helped to preserve and strengthen the taken-for-granted status of full-time work (Bamberg and Andrews, 2004). When we explored how rhetorical strategies were effective in resisting the dominant full-time discourse, we did note that it might not be enough for counter-arguments to simply invalidate existing arguments or boldly suggest their very opposite. Even though these counter-arguments set out to go against the arguments, they did not question their underlying assumptions such as the presumed link between being present and responsibility or the link between working time and commitment, both of which framed part-time workers as being less serious about their work, less emotionally engaged, less approachable in the office and therefore not suitable for responsible management positions. Instead of challenging these underlying assumptions of the arguments, the speakers' counter-arguments – even though they aimed to invalidate or oppose these constructions – remained within the same logic of the arguments they were trying to oppose. Therefore we see these rhetorical strategies as less powerful in breaking out of and resisting the dominant discourse.

We considered that other rhetorical strategies are more forceful and creative in resisting the dominant full-time discourse, as the counter-arguments in these strategies challenged and changed the very assumptions that were underlying the arguments, thereby creatively opening up space for alternative realities. For example, the assumption that the amount of time spent in an office is a reliable indicator of performance (thereby framing part-timers as performing 'less') was challenged by two ideas: that the issue is how one makes use of the time and that better indicators of performance are taking responsibility and having a feeling for people. Moreover, when speakers completely changed the underlying assumptions of arguments, they changed the idea that job demands are fixed and unchangeable into the idea that those demands can be organized in such a way that all tasks – including management tasks – can be accomplished by part-timers. In a similar way, the assumption that tasks are assigned to persons, making certain responsible positions appear indivisible and thus inappropriate for part-time workers, was entirely replaced by the assumption that tasks are assigned by function and thereby always divisible. This rhetorical strategy severely contested the taken-for-granted way of organizing work when full-time work is assumed as the norm. We believe that this rhetorical strategy – of changing the basic underlying assumptions of arguments – offers the most promising way to resist the dominant full-time discourse and to construct part-time work as a valid alternative to the norm.

CONCLUSION

In this chapter, we have drawn attention to a trend in organization studies which depicts organizational control as a matter of normalization through discourse, and resistance as a rhetorical strategy in which counter-arguments question arguments that strengthen a dominant discourse. By framing resistance to the dominant discourse of full-time work as a matter of rhetorical moves, we neither 'romanticized' proponents of part-time work, as Mumby (2005) warns, nor dismissed them as 'unwitting dupes' (Mumby, 2005, p. 38) in the vigorous debate on whether or not resistance to discursive normalization can be deemed successful. On the contrary, we portrayed the resisting individuals as engaging in discursive practices that can be seen as always ongoing and tension-filled, and it is precisely this ongoing rhetorical struggle that may in the long run shift organizational logics around part-time work.

In sum, we believe we have contributed to an understanding of resistance from a rhetorical perspective by zooming in on the micro-discursive mechanisms for achieving resistance through talk and rhetoric. Our investigation of rhetoric has helped to shed more light on how the notion of full-time work is constructed in a dominant way, how arguments are assembled to make it appear normal and how language is used to frame certain reality constructions in a taken-for-granted way by drawing on defensive or offensive rhetoric. Likewise, our rhetorical analysis revealed how counter-arguments can be constructed to successfully introduce alternatives. Showing how resistance can be achieved discursively – by increasing people's sensibility to the way the norm is constructed, and to what arguments are given and what assumptions are put to work – can help evolve a better understanding of what it takes to break out of the norm rhetorically, by contesting the way that reality is constructed in the first place.

Assuming that organizational norms are constructed through dominant organizational discourses that prescribe guidelines for practical action, our rhetorical analysis indicates that these logics may in fact change over time, as people engage dialogically with the arguments that strengthen the discourse in a rhetorically persuasive way and as they undermine these arguments by questioning their underlying assumptions – the argumentative base on which they are built.

REFERENCES

Alvesson, Mats and Hugh Willmott (2002), 'Identity regulation as organizational control: Producing the appropriate individual', *Journal of Management Studies*, **39** (5), 619–644.

Bakhtin, Mikhail M. (1981), *The Dialogic Imagination*, Austin, TX: University of Texas Press.

Bakhtin, Mikhail M. (1986), *Speech, Genres and Other Late Essays*, Austin, TX: University of Texas Press.

Bamberg, Michael and Molly Andrews (2004), *Considering Counter-Narratives: Narrating, Resisting, Making Sense*, Amsterdam: John Benjamins.

Benschop, Yvonne and Hans Dooreward (1998), 'Six of one and half a dozen of the other: The gender subtext of Taylorism and team-based work', *Gender, Work & Organization*, **5** (1), 5–18.

Bevir, Mark (1999), 'Foucault and critique: Deploying agency against autonomy', *Political Theory*, **27** (1), 65–84.

Billig, Michael (1996), *Arguing and Thinking: A Rhetorical Approach to Social Psychology* (Second Edition), Cambridge: Cambridge University Press.

Billig, Michael (1998), 'Rhetoric and the unconscious', *Argumentation*, **12** (1), 199–216.

Burr, Vivien (2003), *Social Constructionism* (Second Edition), New York: Routledge.

Collinson, David L. (2003), 'Identities and insecurities: Selves at work', *Organization*, **10** (3), 527–547.

Dick, Penny and Rosie Hyde (2006), 'Consent as resistance, resistance as consent: Re-reading part-time professionals' acceptance of their marginal positions', *Gender, Work & Organization*, **13** (6), 543–564.

du Gay, Paul (1996), *Consumption and Identity at Work*, London: Sage Publications.

Fleming, Peter and André Spicer (2003), 'Working at a cynical distance: Implications for power, subjectivity and resistance', *Organization*, **10** (1), 157–179.

Foucault, Michel (1976), *The History of Sexuality (Volume 1): The Will to Knowledge*, London: Penguin Books.

Foucault, Michel (1977), *Discipline and Punish: The Birth of the Prison*, New York: Vintage Books.

Foucault, Michel (1982), 'The subject and power', in Hubert L. Dreyfus and Paul Rabinow (eds), *Michel Foucault: Beyond Structuralism and Hermeneutics*, Brighton: Harvester Press, pp. 208–226.

Foucault, Michel (1988), 'The ethic of the care for the self as a practice of freedom', in James Bernauer and David Rasmussen (eds), *The Final Foucault*, Cambridge: Massachusetts Institute of Technology Press, pp. 1–20.

Foucault, Michel (1991), 'Governmentality', in Graham Burchell, Colin Gordon and Peter Miller (eds), *The Foucault Effect: Studies in Governmentality*, Chicago, IL: University of Chicago Press, pp. 87–104.

Fournier, Valérie (1998), 'Stories of development and exploitation: Militant voices in an enterprise culture', *Organization*, **5** (1), 55–80.

Hyde, Rosie (2008), 'Rethinking the response of part-time professionals: The case of the part-time police officer', *International Journal of Public Administration*, **31** (9), 1095–1109.

Kärreman, Dan and Mats Alvesson (2004), 'Cages in tandem: Management control, social identity, and identification in a knowledge-intensive firm', *Organization*, **11** (1), 149–175.

Kärreman, Dan and Mats Alvesson (2009), 'Resisting resistance: Counter-resistance, consent and compliance in a consultancy firm', *Human Relations*, **62** (8), 1115–1144.

Kärreman, Dan and Andre Spicer (2009), 'The school is no more: Managing identity work through dis-identification in an educational organization', paper presented at the 25th EGOS Colloquium in Barcelona, Spain, July.

Lawrence, Thomas B. and Vivien Corwin (2003), 'Being there: The acceptance and marginalization of part-time professional employees', *Journal of Organizational Behavior*, **24** (8), 923–943.

Meriläinen, Susan, Janne Tienari, Robyn Thomas, and Annette Davies (2004), 'Management consultant talk: A cross-cultural comparison of normalizing discourse and resistance', *Organization*, **11** (4), 539–564.

Mumby, Dennis K. (2005), 'Theorizing resistance in organization studies: A dialectical approach', *Management Communication Quarterly*, **19** (1), 19–44.

Nentwich, Julia C. (2004), *Die Gleichzeitigkeit von Differenz und Gleichheit: Neue Wege für die Gleichstellungsarbeit*, Königstein/Taunus: Ulrike Helmer Verlag.

Phillips, Nelson and Cynthia Hardy (2002), *Discourse Analysis: Investigating Processes of Social Construction*, Thousand Oaks, CA: Sage.

Potter, Jonathan (1996), *Representing Reality: Discourse, Rhetoric and Social Construction*, London: Sage.

Smithson, Janet (2005), 'Full-timer in a part-time job: Identity negotiation in organizational talk', *Feminism & Psychology*, **15** (3), 275–293.

Strub, Silvia (2003), *Teilzeitarbeit in der Schweiz: Eine Untersuchung mit Fokus auf der Geschlechterverteilung und der familiären Situation der Erwerbstätigen*, Bern: Eidgenössisches Büro für die Gleichstellung von Mann und Frau.

Suddaby, Roy and Royston Greenwood (2005), 'Rhetorical strategies of legitimacy', *Administrative Science Quarterly*, **50** (1), 35–67.

Swiss Federal Statistical Office (ed.) (2003), *Auf dem Weg zur Gleichstellung? Frauen und Männer in der Schweiz: Dritter statistischer Bericht*, Neuchâtel: Swiss Federal Statistical Office.

Symon, Gillian (2000), 'Everyday rhetoric: Argument and persuasion in everyday life', *European Journal of Work and Organizational Psychology*, **9** (4), 477–488.

Symon, Gillian (2005), 'Exploring resistance from a rhetorical perspective', *Organization Studies*, **26** (11), 1641–1663.

Symon, Gillian (2008), 'Developing the political perspective on technological change through rhetorical analysis', *Management Communication Quarterly*, **22** (1), 74–98.

Tienari, Janne, Sigrid Quack, and Hildegard Theobald (2002), 'Organizational reforms, "ideal workers" and gender orders: A cross-societal comparison', *Organization Studies*, **23** (2), 249–279.

Witzel, Andreas (1996), 'Auswertung problemzentrierter Interviews: Grundlagen und Erfahrungen', in Rainer Strobl and Andreas Böttger (eds), *Wahre Geschichten? Zu Theorie und Praxis qualitativer Interviews*, Baden-Baden: Nomos Verlagsgesellschaft, pp. 49–76.

Witzel, Andreas (2000), 'Das problemzentrierte Interview', *Forum: Qualitative Sozialforschung*, **1** (1).

8. Multilingual organizations as 'linguascapes' and the discursive position of English

Chris Steyaert, Anja Ostendorp and Claudine Gaibrois

INTRODUCTION

This chapter addresses the complexity of multilingual communication by applying a discursive approach. It aims at understanding how people account for the ways in which specific languages are used in multilingual companies, especially considering the emergence of English as lingua franca. A discursive perspective assumes that language use is regulated by various, often contradictory, accounts of how people consider one or more languages in a multilingual context. The questions we are interested in are: How do people account for speaking a given language when different languages are available? How do multilingual organizations differ in the ways they argue for certain options and priorities? How does (the discourse on) English alter the discourses on how a certain language can be adopted and prioritized? And, theoretically, how can the flow of languages that crosses and becomes ordered in a specific organization be conceptualized?

In our study, we compared two multilingual companies, whose markets are globalized in different ways, to understand how both organizations account differently for language use and for the use of English in particular. The discourse analysis allows us to distinguish among the various accounts of language use – we call them discursive practices – that people draw upon to justify the everyday use and adoption of languages. The discourse analysis maps the various tensions between these accounts and helps us to understand how language use is mostly argued for and how English is positioned within one organizational context. These mappings outline the discursive configuration that is formed by the tensions between the various discourses people draw upon to argue for and negotiate a specific language use. In the discussion of our results, we will refer to this discursive configuration as a linguistic landscape or 'linguascape' to conceptualize how the flow of languages that cross a specific organizational space is discursively mediated. With these discursive negotiations, multilingual organizations try to resolve the complexity of their multilingual context.

Following this introduction, we situate our study in the literature, briefly reviewing the various views on 'Englishization' (Dor, 2004) and connecting them to the ways that language policy, language use and English as lingua franca have been framed in international management. Second, we describe the research design and methodology we developed to compare the discursive dynamics within two multilingual companies. Third, we present the results of the discourse analysis by distinguishing the various discursive practices through which people account for language use and map the main tensions that construct the discursive configuration or linguascape of each company. Fourth, in the discussion, we generate the term 'linguascape' as a term that can capture the study of language about languages and the discursive negotiations through which multilingual organizations try to resolve the complexity of their multilingual context. In the concluding section, we discuss the empirical, conceptual and managerially relevant contributions.

LITERATURE REVIEW

Multilingualism and 'Englishization'

Most of the time, the growing dominance of English has been presented in a favourable light based on the argument that it serves as an efficient way to connect speakers from different linguistic backgrounds. This argumentation is based on an instrumental view of language, which is seen to form a neutral and value-free communicative intervention that makes international business efficient and smooth (Steyaert and Janssens, 1997). This perspective comes with a belief in the formation of language policies and seeks to solve the issue of combining languages by introducing a corporate lingua franca. A common corporate language is often seen as an administrative management tool that helps global operations proceed efficiently. This implies that the adoption of English as lingua franca is taken as completely unproblematic. Along with this instrumental focus comes the assumption that language diversity is something which can be 'managed' or 'organized', or which is mainly driven by top management's decisions and strategic choices (Luo and Shenkar, 2006).

Reactions to the dominance of English have been overwhelmingly critical. It has been associated with linguistic imperialism (Phillipson, 1992) in the wake of its increasing spread across many different domains, including science, the economy, culture, politics and the media. It is argued that, through linguistic domination, a next move in the imperialistic game is set up following militaristic and colonial manoeuvres. The central role of English in international business is criticized for the global expansion of capitalism (Tietze, 2004). By addressing how cross-cultural differences (Holden, 2008) and issues of translation (Janssens, Lambert and Steyaert, 2004) are neglected, these critical views show that English can be considered an accomplice in creating a unifying system of knowledge and action and in advantaging the ideological interests of particular elitist groups in society. From this critical perspective, capitalism, managerialism and English form a new trinity of globalization that increases cultural imposition and economic dominance (Tietze, 2004).

Others have suggested that English should not be unilaterally praised or condemned; instead, more attention should be paid to (how to study) the ambivalent and controversial side of what Dor (2004) calls Englishization. According to Phillipson (2001, p. 1), the recurrent emphasis on 'global English' creates a prism 'that obscures the cultural and linguistic diversity of the world's many thousand spoken and sign languages'. English provides us with a false account of the global reality that represents mostly the interests of the English-speaking 'haves' and obscures the position of the 'have-nots' (Phillipson, 2001). Furthermore, Dor (2004) sees the possibility for speakers to resist global pressures and to use, maintain and nurture their local languages. The possibility of such a negotiated multilingualism might sometimes turn into an imposed version as 'the very same global economic pressures that are traditionally assumed to push the global expansion of English may actually be working to strengthen a significant set of other languages – at the expense of English' (Dor, 2004, p. 98). Reversely, in an empirical study, Vaara, Tienari, Piekkari and Säntti (2005) found that, rather than establish a hierarchy between languages during a Swedish–Finnish merger, English was the politically 'neutral' solution. Thus, an ambivalent perspective encourages us to research the multiple and often contradictory effects of Englishization as people come to terms with the complexity of multilingualism in everyday interaction and negotiation.

Aligning itself with this ambivalent positioning of English, our study considers multilingualism as always performed based on a process of negotiation through which language hierarchies are discursively mediated and arranged. We argue that the use of English is not given a priori but is mediated by the various discourses concerning how to adopt one among many available languages. Therefore, in this chapter we examine how multilingualism is negotiated within the context of two multilingual companies with different degrees of global orientation and thus with different relationships to the use of English.

Performing Multilingualism

The above debate about how globalization influences the spread and use of languages and the role of Englishization has been equally taken up in international management research. This is especially true with regard to the possibilities and limits of adopting a common corporate language and its parallel focus on English as lingua franca (Fredriksson, Barner-Rasmussen and Piekkari, 2006). In line with the shifting acknowledgement of the multifaceted character of multilingualism, there seems to be growing consensus that the adoption of a common corporate language is not the endpoint of a language policy but forms one of the possible anchor points around which to deal with multilingual complexity.

Several elements complicate the performance of multilingualism. First, efforts to manage or steer language and communication flows through the prescription of a designated company language such as English have been seen as a simplistic step in dealing with language diversity (Welch, Welch and Piekkari, 2005). What makes this step simplistic is the refusal to recognize that those using English have various degrees of fluency. Managers or employees may not automatically have a shared framework of understanding because of the inevitable variation in the cultural frameworks through which language is understood.

Second, some organizations follow an intentionally emergent approach instead of opting for a strategic decision as documented in the study by Fredriksson, Barner-Rasmussen and Piekkari (2006). Moreover, a formally adopted language choice is often complemented by more complex language practices and performances. 'Introducing a common corporate language will not render the firm monolingual' (Fredriksson et al., 2006, p. 409) but will allow for a parallel use of local languages. Thus, when a shared language is assumed, it should be seen as a necessary but not a sufficient condition (Piekkari and Zander, 2005) which does not exclude the use of other languages.

Third, several studies have looked at power issues with regard to the policy of a common language. The decision to adopt a common language, which is thought to be an integrative measure, can bring with it disintegrative patterns of communication (Piekkari, Vaara, Tienari and Säntti, 2005) or signs of a shadow-language (Marschan-Piekkari, Welch and Welch, 1999). Moreover, several authors (Janssens, Lambert and Steyaert, 2004; Piekkari and Zander, 2005) have made the important point that the mandate of English or any other language as a common language brings along control effects and power imbalances. For instance, in an empirical study Vaara et al. (2005) examined the power implications of language policies during an international merger. They found that the adoption of Swedish as corporate language led to a reification of post-colonial structures of domination.

In short, this review underlines the need to capture the 'complexity and subtle dynamics' (Piekkari and Zander, 2005, p. 7) as well as the substantial 'heterogeneity and complexity' (Fredriksson et al., 2006, p. 407) involved in performing multilingualism. Even when adopting a common language like English, it is necessary to understand how English as lingua franca is positioned, how other languages are being used, and how a language hierarchy is related to other effects in the organization, including those related to power, career trajectories and human capital decisions. We approach this complexity by studying the idea of negotiated multilingualism in a discursive perspective. Through this perspective, we aim at mapping the discursive dynamics that guide the multilingual production of an international company and the role English is said to play in it.

METHODOLOGY

Context and Research Design

To study the different ways that people in organizations account for how they adopt one of various possible languages, a discursive study tries to maximize the variability of accounts. If researchers let variability emerge 'as a focus in its own right, it can be seen that there is complexity and diversity' in discussions and accounts of language use (Marshall, 1994, p. 103). Switzerland, which forms an important element of the context of our study, offers considerable variability in language use. It is known for its official quadrilingualism. The languages spoken, in order of frequency, are German (in northern and eastern Switzerland), French (in western Switzerland, also called Romandy), Italian (southern Switzerland) and Romansh (a minority language in the southeast of Switzerland). Furthermore, Switzerland is recognized for its diglossia in the German-speaking region as it mediates between 'standard' or 'high German' and what is called 'Swiss-German' (Jaworski and Piller, 2008). Diglossia – a technical term for functions being performed in two different languages – refers to the situation that Swiss-German is used in most speech contexts and high or standard German in writing and some formal spoken contexts. Furthermore, English is the 'first' second language and seems to gain importance for the 'linguascaping of Switzerland' (Jaworski and Piller, 2008) through its participation in the new media and the global economy. Thus, Switzerland forms an appropriate setting for studying (accounts of) multilingualism, as more than just the organizations operating in a globalized market are considered multilingual.

Our research design consists of a comparison between two companies, which, for reasons of anonymity, we call respectively Maximal and Globalos. Maximal is mostly oriented towards the Swiss market with its main seat in the French part of Switzerland; it has production units and activities all over Switzerland and employs around 3000 people. Globalos is a global firm with global headquarters in the French part of Switzerland and around 300 000 employees worldwide.

Data Production

Based on intake interviews in Maximal and Globalos, with respectively a HRM manager and a training manager (who acted as brokers during the time of this study), we gained permission to approach employees for an interview. We then asked our interviewees to suggest more possible candidates. At both firms, we made efforts to recruit the most varied possible range of interview candidates with regard to gender, national and linguistic background, educational background, length of experience and hierarchical position in the company. We offered interviewees the chance to choose the language of the interview; this was made possible by the multilingual interview team. This team consisted of two bilingual persons (French and German, and German and Italian, who both speak English as well), and a third member who conducted interviews respectively in German (mother tongue) and English; a fourth member (with mother tongue of Dutch) conducted interviews in French, English and German.

As a consequence, various interviews were conducted in Swiss-German, German, English, or French. Language use during interviews was thus a local accomplishment (Welch and Piekkari, 2006). In each single situation, several options had to be negotiated. Our own findings helped us to be reflexive about these interview performances. In Maximal, we mostly spoke the language of the interlocutor (which we call below discursive practice two); researchers value this practice for its rapport-building qualities (Welch and Piekkari, 2006). In Globalos, we mostly followed the practice of finding a compromise through a third language (in this case English; which we call below discursive practice five), which is usual in international business research (Welch and Piekkari, 2006).

We collected data using semi-structured interviews, thus allowing members of both organizations to account for their experiences and practices of using and adopting one or more languages. As a starting point, we asked our interview partners to tell us about their position in the company and their everyday situation at work. Making the link to the language issue, a next set of questions addressed the linguistic context in which employees move: How do people deal with the fact that employees of different linguistic backgrounds are members of a department, project or team? Which language is used during interactions, and why? Furthermore, we tried to identify the comparative relevance of the local and global contexts by asking questions like the following: When and why does the local language come into play, compared to the use of other international languages like English? To find out whether the issue of linguistic diversity is addressed at a company level, we asked interviewees about the company's strategies and policies with regard to linguistic diversity. We also gave participants the opportunity to express their own preferences: Which language(s) do they prefer to speak? What changes have happened, according to them? We used these questions as probing questions and to structure the interview.

With these questions, we tried to produce interview material that in a discursive study is considered to be 'a basis for understanding the structure and nature of how organizational members talk about organizational phenomena' (Kärreman and Alvesson, 2009, p. 1124). We followed a discursive pragmatist approach, recognizing that language may also represent phenomena (through accounts of language use) at a short distance from the site where it is performed, as is the case in interviews (Kärreman and Alvesson, 2009). In total, we conducted 15 interviews at Maximal and 17 at Globalos; these 32 interviews gave us enough variability to undertake a discourse analysis (Marshall, 1994).

Data Analysis

A discourse analysis explores accounts or discursive practices, namely the varied ways of making sense concerning a certain phenomenon, such as language use. Such accounts form 'regularities at the level of language in terms of recurring patterns' in how we can make sense of a certain phenomenon (Marshall, 1994, p. 93). The terms discourses, interpretative repertoires and discursive practices (Wetherell, 2001) refer to the linguistic resources that are central in the ways that people frame and enact their use of languages. In this study, we opted for the notion of discursive practice which has been defined as 'a source of regularities which people collectively draw on to organize their conduct' (Wetherell, 2001, p. 18), as it underlines the productive aspect of discourse: discourse as social practice produces a certain reality. In everyday utterances, when we make sense of past or current experiences (such as during an interview), language use is not chaotic and arbitrary but follows a certain order, a coherent set of ideas and premises that guides one's interactive accomplishments (Potter and Wetherell, 1987). For instance, when people make sense of and/or respond to an email message in English from a new colleague, they might respond by replying in their own language (for instance, French), following the argument that they can each write emails in a language that is convenient to them. Or they might respond by writing back and asking 'Are we living in England now?', pushing the rule that people use the language of the place where they are working. This message also suggests that the new colleague stepped over the line of viable and appropriate language use in this new professional context.

While any discourse analysis is based on closely reading and becoming immersed in the text, we helped the process by feeding the interview transcripts into the electronic data processing program ATLAS/ti (Kelle, 2000) to organize, compare and categorize recurring accounts of language use. In preparing the analysis, we formulated two analytical research questions that would allow us to retrace the recurrent argumentations or discursive practices that people draw upon to make sense of the ways they and their colleagues deal with a complex, multilingual situation: (1) Which discursive practices do they refer to in order to account for the everyday use and adoption of languages? (2) What tensions can be identified between accounts that characterize in a specific way the configuration of a particular organization?

Using the first analytical question, we read (and reread) and coded the interview texts in search of recurring patterns. By providing summarizing categories for excerpts, we identified a first set of practices, which we then used as a coding system to work systematically through the transcripts, either adding the next excerpt to an existing category or formulating a new category. A category was then identified with a number, company name, identification of interviewee and the lines where the excerpts can be found in the transcript (for example, discursive practice 1, Maximal, interviewee 12, startline in transcript, for instance line 20). As a research team, we checked each other's codings and addressed different interpretations of data material and codings in weekly meetings which helped to distinguish between categories and to stabilize the final list of discursive practices. During discussions, we considered recurrent shortcomings in discourse analysis, such as isolated spottings or overly quick generalizations about specific excerpts with regard to our analysis (Antaki, Billig, Edwards and Potter, 2003).

In the second part of the analysis, we contextualized the discursive practices for each company and re-interrogated the interview texts to identify the tensions between the discursive practices and also the ways that these practices were assumed to be compatible. By comparing the two organizations, we ordered the coded practices and positioned them in relationship to each other. This enabled us to construct a map, a kind of linguistic landscape that ordered the various discourses people draw upon within an organization with regard to how they say they 'choose' among various languages. This ordering or mapping process was done along two dimensions: space and time. First, we reflected that a discursive practice can be oriented towards a local, national or global space. Thus, accounts differed as to whether they related to a local, a national or global space of reference. Second, we could differentiate accounts as they draw upon a different time horizon: sometimes speakers referred to a situational logic (for instance, 'we choose from meeting to meeting which language to speak') while others referred to a persistent logic ('we use English instead of everyone using their mother tongue'). In our search to conceptualize this complex dynamics, we started to name these configurations 'linguascapes', a neologism inspired by the work of Appadurai (1996).

RESULTS

Overview of Discursive Practices

The first discursive practice we call 'adaptation to the viable language of a certain location'. This practice draws upon a spatial dimension, as it is assumed that the local, national or even global space indicates which language should be spoken. Thus, an alignment is constructed between language use and location or territory. This implies that in the German-Swiss part of Switzerland, you speak Swiss-German or that in the French-Swiss part, you speak French. The latter is argued in the following statement, made by a local administrative assistant:

> Sometimes people say: 'But he is already here three years and he does not speak one word of French.' Yes, I have already heard that, and I myself have already said this. Because I find it shocking that someone who comes here has such an opportunity – because it is an opportunity to come to work in Switzerland or in some other country – and after three years he cannot speak another language, just to be able to say something, to go shopping, to order something, to go to a restaurant and order something. (French-Swiss, Globalos, 130, translated from French)

'Adaptation to the language of the other (interlocutor)' is a second discursive practice. This accounts for a person's need to adjust to his or her conversational partner. Thus, what informs one's language use is not the language, which is provided as almost a baseline by one's living or working location, but the more temporary notion of aligning oneself with the language spoken by the person one is interacting with. This implies that individuals will adopt the language of an interlocutor from one situation to another, provided they know the language the interlocutor is speaking, as is the case for this French expatriate with a multilingual background (including French, Turkish, and Japanese):

> I speak six languages and I love to speak to people in their language. I do not like the obstacle of a third language. ... Depending on whom I am talking with, I try to talk in their language ... In order to be more close to the other, I prefer to choose the language of the person in front of me, that is if I know this language sufficiently [laughs]. (Globalos, 56, translated from French)

A third discursive practice can be named 'collective negotiation of a common language'. Instead of a situational and spontaneous adoption to the language of an interlocutor, here we find a situation where depending on the event and persons involved, there is an active moment of negotiation about which common language to use. In particular, the relationship and balance between minority and majority is considered, for instance when a meeting is set up in which both German- and French-speaking people are participating:

> So with regard to meetings ... in principle when the majority ... actually when everyone is speaking French, the meeting will be kept in French, [but] if the majority of people speak German or are more at ease speaking German than French, or have great difficulty with it, then the meetings will instead be held in German. (French-Swiss, Maximal, 17, translated from French)

In a fourth discursive practice, it is suggested that languages can be used simultaneously. When it is thus 'possible that everyone replies in his or her language' (French-Swiss, Maximal, 17), a situation occurs where several languages are mixed. One interviewee drew on this account with regard to written communication: 'It is obvious that, ah, this is somehow a bit of a rule ... that one can write in his or her mother tongue' (French-Swiss, Maximal, 33, translated from French).

'Finding a compromise through a third language' is a fifth discursive practice that employees refer to when it seems feasible to agree to adopt a language other than the mother tongue of both interlocutors involved in the communication. Such a solution is seen as a common platform to work from. As the language is not the mother tongue for either speaker, we refer to it as a 'third language'. When the Swiss context is related to the global situation, English is often the third language:

> The common platform to understand each other today is English ... Even sometimes if I, or we communicate with French-speaking people, I will most

of the time write in English because emails can also be used to be sent to some other people. (French expatriate, Maximal, 57)

A sixth discursive practice we call 'improvisation'; people refer to this one when it is clear that they cannot possibly find a common language and they will need to improvise and actively mix several languages. The following example, from a French expatriate, illustrates how the mix of languages can vary from situation to situation: 'After all, we have many nationalities here. Yes, so the use of languages . . . like in a meeting, we can very easily move from one language to another' (Maximal, 149, translated from French).

The Linguascape of Maximal

The linguistic landscape or 'linguascape' of Maximal is constructed around a central tension among two discursive practices: the first – adaptation to the viable language of a certain location – and the fifth – finding a third language as compromise. On the one hand, there is a recurring reference to the argumentation of the first discursive practice. This holds that people should adapt to the language of the location where they are interacting. As Maximal is located in the French part of Switzerland, people in the firm traditionally argue that employees should speak French; when people work in other locations of Switzerland, such as the German part, they are expected to speak Swiss-German. Whatever the location, an expectation is raised that the 'guests' – read employees who speak other languages – will learn the local language. This is illustrated in the following example:

> The middle and higher management of companies which are established in the French part of Switzerland: of them one can in a very natural way demand that they will speak the local language, and thus French. (French expatriate, Maximal, 67, translated from French)

This somehow traditional discursive practice is in competition with the increasingly significant discursive practice five, in which English is viewed as an acceptable language of compromise. Rather than adopting a local point of reference, Maximal is inscribed in its global context:

> There is always a language that people don't speak at a table. Then you should choose one, you have to do some sort of compromise towards whoever is in the meeting. (Brazilian expatriate, Maximal, 115)

We thus find two incompatible standards that people draw upon and which hold one another in a strong grip. There is an ongoing negotiation between favouring the local or the global option. To illustrate this negotiation, we see a strong resistance – 'a pushing back' – to the global compromise language based on sending sharp comments to a new colleague who just entered Maximal as an expatriate and is not able to write in German or French:

> [A]t the beginning I was sending emails in English, but I got a comment: 'Are we in England?' And since then I haven't done that. It's really not taken well. (Maximal, 168)

In a second illustration, a French expatriate refers to the tension in terms of a 'battlefield' and criticizes the battle between the global lingua franca and the local language:

> [T]he people who orient the debate towards a battle between . . . English and the local language, this is not a good debate, this is not a good battlefield. We need a universal language. The economy, everything is globalized, so in the end it goes against our common interests to refuse such exchanges and to withdraw within the walls of the national languages. (French expatriate, Maximal, 91, translated from French)

The tension between discursive practices one and five can be framed in a political sense as a clash with regard to power and influence. It is a conflict between a local 'majority' of French-speaking employees, and a group of expatriates who import languages other than the Swiss national ones and increase the pressure to speak English. The expats, even if they form a minority, are able to impose their language on others. As a Russian expat suggests, 'if they want me to understand, we speak English' (Maximal, 739). As a consequence, employees who come from the region around the company or from other parts of Switzerland realize they are confronted with a linguistic glass ceiling which sets limits on their possibilities:

> [There] is also a limit for people working here who are not good in English. They're going to have some limits working together with [multinational company] or going into another country. (Belgian expatriate, Maximal, 175)

On the other hand, the fact that the global lingua franca is English does not always imply a one-sided imposition. It can also be considered a 'democratic moment'. English is a second language for most people and the choice implies that no one can outperform others with regard to language:

> [H]ere, English is not the native language for my colleagues either, so I don't see big problems, so . . . We both speak English as a second or third or fourth language. (Russian expatriate, Maximal, 101)

Employees who have the local language as a mother tongue show more signs of resistance. They argue that the workplace and the place where people live have historically developed into a strong union that should not be broken up: 'We are here in Romandy [the French-speaking part of Switzerland], a French stronghold if you like' (French-Swiss, Maximal, 121, translated from French). This situation was also noticed by an expatriate in Maximal who said people signalled that the Swiss tradition should not be altered; they told her: 'Why should we talk English here? . . . We have French and Swiss-German' (Belgian expatriate, Maximal, 32). This tension between a nationally-oriented argumentation and a global option is mediated by the reference to other discursive practices such as practice three, collective negotiation, and practice six, improvisation. Practice three draws on the tradition of collective negotiation which is part of the Swiss historical balance between German, French and Italian:

> When there are presentations, or when they are going to participate in meetings, there is always a moment where people will say 'What will we speak? High German, Swiss-German, in French, a little of both or how are we going to do it?' Thus there is goodwill about having people participate . . . In general, and it is 99% of the people, there is an urge to find an agreement. (British-French expatriate, Maximal, 55, translated from French)

This discursive practice, through which people negotiate in each situation what language(s) will be spoken, is increasingly under pressure from practice five, which opts for a third language. Rather than alternate between French or German, English has become an additional option; as a consequence, English becomes more and more the option used after negotiation, instead of a more situational solution.

A similar trend can be seen with regard to practice six, improvisation. This practice resembles collective negotiation as it argues for opting for a specific language on a situational basis. In the case of practice six, a spontaneous mixture of languages is practised:

> I refer again to my boss as an illustration. So for example, sometimes she wants to send out a message in French, but she has a little difficulty, so she will say: All right, I will speak in English, and this is really accepted and seen as acceptable, and this happens all naturally. Myself, I don't even pay attention to it, you see. (French expatriate, Maximal, 110, translated from French)

Both the practice of collective negotiation and of improvisation, which draw upon a situational argumentation, form a field of tension with practice five, which suggests a third language as a more enduring option.

In summary, the 'linguascape' of Maximal is characterized by an ongoing negotiation process where tensions among various discursive practices are reconfigured. The discursive practice that the location should orient people to adopt the local language used to be dominant but is increasingly in tension with the discursive practice which prompts people to use English as a third language. This tension is mediated by other options which are instigated by drawing upon more situational practices, where people negotiate a common solution or where they improvise and actively mix different languages. On a national level, Maximal oscillates between adapting to the local language, collective negotiation and improvisation, but the growing presence of expats increases the orientation towards a compromise language. Even when negotiation occurs, the pressure to take on English as a negotiated solution is rising, while improvisation allows people to switch among languages. Thus the adoption of English is not a one-sided process but is enacted in a process with signs of resistance and tensions where viable discursive practices are reconsidered and other language options (than English) remain significant for a large group of employees.

The Linguascape of Globalos

The linguistic landscape or 'linguascape' of Globalos is shaped mainly by an apparently similar tension between the reference to discursive practices five and one. The landscape takes on a very different appearance, however, when we consider how other discursive practices are positioned and different kinds of English are distinguished. As the headquarters of a global company, the most common choice is English, a language of compromise. This is seen to guarantee smooth communication, at least when considered from a certain hierarchical level:

> [W]e are making sure that our meetings are all in English . . . all the communication is in English. [Things] like the performance assessment [have] to be in English, because [there] could be another manager who is looking at that who doesn't understand French. (Indian expatriate, Globalos, 177)

This also implies that two French-speaking employees need to communicate in English as every communication is also embedded in a larger conversation, according to this Italian expatriate:

> Well here, everything is in English, even between people who have French as their mother tongue, especially because of emails. You see, you might have to forward them to somebody who does not speak French, so he would need to understand what has been written in that mail. (Globalos, 21, translated from French)

If another language is spoken than English, reference is recurrently made to discursive practice one, as Globalos has its headquarters in the French part of Switzerland. Thus people draw upon the location of the headquarters to suggest adapting to the local language; this is especially true for people from the local area who work for Globalos:

> [I]n general, local people like me who are assistants or something like that, they, they will speak French, since we engage them on a local basis, and all those that we invite to come here, in fact, we have them come here for an experience in Globalos. So we don't oblige them to know French in the beginning. (French-Swiss, Globalos, 65, translated from French)

Indeed, reference to discursive practice one is often made in association with the lower hierarchical level on which people operate:

> [W]hen you get down to levels below that or to the guys who drive the trucks . . . you get into the language of the country more and more . . . with less and less people understanding English. (Australian expatriate, Globalos, 80)

Even if practice five, finding a compromise language, gives English a central role in Globalos, its positioning is less than fixed. In a certain sense, employees speak of two kinds of English: English as a 'real' language (known by people from English-speaking countries) and as a learned language. In Globalos, people emphasize again and again that their lingua franca is a simplified version, which has nothing to do with English as a 'real' language:

> [I]t is true that one is inclined to create an English [laughs] that is no longer really a kind of real English, which is rather a kind of . . . it is rather a kind of jargon. But, all right, we succeed in understanding each other [laughs]. (French expatriate, Globalos, 60, translated from French)

This simplified English can be described as a 'business tool' as shown in the following quote by the Italian expat: 'Sometimes a colleague defines English as a "business tool". It is indeed almost a work instrument . . .' (Globalos, 21). This simplified language must be distinguished from the 'real' English language, which people speak as their mother language, as is the case in Great Britain:

> The English maybe with English as mother tongue, maybe they would be horrified when they see how we have made their language evolve, but it is true that very often one can write it very quickly without having to care about form, accents, and so on. (Italian expatriate, Globalos, 21, translated from French)

If somebody speaks 'real' English, there is a possibility of drawing upon a richness of nuances and precision, while it is argued that many of those who speak a simplified English experience plenty of difficulties in doing so:

> I think in terms of expressions some people used to feel frustrated that . . . you know, 'we are not able to express what we really want to say . . . you know, we are using . . . because we are not that fluent or that coherent or we don't know the language that well'. (Indian expatriate, Globalos, 97)

On the other hand, English is not experienced as a homogeneous language. This creates other difficulties, even for native speakers of English:

> [W]e had another Australian in the group . . . who speaks much faster than me. He comes from a different part of Australia . . . So, he has a different . . . another accentuation of words and some people had to struggle with him. (Australian expatriate, Globalos, 216)

The various accents and rhythms practised in the various regions that make up the Anglophone linguistic space are distinguished as a variety of sub-languages each with their own colour.

In summary, the 'linguascape' of Globalos, as would be expected for a global firm, is apparently dominated by its adherence to discursive practice five: finding a compromise in a third language, in this case English. However, looking at things more closely, this English shows two different features which are in strong tension with each other. On the one hand, a simplified version of English is used as a 'business tool' by people from different linguistic backgrounds. On the other hand, English is the language that employees from the Anglophone linguistic space speak as a mother tongue – a 'real' language with all the cultural connotations and subtleties of a 'real' language. In the latter case, English functions as discursive practice one: 'adaptation to the viable language of a certain location', here the Anglophone linguistic space. This distinction brings along a variety of political meanings where English is simultaneously considered as offering a chance at democratization and assessed as a form of power imbalance: because a minority of employees can speak their mother tongue, non-native speakers of English are forced into a subordinate position. This might have an interesting effect: locals defending the practice of adapting to the local language as shown in the configuration of Maximal might situatively become 'allies' with non-native speakers of English who come from other countries, that is, expats from the non-Anglophone linguistic space.

DISCUSSION

Our literature review indicated that a common language policy is only a starting point for dealing with the complexity of language diversity and requires us to understand how multilingualism is performed in everyday communication. The way that languages are prioritized in their use is the effect of a negotiation process among various discourses concerning how a specific language comes to be adopted. Through a discursive study, we have tried to analyse carefully how multilingual organizations account for the ongoing language use and how they position English during everyday communication. Considering that 'corporate language policies are easily seen as "practical", "inevitable" and even "natural"' (Vaara et al., 2005, p. 522), our study shows that nothing about language use is 'natural' or easily solved using general rules. First, our findings identified six different discursive practices which enable us to show that people draw upon a varied repertoire of often contradictory accounts concerning the ways languages are used. If people think it is important to speak the language of the location where they work, or believe they should adapt to their conversational partners, those beliefs might influence them to speak a different language. We do not believe our list of discursive practices is exhaustive; in other organizations and countries other rules might have been identified. For instance, a seventh discursive practice – that everyone speaks his or her own mother tongue – is an account people drew upon in the past in Switzerland and one we found in a public organization.

Second, we have shown how organizations form specific linguistic landscapes or 'linguascapes' where a different plethora of languages is created as different discourses about language use are considered and combined. While Maximal and Globalos draw upon the same discursive practices, their configurations accommodate different tensions, provoke different possibilities for language use, and effect different positions through which certain language options are either prioritized or marginalized. In fact, then, there is nothing natural about language policies; as one looks behind such policies, one discovers that the discursive dynamics through which English is positioned in the ongoing negotiation of a language hierarchy is quite complex, yet in different ways. For instance, the configuration of Maximal is much more embedded in the Swiss national context and its own quadrilingualism. It forms an interesting contrast with Globalos where, in strong resemblance to other global firms, speakers do not regularly draw upon the Swiss-French territorial and linguistic space.

In order to conceptualize this complex and heterogeneous flow and adoption of languages, we suggest the notion of linguistic landscape or 'linguascape' as inspired by the transnational anthropology developed by Appadurai (1996). This allows us to relate the different (empirically derived) configurations of discursive practices in multilingual organizations in a wider context of current research and thinking on globalization. Appadurai (1996) addresses questions of culture, globalization and transnationalism, looking at how their relationship produces locality. He conceives of globalization not as an abstract process but as something being articulated at given moments and in particular geographies, thus turning the global into a now and here, a globalization from below. To describe these cultural processes from below, Appadurai (1996) distinguishes between several flows, including ethnoscapes, technoscapes, financescapes, mediascapes, and ideoscapes; these refer respectively to the flow of people, technologies, money, images and ideas in which we are continuously immersed. A linguascape has been called a neologism in the vein of Appadurai (Bellier, 2004) to describe the flow of languages that cross a specific space (for instance, a nation; see Jaworski and Piller, 2008).

While some have used the notion of linguascape in a normative sense to envisage a balanced ecology of languages where interaction between users of languages does not allow one or a few to spread at the cost of others (Skutnabb-Kangas and Phillipson, 2008), we use the term in a sociopolitical, yet descriptive, sense to point at the dynamics of accounting for language use and of their consequences for (im)balances among languages and the respective minorities and majorities these languages represent. Thus, a linguascape refers to the discursive space in which an organization or any other actor frames and imagines how it can deal with its (de facto) multilingual composition by negotiating among various discursive options that distinguish between local, national or global spaces and that are oriented to more situational or enduring solutions.

By using the notion of linguascape, we conceptualize the multilingual organization as an effect of the way it relates to different concepts of space and time: while some refer to the space of one meeting and an ad hoc decision, others refer to the space of the national state and its relatively enduring language options. With regard to Maximal and Globalos, their respective linguascapes concern different ways of relating to and imagining the space in which one operates. As we pointed out, at Maximal the Swiss-French territorial and linguistic space plays an important role, but at Globalos it is the Anglophone one which becomes localized as people address various uses of English. However, what unifies each company is the fact that the discursive practice requiring the adaption to the language of a certain location is in strong tension with a new discursive practice which has emerged as a result of globalization: the use of a simplified English as a compromise language throughout the world. In the wake of this trend, more enduring discursive practices are used at the expense of more situational options.

This linguistic space differs from traditional linguistic spaces because it lacks connection to a territory. Instead, the use of this compromise language anchors people in a transnational cultural flow: a wave that unites its users to an international, not territorially bound community, often in the field of work, but also in travel, consumption, art and mass media. As we have shown, the creation of this new linguistic space excludes non-English speakers, but it also can have a democratizing effect: it allows people to join it temporarily or constantly without requiring perfect command of the English language as its basis is rather a simplified English.

CONCLUSION

This chapter responds to the observation that the field of organizational discourse and the study of multilingualism in organizations so far have been little connected. Their respective fields of international management and organization studies do not easily 'talk to each other' (Tietze, 2008, p. 3), even if they have a common interest in language. Our study has documented how a discursive perspective is useful to understand how multilingualism is performed in two organizational contexts. We looked into the everyday consequences of establishing language policies by moving to the process of linguascaping, the ongoing negotiation among accounts of how to 'choose' between languages. More specifically, our contribution is empirical and conceptual, and also relevant to management.

First, we have tried not to approach the rise of English as an abstract, global phenomenon but as a global process that can be studied as an everyday negotiation process from below, where the discourse on English is situated in a broader conversation on how organizations can deal with their multilingual complexity. Therefore, we compared two organizational contexts with different globalized orientations. Our findings show that in Maximal the option of using English as a compromise language is embedded in a broader variety of options and that some actively resist it by referring to the Swiss territorial space and its specific concern for equality among languages. In the global context of Globalos, English is considered not as a homogeneous and static resource, but as a hybrid platform, where possible versions of English are distinguished and the meanings of these different Englishes are negotiated.

In this study, we have thus followed the idea that an initiated process of 'Englishization' (Dor, 2004) brings with it a new interplay and mixing of languages where a specific hierarchy of languages becomes negotiated and practised. Our study thus empirically supports a more ambivalent understanding of the rise of English in corporate organizations. This is in line with how House (2003, p. 557) questions that English as lingua franca forms a threat to multilingualism. She presents a view of lingua franca as an inter-language; features include 'negotiability, variability in terms of speaker proficiency, and openness to an integration of forms of other languages'. Language users are not necessarily pawns directed by a blunt kind of linguistic dominance but can be seen as sometimes developing a multiple competence which allows them to live in a multi-optional context, combining English with other language options. However, as not everyone has similar resources or interests, future research should help us better understand the identity effects of adopting certain languages and how certain options people pursue create symbolic power effects as languages act as symbolic capital.

Second, this study makes a conceptual contribution by considering the importance of discursively understanding how people deal with language diversity. Using the notion of linguascape, we can theorize how multi-lingual communication is performed through the ways that discourses are drawn upon to account for and negotiate specific language use. Linguascape is a conceptual suggestion that relates well to the current interest in the power processes of multilingual organizations (Tietze, 2008; Vaara et al., 2005). Through the notion of linguascape, it becomes possible to describe the complex socio-political processes that underlie multilingual corporate communication. In future research, organizational linguascapes can be used as a conceptual notion to describe and research linguistic diversity as a complex process of signification, where discussions of globalization and the role of English are embedded in complex reper-toires of various discursive practices. In that sense, the notion of lingua-scape responds conceptually to Maclean's (2006, p. 1386) prediction that 'interest will grow in sophisticated, multilingual approaches to resolving language problems, rather than the avoidance of complexity by imposing monolingual solutions universally'.

Our study also has practical implications. We have developed a rep-ertoire of discursive options that people in organizations consider with regard to the ways they mobilize and/or exclude languages in everyday work life. Mapping these discourses and their tensions through linguas-capes can allow managers to acknowledge how language diversity is dealt with on the 'work floor' and the implications that process has for reconsidering language policies. We believe linguascapes can form heu-ristics that enable managers to better capture the complexity through which they deal with multilingualism. Rather than focus only on policy and planning, a discursive approach can help validate the dominant and non-standardized discursive practices as part of the overall complexity in which they operate. While organizational linguascapes might not become less unequal (Coupland, 2003), multilingual organizations might become more reflective about why and how they use and negotiate linguistic resources.

REFERENCES

Antaki, Charles, Michael Billig, Derek Edwards and Jonathan Potter (2003), 'Discourse analysis means doing analysis: A critique of six analytic shortcomings', *Discourse Analysis Online*, **1** (1).

Appadurai, Arjun (1996/2005), *Modernity at Large. Cultural Dimensions of Globalization*, Minneapolis, MN: University of Minnesota Press.

Bellier, Irène (2004), 'Review of English only Europe? Challenging language policy by Robert Phillipson', *Journal of Language and Politics*, **3** (1), 168–173.

Coupland, Nikolas (2003), 'Sociolinguistics and globalization', *Journal of Sociolinguistics*, **7** (4), 465–472.

Dor, Danny (2004), 'From Englishization to imposed multilingualism: Globalization, the internet, and the political economy of the linguistic code', *Public Culture*, **16** (1), 97–118.

Fredriksson, Riikka, Wilhelm Barner-Rasmussen and Rebecca Piekkari (2006), 'The multinational corporation as a multilingual organization. The notion of a common corporate language', *Corporate Communication: An International Journal*, **11** (4), 406–423.

Holden, Nigel (2008), 'Reflections of a cross cultural scholar: Context and language in management thought', *International Journal of Cross Cultural Management*, **8** (2), 239–251.

House, Juliane (2003), 'English as lingua franca: A threat to multilingualism?', *Journal of Sociolinguistics*, **7** (4), 556–578.

Janssens, Maddy, José Lambert and Chris Steyaert (2004), 'Developing language strategies for international companies: The contribution of translation studies', *Journal of World Business*, **39** (4), 414–430.

Jaworski, Adam and Ingrid Piller (2008), 'Linguascaping Switzerland: Language ideologies in tourism', in Miriam Locher und Jürg Strässler (eds), *Standards and Norms in the English Language*, Berlin: Mouton de Gruyter, pp. 301–321.

Kärreman, Dan and Mats Alvesson (2009), 'Resisting resistance: Counter-resistance, consent and compliance in a consultancy firm', *Human Relations*, **62** (8), 1115–1144.

Kelle, Udo (2000), 'Computergestützte Analyse qualitativer Daten', in Uwe Flick, Ernst von Kardoff and Ines Steinke (eds), *Qualitative Sozialforschung: Ein Handbuch*, Reinbek: Rowohlt Taschenbuch Verlag, pp. 485–501.

Luo, Yadong and Oded Shenkar (2006), 'The multinational corporation as a multilingual community: Language and organization in a global context', *Journal of International Business Studies*, **37** (3), 321–339.

Maclean, Dirk (2006), 'Beyond English. Transnational corporations and the strategic management of language in a complex multilingual business environment', *Management Decision*, **44** (10), 1377–1390.

Marschan-Piekkari, Rebecca, Denice E. Welch and Lawrence S. Welch (1999), 'In the shadow: The impact of language on structure, power and communication in the multinational', *International Business Review*, **8** (4), 421–440.

Marshall, Harriette (1994), 'Discourse analysis in an occupational context', in Catherine Cassell and Gillian Symon (eds), *Qualitative Methods in Organizational Research*, London: Sage, pp. 91–106.

Phillipson, Robert (1992), *Linguistic Imperialism*, Oxford: Oxford University Press.

Phillipson, Robert (2001), 'Global English and local language policies. What Denmark needs', *Language Problems & Language Planning*, **25** (1), 1–24.

Piekkari, Rebecca and Lena Zander (2005), 'Language and communication in international management', *International Studies of Management & Organization*, **35** (1), 3–9.

Piekkari, Rebecca, Eero Vaara, Janne Tienari and Risto Säntti (2005), 'Integration or disintegration? Human resource implications of a common corporate language decision in a cross-border merger', *International Journal of Human Resource Management*, **16** (3), 330–344.

Potter, Jonathan and Margaret Wetherell (1987), *Discourse and Social Psychology: Beyond Attitudes and Behavior*, London: Sage.

Skutnabb-Kangas, Tove and Robert Phillipson (2008), 'A human rights perspective on language ecology', in Angela Creese, Peter W. Martin and Nancy Hornberger (eds), *Encyclopedia of Language and Education*, New York: Springer, pp. 3–14.

Steyaert, Chris and Maddy Janssens (1997), 'Language and translation in an international business context: Beyond an instrumental approach', *Target, International Journal of Translation Studies*, **9** (1), 131–154.

Tietze, Susanne (2004), 'Spreading the management gospel – in English', *Language and Intercultural Communication*, **4** (3), 176–189.

Tietze, Susanne (ed.) (2008), *International Management and Language*, London: Taylor & Francis.

Vaara, Eero, Janne Tienari, Rebecca Piekkari and Risto Säntti (2005), 'Language and the circuits of power in a merging multinational corporation', *Journal of Management Studies*, **42** (3), 595–623.

Welch, Catherine and Rebecca Piekkari (2006), 'Crossing language boundaries: Qualitative interviewing in international business', *Management International Review*, **46** (4), 417–437.

Welch, Denice E., Lawrence S. Welch and Rebecca Piekkari (2005), 'Speaking in tongues: The importance of language in international management processes', *International Studies of Management & Organization*, **35** (1), 10–27.

Wetherell, Margaret (2001), 'Themes in discourse research: The case of Diana', in Margaret Wetherell and Stephanie Taylor (eds), *Discourse Theory and Practice*, London: Sage, pp. 14–28.

PART IV

Creativity and change

9. The expectations gap and heteroglossic practices of (non-) compliance in banking regulation

Roland Pfyl

INTRODUCTION

Over the past two decades, banking regulation has been tightened, risk management and control systems have been refined through an enormous investment of effort and sophistication and financial institutions have multiplied their numbers of auditors, risk managers and compliance officers. Nevertheless, the banking system has suffered from the worst crisis in its post-war history, the Great Financial Crisis in the words of Foster and Magdoff (2009). Regulations did not stop institutions and individuals from engaging in high-risk financial transactions; meanwhile auditing reports failed to uncover the underlying control weaknesses, and rating agencies and risk managers massively underestimated the amounts at risk in financial institutions. In short: banking regulation has not lived up to the inherent expectations for it, and it seems to have failed. We see clear evidence of the so-called expectations gap (Liggio, 1974) between what banking regulation *should do* and what it *has done* effectively in practice.

One of the most influential economists working in the field of banking regulation, Martin Hellwig (2010, p. 2), describes the situation trenchantly:

> Is it really enough to tighten a screw here and put in a new nail there? Or doesn't the entire ship of banking regulation need a thorough overhaul? The regulatory community seems unwilling to even ask such questions. It sticks to a tradition of discussing the rules of capital regulation among the bureaucratic cognoscenti, in some interaction with the industry, without ever providing any theoretical or empirical analysis of the effects that the measures under consideration are deemed to have and without heeding demands that such analyses should be just as much a precondition for the implementation of new regulatory rules as for the introduction of new pharmaceutical drugs into the market.

Unfortunately, Hellwig himself does not provide a theoretical or empirical analysis of the effects that regulation has on everyday banking practices.

Moreover, while he postulates the need for a fundamental overhaul of the regulatory system, he does not break the rationalist chains around the moral hazard arguments that are used to frame individual and organizational behaviour. A clear gap remains between the rationalistic expectations of banking regulation and the actual malfunctions, irrationalities and inefficiencies that many have observed.

In this chapter I provide an empirical analysis (Pfyl, 2010) of the effects that banking regulation has on everyday practices of (non-)compliance, and I develop a model to sharpen our theoretical understanding of the expectations gap in banking. I argue that in order to understand how banking regulation works – and how it fails – it is indispensable to move beyond a rationalistic understanding of individual and organizational behaviour. Therefore, taking a micro-perspective, I investigate how managers respond to regulations in their everyday practices, and I frame these everyday encounters with regulation as practices of (non-)compliance. My goal in this chapter is to increase our understanding of how regulations, in effect, come to life in organizations through practices of (non-)compliance and how these practices continuously open and close the expectations gap of banking regulation.

To capture the complexities of everyday practices of (non-)compliance, I draw upon the linguistic turn in organizational psychology and place my work within the Bakhtinian conception of the organization as heteroglossic. In this conception, everyday practices of (non-)compliance are immersed in a variety of discourses that are simultaneously contradictory but that collectively support the hegemonic rationality discourse that underpins regulatory expectations. Consequently, practices are seen not as catering to a priori structural or individual variables or essences, but as resulting from discursive processes that underlie everyday encounters with regulation. Hence, I focus on the expectations gap around banking regulation in order to better understand two phenomena: the discursive processes at work within organizations through which people structure their everyday encounters with regulation, and the systemic consequences that arise out of these encounters. Therefore, I will consider regulation not as fixed but as constantly being created, as banking professionals make sense of them in their everyday practices of (non-)compliance.

To ground my analysis empirically, I examine data from interviews with managers of an international bank. Focusing on the expectations gap of banking regulation, I use two analytic questions to structure my analysis: (1) What discursive patterns can be identified in everyday encounters with regulation, that is, in everyday practices of (non-)compliance? (2) And how are these discursive patterns (re-)constructing the expectations gap of banking regulation? Before I present my analysis, I situate the problem formulation in the literature and introduce the conceptual framework and the methodological considerations that have guided this study.

LITERATURE REVIEW

The concept of the expectations gap first appeared in the academic literature on auditing. It depicts the gap between the broad assurance that the public expects from auditors, such as detecting fraud, and the much narrower focus of what auditors really do, such as review control systems for weaknesses (Liggio, 1974; Porter, 1993). It was later extended to other areas such as risk management (Power, 2004), investor protection (Eckstein, 2014; Langevoort, 2003) and monetary policy (Borio, 2014) to depict the mismatch between high public expectations for regulations and the much narrower capability for control in practice.

The insight that a mismatch exists between social expectations and organizational 'realities' is a prevalent but variegated theme in the organizational literature. In addition to the dominant economist argument derived from principal–agent theory – that information asymmetry is responsible for the expectations gap – two other major discussions provide alternative explanatory routes. First, neo-institutionalist arguments focus on decoupling the formal structures (that is, regulations) of organizations from their actual day-to-day work activities. Second, sociological and psychological arguments focus on how regulatory expectations are reconstructed in the micro-processes of everyday practices of (non-)compliance.

According to the institutionalist argument of decoupling, organizations build up their formal structures according to outside expectations, and not primarily according to internal needs (Meyer and Rowan, 1977). Organizations tend to be isomorphic with the institutional environment. For an organization it is vital to uphold the myth of compliance with the external, for example, regulatory, demands in order to assure legitimacy and the capacity to survive. Conflicts with internal structures and cultures are solved by 'decoupling' the actual work activities. A similar concept was introduced by Argyris and Schön (1974), who differentiate between 'espoused theories' and 'theories in use'. The former construct the formal organizational structure by espousing the external norms and the latter reflect the informal ideology or implicit assumptions that govern actual behaviour. This decoupling is also the starting point for Brunsson's (1993; 2003) theory of 'organized hypocrisy', with the separation of 'talk', 'decisions' and 'actions'. Organized hypocrisy, as distinct from ordinary hypocrisy, refers to decoupled and compensatory organizational responses to conflicting external pressures.

A neo-institutionalist perspective has also served those analysing the Great Financial Crisis. For instance, Abolafia (2010) analysed the institutional embeddedness of market failures and identified ideological blinders that prevented organizations from reducing their involved risks. In another study, Rubtsova, DeJordy, Glynn and Zald (2010) investigated the effects of institutional myths on financial regulation and showed how older field logics are retained and re-emerge throughout history.

Common to this neo-institutionalist stream of organizational literature is a focus on the institutional myths of formal institutions, such as regulations, and the decoupling of informal organizational behaviour, which is seen as logically leading to the expectations gap. While neo-institutionalist arguments point to important 'irrationalities' in the conception of regulation, they typically focus at the level of a field or institution. Such a focus fails to acknowledge the complexities and idiosyncrasies of encounters with regulation in everyday practices. Thus, analysts need a closer view of the micro-processes involved in everyday practices of (non-)compliance.

These micro-processes are the focus of the second stream of literature I introduce here. The conflicting tensions between the formal demands of regulatory institutions and the informal pressures in everyday practices are the starting point. These conflicts can be framed as the practices of (non-)compliance in an environment of scarcity and competition, of bargaining in decision-making, of uncertain technology, of incremental developments, of complex patterns of information flows, and of routinization.

Several studies provide this kind of closer look at the micro-processes by examining how regulatory requirements are enveloped in organizational practices. Edelman and Suchman (1997) provide a good overview of the literature on legalistic practices in organizations. A crucial insight is that compliance – and thus non-compliance – is more than a simple organizational consequence of formal structures; rather, it requires institutional work. (Non-)compliance as the everyday encounter with regulation is a practice in its own right (Sitkin and Bies, 1994). Following this logic, the expectations gap is a result of muddling through a fragmented regulatory space by engaging with formal structures, rather than by decoupling them from everyday practices (Feldman and Levy, 1994). Some have observed, for instance, that professionals tend to offer the illusion of responsible actions through 'selective compliance' with some of the numerous competing regulatory requirements, which in turn ensures 'plausible deniability' of responsibility for any action taken (Browning and Folger, 1994; Edelman, 1990).

Once analysts focus on the micro-processes, they can explain organizational failures by looking at both practices of non-compliance and practices of compliance. Diane Vaughan (2005) describes how non-compliance can be incrementally transformed into acceptable behaviour in a process she refers to as normalization of deviance that can result in major failures. On the other side – that of compliance – Perrow's (1984) study of 'normal accidents' investigates how everyday failures may be inevitable, not because people do not comply with regulatory requirements, but because the failure is triggered by the complexity and tight coupling of a system even though people do comply. The normal accident theory has also been applied to the Great Financial Crisis. Analysts have argued that the combination of high complexity and the lack of built-in buffers triggered that crisis, rather than individual wrongdoings (Guillén and Suárez, 2010; Schneiberg and Bartley, 2010).

While the first, institutionalist stream of literature emphasizes the role of formal structures, the second stream focuses on individual agency involved in banking regulation. Common to this literature is a shared view of complex and dynamic interrelationships between the effects of regulation *on* everyday practices and the role of individual agency *in* everyday practices. The concept of *everyday practice*, in turn, is the common ground for analysis of the emergence and existence of expectations gaps in regulatory regimes.

However, this literature also contains shortcomings. It has not convincingly explained the paradox that public expectations – and thus regulatory institutions – are highly stable in the face of ample evidence of malfunctioning, irrationalities or inefficiencies. Both the institutionalist perspective of the (partial) decoupling of formal structures from everyday practices, and the micro perspective of muddling through the complexities and irrationalities of everyday activities offer interesting insights, but they both fail to provide an integrative explanatory framework.

Such a framework would allow us to conceive of the organizational struggle underlying efforts to uphold the rationalist regulatory expectations while everyday practices are immersed in an environment of competition and of bargaining in decision-making, of uncertain technology, of incremental developments, of complex patterns of information flows, of time pressures, and of routinization. Thus, we see a struggle between contradictory pressures: convergent forces push towards accommodating regulatory expectations while divergent forces undermine the very same expectations.

In this chapter I contribute an explanatory model to frame this dynamic struggle underlying the expectations gap of regulation. Based on empirical evidence, I will develop a Bakhtinian model to frame both the reproductive and the paradoxical effects of regulation in everyday practices of (non-) compliance.

CONCEPTUAL FRAMEWORK: REGULATION AS HETEROGLOSSIA

To frame the dynamic struggle underlying the expectations gap, I have chosen a discursive approach and framed the organization in a Bakhtinian conception (Bakhtin, 1981; 1986) as heteroglossic. That is, I conceive of banking regulation as an overarching organizational language that breaks down into different organizational discourses. Organizational discourses are the phenomena that bring into existence, and then maintain and develop, 'organized' states – such as regulation. The term regulation refers not to an extra-linguistic reality, but to a discursively constructed state. Everyday encounters with regulation, that is, practices of (non-)compliance, involve (re-)producing shared codes of behaviour and understandings, which are institutionalized as organizational discourses (Chia, 2000). The different organizational discourses represent different ways of sensemaking, and thus different ways of structuring everyday encounters (utterances, to use Bakhtin's term) with regulations.

Four defining characteristics of a heteroglossic understanding of organizations are relevant to this study. First, my analysis is inscribed within a wider 'practice turn' in contemporary social theory (Schatzki, Knorr Cetina and von Savigny, 2001). The practice turn directs the researcher's attention to micro-processes, that is to the 'everydayness' of social action (Steyaert, 2004). Central to the practice turn is the effort to move beyond the problematic dualism of agency and structure and merge them into the single concept of practice. Thus the researcher focuses on understanding the continuous (re-)production of regulation in the mundane, the ordinary or the customary of everyday practices.

Second, the various discourses that cohabit the heteroglossic organization are not politically neutral. For instance, one can assume that the rationalist discourse holds a hegemonic (authoritative) position that legitimates the logic of contemporary banking regulation. This position, however, cannot suppress other counter-hegemonic discourses, but lives in a dynamic struggle with them.

Third, the various discourses are not only simultaneously present in everyday encounters with regulation, that is, in everyday practices of (non-)compliance, but also interdependent. Hence, the practices of (non-)compliance embody multiple organizational discourses that are at once contradictory but also mutually constitutive. To use Bakhtin's term, we are seeing the dialogic nature of discourses (Valsiner, 1991).

Fourth, each encounter with regulations is conceived of as a dialogical struggle between convergent (centripetal) and divergent (centrifugal) discursive meanings (Clark and Holquist, 1984; Holquist, 1990). Centripetal forces tend to standardize around the hegemonic (authoritative) rationality discourse of regulation in that these forces fix and close meanings. Centrifugal forces de-standardize and diversify meanings; they resist discursive closure by producing counter-hegemonic (counter-authoritative) worldviews. Heteroglossia alludes to the dynamic conflict between these two forces. Bakhtin (1981, p. 272) notes how this occurs in relation to utterances that are defined as practices:

> Every concrete utterance ... serves as a point where centrifugal as well as centripetal forces are brought to bear. The processes of centralization and decentralization, of unification and disunification, intersect in the utterance; ... Every utterance participates in the 'unitary language' (in its centripetal forces and tendencies) and at the same time partakes of social and historical heteroglossia (the centrifugal, stratifying forces).

The dynamic interrelatedness of the centripetal forces around a hegemonic (or 'official') rationalist discourse of regulation and the centrifugal forces of counter-hegemonic noise attach a political aspect to heteroglossia. From this perspective, practices of (non-)compliance are not just about formal (re-)production of official regulatory requirements; they constitute a continuous heteroglossic struggle. As a result, my aim in this study goes beyond identifying various discourses that structure everyday encounters with regulation. I also aim to show how these discourses relate to each other, by highlighting the centripetal and centrifugal forces in everyday practices of (non-)compliance and by investigating how these practices both reinforce and undermine the hegemonic rationalist regulation discourse in the organization – and thus create and maintain the expectations gap in banking regulation.

METHODOLOGY

In order to trace the presence and consequences of the expectations gap in everyday practices of (non-)compliance, it is important to understand how managers experience and interpret regulation in everyday practice as they engage with, avoid or resist it. Grounding the study in a heteroglossic understanding of organizational discourse requires a methodological approach that shares its practice and language focus. To ensure a practice focus, I chose to focus on concrete everyday experiences in the organizational environment of a medium-sized international bank in which I had previously worked as an internal auditor. To reflect my focus on language I have chosen interviewing as my method of data collection and discourse analysis as my method of interpretation. I will describe my approaches to interviewing and discourse analysis in turn.

Data Collection

I chose interviewing as my primary method of data collection. Rather than a neutral exercise involving questioning, in this study interviewing meant an unavoidably collaborative and interpretively active endeavour, in which both interviewers and interviewees engaged in discursive constructions (Alasuutari, 1995). In order to expose the centripetal and centrifugal forces, I took this active interviewing approach to 'cultivate the respondent's narrative activity' (Holstein and Gubrium, 1995, p. 76) and to promote multivocality, or 'multivoicedness' (Bouwen and Steyaert, 1999).

Methodologically, this understanding of interviewing meant that I did not adhere strictly to a detailed questionnaire, and instead engaged in relatively open conversations. After a general warm-up question about what comes spontaneously to mind when talking about regulation, I first asked the interviewees to evaluate the advantages and disadvantages of regulation in everyday practice. I intended for this rather abstract first set of questions to lay open the 'official' story of regulation: the hegemonic discourse. Second, I explored the power positions within the organization with regard to designing, controlling and interpreting regulations. This triggered stories about how they experience regulation in everyday practice. Third, I directed the conversation towards reflections on challenges and problems in everyday encounters with regulation. By problematizing regulation, I was able to ground the analysis in the centrifugal and centripetal forces. Finally, I asked the interviewees to speculate about future regulatory developments, in order to generate normative stories about how they thought regulation should operate. Throughout the interviews, I asked for concrete examples to ground the analysis in practice.

I conducted interviews with a total of 25 employees, all of them at managerial level. The interviews were held in English or German and lasted 60 to 90 minutes. The sample included general managers at the strategic apex of the organization, operations managers, and relationship managers as well as professionals in regulation: experts with professional qualifications in the fields of auditing, risk management or legal practice. This broad mix of managers provided ample stories about lived experiences. By focusing exclusively on managers I risked suppressing the voices of employees below the managerial level. I made the decision to limit my sample to managers based on my conviction that managers are the opinion leaders in the organization with the most impact on how everyday practices of (non-)compliance are structured.

Data Analysis

To analyse the interview data, I relied on discourse analysis as my main method of interpretation. The very nature of a discourse is that it imbues everyday practices with meaning. In that sense, any account of everyday encounters with regulation is not just a description of a practice, but also includes – at least implicitly – the reasons for those practices and the normative ground that people use to justify them (Giddens, 1984, p. 30). In that sense, discourses determine how rationalistic regulation is subsumed within a particular discourse (through centripetal forces) and what type of counter-hegemonic noise is generated (through centrifugal forces).

In order to discern the discourses that constitute a heteroglossic organization, I developed a four-phase research approach. First, I converted the interviews to text by taking notes after each interview and transcribing the interview audiotapes. Second, to generate a first set of interpretative patterns and codes to use in further analysis, I performed an in-depth analysis of three interviews, following Froschauer and Lueger's (2003) approach to systems analysis. Third, I applied that analytic process to the other interviews. Fourth, I looked for discursive patterns across all the coded interview transcripts and synthesized the discursive patterns into a coherent set of discourses on (non-)compliance. Table 9.1 illustrates these four phases.

Froschauer and Lueger's (2003, p. 142ff.) systems analysis is designed for exploring processual dynamics in complex social spaces. This approach fits particularly well with the heteroglossic conception of the organization in that it reveals discursive patterns as well as interaction and system effects. The in-depth analysis was subdivided into three steps: to paraphrase, to deconstruct and to reconstruct. Table 9.2 illustrates these three analytic steps.

To analyse the interview data, I gathered similar underlying assumptions, positions and metaphors in a 'basket' of patterns. This analytic process resulted in four clearly discernible 'baskets' representing a discursive pattern. The discursive patterns determine the sphere of possible actions. Finally, I constructed the discourses by speculating on the interactional and systemic consequences of the four discursive patterns. This final analytical step brought to light coherent but often conflicting logics: the centripetal and centrifugal forces of everyday practices.

Reflexivity

Interviewing and interpreting is always an active process of reconstruction and never a neutral representation of the actual practices involved in (non-)compliance. Interviewees tend to respond to what they imagine to

Table 9.1   Data analysis process

---

1. Convert interviews to text

Write notes after each interview	Write down first thoughts after each interview (important for later contextualisation).
Transcribe first three interviews	Transcribe three interviews. Sequence text according to the conversational agenda and link it directly to the audio file.

2. Conduct in-depth analysis

'Systemanalyse'	Analyse three interviews following the approach of Froschauer and Lueger (2003), called 'Systemanalyse'.
Define codes	Define codes. Based on my results in the 'Systemanalyse' step, I identified a set of meaningful codes and applied them to the transcripts.

3. Extend analysis

Transcribe and (re-)code the remaining interviews	Transcribe and (re-)code the other taped interviews. After coding three to four additional interviews, I returned to the earlier coded interviews and adapted them, if necessary, based on the latest coding structure.

4. Look for discursive patterns

Analyse codes	Explore for patterns of codes, including an analysis of the co-coding frequency and the co-variation of codes and text sequences.
Contextualize interviews	Analyse patterns of codes in relation to contextual factors, including the organizational position and the interviewees' relationship to me.
Identify discursive patterns	Based on the analysis of codes, various discursive patterns emerged. I condensed these patterns into four distinguishable discourses of (non-)compliance.

---

be the researcher's expectations. Studying the organization where I had worked as an internal auditor provided several advantages in relation to access, data availability and background understanding; however, it also raised difficult methodological and ethical problems in relation to personal relationships to some of the interviewees. To reduce these problems and thus control my results, I used two research strategies.

First, I focused the interview narratives on concrete examples of everyday encounters with regulation, that is, on descriptions of how the managers being interviewed, and others they knew, dealt with the regulatory requirements in everyday practice. This focus on concrete examples allowed them to be objective in a way that was independent from my position in the bank. My professional background knowledge and my status as 'internal' contributed to creating interview situations that were

Table 9.2   Discourse analysis process

Paraphrase	Deconstruction				Reconstruction	
Determine and paraphrase thematic units	Look for underlying assumptions	Determine position towards formality	Look for metaphors		Speculate on interaction effects	Speculate on system effects
Defines the field of formality	Generates discursive patterns as the building blocks of discourse				Defines the actional and systemic components of discursive patterns	

quite similar to concrete experiences of practice. The interviewees used many abbreviations, and referred to generally known projects, processes, events and people during the interviews. These conversational elements would have represented a major barrier for any researcher external to the organization. Second, I mixed the types of relationship I had with the interviewees, by including people I did and did not know personally. I also shifted perspectives within each interview to generate some variation in the narratives.

RESULTS: PRACTICES OF (NON-)COMPLIANCE AS RATIONALITY, MYTH, GAME AND FATE

The discourse analysis yielded four discernible discourses of (non-)compliance which I have named the discourses of rationality, myth, game and fate. The rationality discourse has been established as the hegemonic (authoritative) discourse within the heteroglossic practices of (non-)compliance. The hegemonic position, however, is deployed not by overt force, but by centripetal forces; that is, it integrates and envelops people rather than dominating them. The hegemonic position of the rationality discourse could be recognized in all of the interview accounts. As I analysed the interview texts sequentially I discovered that the participants tended to argue using a rationality discourse logic at the beginning of our interview conversations. This reflects the tendency to draw on hegemonic discourses in unknown interactional situations – such as an interview – in order to insure against interactional conflicts.

Establishing the rationality discourse as hegemonic is important for my analysis of centrifugal and centripetal forces as the main explanatory factors for the expectations gap in banking regulation. The co-existence of multiple discourses that are contradictory but collectively supportive of the hegemonic rationality discourse provides the discursive web of practices of (non-)compliance.

In order to highlight the practices of (non-)compliance, I focus my presentation of the discourses on the patterns of the managers' reactions to emerging problems in their encounters with regulation. Focusing on problems is a fruitful approach for analysing discursive patterns since people have to rationalize the causes *of* and the solutions *to* these problems. Rationalizing means building a coherent argumentation that draws on available discourses.

In a heteroglossic conception of regulation, a problem can be framed as a discursive tension between the hegemonic rationality understanding of regulation and the simultaneously present but counter-hegemonic noise of other discursive logics. A solution, in turn, does not mean resolving discursive tensions but rather altering the discursive emphasis. In that sense, everyday practices of (non-)compliance are never neutral, but always function as the source of both centrifugal and centripetal forces. By centripetal forces I mean the propensity of each discourse to mimic the hegemonic rationality discourse without employing its underlying discursive logic. In turn, the centrifugal forces inherent in competing discursive logics result in effects that undermine the rationalist expectations. I found that this simultaneous presence of centripetal and centrifugal forces is the key mechanism for (re-)constructing the expectations gap in everyday encounters with regulation. For each discourse, I will reconstruct the discursive seeds of both the centripetal and centrifugal forces, and thus of the expectations gap.

Rationality Discourse

The rationality discourse has been established as the hegemonic discourse – as regulation's own story. The rationality discourse embodies the scientific aspiration that one approach to regulation is objectively the best, and a view that regulations take on a life of their own, once they have been rationally designed and institutionally established. Through this process, regulations are reified and thus decoupled from concrete everyday situations. In turn, everyday practices of (non-)compliance are seen to be the logical consequence of regulation.

The rationalist discourse tends to be self-reinforcing. I identified three centripetal reaction patterns to problems in everyday practices of (non-)compliance. The first is a tendency to solve problems by increasing regulation. As a relationship manager trenchantly remarked, 'Got a problem? Invent a rule. We solve problems by inventing rules' (Interview 16). The very logic of the rationality discourse maintains that good regulation precludes failures. As a consequence, failures are conceived of in terms of regulatory loopholes or badly adapted regulation rather than individual wrongdoings.

Second, the rationality discourse reinforces the power status of regulation professionals such as auditors, risk managers and lawyers. For those operating in a rationalist logic, the appropriate response to a problem is to engage in a quasi-scientific task rather than to make a management judgement. Regulation professionals build their legitimacy on this quasi-scientific nimbus of professionalism, which incorporates the rationalistic values of objectivity, neutrality and scientism. The third centripetal pattern relates to materialization. The propensity of formalizing, the virtual detachment of regulation from persons and the idea of organizing everyday practice in a series of logical steps are materialized in detailed documentation and high level of automation.

Even though the rationality discourse has been established as hegemonic, it nevertheless contains within itself the seeds of centrifugal forces in everyday practices of (non-)compliance. It seems counterintuitive to discuss the centrifugal forces of the hegemonic discourse. This discourse, however, is not simply self-reinforcing, but also entails unintended or even paradoxical consequences in everyday practices. These are based on blind spots: cases of people relying excessively on one type of discursive logic, and thus omitting the other aspects that constitute a heteroglossic organization. My analysis revealed three kinds of blind spots.

First, the rationality discourse casts failures in terms of generic risks rather than individual problems. Casting a failure in terms of a general risk to the organization amplifies the impact of that failure beyond the individual concrete practice that is found to be deficient. Risks and failures become relevant in all parts of the organization. In the face of ample evidence of malfunctioning, irrationalities or inefficiencies of regulation in everyday practices, the amplification effect leaves the bank looking like a precarious place fraught with failures. An operations manager clearly portrayed this sense of a focus on omnipresent risk, combined with high risk aversion: 'Risk is the central driver of internal regulation. Or, to put it more accurately, no incidents are tolerated at our bank. None!' (Interview 14). With such a rationalist focus, risk avoidance becomes a dominant driver in regulatory practice, while other aspects such as justice – or even profit – are marginalized.

A second blind spot is the marginalization of business managers; this is the logical drawback of regulation professionals having a high power status. The focal point of managing tends to become problems cast as risks, and solutions cast as regulations. This situation hampers those who would make quick and targeted management solutions to concrete problems. A third blind spot is the irrelevance of output. Reflecting technico-scientific assumptions, output is reduced to the logical consequence of proper formal procedures. Such a focus on procedures carries the risk that managers will turn their attention away from the underlying regulatory goals. All three blind spots of the rationality discourse nurture the expectations gap of banking regulation.

Myth Discourse

The logic of the myth discourse comes close to the neo-institutionalist insights about decoupling and to the ceremonial practices that foster the myths of regulation; for those reasons, I have attached the neo-institutionalist label to it. The myth discourse decouples practices of everyday work from practices that demonstrate compliance with regulations. In the interviews, managers often conceived of regulations as ceremonial exercises – such as ticking boxes and filling in forms – whose goal was to satisfy the myth that their organization was compliant. In contrast, in everyday work, the emphasis is put on common sense and interpersonal trust as the driving energy of everyday practices. In the following quote about the formal requirements for opening a bank account, a relationship manager tellingly dissociates the regulatory logic of ticking off documentation requirements from the myth discourse's normativity of common sense and trust:

> Nowadays, for me to say I trust this guy, what I mean is that I have a copy of a utility bill and a copy of a passport. All of these, let's be honest, if I was faced with a fraudster or a money launderer, the first thing you can be sure they will have from the get-go is the passport copy and the address verification. That, they will have done. But what is missing is the bit that goes beyond the [regulatory requirements]: filling in all the soft details that create a picture, a consistent picture that makes sense to someone, so that I actually can say, I do trust this guy. (Interview 16)

As we consider the decoupling that is this manager's solution to his inter-discursive struggles, we see two types of centrifugal forces in play. The first is a normalization of deviance. While rationalistic expectations would presuppose that, in practice, people observe regulations according to the letter of the law, the myth discourse underscores that, in their everyday encounters, managers screen regulations through their own combination of common sense and interpersonal trust.

As result, it was possible to identify typical practices of non-compliance; for example managers would bypass the more time-consuming, burdensome or nonsensical aspects of regulations but still report that they had performed the controls. An operations manager noted:

What I have heard is that private bankers regularly check off 'signature confirmed', when the signature is not confirmed at all, [I could provide] some blatant examples. . . . The point is, I think, that when you go through routines, after some time, you say . . . if something is correct today, it is surely correct tomorrow. Why should I examine it every day? . . . When something happens that is outside the routine, then we still mark it. It'd be even worse if we were to introduce a six-eyes or even eight-eyes principle. Because this would certainly then lead to a practice where the last one would say, 'What should I check? The others have done it already'. (Interview 12)

I use the term 'lulling effect' for the second centrifugal force. The apparent effectiveness of the regulations portrayed within the practices in the myth discourse may lead to complacency with the quality of the bank's control framework. Such complacency in turn may lead to blindness and inertia with respect to actual problems that arise in the bank. The lulling effect is seen as the consequence of the unrealized promise of regulation. Most interestingly, managers seem to be fully aware of practices associated with the myth discourse, as we see in this statement from a legal manager:

I assume that the board of directors, the audit committee and the executive board believe that we have a very good regulatory control framework. Or at least they are pretending to. The board of directors believes it, the audit committee acts as if they believe it, and the executive board makes sure that the others believe it. (Interview 13)

Rationalistic expectations hold that management attention tends to be turned exclusively toward what appears on the radar screen of formal reporting. From a myth perspective, the managerial radar screen is decoupled from the reality of everyday practices. The myth discourse sees both the normalization of deviance and the lulling effect grounded in a flawed assumption that regulation and everyday practices are directly coupled.

However, the myth practices of (non-)compliance also involve centripetal forces supporting the hegemonic position of the rationality discourse. The typical pattern of reacting to problems is also to amend regulations and to adopt practices for managing risk in new situations, but without necessarily changing everyday work practices. Underpinning this pattern is a common-sense logic about upholding the myth of compliance. Upholding that myth protects the trust-based work environment from unwanted external disturbance.

The dynamic struggle between the decoupling of regulation from everyday practices and the practice of upholding the myth of regulatory compliance provides an explanation both for the expectations gap and for its apparent stability.

Game Discourse

A somewhat different logic underpins the practices of (non-)compliance driven by the game discourse. Instead of decoupling, it frames practices of (non-)compliance as processes of influencing and interpreting through which regulations set the boundaries in game-like interactions. Contrary to general expectations, regulation does not predetermine any outcome. What makes the difference here is the skills people apply in strategically manoeuvring through the various options on the playing field of regulations. As a credit manager puts it in the following quote, everyday practices of (non-)compliance are part of a continuous negotiation process and are not objectively given:

> Well it happens every day. Those whose responsibility it is to earn money for the bank, they want to weaken the credit conditions in order to make a particular credit and they will try to pressure us on the policy requirements and push the boundaries [to find out] what we are prepared to give. . . . It is not easy to handle. (Interview 10)

While the rationalistic regulatory aspiration is to control everyday practices comprehensively and exclusively, the game discourse plays on the high complexity of everyday interactions, the regulatory contradictions, and the considerable leeway that remains. Responding to the expectations of the hegemonic rationality discourse, the game discourse limits its interactional logics to formal requirements, which render irrelevant every consideration that is not explicitly included in regulatory blueprints – such as ethical or moral ones. As a result, the skilful player is freed up rather than constrained by the limited rationalist focus of regulations and can deploy them as resources to pursue his or her self-interest, as a general manager noted:

> To those who want to open an account with fraudulent intentions, [the anti-money-laundering regulation] provides a proper manual on how to do it . . . And [if something goes wrong, the responsible relationship managers] will insist that they have done everything as required. (Interview 8)

Again, the game discourse is both centrifugal and centripetal. In its dynamic struggle with the rationality discourse, the focus is on the spaces and options created by rationalist regulations rather than on the constraints they induce. In this discourse, managers' reactions to problems typically consist of strategically selecting and moulding regulations and choosing the playing field that allows individuals to best achieve their self-interest.

A first centrifugal force connected to this discourse refers to the difficulty of rational long-term planning. In a game logic, everyday practices result not from planning at the strategic apex, as postulated by the rationality discourse, but from continuous and messy everyday negotiation practices. The result is a maze of partly contradictory regulations and omnipresent exceptions that open a wide playing field in everyday practice.

A second centrifugal effect is grounded in the fact that the rationality discourse marginalizes subjectivity. The general and abstract logic of regulations can contribute to obscuring the subjective nature of everyday decisions instead of eliminating subjectivity from everyday practice. In other words, regulation offers a legitimating cover for almost any action. A legal specialist tellingly referred to the art of dealing with regulations during internal approval processes:

> Personally, you always have to consider that you are standing your ground – . . . That is the art and the duty – without giving the impression of being uncooperative or cross-grained – to give the approval . . . with the right qualifications and reservations. (Interview 13)

For both the one seeking approval and the one granting it, adherence to formalized procedures makes it possible to shirk responsibility. Individual responsibility is replaced by a concern for plausible deniability based on reference to due compliance, whether through formal approval or through the artful drafting of the right qualifications and reservations.

The game discourse also embodies a propensity toward reinforcing rationality's hegemonic position by catering to regulatory logics of regulating. The game discourse tends to seek new regulations to create new opportunities of regulatory arbitrage in everyday practices of (non-)compliance. As a general manager noted, 'the more something is regulated, the more the regulatory uncertainty increases' (Interview 8). By promoting opportunities for skilful players, the game discourse also contributes to the (re)production of professionalism at the bank. The rationality logic allows regulation professionals to acquire an important power position while disguised as the gatekeepers of regulation.

A final centripetal force is the shared propensity to materialize interactions through documentation. Contrary to the rationality discourse logic, documents are not neutral representations of reality, but are fundamentally self-conscious and self-interested. As the following quote from an operations manager highlights, documents are purposely designed to produce an effect of some kind, such as self-protection: 'We are documenting everything, because we want to be protected against regulation, internal or external' (Interview 1). Conversely, if managers choose not to document certain types of interactions and deliberations, they withdraw these interactions from regulatory or managerial focus. Both strategic documentation and non-documentation are important practices of (non-) compliance. The rationality discourse provides no room for these aspects as they fundamentally contradict its view that documentation is objective.

This play, with its ambiguous and sketchy set of rules, reflects another dynamic struggle: between the rationalistic aspirations of regulation and the self-interested individuals undermining these aspirations. Once again, this dynamic struggle between centrifugal and centripetal forces helps to explain both the existence and the persistence of the expectations gap of banking regulation.

Fate Discourse

What distinguishes the fate discourse is its lack of an appropriate normativity underlying everyday practices of (non-)compliance. Fate steps in as the normative guidepost. The fate discourse frames people as organizational automatons, formulaically complying, to the letter, with regulatory items. As one relationship manager expressed it, 'The sad thing . . . is that all that regulation does . . . is that we tick boxes or we fill in forms' (Interview 16).

Unlike the other three kinds of discourse, in which people adapt regulations according to an underlying logic of common sense (as in trust-based interactions typical to the myth discourse), self-interest (as in game-like interactions) or rationality, the fate discourse turns towards blind compliance. As a consequence, there is no dynamic struggle between the hegemonic rationality logic and a counter-hegemonic logic. Non-compliance is not an option in such an automatic logic. In the absence of any normative reference, compliance is elevated to a normative value in itself. Accordingly, the relationship manager quoted above elaborated further:

> I don't know whether we have much choice. Because many of the pressures that arrive on our desk come from on high. There is an element – I use the expression of JFDI – 'just f****** do it' . . . or you needn't bother to come in to work next year. That kind of thing. (Interview 16)

Despite its passive and fundamentally pessimistic nature, the fate discourse also breeds the (re-)production of formalization and professionalization – the centripetal forces of rationalistic regulation. The fate discourse embodies the fatal view that every regulation is prone to failure. Problems are solved by blindly adapting regulations without any underlying justification and without participating in an active search for a good solution. This facilitates further regulation and professionalization.

The passivity of human agency and the absence of a normative frame of reference beyond formal compliance engender what I call blind compliance in interactions. I call it blind because no normative grounding is present to guide everyday practices of (non-)compliance. The absence of a normative grounding paves the way for functional disruptions in everyday practices. Functional disruptions are paradoxical organizational phenomena in which strict compliance might jeopardize the original intentions of a regulatory requirement. Discarding the rationalist underpinning of a regulation without replacing it with another normative logic makes the results of interactions unpredictable. The consequence of a new regulation can be an increase in risk, rather than a decrease. A general manager voiced his concerns about it this way:

> The biggest risk is that you try making the banking business more secure and in the end, you increase the inherent risk, because people start switching off their minds. (Interview 8)

With the phrase 'switching off their minds' this manager refers to the absence of a normative value, one that could adapt regulation to concrete everyday situations through a dynamic discursive struggle. The lack of a compensatory counter-hegemonic noise that we witnessed within the other discourses leaves the organization vulnerable to failures and thus contributes to the expectations gap of banking regulation.

DISCUSSION

I have condensed the complexity of everyday practices of (non-)compliance into four discourses of regulation and examined their dynamic struggles with the hegemonic rationality discourse of regulations. Each discourse opens the expectations gap of regulation through its centrifugal forces; at the same time, it closes the gap by bolstering the hegemonic position of the rationalist regulatory logic through its centripetal forces.

For analytical purposes, I treated each discourse in isolation, but any such approach inevitably leads to a simplification of the complexity of everyday practices. The separate treatment of the four discourses separates what people experience as dynamically interconnected. In the face of this heuristic device of disconnection, a question about contingency arose: Do the four identified categories truly represent four organizational discourses, or are the discourses merely representations of idiosyncratic situations or individual persons? By investigating the heteroglossic nature – that is, the simultaneous presence of contradictory but mutually reinforcing discourses – I found that all four discourses appeared during the course of every single interview. Typically, the managers I interviewed enacted various discourses in the same line of argumentation without displaying an obvious sense of rupture. I found that the apparent absence of discursive coherence in reasoning about regulation was a defining characteristic of everyday practices of (non-)compliance. Therefore, the heteroglossic nature of regulation is characterized not only by the mere co-existence of various (non-)compliance discourses within everyday practice, but by their simultaneous presence in a state of contradictory tensions.

The simultaneous presence of centripetal and centrifugal forces in everyday practices of (non-)compliance helps to explain both the existence and the persistence of the expectations gap of banking regulation. While the rationalist conception of regulation as an impersonal, quasi-scientific process for structuring everyday practice can hardly hold up in the face of ample evidence of deviance, malfunctioning, irrationalities and inefficiencies, my discourse analysis showed that these managers consistently accepted the rationality basis throughout our interviews and rarely made any serious attempt to question regulation as an organizational concept. In other words, the expectations gap is clearly visible, but it also stands on a very solid foundation.

Opening the Gap . . .

To resolve the heteroglossic tensions that underpin the expectations gap, managers typically used the practice of decoupling reified regulation from the discursive (re-)constructing process. Arguably, then, the discursive mechanism of decoupling – and thus the expectations gap itself – is grounded not only in the counter-hegemonic discourses, but also in the hegemonic rationality discourse itself. The rationality discourse starts with the assumption that one objective best way exists for doing everyday work, an approach that is independent of any personal adaptation. Once regulations are designed, they are thought to take on a life of their own. Its discursive mechanism of depersonalization and of 'de-concretization' leaves the rationality discourse looking like an untouchable truth despite the 'reality' that regulation can be dysfunctional, irrational or inefficient.

When the managers talked about abstract organizational themes, they consistently upheld the rationalistic concept that regulations are generally applicable. They switched discourses, however, when they discussed concrete and particular situations connected with everyday practices. This decoupling of the general and abstract regulations from the concrete and particular practices appeared, for example, as one manager used discursive hedges while recounting experiences that openly contradict the rationality logic of the formal structure:

> Yes, I can see the need to regulate, I can see the need to combat money launder-ing, I can see the need [to ensure] that we are not selling people duff investments, I can see the need to be able to provide the reason for doing a transaction. But I do think somewhere the actual art of banking has been forgotten. (Interview 16)

I noticed another way to decouple everyday practices from the impersonal realm of regulation: managers tended to ascribe a deficiency to a concrete everyday practice instead of questioning the underlying rationality logic of the given regulation. They typically compared how things are done to how they should be done. By establishing the rationalistic reference structure as good and the actual situation in everyday practice as bad, they again elevated regulation to an untouchable hegemonic position.

This open contradiction between the discursive patterns in everyday practices and the respected status of the rationality discourse of regu-lation is central for understanding the discursive underpinning of the expectations gap. Decoupling regulation from everyday practices is a key discursive mechanism for reconciling open contradictions. Arguably, this discursive decoupling is the very source of the hegemonic power of the rationality discourse in regulation. An everyday expression of this decou-pling is the saying that the exception proves the rule. Evidence contradict-ing the hegemonic logic of regulation is typically declared to be irrelevant or an idiosyncratic point that does not disprove the value of regulation. On the contrary, decoupling everyday practices of (non-)compliance from an objective and transcendent truth strengthens the hegemonic position of regulation.

... and Bridging the Gap

The phenomenon of decoupling regulation from everyday practices may explain how people ward off discursive challenges and therefore how the expectations gap opens up. The decoupling does not offer any explanation about how regulations effectively structure everyday practices. In short: How can everyday practices be reconnected to regulation in the face of this apparent decoupling?

This reconnection is arguably the main underlying function of all four discourses in their everyday encounters with regulation. Paradoxically, the counter-hegemonic seeds in the game, myth and fate discourses help to reconcile contradictory evidence rather than fundamentally challenging the hegemonic rationality discourse. I found multiple examples in which a 'creative' or even non-compliant engagement with regulation, based on common sense or self-interest, did not undermine a rule in a specific situation; in fact it effectively ensured the very intentions, the spirit, of that rule. Illustrative is the relationship manager's statement that I introduced above:

> the bit that goes beyond the [regulatory requirements]: filling in all the soft details that create a picture, a consistent picture that makes sense to someone, so that I actually can say, I do trust this guy. (Interview 16)

The plurality of discourses allows managers to flexibly reconnect the complexities of everyday experience with the rationality of regulation. This heteroglossic essence of everyday practices of (non-)compliance stabilizes or even strengthens the hegemonic position of rationalistic regulation. In that sense, the rationalistic regulation depends directly on the irrationalities of the game, myth and fate discourses which allow managers to flexibly handle the variations, malfunctions, irrationalities or inefficiencies of regulation that they encounter in everyday practice.

Thus, a key characteristic of the expectations gap is the complex nature of the centripetal and centrifugal forces revolving around a hegemonic rationality discourse. As practices of (non-)compliance exist at the intersection of centripetal and centrifugal forces, they continuously reproduce the heteroglossic diversity and thus the expectations gap of banking regulation. However, from a heteroglossic perspective, the continuous reproduction of the expectations gap is not bad news. The heteroglossic nature of contradictory but mutually constitutive discourses helps people cope with the complexities and idiosyncrasies of everyday practices. It often lifts the rationalistic blinders to allow people to muddle through the mess of everydayness – and thus helps organizations work.

CONCLUSION

In this chapter, I have discussed the expectations gap in banking regulation, the gap between the high public expectations of 'good' banking regulation and the ample evidence of malfunctioning, irrationalities or inefficiencies in everyday practices. Starting from a heteroglossic conception of organizations, I have conceived of banking regulation as an overarching organizational language that breaks down into four different organizational discourses. I have shown, the contradictory but mutually constitutive nature of these four discourses in the micro-processes of everyday practices of (non-)compliance with regulations. By framing the organization as heteroglossic, I believe I have contributed to an understanding of how banking regulation works in everyday practice and how the expectations gap is constantly (re-)constructed in a dynamic struggle. Looking through a heteroglossic lens at the Great Financial Crisis, I return to the thoughts of Martin Hellwig (2010) I cited at the beginning: Is it in fact 'enough to tighten a screw here and put in a new nail there?' Maybe the 'entire ship of banking regulation' does 'need a thorough overhaul'. The heteroglossic conception of banking regulation offers interesting insights for understanding regulation. My focus on practices in analysing banking regulation makes it possible to move beyond the theoretical distinction between formal structure and everyday action. Once we better understand the micro-processes of everyday practices of (non-)compliance, we understand that attempts to micro-regulate these practices tend to be more difficult than commonly assumed. On the negative side, centrifugal forces are moulding regulations into their respective logics and thus undermine the rationalist expectations that people have of regulations. On the positive side, compensatory discursive logics are available that can step into the breach of regulatory shortcomings. As a result, taking the heteroglossic nature of everyday practices of (non-)compliance into account might not close the expectations gap, but it might help to adapt regulatory expectations to it.

REFERENCES

Abolafia, Mitchel (2010), 'The institutional embeddedness of market failure: Why speculative bubbles still occur', in Michael Lounsbury and Paul M. Hirsch (eds), *Markets on Trial: The Economic Sociology of the U.S. Financial Crisis*, Bingley: Emerald, pp. 177–200.

Alasuutari, Pertti (1995), *Researching Culture: Qualitative Method and Cultural Studies*, London: Sage.

Argyris, Chris and Donald Schön (1974), *Theory in Practice*, San Francisco, CA: Jossey-Bass.

Bakhtin, Mikhail M. (1981), *The Dialogic Imagination*, Austin, TX: University of Texas Press.

Bakhtin, Mikhail M. (1986), *Speech, Genres and Other Late Essays*, Austin, TX: University of Texas Press.

Borio, Claudio E.V. (2014), 'Monetary policy and financial stability: What role in prevention and recovery?' *BIS Working Paper*, **440**, Basel: Bank for International Settlements.

Bouwen, René and Chris Steyaert (1999), 'From a dominant voice toward multi-voiced cooperation: Mediating metaphors for global change', in David L. Cooperider and Jane E. Dutton (eds), *Organizational Dimensions of Global Change: No Limits to Cooperation*, Thousand Oaks, CA: Sage, pp. 291–319.

Browning, Larry D. and Robert Folger (1994), 'Communication under conditions of litigation risk: A grounded theory of plausible deniability in the Iran-Contra affair', in Sim B. Sitkin and Robert J. Bies (eds), *The Legalistic Organization*, Thousand Oaks, CA: Sage, pp. 251–280.

Brunsson, Nils (1993), 'Ideas and actions: Justification and hypocrisy as alternatives to control', *Accounting, Organizations and Society*, **18** (6), 489–506.

Brunsson, Nils (2003), 'Organized hypocrisy', in Barbara Czarniawska and Guje Sevón (eds), *The Northern Lights: Organization Theory in Scandinavia*, Oslo: Copenhagen Business School Press, pp. 201–222.

Chia, Robert (2000), 'Discourse analysis as organisational analysis', *Organization*, **7** (3), 513–518.

Clark, Katerina and Michael Holquist (1984), *Mikhail Bakhtin*, Cambridge, MA: Harvard University Press.

Eckstein, Asaf (2014), 'Great expectations: The peril of an expectations gap in proxy advisory firm regulation', *Delaware Journal of Corporate Law (DJCL)*, **40** (1).

Edelman, Lauren (1990), 'Legal environments and organizational governance: The expansion of due process in the American workplace', *American Journal of Sociology*, **95** (4), 1401–1440.

Edelman, Lauren and Mark Suchman (1997), 'The legal environments of organizations', *Annual Review of Sociology*, **23**, 479–515.

Feldman Martha S. and Alan J. Levy (1994), 'Effects of legal context on decision making under ambiguity', in Sim B. Sitkin and Robert J. Bies (eds), *The Legalistic Organization*, Thousand Oaks: Sage, pp. 109–136.

Foster, John B. and Fred Magdoff (2009), *The Great Financial Crisis: Causes and Consequences*, New York: Monthly Review Press.

Froschauer, Ulrike and Manfred Lueger (2003), *Das qualitative Interview*, Vienna: WUV-Universitäts-verlag.

Giddens, Anthony (1984), *The Constitution of Society*, Cambridge: Polity.

Guillén, Mauro F. and Sandra L. Suárez (2010), 'The Global Crisis of 2007–2009: Markets, politics, and organizations', in Michael Lounsbury and Paul M. Hirsch (eds), *Markets on Trial: The Economic Sociology of the U.S. Financial Crisis*, Bingley: Emerald, pp. 257–279.

Hellwig, Martin (2010), 'Capital regulation after the crisis: Business as usual?', *Preprints*, (31), Bonn: Max Planck Institute for Research on Collective Goods.

Holquist, Michael (1990), *Dialogism: Bakhtin and His World*, London: Routledge.

Holstein, James A. and Jaber F. Gubrium (1995), *The Active Interview*, Thousand Oaks, CA: Sage.

Langevoort, Donald C. (2003), 'Managing the "expectations gap" in investor protection: The SEC and the post-Enron reform agenda', *Villanova Law Review*, **48** (4), 1139–1165.

Liggio, Carl D. (1974), 'The expectation gap: The accountant's Waterloo', *Journal of Contemporary Business*, **3** (3), 27–44.

Meyer, John W. and Brian Rowan (1977), 'Institutionalized organizations: Formal structure as myth and ceremony', *The American Journal of Sociology*, **83** (2), 340–363.

Perrow, Charles (1984), *Normal Accidents: Living with High-Risk Technologies*, Princeton, NJ: Princeton University Press.

Pfyl, Roland (2010), *Formality at Work: Organisational Discourses of Formality in Everyday Management at a Swiss Private Bank*, Norderstedt: Books on Demand.

Porter, Brenda (1993), 'An empirical study of the audit expectation-performance gap', *Accounting and Business Research*, **24** (93), 49–68.

Power, Michael (2004), *The Risk Management of Everything: Rethinking the Politics of Uncertainty*, London: Demos.

Rubtsova, Anna, Rich DeJordy, Marry Ann Glynn and Mayer Zald (2010), 'The social construction of causality: The effects of institutional myths on financial regulation', in Michael Lounsbury and Paul M. Hirsch (eds), *Markets on Trial: The Economic Sociology of the U.S. Financial Crisis*, Bingley: Emerald, pp. 201–244.

Schatzki, Theodore, Karin Knorr Cetina and Eike von Savigny (eds) (2001), *The Practice Turn in Contemporary Theory*, New York: Routledge.

Schneiberg, Marc and Tim Bartley (2010), 'Regulating and redesigning finance: Market architectures, normal accidents and dilemmas of regulatory reform', in Michael Lounsbury and Paul M. Hirsch (eds), *Markets on Trial: The Economic Sociology of the U.S. Financial Crisis*, Bingley: Emerald, pp. 281–308.

Sitkin, Sim B. and Robert J. Bies (eds) (1994), *The Legalistic Organization*, Thousand Oaks, CA: Sage.

Steyaert, Chris (2004), 'The prosaics of entrepreneurship', in Daniel Hjorth and Chris Steyaert (eds), *Narrative and Discursive Approaches in Entrepreneurship: A Second Movements in Entrepreneurship Book*, Cheltenham, UK and Northampton, MA, USA: Edward Elgar Publishing, pp. 8–21.

Valsiner, Jaan (1991), 'Building theoretical bridges over a lagoon of everyday events', *Human Development*, **34** (5), 307–315.

Vaughan, Diane (2005), *The Challenger Launch Decision. Risky Technology, Culture, and Deviance at NASA*, Chicago, IL: The University of Chicago Press.

10. Anticipating intended users: prospective sensemaking in technology development

Claus D. Jacobs, Chris Steyaert and Florian Ueberbacher

INTRODUCTION

How do developers and designers of a new technology make sense of those who are expected to use it? In information systems development (ISD), user-centred development methods assume that user-centredness improves both the process and the outcome of an ISD effort, in terms of actual users adopting the system as expected. While a *user involvement* perspective refers to the activities *of actual users* in ISD processes, a *user focus* perspective is concerned with identifying and representing *intended users*. Thus if we are to better understand user focus, we need to understand and conceptualize the ways that *intended users* are being anticipated by key stakeholders in the technology development process.

Using a perspective based on the social construction of technology (SCOT), we offer a social constructionist approach to understand *intended users*. We conceptualize the way that designers and developers anticipate intended users as a form of *prospective* sensemaking. We then ask: *How do key stakeholders in technology development – such as developers and designers – make sense of intended users?*

We examine the prospective sensemaking of four key stakeholder communities involved in developing grid technology in the Grid of E-SciencE (EGEE) project, a pan-European project headquartered at the European Organization for Nuclear Research (CERN). Through our analysis we identify four distinct prospective sensemaking narratives about grid computing (the grid as saviour, as resource option, as cost saver, and as European integrator) as well as four corresponding conceptions of intended users: the grid user as author, exegete, translator, and reader. In turn, these four conceptions of intended users can be considered ideal types that differ with respect to two dimensions: the *intended possibility of inscribing user needs into the technological artefact* and the *intended scope of the application domain.* Based on these two dimensions, we then propose that user anticipation is an antecedent of user focus and aim to systematize the concept, offering both a corresponding terminology and an initial step towards developing a generic typology of intended user concepts.

THEORETICAL BACKGROUND

Why Intended Users Matter in Technology Development

Users matter in technology development. Over the last 30 years or so, especially during the early stages of information system development (ISD), they became more and more interesting and recognized (Barki and Hartwick, 1989). Accordingly, scholars of ISD have paid considerable attention to user-centred development approaches (Barki and Hartwick, 1994; Hartwick and Barki, 1994; Iivari and Iivari, 2011; Spears and Barki, 2010). Most broadly, user-centred development methods are grounded in the assumption that such approaches increase the quality of both the process and the outcome of an ISD effort (Harris and Weistroffer, 2009; Iivari, Isomäki and Pekkola, 2010; Markus and Mao, 2004). Specifically, an ISD effort is considered to be of high quality if 'the *intended users . . .* adopt the system, use it as expected, and/or use it with the desired effects' (Markus and Mao, 2004, p. 525; our emphasis).

Loaded with a variety of meanings, the concept of user-centredness has recently been discussed in terms of two perspectives most relevant to our endeavour: user involvement and user focus (Iivari and Iivari, 2011). The *user involvement* perspective has been most broadly referred to as the activities and behaviours of *actual users* during ISD processes (Barki and Hartwick, 1989; Iivari et al., 2010; Markus and Mao, 2004). The systematic challenges of this strand of user-centredness include the overall rationale for involving users and the modus operandi of user involvement (Iivari and Iivari, 2011).

Related, yet distinct, the *user focus* perspective initially referred to the ideal of fully satisfying every user's needs and requirements. Such an ideal faces practical limitations such as total numbers of users, their geographical spread, and their heterogeneity in general. In turn, this situation has led developers to consider design strategies that depend on a 'fictive user' or 'hypothetical archetype' (Iivari and Iivari, 2011, p. 130). Thus, the main challenge for the user focus perspective is to identify and represent *intended users* since 'an information system is not successful if it is not used by its *intended users'* and 'failure to get the *intended users* to use the system may be fatal to an organization' (Iivari et al., 2010, p. 110; our emphasis).

A Social Constructionist Perspective on Intended Users

Proponents of social studies of technology and science (STS) in general (Dawson et al., 2000; MacKenzie and Wajcman, 1999; Wajcman, 2002) and especially those who hold the SCOT view (Pinch and Bijker, 1987) have suggested that, in the early stages of development, a technology and its intended users are subject to processes of discursive meaning negotiations. Oudshoorn and Pinch (2003) focus specifically on how the concept of intended users is socially constructed. In particular, such a view conceives of 'users as *imagined* by the designers of a technology' (Oudshoorn, Rommes and Stienstra, 2004, p. 31). These initial ideas and images of intended users are at the core of what we conceive of as anticipating the intended user: 'technologists *anticipate* the interests, skills, motives, and behaviour of future users' (Oudshoorn and Pinch, 2003, p. 9; our emphasis; on a related note see Rau et al., 2012). Pointing to the interpretive flexibility of intended users, Oudshoorn et al. (2004, p. 37) assert that 'design practices are usually characterized by the construction of a wide variety of (sometimes conflicting) user representations that are intentionally (or unintentionally) produced by a variety of actors, including policy makers, designers, producers, marketers, journalists, and test users'.

It is crucial to understand how these different concepts of intended users come into being, because if 'the user representations incorporated into the artefact fail to match the actual users, it is very likely that the technology will fail' (Oudshoorn et al., 2004, p. 31).

The Anticipation of Intended Users as Prospective Sensemaking

We propose that when designers and developers of a new technology anticipate a conception of their intended users, they engage in a form of *prospective* sensemaking (Cornelissen and Clarke, 2010; Gioia and Mehra, 1996). Most broadly, sensemaking refers to a process of interpreting and generating meaning in order to develop 'a coherent account of what is going on' (Fiss and Hirsch, 2005, p. 31) and to turn 'circumstances into a situation that is comprehended explicitly in words and that serves as a springboard into action' (Taylor and van Every, 2000, p. 40). Albeit more tentative than its retrospective 'cousin', prospective sensemaking is 'an attempt to make sense for the future' and aims at 'creating meaningful opportunities for the future' (Gioia and Mehra, 1996, p. 1229). The content of such prospective sensemaking is concerned with two concepts. The first is what Leonardi

(2011, p. 347) referred to as a *technology concept*: 'an innovator's vision of what functionality the built technology (the technological artefact) should have' (p. 349). Second, and fundamental, is the *user concept*: the vision that a designer, developer or other technology development stakeholder has of the intended user. Summarizing the above conceptual considerations, our research question is: *How do key stakeholders in technology development (such as developers and designers) make sense of intended users?*

METHODOLOGY

Empirical Context of Case Study

We selected the case of grid computing, a precursor of the currently much hyped and popularized cloud computing. It is an approach to high-performance distributed computing that relies on sharing resources within and between communities. We ground our analysis in data gathered between July 2004 and August 2006 within the European EGEE project, funded by the European Commission (EC) and concerned with establishing a pan-European multi-science grid infrastructure headquartered at CERN. Between 2004 and 2010, EGEE was the largest computing infrastructure project funded by the EC (www.eu-egee.org). By April 2010, EGEE ended and the distributed computing infrastructure developed within and through EGEE is now supported and maintained by the European Grid Infrastructure (www.egi.eu). As a not-yet stabilized technology 'under construction', we selected grid computing as our case based on its theoretical relevance; we used it to focus on the prospective sensemaking in four distinct communities of the EGEE project. These were high-energy physicists (HEP); scientists from other disciplines (identified by project jargon as 'non-HEP'); IT service providers such as IBM, Atos Origin and EDS; and the EC as funder of the project.

In the early 2000s, based on CERN's computational needs, the EC acknowledged the need for a large-scale, transdisciplinary grid infrastructure; therefore it funded the EGEE project with the aim of having more than 90 institutes from over 30 countries collaboratively develop a single grid computing infrastructure for multiple scientific uses. Initially, two pilot applications were selected to guide the implementation of the evolving technological infrastructure and certify its performance and functionality. One was the Large Hadron Collider Computing Grid (LCG) supporting high-energy physics experiments at CERN; the other was biomedicine, reflecting the need for high-level computation in biomedical treatment and diagnosis. At the time we gathered our data, other so-called scientific 'non-HEP' communities, including computational chemistry, geosciences, and fusion, were joining EGEE. HEP and non-HEP thus formed two of our four communities. Early on, a further distinct community was invited to join EGEE: industry partners in the form of large IT service providers such as IBM, EDS or Atos Origin. The fourth community we tracked was the EC as the funding body of the entire project. All four communities experienced high degrees of ambiguity and uncertainty and thus engaged in prospective sensemaking regarding both the technology concept and the user concept.

Data Collection

Sensemaking can be reconstructed from a variety of data (Maitlis, 2005). Thus, we used semi-structured interviews with informants from these four distinct EGEE communities as our primary source of data, along with archival data and field notes, to contextualize and continuously refine our analysis.

Over the course of two years, we conducted three rounds of semi-structured interviews with members of the four EGEE communities. In each round we met with six to eight members of the HEP and non-HEP communities, three to four from industry, and two from the EC, for a total of 56 interviews. The first author conducted all the interviews; he began by asking informants general questions about their professional role in general and within EGEE in particular, then focused on the specific nature of that work and contribution as well as their community's specific expectations and requirements for grid computing. The interviews, each lasting 45 to 80 minutes and based on prior informed consent, were digitally recorded and transcribed verbatim.

Seeking secondary data to contextualize and refine our analysis, we supplemented these core data with archival data. These included EGEE project proposals; presentations at EGEE conferences, industry forums and user forums; and the websites of the EGEE, the EC, and grid vendors. We also observed EGEE project office meetings, workshops, EU progress reviews, and three major grid technology conferences in The Hague, Athens and Geneva, as well as the first grid user forum in Geneva.

Analytic Procedure: Narrative Analysis

Various authors have suggested that sensemaking is fundamentally made up of, and relies on, narratives (Maitlis, 2005; Pentland, 1999; Sonenshein, 2010; Weick, 1995); therefore we employ techniques from the elaborate toolkit of narrative analysis to structure our investigation of prospective sensemaking. Narrative has been conceptualized as a 'discursive construction that actors use as a tool to shape their own understanding (sensemaking)' (Sonenshein, 2010, p. 480). Among the main properties that Pentland (1999, pp. 712–713) suggests, we focus particularly on two that are most relevant for our research questions: the concepts of a 'focal actor' and an 'evaluative frame of reference'. In conjunction with a narrative's temporal sequence, the *focal actor* is what provides a story with continuity and an integrative thread. Although not always fully developed, protagonists and often antagonists are those elements of a story that are typically credited with agency (Pentland, 1999, p. 714). For instance, we anticipate that as designers and developers create their prospective sensemaking narratives, they may credit both the technology concept and the intended user concept with agency; thus either concept, or both, can take on the role of a focal actor. A second important element of a prospective sensemaking narrative is the *evaluative frame of reference* since narratives 'embody a sense of what is right and wrong, appropriate or inappropriate' and provide 'standards against which actions of the characters can be judged', and thus 'can provide a window onto the values of a cultural group' (Pentland, 1999, p. 716).

In narrative analytical procedures, the 'collective constructions of meanings' in compound narratives (Sonenshein, 2010, p. 479) have been shown to effectively summarize a large, narrative dataset as well as to credibly account for the major semantic trajectories in a given dataset (Currie and Brown, 2003; Dunford and Jones, 2000; Sonenshein, 2010). Thus, the goal of our narrative analysis is to identify different types of intended users within these main compound narratives.

FIELD ANALYSIS: FOUR PROSPECTIVE SENSEMAKING NARRATIVES AND THEIR FOCAL ACTORS

In our dataset we identified four prospective sensemaking narratives that are distinct in terms of their evaluative frame of reference and their focal actors. These are the grid as 'saviour', 'resource option', 'cost saver', and 'European integrator'. In the following sections, we reconstruct these four prospective sensemaking narratives and describe the focal actors in terms of both their technology concept and their user concept. Our first-order findings culminate in a case-specific set of focal actors, namely the intended user as 'author'; 'exegete'; 'translator' and 'reader'. Table 10.1 summarizes our findings of this section. From these first-order findings, we conclude an initial typology of intended users, which we outline and discuss in detail in the subsequent discussion section.

Table 10.1 Summary of prospective sensemaking narratives

Prospective sensemaking narrative		I Grid as saviour for HEP	II Grid as option for non-HEP	III Grid as cost saver	IV Grid as European integrator
Authoring community		HEP	Non-HEP	IT service providers	European commission
Evaluative frame of reference	Core problem identified	Performance: speed and storage capacity	Switching cost/benefit; data security	Cost considerations and data security	Digital divide within EU and competitiveness of EU
	Main criterion of goodness	'A fast and reliable IT infrastructure is critical to the success of the LHC mission at CERN.'	'Non-HEP scientists might gain from the grid but are sceptical about the costs of switching.'	'Reducing IT costs leads to higher margins for us and our clients.'	'Pan-European science and technology projects foster European integration and competitiveness.'
Focal actors	Technology concept	Saviour	Resource option	Cost saver	European Integrator
	Intended user concept	Author	Exegete	Translator	Reader

224

Prospective Sensemaking Narrative I: The Grid as Saviour

This narrative revolves around the idea that grid computing is the pivotal technology that is enabled by the Large Hadron Collider at CERN to produce grand scientific results; thus it is mainly authored through the high-energy physics community at CERN. (Figures 10.1 and 10.2 offer exemplars of our data structures; analogous figures II through IV are available from the authors.)

Evaluative frame of reference of narrative I
The frame of reference of this narrative is based on the premise that societal – or even human – progress ultimately results from insights derived from science on a grand scale. Examining the narrative sequence of this narrative, we identified four core components. First, since *grand science* is likely to advance humanity's progress, CERN's *LHC, as one of the most prominent physics experiments*, must not fail. Hence, an effective and reliable *grid computing infrastructure is indispensable for the HEP community* at CERN. In particular, such an infrastructure needs to live up to the *high capacity demands and requirements* of the HEP community. Finally, the people most likely to live up to the challenging development tasks are the *highly skilled scientists-turned-developers within the HEP community*.

Such a large-scale technology challenge can – supposedly – only be handled by people with expertise in large-scale, pioneering science:

> There are all these other grids; every university has its grid, but they are just toys. For researchers, they play and do this and that. The LHC grid is the only grid which really has to work – it must work! In this sense, it is the only serious grid at the moment. (LCG developer at CERN)

On a similar note, a senior HEP scientist admitted that his team uses only a negligible 'quantity of technical aspects developed by other disciplines'.

Focal actors of narrative I
Technology concept: The grid as saviour of HEP. The immediate technical problem of HEP – providing high-capacity computing for a physics experiment – is legitimized through a broader premise: that in finding 'God's particle', humanity will be in a position not only to understand nature ('everything around us') but ultimately 'us' ourselves. Narrated in this broader trajectory, the grid as focal actor gains the status of almost a saviour-like figure; without it, the entire endeavour – and thus the prospect of an ultimate explanation of nature and human existence – could vanish. In turn, such a focal actor requires a corresponding concept of the intended user.

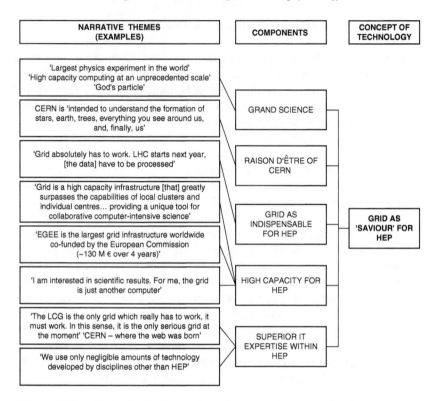

Figure 10.1 Narrative I: Exemplary data structure of technology concept

Intended user concept: Grid user as author. Within this narrative the intended user of grid computing is suggested as a developer-user who is 'naturally' an expert in HEP. Thus, the concept of the user emerges as speakers point to HEP as the intended primary user community: a community of people with superior knowledge in both scientific and computing terms. This exclusivity among the intended users obviously brings with it the risk of excluding other potential users. The concept of an expert developer-user as the intended user of grid computing deliberately dilutes the established dichotomy between user and developer in portraying the *HEP community as the grid's intended main user.* As an officer of the EC admitted, 'frankly, this whole project . . . is all really set up largely with the LHC project in mind'. Similarly, a particle physicist and senior EGEE project officer observed that 'The four LHC experiments are currently the main users of the grid'.

Thus, the concept of the intended user as a focal actor who is constructed as substantively shaping the meaning generation – in this case, literally

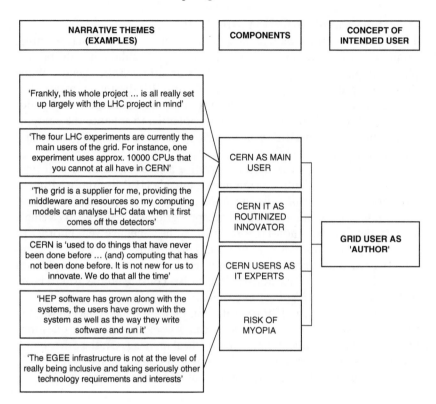

NARRATIVE THEMES (EXAMPLES)	COMPONENTS	CONCEPT OF INTENDED USER

'Frankly, this whole project ... is all really set up largely with the LHC project in mind'

'The four LHC experiments are currently the main users of the grid. For instance, one experiment uses approx. 10000 CPUs that you cannot at all have in CERN'

CERN AS MAIN USER

'The grid is a supplier for me, providing the middleware and resources so my computing models can analyse LHC data when it first comes off the detectors'

CERN IT AS ROUTINIZED INNOVATOR

CERN is 'used to do things that have never been done before ... (and) computing that has not been done before. It is not new for us to innovate. We do that all the time'

CERN USERS AS IT EXPERTS

GRID USER AS 'AUTHOR'

'HEP software has grown along with the systems, the users have grown with the system as well as the way they write software and run it'

RISK OF MYOPIA

'The EGEE infrastructure is not at the level of really being inclusive and taking seriously other technology requirements and interests'

Figure 10.2   Narrative I: Exemplary data structure of intended user concept

writing the grid artefact using software code – can best be conceptualized as an author.

Narrative II: Grid as Resource Option

This narrative is mainly authored by members of scientific communities including bioinformatics, earth science, and plasma physics; it revolves around these communities' efforts to appreciate the grid's contribution to their respective analytic challenges. While each of these disciplines has its distinct scientific identity, these differences were glossed over by the EGEE jargon that refers to them colloquially as 'non-HEP' sciences. For pragmatic reasons, and in accepting HEP as their point of reference, most non-HEP scientists eventually self-identified with this label.

Evaluative frame of reference of narrative II

This narrative's frame of reference is based on the premise that scientific results contribute to societal progress at large – although only plasma physics might come anywhere near HEP's grand scientific agenda. While the diversity and geographical spread of non-HEP disciplines creates less urgency to develop a joint computing resource, the main criterion of goodness regarding grid computing lies in its potential to enhance the computing resources for non-HEP sciences, as long as concerns about privacy and security can be provided for.

The narrative sequence of this narrative also exists in several distinct core components. Scientific communities outside HEP, like those within it, strive for *scientific results that might be enhanced through additional computing resources*. While HEP could accept a grid oriented towards a single science, the EC urged non-HEP scientists to become involved, in order to direct the project *towards a multi-science grid*. Thus, while the HEP community needed the participation of non-HEP communities to comply with EC funding requirements, non-HEP scientists considered the grid to be *an additional, but not critical, resource option*.

For many in the non-HEP scientific community, a main concern was the then unresolved *issues of data security and privacy*, especially for questions like how to handle patient data in biomedical imaging. On the other hand, enhancing security through encryption would come at the *expense of the grid's computing speed* – a core criterion of goodness for those in HEP.

Focal actors of narrative II

Technology concept: Grid as resource option. For most non-HEP scientists, the grid remained a resource option in which the actual costs of switching and the associated risks of changing the information technology were balanced against the grid's potential for improved performance. The initial relationship in which the grid was a solution to a specific scientific community's analytical problem became inverted here; now it became a solution in search of a problem. As a European Commission officer observed, 'for a long time EGEE I was actually the HEP grid, to put it bluntly. In the first contract, they had biology, but it was always the follower'.

Intended user concept: Grid user as exegete. This narrative mainly constructs the intended user as a test bed of grid computing. It mobilizes concepts such as non-HEP science as follower; solution in search of a problem; slow uptake in non-HEP scientific communities; non-HEP users as lay users; and lack of skills and community characteristics. Especially when we juxtapose HEP with non-HEP, we see that the implied lack of skills, in conjunction with the supposedly 'wrong' characteristics for a scientific community, are further characteristics in constructing the intended

user as test bed. As a senior HEP physicist put it, 'While HEP has traditionally been set up very well in large organizations, it naturally fits into
the role of a virtual organization, and biomedicine fits much less so. There
are problems involved in actually forming a biomed virtual organization.'
In contrast to the view of the HEP developer-user, in this intended user
concept they are viewed as separate. Thus, the test bed user is someone
for whom a technology is being designed: 'From what I know, I think
there are currently no normal biologists using the grid in their daily business' (EGEE officer). Such users are considered secondary because their
research agenda is supposedly less relevant, and also because it contributes
less to the development of the grid as a whole.

A focal actor who is constructed as not initially authoring, but as critically interpreting or explaining a text to others – in this case, grid software
code in action – can best be conceptualized as an exegete.

Narrative III: Grid as Cost Saver

Authored by IT service providers, this narrative revolves around the relevance of grid computing for cost-efficient use of IT infrastructures. In contrast to the first two narratives, this one is authored by EGEE's industry
partners, including ATOS Origin, IBM, and EDS.

Evaluative frame of reference of narrative III

The frame of reference is fundamentally based on an economic consideration that seeks at least to increase resource efficiency, and at best to
maximize return on invested capital. Sharing resources, for instance by
outsourcing computing power and data storage to IT service providers,
is a 'natural' cost saver. But in any such outsourcing process, it is crucial
to protect the technology's privacy and security in order to protect trade
secrets and client data.

The narrative sequence of this narrative involves three core components.
First, IT costs are mainly driven by the *utilization rate of the invested IT
infrastructure*. Thus, a *commoditized IT usage* (for example, manifest by
IBM's 'on demand' slogan) would offer IT service providers and their
clients a new business model of IT service usage. And therefore sharing
the use of this infrastructure would help increase the rate at which the IT
investments were utilized.

Focal actors of narrative III

Technology concept: Grid as cost saver. Among the many possible ways to
make sense of the grid, this narrative focuses mainly, if not exclusively, on
its implications for cost-effective IT usage. Thus, the grid is conceptualized

as a 'next generation' form of IT usage: firms would not themselves be owners of IT infrastructure but could be on-demand users of an infra-structure owned, managed, and shared by a grid vendor or service provider.

Intended user concept: Grid user as translator. As one informant, a member of the EC staff, succinctly noted, 'the grid has not been designed with a user in mind'. With regard to this narrative, the intended user has been conceptualized, albeit implicitly or unconsciously, as a translator, one who mobilizes several dimensions such as *a technology in search of business users*; a *technology whose proof of concept is still outstanding*; and *lack of skill and capabilities*.

The non-scientific expert user is mainly constructed as speakers acknowl-edge that businesses are indeed interested in reducing the costs of IT but they remain sceptical about the technology. Thus, the grid technology needs someone to translate it to the end users among the IT service providers. A senior project officer reflected this search: 'we felt that we needed some refer-ences, some case studies, successful case studies to show that grid technology can be useful for business'. Equally, a senior manager of an IT service pro-vider emphasized that 'because grid technology has been pushed by the tech-nology people, it has not been demanded by the users'. The challenge for grid vendors to act as translators is evident in this consideration by an EC staff member: 'I do not think [the EC-funded grid projects] are really addressing industry needs; they don't talk industry language'. Most importantly for non-scientific expert users, they still have no proof of concept: 'We need to show what the grid could be for our customers' (CTO of a grid vendor).

Thus, we believe the concept of translator is the best way to conceptualize the intended user as focal actor who is constructed neither as author nor exegete but as transferring the meaning from a source to a target language – in this case, scientific grid applications to business applications.

Narrative IV: Grid as European Integrator

Mainly authored by officers of the European Commission, the main funding body of the EGEE project, this narrative revolves around the grid's potential contribution to European integration and to enhancing the EU's international competitiveness.

Evaluative frame of reference of narrative IV
This frame of reference is based on the prospect of a united and prosper-ing Europe. The EC grounds its funding policy on two main political goals: fostering Europe's integration and its international competitiveness. Thus, in funding a pan-European grid infrastructure it first aims to enable scien-tists to collaborate throughout Europe in both technological and scientific

terms. Second, and provided that industry will in fact adopt the grid as planned, the EC views it as one of the technologies that will place Europe on par with other major world regions.

The narrative sequence of this narrative is based on two elements. First, in its identity as a benevolent, politically oriented technology investor, the EC aims to support the development of grid computing as a democratizing and politically integrating technology. Second, in the middle term, it expects to gain economic and political dividends as the grid enhances European competitiveness. The constitutive components of this narrative include the *grid as an expert technology; keeping the end user ignorant* and a *slow uptake within a wider audience*. The concept of the intended user as a non-scientific lay user is close to the classic position of a passive recipient user of a technology, one that is typically portrayed as being driven by designers or developers.

Focal actors of narrative IV
Technology concept: Grid as European integrator. The political impetus of this narrative becomes evident as a senior officer of EGEE suggests that the grid is 'a democratic, collective computer network paradigm'. Furthermore, as a benevolent technology investor the EC anticipates political dividends including European *competitiveness* and *integration*. As an EC officer suggested, 'everything that we do – even in a research program in a pre-competitive stage . . . has to have as an object the competitiveness of European industry'. Furthermore, 'EGEE-II will reinforce its position, will act as a coordinating body for related grid projects, and will help reduce the "digital divide" between European States'.

Intended user concept: Grid user as reader. This narrative conceptualizes the intended grid user as exactly opposite to the HEP developer-user. In this narrative the user is a non-scientific lay user, or the reader of a technology who does not author the technology in any way. Put differently, the anticipated user is 'everybody'. Another key component in constructing the non-scientific lay user is the idea of keeping the end user deliberately ignorant. As a particle physicist observed: 'hiding the complexity is the key issue here'. An IT consultant confirmed this idea:

> What you see if you are a user is your particular business problem, screen and instructions. You don't understand anything – and you don't want to understand – of how it is managed in the grid. . . . All they see is the tablecloth and the applications. The dishes itself – the table itself – that structure is completely hidden by the tablecloth.

Thus, the focal actor is constructed as a passive recipient of a text, someone from whom the complexity of text production is deliberately hidden. Such a person is typically conceptualized as a reader.

DISCUSSION

Acknowledging that the intended users are highly relevant to a user focus perspective in ISD, we investigated the case of developing grid computing in the EGEE project in order to reconstruct how intended users were being conceptualized in the prospective sensemaking narratives of four communities that were key to the development process.

Through our analysis we identified four distinct prospective sensemaking narratives of these key stakeholders to conceptualize the technology of grid computing: they saw the grid as saviour, as resource option, as cost saver, and as European integrator. We also identified four conceptions of intended users: grid user as author, exegete, translator, and reader. While these four concepts of intended users are grounded in our analysis, we believe that they have broader relevance and can be considered ideal types of intended user concepts. As we demonstrated in describing our analysis, an intended user who is conceptualized as an author (such as an HEP scientist) is anticipated as having a comparatively high level of agency and autonomy, compared to a simple reader of a technology, who is to be somehow protected from having to see the complexity of a new technology. An intended user conceptualized as an exegete, such as a non-HEP scientist, is one who is not directly contributing to the development of the technological artefact but is crucial in explaining and demonstrating the technology's potential to others in a similar domain (in this case, their specific scientific community). Finally, an intended user conceived as a translator is anticipated as having even less influence over the technological artefact but carrying a higher burden: this user has to transfer the potential contribution from one domain (in our case, science) to another domain (in our case, business and industry).

As we reflected critically on the differences and commonalities of these four ideal types of intended users, we organized them in terms of an initial typology that is structured along two key dimensions. First, and as we demonstrated in the case, one dimension that differentiates the intended user concepts is the intended possibility of inscribing user needs into the technological artefact. For instance, HEP scientists as active specialists ('authors') consider the grid to be 'their' technology and thus believe they can legitimately claim to inscribe their needs into its software code. Equally, a passive generalist ('reader') has virtually no possibility of inscribing his or her needs into the artefact.

Second, the intended user concepts differ in the scope of the domain where their needs and interests will apply. While some intended users might be conceptualized as having a rather narrow domain, and thus be seen as specialists (such as HEP scientists or non-HEP scientists), others, such as

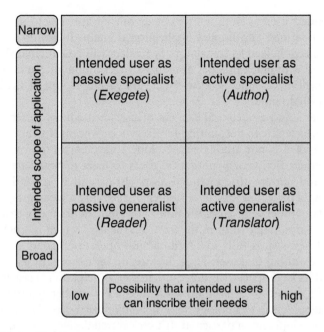

Figure 10.3   Typology of concepts of intended users

those in industry, and general lay users, might be anticipated as generalists involved in a broader domain.

Thus, we propose that those who are conceptualizing intended users will use two key aspects as they do so: the intended possibility of inscribing user needs into the technological artefact and the scope of the domain where the technology will be applied. Considering each of these two dimensions in turn, we see several ways that the four intended user concepts differ. An intended user seen as author will be anticipated with the comparatively highest possibility to inscribe user's needs into the technological artefact. The exact opposite is true if the intended user is seen as a reader: which will be granted the least possibility for inscription. Although not anticipated as inscribing user needs directly into the technological artefact, intended users such as the exegete and translator will have an indirect possibility through their hermeneutic power to explain and interpret the technology for others. Correspondingly, we suggest that the concepts of intended users will vary based on the possibility of their needs being inscribed into the artefact.

Equal differences apply to the second dimension: the intended scope of the application domain. In the early stages of technology development, intended application domains are typically rather narrow. Thus, an intended user as author or exegete will be anticipated as operating in a well-defined and limited application domain. In contrast, intended users conceptualized as translators or readers will be anticipated as being concerned with much broader domains. Correspondingly, we propose that the conceptions of intended users will vary with the scope of the intended application domain.

Further – and as a central element of user-centredness – user focus has been concerned with accounting for every user's needs. In acknowledging that this ideal is not attainable, developers have embarked on operating with average, fictive or hypothetical users to meet the challenge of identifying and representing intended users (Iivari and Iivari, 2011). In the early stages of technology development, specifying a clear user focus is a challenging process, because the notion of an intended user carries such a variety of meanings. In turn, the focus on the user, which is crucial if that user is to be successfully involved, should operate on solid assumptions and images about that user. Thus, drawing on the concept of user anticipation and its key aspects, we suggest that user anticipation is crucial to user focus. We set out to explore how intended users are being anticipated by key stakeholders in technology development in general, and in information system development in particular. If user-centred development approaches are to make ISD processes more successful (Harris and Weistroffer, 2009; Markus and Mao, 2004), it is crucial to understand intended users.

In particular, the user focus perspective has been oriented towards design and development strategies that operate from a fictive, hypothetical or archetypical user in this respect (Iivari and Iivari, 2011). Yet, despite the acknowledged relevance of intended users, the concept seems to be undertheorized in ISD research in general and user focus in particular. Our study contributes to filling this gap; we offer a concept of user anticipation in conjunction with a corresponding initial typology of intended user concepts that provides both a systematic approach and adequate terminology for exploring and understanding how intended users are being anticipated by key stakeholders of a technology development process.

Further, we suggested conceptualizing user anticipation as a form of prospective sensemaking (Gioia and Mehra, 1996): a hermeneutic process of interpreting and creating the future possibilities of an emergent technology. Although we are not the first to introduce sensemaking as an important focus for technology development research (for example, Davidson, 2002, 2006), we believe nevertheless that employing a prospective sensemaking perspective on intended users seems very appropriate and formative for future studies. We echo an adjacent research perspective on technology frames that suggests sensemaking as an important manifestation and evidence of such frames (Davidson, 2002; Orlikowski and Gash,

1994). In particular, we suggest that a technology frame does not merely refer to or consist of ideas about a technology – a technology concept (Leonardi, 2011). In addition, it fundamentally implies ideas of future users: a concept of intended users. This is particularly relevant since this strand of scholarship does not seem to have sufficiently and systematically explored the user in technology frames. Thus, we have demonstrated how a prospective sensemaking approach can contribute to a more balanced investigation of these equally relevant components of technology frames.

While a social constructionist view of technology development (Pinch and Bijker, 1987) has highlighted that both the technology concept and the user concept are subject to discursive meaning negotiations, it has rarely explored the interpretive flexibility that surrounds the concept of intended users. Given the wide variety of conflicting or competing concepts of intended users, Oudshoorn and Pinch (2003) have called for more studies to understand how key stakeholders in technology development anticipate intended users. With our study, we have answered this call both by extending the conceptual repertoire of SCOT with the notion of user anticipation and by offering an initial typology of intended user concepts. The latter in particular provides an initial starting point for future investigations into the ways that intended users are being anticipated.

Our framework also has implications for the challenge of integrating potentially conflicting user needs. This challenge will manifest itself in distinctively different ways, depending on whether one refers to technology *implementation* or technology *development*. In implementation the challenge lies in integrating the needs voiced by actual users; in development it lies in achieving convergence in meaning among the various needs of intended users that developers describe. Thus we might paraphrase the integration challenge as *achieving a convergence of intended user needs in technology development*. While this would clearly make for an interesting study, it would be beyond the scope of a single chapter, in terms of both concept and dataset, to offer any prescriptions on how to achieve convergence between the conflicting needs of the intended user types. Still, our framework allows us to provide a more nuanced and systematic framing of the convergence challenge.

For instance, Griffith (1999) compellingly reminds us of both the challenge and the costs of non-convergent, unanticipated needs of intended users; she points to the discomfort many patients experience with an MRI tube and Intel customers who take issue with a flawed chip technology. We find Griffith's approach, describing how technology features trigger (prospective) sensemaking in developers, to be a useful foundation, as it offers initial propositions about the likelihood of convergence among the needs of intended users, based on the anticipated features of a given technology.

In terms of technology features, using our framework we can distinguish between two dimensions of emergent technologies: the scope of a novel technology and the possibility that users can inscribe their needs into that technology. So, how challenging is it to find convergence among intended user needs along these dimensions? Most generally, we would anticipate that the narrower the scope and the lower the possibility that users can inscribe their needs, the more agony we would witness as stakeholders try to achieve convergence among the needs of intended users. More specifically, we suggest that the more 'authors' (that is, active specialists) are anticipated, the harder it will be to achieve that convergence. In contrast, the more 'readers' (that is, passive generalists) one anticipates, the easier it will be to achieve that convergence. Looking at intended users who are exegetes or translators, we suggest it will be a moderate challenge to achieve that convergence. The main challenge, however, of achieving this convergence consists in the effort to integrate competing, conflicting user needs that cut across the different intended user types. Exploring this challenge would clearly make for a pertinent future investigation.

Finally, we believe that the concept of anticipation and the typology of intended users we suggested can be brought to bear on phenomena and topics beyond the immediate realm of ISD and technology studies. Disciplines concerned with uncertain and ambiguous futures and thus amenable to prospective sensemaking – such as entrepreneurship and strategic management – might consider the concept of anticipation in terms of conceptualizing a future opportunity, state or actor, and that anticipation might, in turn, inform the process of making a decision and taking action. Both entrepreneurs and strategic managers are fundamentally concerned with anticipating and exploring future opportunities in terms of novel products and markets (Cornelissen and Clarke, 2010; Hitt et al., 2001; McGrath, 2001; Lawlor and Kavanagh, 2009). Thus, and by way of analogy, they may ground their prospective sensemaking and subsequent resource allocation on their 'market concepts' and in particular on their 'consumer concepts'. Accordingly, as it is crucial for entrepreneurs and strategists to anticipate their prospective customers adequately, we believe that our initial typology of user concepts may also contribute to a more fine-grained understanding of prospective consumers and clients in the disciplines of entrepreneurship and strategic management.

Thus, we can underline the relevance of understanding how technology developers and other strategic actors prospectively make sense of intended users, consumers, and clients in terms of the degree of agency they are granted and then whether the technology or product is assumed to be of single or multi-purpose. We believe our study paves the way towards developing a generic typology in this respect.

REFERENCES

Barki, Henri and Jon Hartwick (1989), 'Rethinking the concept of user involvement', *MIS Quarterly*, **13** (1), 53–63.

Barki, Henri and Jon Hartwick (1994), 'Measuring user participation, user involvement, and user attitude', *MIS Quarterly*, **18** (1), 59–82.

Cornelissen, Joep P. and Jean S. Clarke (2010), 'Imagining and rationalizing opportunities', *Academy of Management Review*, **35** (4), 539–557.

Currie, Graeme and Andrew D. Brown (2003), 'A narratological approach to understanding processes of organizing in a UK hospital', *Human Relations*, **56** (5), 563–586.

Davidson, Elizabeth J. (2002), 'Technology frames and framing: A socio-cognitive investigation of requirements determination', *MIS Quarterly*, **26** (4), 329–358.

Davidson, Elizabeth J. (2006), 'A technological frames perspective on information technology and organizational change', *Journal of Applied Behavioral Science*, **42** (1), 23–39.

Dawson, Patrick, Christian Clausen and Klaus T. Nielsen (2000), 'Political processes in management, organization and the social shaping of technology', *Technology Analysis & Strategic Management*, **12** (1), 5–15.

Dunford, Richard and Deborah Jones (2000), 'Narrative in strategic change', *Human Relations*, **53** (9), 1207–1226.

Fiss, Peer C. and Paul M. Hirsch (2005), 'The discourse of globalization: Framing and sensemaking of an emerging concept', *American Sociological Review*, **70** (1), 29–52.

Gioia, Dennis A. and Ajay Mehra (1996), 'Sensemaking in organizations', *Academy of Management Review*, **21** (4), 1226–1230.

Griffith, Terri (1999), 'Technology features as triggers for sensemaking', *Academy of Management Review*, **24** (3), 472–488.

Harris, Mark A. and Heinz Roland Weistroffer (2009), 'A new look at the relationship between user involvement in systems development and system success', *Communications of the Association for Information Systems*, **24** (1), 739–756.

Hartwick, Jon and Henri Barki (1994), 'Explaining the role of user participation in information system use', *Management Science*, **40** (4), 440–465.

Hitt, Michael A., R. Duane Ireland, S. Michael Camp and Donald L. Sexton (2001), 'Strategic entrepreneurship: entrepreneurial strategies for wealth creation', *Strategic Management Journal*, **22** (6–7), 479–491.

Iivari, Juhani and Netta Iivari (2011), 'Varieties of user-centeredness: An analysis of four systems development methods', *Information Systems Journal*, **21** (2), 125–153.

Iivari, Juhani, Hannakaisa Isomäki and Samuli Pekkola (2010), 'The user – the great unknown of systems development', *Information Systems Journal*, **20** (2), 109–117.

Lawlor, Jim and Donncha Kavanagh (2009), 'The relationship between new technologies and strategic activities', *Technology Analysis & Strategic Management*, **21** (5), 587–598.

Leonardi, Paul M. (2011), 'Innovation blindness: Culture, frames, and cross-boundary problem construction in the development of new technology concepts', *Organization Science*, **22** (2), 347–369.

MacKenzie, Donald and Judy Wajcman (1999), *The Social Shaping of Technology* (Second Edition), Buckingham: Open University Press.

Maitlis, Sally (2005), 'The social processes of organizational sensemaking', *Academy of Management Journal*, **48** (1), 21–49.

Markus, M. Lynn and Ji-Ye Mao (2004), 'Participation in development and implementation', *Journal of the Association for Information Systems*, **5** (11), 514–544.

McGrath, Rita G. (2001), 'Exploratory learning, innovative capacity, and managerial oversight', *Academy of Management Journal*, **44** (1), 118–131.

Orlikowski, Wanda and Debra Gash (1994), 'Technology frames: Making sense of information technology in organizations', *ACM Transactions on Information Systems*, **12** (2), 174–207.

Oudshoorn, Nelly and Trevor Pinch (2003), *How Users Matter. The Co-Construction of Users and Technologies*, Cambridge, MA: MIT Press.

Oudshoorn, Nelly, Els Rommes and Marcelle Stienstra (2004), 'Configuring the user as everybody: Gender and design cultures in information and communication technologies', *Science, Technology & Human Values*, **29** (1), 30–63.

Pentland, Brian T. (1999), 'Building process theory with narrative: From description to explanation', *Academy of Management Review*, **24** (4), 711–724.

Pinch, Trevor and Wiebe E. Bijker (1987), 'The social construction of facts and artefacts', in Wiebe E. Bijker, Thomas P. Hughes and Trevor J. Pinch (eds), *The Social Construction of Technological Systems*, Cambridge, MA: MIT Press, pp. 17–50.

Rau, Christian, Anne-Katrin Neyer and Kathrin M. Möslein (2012), 'Innovation practices and their boundary-crossing mechanisms: A review and proposal for the future', *Technology Analysis & Strategic Management*, **24** (2), 181–217.

Sonenshein, Scott (2010), 'We're changing – or are we? Untangling the role of progressive, regressive, and stability narratives during strategic change implementation', *Academy of Management Journal*, **53** (3), 477–512.

Spears, Janine L. and Henri Barki (2010), 'User participation in information systems security risk management', *MIS Quarterly*, **34** (3), 503–522.

Taylor, James R. and Elizabeth J. van Every (2000), *The Emergent Organization*, Mahwah, NJ: Erlbaum.

Wajcman, Judy (2002), 'Addressing technological change: The challenge to social theory', *Current Sociology*, **50** (3), 347–363.

Weick, Karl E. (1995), *Sensemaking in Organizations*, Thousand Oaks, CA: Sage.

11. Career change: the role of transition narratives in alternative identity constructions

Patrizia Hoyer

INTRODUCTION

While the core literature on career change has mainly focused on people's attempts to most adequately match their personality traits, individual skills, values and preferences with the characteristics and requirements of a certain profession (Schein, 1978, 1990), in this chapter I highlight how the choices involved in career change are often embedded in larger discourses about what a 'good career' looks like. In doing so I introduce a new conceptualization of career change, one in which motivations to enter, exit or stay within a given working context are not just personal and internally developed choices, but instead are constructed socially and in dialogue with others, often influenced by discourses around career progression, professional development, individual achievement and self-actualization.

A change in career may be deemed successful when a career changer, over time, departs from a self-image that is primarily grounded in a past working context, by gradually adopting and stabilizing an alternative identity in the new working context (Ibarra and Barbulescu, 2010). With an interest in the varieties of career change experiences, and especially the question of why some career changers are more successful than others in constructing an alternative self-image in a new working context, in this chapter I depart from traditional references to congruence between personality type and job characteristics. Instead I draw attention to the role of 'transition narratives' (LaPointe, 2011) and how they enable or inhibit people as they develop alternative identity concepts.

Some scholars argue that in times of career change, people's self-concepts and professional identities may become severely jeopardized, particularly when they are not able to draw a continuous link between their past and present sense of self in their career narratives (Brown, Gabriel and Gherardi, 2009). I therefore propose that in order to respond to these potential disruptions in the narrative, people may try to construct a 'transition bridge' (Ashforth, 2001) across gaps between their old and new roles, by making use of 'transition narratives' (LaPointe, 2011). Transition narratives, which are often a product of hindsight (Weick, 1995), may be understood as individual strategies to deal with interruptions in one's work life history. Following LaPointe (2011), I suggest that transition narratives function as legitimizing resources; they allow people to distance themselves from previous discourses or to place some aspects of identity into the past, and at the same time imagine, and experiment with, new sources of meaning and alternative identities.

Ibarra and Barbulescu (2010) argue that, in order to legitimate a change in career that departs from conventional career scripts, people have to tell compelling (transition) stories. A 'good' (fitting, adequate) transition narrative would allow them to show that two seemingly discontinuous professions are actually closely related or that discontinuity is not problematic as the career shift aligns well with their personal values and motives (see also Ibarra, 2005; Rossiter, 2009). Providing a compelling narrative thus helps career changers to endow their transition with meaning and to increase the likelihood that alternative identity claims will be granted and socially accepted (Keupp and Höfer, 1998; Keupp, Ahbe, Gmür, Höfer, Mitzscherlich, Kraus and Straus, 1999).

Moreover, Ibarra and Barbulescu (2010) maintain that those career changes that mark a more radical discontinuity in a progressive career path often require more convincing narratives to justify the shift, and thus may provide greater resources for constructing an alternative image of self in which a person questions and to a certain extent disengages from a previously held identity in the course of exploring and eventually adopting alternatives (Ibarra, 2005). In that sense, a more radical career shift may lead to the person telling a stronger transition narrative, and thus increasing the possibility of alternative identity constructions.

In this chapter I examine in particular the transition narratives that former management consultants draw upon as they try to make sense of their career shift, away from the elite working context of a prestigious management consultancy towards a different working context (Table 11.1). By subscribing to the processual understanding (Steyaert and Van Looy, 2010) that, during times of career change, identities are enacted through such identity constituting transition narratives (LaPointe, 2011), in this chapter I take an interest in the potential variations which transition narratives may provide for alternative identity constructions in response to career change.

And indeed, as the narrative analysis of 30 life story interviews with former management consultants will show, different organizational contexts, also depending on the radicalness of an experienced career change, provide different contextual resources for telling a more or less compelling transition narrative, thereby allowing for different modes of adjustment and variations in the construction of post-exit identities. More concretely, among the different organizational contexts that ex-consultants have moved into, four different transition narratives were identified for (more or less compellingly) constructing an alternative self-image in the new working environment. These four transition narratives were labelled as re-invention, alteration, re-enactment and stagnation narrative.

Before describing the analysis and reporting the results, however, I will first situate the formulated problem in the literature on identity transition in times of career change, drawing attention to the peculiarities of the management consulting context in relation to career shifts. Second, I will introduce the conceptual framework around narrative identity and contextual resources in transition narratives, which determined the methodological setup of the study and guided the analysis. And finally, I will describe the contributions that this study can make by elaborating upon the link between career change, transition narratives, contextual resources, modes of adjustment and alternative identity constructions in the post-exit arena.

LITERATURE REVIEW

Identity Transitions in Times of Career Change

Traditional theories have conceptualized careers as bureaucratic, linear, hierarchical and rigid developments where people progress, throughout their working lives, along a set of institutionally defined occupational stages within the confines of one single organization. This norm, however, is increasingly being supplemented by emerging concepts of career as ever-evolving, dynamic, boundaryless and multi-directional, where people periodically change their career trajectories (Ibarra, 2005; Louis, 1980a; Sullivan and Arthur, 2006; Wise and Millward, 2005). A change in career may by definition be regarded as non-institutionalized as it does not follow the logic of a pre-defined role progression or organizational career path, but instead marks a move into a new and sometimes considerably different line of work (Ibarra, 2005).

The impetus for a change in career may be a voluntary choice, but it can also be imposed, for example by a job loss. Involuntary unemployment can be assumed to pose considerable identity threats (Ibarra, 2005; Louis, 1980a), but even voluntary career changes, my focus in this study, are rarely experienced as smooth processes. This is because non-institutionalized transition processes are often not well established, but rather disjunctive (Ibarra and Barbulescu, 2010). Moreover, it would be naïve to assume that when people voluntarily make career changes, they are entirely free to choose a new profession and thus to freely reconstruct an alternative image of their professional self. Instead, certain institutional environments can be rather directive in providing career scripts that influence people's future career choices (Chreim, Williams and Hinings, 2007). In these scripts only a succession of jobs – that is, progress in terms of salary, title, hierarchy and prestige – is framed as socially desirable. Any career move that departs from this convention would represent a major discontinuity and thus require extensive justification (Ibarra and Barbulescu, 2010).

Despite a predominance of reported benefits, people often experience career shifts as difficult and destabilizing. When moving from one career to another, they necessarily have to learn, internalize and make sense of new skills and daily routines (Wise and Millward, 2005). They often experience all this with a sense of foreignness, disorientation and sensory overload, as the moment of entry brings multiple professional and social changes simultaneously, with no opportunity to adjust gradually (Louis, 1980b). Feelings of ambiguity, conflict and role overload arise especially when career changers receive conflicting signals in the new working about what is expected of them. Wise and Millward (2005) observed that transitioners, when moving from one career to the other, were often keen to hold on to the knowledge, skills and abilities they had acquired in previous jobs.

In line with this observation, other scholars found that career changers describe their personal identities as being based in both the past and the present (Beyer and Hannah, 2002; Rossiter, 2009), where 'people oscillate between "holding on" and "letting go", between a desire to rigidly clutch or grieve for the past and the impulse to rush exuberantly into the future' (Ibarra, 2005, p. 26). When people are still intensely involved in their old work identity (even though it was no longer appealing), while they are already committed to, yet unsure about what the future holds, the question arises: How are career changers able to develop alternative identities that are not primarily grounded in the past? Given my particular interest in the variation in career change experiences, and the related variation in alternative identity constructions in a new working context, in the following section I will delineate a model around different modes of career change adjustment that illuminates some of this variation.

Different Modes of Career Change Adjustment

The career change literature has often depicted the link between career shifts and corresponding identity transitions as a unilateral process where adjustment only occurs on the side of the career changer; however, in a negotiated adaptation process, not only identities but also the new working roles and sometimes even the new working conditions can be adjusted (Black, 1988; Chreim et al., 2007; Ibarra, 1999; Nicholson, 1984). Nicholson (1984) found that the mode of adjustment is closely related to the parameters of a given career change, or as Ibarra and Barbulescu (2010) would claim, to the radicalness of a career change. For instance, when changing to a new working environment that is relatively similar to the old one, little change can be anticipated on both dimensions: the identity of the career changer and the new working conditions. We would expect to observe quite the opposite during a more significant career shift with higher degrees of change being imposed on both ends. To depict this variation in possible adaptations, Nicholson described four different modes of adjustment which he labels replication, absorption, determination and exploration.

The first mode of adjustment, *replication*, can be observed when a person changes a career or even just a job across similar contexts. In this mode the career changer makes few adjustments either to his own identity or to the new working role, thus preserving valued skills and the feeling of stability throughout the entire transition period. At the same time this mode of adjustment may bear the danger of making people feel trapped 'in a rut' where they experience little scope for change of any kind (Black, 1988; Nicholson, 1984).

The second mode of adjustment, *absorption*, can be observed when the new working context is in sharp contrast to the previous one. In such a situation the burden of adjustment is often exclusively borne by the career changer who has to engage in some significant amount of role learning, while the new working parameters remain mostly unmodified. Even though this steep learning curve may be experienced as a positive identity development, the person may likewise face a disconfirmation of existing and valued self-images, leading to feelings of anomie and questions about his/her skills.

The third mode of adjustment, *determination*, can be observed when the career changer considers the previous working context to be superior to the new one. In that situation, rather than adjusting her identity to the demands of the new role, the person is determined to change the content and structure of the newly assigned role, thereby imprinting her stamp of identity upon the new working context (Black, 1988; Nicholson, 1984). This mode of adaptation is often associated with positive feelings deriving from a sense of one's own capacity for innovation and reform within the new context. On the negative side, however, this mode of adjustment bears the danger of being judged by others in the new context as thoughtlessly destroying valued elements within the existing setup.

In the fourth mode of adjustment, *exploration*, career changers experience an opportunity both to develop their own identity and to change some of the new working (role) parameters. Positive experiences regarding the exploration mode are the pleasures of thoughtful experimentation and a sense of personal as well as organizational growth. On the negative side, people may experience confusion and anxiety as they lose both internal and external stability in an incoherent turmoil of change.

I would argue that these different modes of adjustment provide a good starting point for investigating variation in career change experiences, as they account for different ways in which people adopt their identity concepts to a new working context. In the discussion section I will further elaborate upon these different modes of adjustment, arguing that the actual processes of adjustment, which are underspecified in Nicholson's model, could well be explained through a narrative framework. More specifically, I will illustrate how certain transition narratives can be associated with these modes of adjustment, thereby explaining the dynamics and contextual parameters that lead people to choose one mode over the other.

In the next section I describe how the context of management consultancies is a particularly interesting research field for investigating alternative identity constructions in the course of career change.

Career Change in the Context of Management Consultancies

Organizational scholars have depicted management consultancies as quite effective in inviting strong identifications among their employees (Meriläinen, Tienari, Thomas and Davies, 2004), especially through discourses of elitism (Alvesson and Robertson, 2006; Armbrüster, 2004). Identification with a highly prestigious company allows employees to take pride in their organizational membership and to construct a positive self-image which mobilizes enthusiasm. Aware of this decisive factor, management consultancies invest heavily in their external brand image, engaging in marketing activities that ensure it will succeed and survive – along with the prestige associated with it (Kärreman and Rylander, 2008). This behaviour certainly helps to explain why young graduates find it so compelling to work for prestigious companies such as management consultancies.

As a result, however, management consultants may find it difficult to let go of their consultant identity when they exit the consulting context, and they may maintain their strong ties with the previous employer (Alvesson,

2000). Indeed, Sturdy and Wright (2008) observed that when consultants move into new working environments their identities are often still linked to the prestige and status of their former job. This may also have consequences for the way they adjust to their new working conditions. More concretely, if they ground their sense of self primarily in discourses linked to the past, career changers may feel discouraged about exploring and embracing new opportunities for identification, and thus constrain their own processes of re-orientation (Brown and Humphreys, 2002).

Given this tension among former management consultants – on the one hand seeking an alternative career path and on the other wanting to maintain an elite identity associated with their consulting past – I argue that the context of management consulting poses an interesting field for empirically investigating alternative identity constructions in response to career change. In the next section I describe the narrative framework I used to investigate former consultants' alternative identity constructions.

CONCEPTUAL FRAMEWORK

Narrative Perspective on Identity in Light of Career Change

The creation of identity has been conceptualized from a wide variety of disciplines (Horrocks and Callahan, 2006) and a seemingly endless number of different avenues (Alvesson, 2010). In this chapter I take a narrative perspective on identity which assumes that identities are moulded and fashioned through narratives people tell about themselves (Somers, 1994). More generally, identity scholars assume that we live in a 'storytelling society' (Benwell and Stokoe, 2010) where people make sense of their lives through processes of arranging characters and events in meaningful ways (Czarniawska, 1998; Kenny, Whittle and Willmott, 2011). The philosophical work of Paul Ricoeur and his narrative identity theory have been particularly influential in identity research. Ricoeur (1988) suggests that through narratives people develop a conception of self-identity where, in a reflective process, the self is discovered in its own narrational acts.

Moreover, he highlights the importance of 'emplotment' which is 'the process that synthesizes experience in a narrative' (Ricoeur 1991, p. 21), and which integrates a complex set of episodes into a single story. In line with the idea of emplotment, researchers have tended to locate and analyse identity constructs in the context of biographical self-narratives (Humphreys and Brown, 2002). Many narrative identity scholars have in fact followed the influential work of McAdams (1987, 2001) who proposed that identity itself takes the form of a unified and meaningful life story, where open-ended, confused and ambiguous stories become 'readable' as the individual creates an internalized sense of coherence and self-continuity.

Moving away from an approach of studying narratives as text, which may be regarded as the first wave of narrative investigations, a second wave of studies has emphasized the concept of narrative-in-context (Georgakopoulou, 2006). Framing narrative as practice (De Fina and Georgakopoulou, 2008) with a particular interest in what people *do* when they tell stories (Bamberg, 2004), this group of researchers assumes that people do not simply tell stories but rather enact them (Pentland, 1999) in order to accomplish and perpetuate a sense of who they are.

Following this notion of narrative-in-context, Taylor (2007) puts forward the idea that larger social and cultural contexts can be understood to provide resources for people to make sense of the world and of themselves. In that view people do not completely reinvent their identities in the telling of life narratives; instead they construct them by drawing on the discursive resources accumulated over time within a given context. Moreover, in this framework, context-related biographical narratives are assumed to become resources as well, or even rehearsals for imagining and actively shaping a future image of self. Conversely, when people move to a new working environment which lacks contextual resources, they may not be able to enact a compelling transition narrative through which to construct a plausible alternative identity. In such situations, their identity constructions may still be primarily grounded in the previous working context.

In the narrative analysis of interviews with former management consultants, I focused on the link between four elements – transition narratives, the radicalness of career change, contextual resources, and different modes of adjustment – to observe how people construct alternative identities in a new working context.

Research Questions

My focus in this study is the alternative identity constructions of former management consultants. Assuming that management consultancies mark a special working context as they are particularly successful in shaping their employees' identities through the construction of a self-pleasing elite image, in this study I examined the question: *How can ex-consultants construct an alternative identity in the new working context that is not primarily grounded in their consulting past?*

By taking into account the radicalness of people's career changes, along with their mode of adjustment and the contextual resources that shape their transition narratives, I have further refined this general research question into two analytical questions that helped me to analyse and better understand the variations in the ways ex-consultants produce alternative identities:

1) How do ex-consultants experience the degree of radicalness in their career shift from the consultancy to a certain new working context and how is this experienced degree of radicalness reflected in the mode of adjustment?
2) Which different contextual resources do former management consultants draw upon (or lack) in telling a compelling transition narrative and in constructing an alternative self-image within the new working context?

Based on these analytical questions, in the next sections I describe my methods for collecting and analysing my data.

METHODOLOGY

Data Collection and Sample

I conducted 30 life story interviews (Atkinson, 1998; McAdams, 2001) with former consultants of large global management consultancies, mostly (but not exclusively) based in Switzerland and Germany. All of these consultancies, which are headquartered in the United States but operate internationally, are regarded as highly prestigious and elite companies. While all 30 interviewees had similar backgrounds, having worked at major global management consultancies, their new work contexts fell into six different categories: academia, NGO, industry, financial services, in-house consulting and their own start-ups. This diversity enabled me to explore a variety of transition narratives that they drew upon in developing alternative self-concepts.

At the beginning of each interview, I provided some brief information on my research interest: how people construct their identities across changing organizational contexts. I explained that I was above all interested in stories rather than pure facts and encouraged the interviewees to share their stories by imagining that in a couple of years from now they would have the idea of writing up their personal life story in a book (Atkinson, 1998; McAdams, 2001). I asked them to delineate the important chapters and think of interesting episodes that they would feel were worth sharing in such a book. Given the time constraint of approximately one hour (interviews ranged from 45 to 135 minutes), I asked them to share their stories starting from the day they entered university up to the current date of the interview. Most interviews were conducted in German, while three were also conducted in English and three in Swiss German, depending on the interviewees' preferences.

Since all 30 interviewees had pursued a university degree, spent several years in a management consultancy, and then at least entered one new organizational context, everyone reported on a minimum of two major changes in his or her life: first the transition from university to a working context and then from the consultancy to a new work environment. The time spent in consultancy ranged from under one year to 10 years with an average of three years; the time they had been out of the consultancy when doing the interview ranged from under one year to nine years, with an average of two years.

Concerning the conduct of the interviews, for the most part I tried not to interrupt the interviewees as they unfolded their stories. In some instances, however, when they did not explain or elaborate upon certain decisions, I asked follow-up questions such as 'Why did you choose to go into/leave consulting?' Or if they implied that I already understood too many aspects within the story, I suggested 'Now imagine someone does not know what this particular working context is like at all. How would you describe it in the book so that everybody could get a good idea of what was going on?' Additionally, I asked some probing questions around their decisions concerning transitions and career shifts.

Data Analysis

After I fully transcribed all the interviews in their original language, I ana-lysed the data in English, guided by the two analytical research questions above. I aimed to identify four aspects: the radicalness of the career change, the mode of adjustment, the contextual resources for telling a more or less compelling transition narrative, and their ability to formulate alternative identities. To analyse these aspects, I first colour-coded all the interview transcripts using the highlighting function in MS Word. This allowed me to highlight passages in which they made comparisons between the past and the present, or described their process of adapting to the new working context.

The first stage of the analysis turned out to be an iterative process of moving back and forth between data, literature and analysis. For that stage, I compared and contrasted all the selected interview passages to filter out the overarching narratives around the radicalness of a career shift and the related mode of adjustment according to a certain organi-zational context. Through this process four different transition narratives (re-invention, alteration, re-enactment and stagnation) were identified that these former management consultants made use of when constructing an alternative identity in the new working context.

In the second stage of the analysis, I further investigated the contextual resources for alternative identity constructions. I coded the coloured (mostly German) text passages using Atlas.ti in an open coding process (in English) (Turner, 1981), generating 22 codes on reported contextual resources and 21 codes for reported obstacles, that is, the lack of contextual resources. In a next step of axial coding (Strauss and Corbin, 1990), I summarized related codes and condensed them into broader themes for each category, touching upon issues of job characteristics (for example, meaningful work, balanced lifestyle), interpersonal dynamics (for example, good working climate, strong firm culture) and a person's self-image (for example, the decision-maker, the change agent) created in the new context. I then explored these themes within each of the six different work contexts in order to highlight recurring patterns as well as similarities and differences in their transition narratives. I will now describe each transition narrative and its characteristics. All names used in the following are pseudonyms.

RESULTS

Re-invention Narrative: 'It's All Better'

The first transition narrative that these former management consultants drew upon to bridge the gap between their past and their present self-concept was the 're-invention narrative'. In this narrative they described the new working context positively, as better or more likable compared to the consulting context. Most of those who enacted this narrative had left the consultancy in order to become self-employed entrepreneurs. They described working in one's own start-up as considerably different from the past profession, thus signifying what Ibarra and Barbulescu (2010) would refer to as a radical change in career. This radical change was positively associated with a range of contextual resources for alternative identity construction including 'greater reported degrees of ownership' and 'decision-making responsibility':

> As a consultant you can sell things very nicely and you can impress people with slides and then you leave again. But yes, whether it works or not, that you will never find out. . . . I find it much more exciting to push your own topic. . . . The decisions I made six months ago, they still have an impact today. And you see how something grows, how it moves forward, the products become better. Problems are being solved. People are becoming better, they are learning, they are growing along. That's just super exciting. (Michael, entrepreneur)

As they were so absorbed by their own projects, it is not surprising that the entrepreneurs who used the re-invention narrative dedicated most of their interview time to talking about the new (rather than the previous) working context, which they enthusiastically described as a challenging project.

Another radical difference between the consulting past and the entrepreneurial present was manifested in their reported experience of 'greater freedom'. While they often described the consulting context as highly restrictive with long working hours and a meticulous monitoring of working results, they described the new context as just the opposite:

> I actually define my current working situation as totally not bound by anything. That means I could basically do anything. I could go to the Antarctic and study dolphins. (Josha, entrepreneur)

Though Josha might not really be contemplating a trip to the Antarctic, this somewhat exaggerated statement (or even fantasy) still provides a good example of how the re-invention narrative compellingly produces the new working context as liberating in comparison to the past.

Even though the new context is actively shaped by the person itself, the mode of adjustment is mostly one of absorption (Nicholson, 1984), where the career changer is totally sucked in by the new context and its various new demands. Thus, change occurs above all on the interviewee's part. Yet this change, which some described as rather radical and overwhelming, is almost exclusively framed in a positive way, as a great learning experience:

> I really believe that with this step of becoming self-employed I have pushed my professional development very far forward. Because you do a lot of things wrong, so the learning opportunity. . . . How can I say it? Mistakes are one thing. The other thing is learning opportunity. Suddenly you make enormous progress in your own development. (Nick, entrepreneur)

The interviewees in this new organizational context were hardly negative about anything in their new work environment. The re-invention narrative at best (or worst) encompassed passages that revealed the difficulties associated with starting one's own business, such as finding the required funding or 'having to start at zero' and establishing oneself in a certain field:

> Of course the competitive pressure is much higher, because you have to imagine, you are selling yourself as a private person. You don't have an organization, you do not have research staff, you have no branding. You're selling

yourself based on competence. And that of course is extremely difficult. (Timon, entrepreneur)

Even though most of the entrepreneurs reported such initial difficulties, they mostly framed them as challenges rather than obstacles within the new working context, thereby strengthening the overall compelling story of positive career change which can be assumed to carry strongly identity-constituting effects:

> I can tell that this is the place where I belong. [A place] where on the one hand I can learn something, where I move on, where I feel good, but on the other hand I am also needed here. And I have the feeling that I am the ideal person to make this happen in Switzerland. (Karl, entrepreneur)

In summary, the re-invention narrative is a compelling narrative of radical career change towards a new and better working reality. Based on a range of contextual resources the re-invention narrative provides great room for constructing an alternative identity in the new working context.

Alteration Narrative: 'It's Different, but Similar'

A second transition narrative that some of these ex-consultants applied was one of alteration. On the one hand they constructed the new working context as radically different from the past, and on the other they described the past and current working contexts as quite similar. Most of the ex-consultants who offered this narrative had moved into a career in an NGO or academic context. Some did describe a radical difference; several now in the NGO context stated that the new work setting provided them with contextual resources they did not have in the consultancy: 'a sense of purpose' and 'the feeling of doing meaningful work'. They then reported this newly found meaning as a strong basis for their alternative identity construction:

> If at the end of the day it is only a matter of maximizing shareholder value, then this is simply not my thing. That's simply not enough.. . . So towards the end of my consultancy time I started looking for something that would provide me with a sense of purpose. . . . And now I cannot imagine ever not working for an NGO. I cannot imagine working for a company where in the evening I would put down my [professional] identity. (Steve, NGO)

In a similar vein, ex-consultants moving to an academic context raised the positive point that their new work environment was considerably different from their consulting past in that it let them produce more innovative and avant-garde knowledge:

> In the university context we are involved in the early phases of this knowledge creation process. That means we work on problems which cannot be sold to a client today or tomorrow. . . . Consulting firms work with tools and concepts that are actually not so new from a scholarly standpoint. (Ferdinand, academia)

While these interviewees describe their career shift as radical and positively connoted change, it almost comes as a surprise when some of them later emphasize the similarities they have found across the changing contexts. In the NGO context respondents mainly grounded this similarity in the nature of the work they conducted; for nearly all of them, their new work in the non-profit sector was very similar to that in the consultancy:

> It's not a huge shock that suddenly I am standing there distributing sacks of rice. That's not how it is, quite the opposite. From day one onwards I could bring in my consultant skills. . . . In functional terms the work is very similar to the consultancy work. (Jeremy, NGO)

Similarly, the academic context – which in the earlier example was depicted as radically different from consulting – was later constructed as very comparable to the consulting past, especially as they pointed to the professionalism of their new colleagues and the quality of the results they obtain:

> [I have] very competent colleagues with a lot of experience and I have to say that at the end of the day we come to very good results too [like in the consultancy]. (Paul, academia)

Given this combination of both radical change and considerable similarities across contexts on the other, the adjustment often seemed to be one of exploration. That is, these respondents seemed to change their identity to a certain extent (such as becoming a passionate NGO employee), but also slightly changed their working habits within the new environment. They often connected this changing of habits to a lack of contextual resources, as they experienced the new context as inferior to the consulting past. In the academic context they mostly directed their critique towards a slow working culture and a lack of efficiency:

> Of course the environment is different. The way I immediately attend to something, such as immediately replying to emails: that is not so common in the academic context. . . . Sometimes I actually find people to be a bit out of it, that they cannot get to the point. They talk about something for hours, totally impractical stuff, so I realize they are wasting a lot of time. That irritates me a bit. (Petra, academia)

A similar discontentment was reported in the NGO context. Particularly in situations when new colleagues did not show the level of professionalism they had experienced in consultancy, they actively reproduced their previous self-image as a consultant:

> I can put a lot of pressure on people, or I can be really authoritative and say: 'this needs to be reworked all over again'. And there I believe that what drives me is my previous [consulting] job. (Lea, NGO)

Overall, the alteration narrative is a somewhat compelling transition narrative, indicating a balance between having and not having the contextual resources needed to construct an alternative identity in the new work context.

Re-enactment Narrative: 'It was Better in the Past'

In the third transition narrative, that of re-enactment, former management consultants depicted their new work context as relatively comparable to the consulting context, but inferior, thereby allowing themselves to re-enact a past identity in the new work environment. Promoting the notion that 'things were better in the past', the re-enactment narrative may be considered as a transition narrative that does reflect a change, but one that is not radical and certainly not desirable. Moreover, given how much similarity they reported between their old and new work contexts, they showed they had relatively few contextual resources to draw upon to construct an alternative image of self in the new context.

Those who engaged the re-enactment narrative were mostly moving to positions in either industry or financial services. Those moving to a management position in industry were more likely to describe the new context as (considerably) less professional and therefore inferior to their consulting past:

> When you go into industry and you do your work just like you did in the consultancy, then you already do things 200 times better than everyone else. . . . When you get something back, it mostly comes too late. . . . And when it comes back, either on time or not, only half of the work is done or something is done completely wrong. They don't even ask for clarification. (Daniel, industry)

Those moving from consultancy to a bank mostly experienced the negative change as involving an unpleasant working culture or atmosphere:

> To be honest, in my first year [at the bank] I had culture shock, especially with private banking. It's very much single runners, very much. In private banking

the business is based a lot on contacts, on your relationship with the client. And once you have built this relationship, everybody else becomes a threat. You know, in the sense that someone else will take it. It's very much single runners, very much. (Andrea, financial services)

Since they considered their new working context to be inferior and less appealing, these interviewees seemed to be using determination as their way of adjusting: they attempted to improve their new work environment while holding on to their past work routines and skills which seemed to be appreciated within the new work context. Even though the kind of work they were doing and the way of doing it had not changed, at least the greater appreciation they experienced in the new context became a contextual resource for constructing an alternative identity:

They totally appreciate my work. And sometimes I think, in the consultancy I would have done something similar and they would have said it's not enough. (Amelie, industry)

Another contextual resource associated with moving to a similar yet inferior work context is having more career opportunities while being rated as a superior new employee:

I have already had several discussions with my boss and HR on how I see my future in the company or outside the company, what kind of position I would like to have in the future and everything. There are a lot of options, opportunities for the future. . . . I could say, okay, in the next five years or ten years I want to be general manager of Barrington [pseudonym] Switzerland. So then they would make sure that I have [experience in] the different positions that will lead me to that role. (Francesco, industry)

To conclude, the re-enactment narrative may be considered as a relatively weak and not overly compelling transition narrative as it only provides a few contextual resources that are not grounded in the consulting work, for constructing an alternative identity in the new work context.

Stagnation Narrative: 'Nothing has Changed'

A fourth transition narrative that ex-consultants drew upon was that of the stagnation; it mainly promotes the idea that 'nothing has changed' as they changed jobs. Most of those offering this narrative had left the consultancy to work as in-house consultants in a large Swiss bank. In particular, they reported that the type of work they did and the way they did it were almost identical across the two working contexts. In line with that depiction, they often mentioned that they shared their work history with their other new in-house consultant colleagues, as most of them also had a background in external consulting. It was not surprising then that they maintained a positive connotation of consultants as belonging to 'a smart and hardworking elite' and could carry it on from their consulting past into the new work context:

> We also work a lot, especially compared to the rest of the organization. We do not drop our pens at 5 pm, but instead, the spirit, the culture here is probably driven by the ex-consultants. . . . That's also what we have a good reputation for among the management of the organization. (John, in-house consulting)

Given the considerable similarities they reported between their former and current jobs, one could hardly speak of a radical career shift here, as most parameters of the interviewees' working reality remain constant. Accordingly, the observed mode of adjustment was one of 'replication' (Nicholson, 1984), where little change was required – in either the identity of the career changer or the parameters of the new work context.

Given the great similarity in old and new contexts, these former management consultants had only a few contextual resources to draw upon to construct an alternative image of self in the new working context. One aspect of the new context that several mentioned, and appreciated, was the perception that they had at least achieved a more balanced lifestyle which then allowed them to construct an alternative identity beyond the professional context, grounded in their private lives:

> Now I have the freedom, let's say, first of all to have children and to be deeply involved as their father. (Klaus, in-house consulting)

Another contextual resource these in-house consultants drew upon in their transition narratives was the perception that they were now doing more meaningful work, as they could follow their consulting projects all the way through to the implementation phase rather than just suggesting strategies.

These few positive aspects of change were immediately balanced out, however, by several unpleasant characteristics which together reinforced a feeling of stagnation in the transition from the old to the new work context. What they most complained about as a lack of contextual resource was the fact that, compared to the consulting context, they experienced working in the bank as much more political, hostile and hence discomforting:

> Management consultancies are usually meritocratic. . . . The corporate world is much more political, especially at higher levels. As I said, this might correlate with this 'blame me, blame you' or 'who can prove what' culture. . . . And of course this is a huge difference compared to a management consultancy where you have a completely different code of ethics. (John, in-house consulting)

Moreover, some claimed that this highly political firm culture also had a negative impact on their own career advancement within the corporate setting. Given their discovery that the new work context was so remarkably similar to their consulting past, and that various downsides overshadowed their feelings of positive change, in their stagnation narrative many ex-consultants actually questioned their decision to make the switch, or even considered returning to their previous employer:

> In hindsight I have the tendency to glorify things. There I have to be a bit careful. Well, in hindsight . . . when I see that it's the same shit for less money, then I think maybe I should have stayed for a year longer, until the next level or so. . . . Let's say if in three years from now I should bump into the office head [of the previous consultancy] downtown and he would say: 'Look, we still need a manager for our financial services practice', then at least I would not dismiss that option altogether. (Jan, in-house consulting)

In conclusion, the stagnation narrative may be seen as a relatively weak transition narrative, providing the fewest contextual resources for ex-consultants to draw upon to develop an alternative image of self within the new working context.

Table 11.1   Overview of transition narratives and parameters of transition

Transition narrative	Re-invention narrative	Alteration narrative	Re-enactment narrative	Stagnation narrative
New context	Entrepreneurship	NGO, Academia	Industry, Financial services	In-house consulting
Radicalness of career change	High	High and low in different aspects	Relatively low	Almost none
Contextual resources (or lack thereof)	Responsibility, ownership, freedom	More meaningful work, but lack of professionalism	Positive self-image and appreciation of one's work, but new context seen as inferior	High performance culture and balanced lifestyle, but too political
Mode of adjustment	Absorption	Exploration	Determination	Replication
Compellingness of transition narrative	Very compelling	Somewhat compelling	Relatively weak	Weak
Alternative identity construction	Enabling alternative identity constructions	Partly enabling alternative identity constructions	Limiting alternative identity constructions	Preventing alternative identity constructions

DISCUSSION AND CONCLUSION

In this chapter I have investigated the notion of career change through a narrative perspective. More concretely, by identifying and analysing four different transition narratives (re-invention, alteration, re-enactment and stagnation) that former management consultants drew upon to make sense of their past career move – away from a prestigious management consultancy towards a new working context – I was able to show some variation in their experiences of career change. Moreover, the narrative analysis has provided interesting insights into why some career changers may be more successful than others in developing an alternative professional identity upon entering a new work context. First, I observed that a more radical career change experience allows people to draw on a richer repertoire of contextual resources, which enables them to create more compelling transition narratives. Second, it became evident that the more compelling a transition narrative, the more likely a person would be to successfully construct an alternative self-image in a new work context.

While some of this understanding has already been theorized and conceptually developed elsewhere, for instance regarding the role of radical career change (Ibarra and Barbulescu, 2010), in this chapter I have tried to investigate these questions empirically and have added some complexity to the analysis of career change by taking a narrative lens. Instead of just translating some theoretical insights by other scholars into an empirical study, however, in the following section I will also try to do the reverse by conceptualizing and theoretically substantiating some of my own findings. In this way I hope to make explicit the various contributions I aspire to make in this study.

My first contribution is in theorizing career change through a narrative framework, thereby rendering (successful) alternative identity constructions in a new working context as the result of different narrative practices (Bamberg, 2004; De Fina and Georgakopoulou, 2008). This narrative understanding departs from some generalizing claims that career change is simply a matter of matching personality traits with job characteristics. Instead, I suggest that by drawing on one of the four delineated transition narratives, people engage in practices of re-invention, alteration, re-enactment or stagnation with regards to their identity projects. This highlights the performative power of narratives as they may not only describe social and organizational phenomena, but instead help to constitute them (Heracleous, 2006; Maitlis, 2012). Likewise, it emphasizes the identity constituting effects of narratives; this goes back to the claim that narratives *are* in fact identities since 'we become who we are through telling stories about our lives and living the stories we tell' (Bruner, 1994, p. 53).

In that sense, transition narratives may be considered 'ontological narratives', to use Somers' (1994) term:

> Ontological narratives are used to define who we *are*; this in turn can be a precondition for knowing what to *do*. This 'doing' will in turn produce new narratives and hence, new actions; the relationship between narrative and ontology is processual and mutually constitutive. Both are conditions of the other; neither are a priori. . . . Ontological narratives make the self something that one *becomes*. (Somers, 1994, p. 618, italics in original)

Going back to the analysis, we may then understand the various transition narratives as ontological practices of constituting alternative identities in a new working context. While some transition narratives (re-invention, alteration) seem to be more effective in enabling new identity formations, others (re-enactment, stagnation) seem more limiting or even preventive with regards to a 'becoming' trajectory. The way that people *narrate* a transition experience is hence not trivial with regards to *shaping* this very experience and its respective outcome.

Second, and going back to the notion of narrative-in-context (Georgakopoulou, 2006), another aspired contribution is my emphasis on 'context' as a relevant parameter in career change experiences. This focus on context, one could argue, is not entirely novel as other scholars, including Nicholson (1984) in his model on different modes of adjustment, have also taken this element into account – actually calling it a 'variable'. Nicholson in particular has proposed that one can expect to find differences in the ways people adopt to a new working context: they either adjust their own identities or adjust some working conditions in the new environment. Similar to my own approach, Nicholson (1984) explained this variation by looking at the contextual parameters in the course of a career change, or what Ibarra and Barbulescu (2010) would refer to as the 'radicalness of career change'. While I consider this a good starting point for integrating 'context' into the equation of career change experiences, I suggest that Nicholson's model falls short of capturing the discursive and processual dynamics that underlie these modes of (identity) adjustment.

What I try to offer instead is an understanding of contextual variation, again through the lens of narrative. Going back to the analysis, I have observed that ex-consultants moving to the reportedly most different working context of entrepreneurship also seemed to have the most compelling transition narrative for constructing an alternative identity with a rich repertoire of contextual resources to draw upon. At the other end of the continuum, in-house consultants struggled most to construct interesting transition narratives as they found their new working context to be all too similar to their past consulting reality. As a result they could find few contextual resources for constructing an alternative identity in the new context.

My understanding of context, here, is comparable to an image of 'narrative reservoir' that can be drawn upon by anyone passing through this context. This may explain why people do not freshly construct a new identity each time they enter into a new working context, or why former management consultants moving to a new work context that is very similar drew upon the same contextual resources and transition narratives when making sense of their career change. More generally this finding shows that, rather than being an individual endeavour, career change experiences are always embedded in existing repertoires of cultural narratives, and are therefore socially constructed and mediated. This, I hope, provides a more nuanced, dynamic and relational understanding of how people construct their career change experience as they move from one organizational context to another. Given the observation that contextual resources may become important for compelling career change narratives, and thus, for alternative identity constructions in a new working context, I contend that matters of context should not be taken lightly in the study of career change.

Third, given my particular focus on the context of management consultancies, I dare to claim that some working contexts – especially those with a strong hold over employees' identities – make it more difficult for people to exit a firm and to freely construct an alternative self-image in a new working context. Even though the interviewees offered quite a variety of transition narratives and drew upon diverse contextual resources to construct their alternative identities, I did observe overall that they still reported extensively upon their past consulting experience. Especially during times of transition, attachment to the past may increase people's psychological well-being and their emotional capacity to cope with challenges in the present (Routledge et al., 2011), but overall I suggest this continued identification with the past may prevent career changers from adopting a new professional identity. I hope that by drawing attention to these long-lasting effects that certain organizations may have on their employees, I am inviting people to be more reflexive about entering or exiting certain working contexts.

Finally, with regards to career change, I hope this study invites some greater awareness and more active engagement with what people would actually like to do rather than continuing to be preoccupied with what options are the most prestigious and externally recognized. I would argue that greater sensitivity to the role of transition narratives may allow people to break out of pre-defined career (change) scripts, that is, discourses in which only a succession in status and hierarchy can mark a desirable career move. This could allow people to re-invent themselves more actively in the new working context and to include in their repertoires contextual resources that may still be hidden beneath the surface. Over time, I hope, this may lead to new and more varied transition narratives which may help people to dilute some of their normative assumptions about what constitutes a 'good career'.

REFERENCES

Alvesson, Mats (2000), 'Social identity and the problem of loyalty in knowledge-intensive companies', *Journal of Management Studies*, **37** (8), 1101–1123.
Alvesson, Mats (2010), 'Self-doubters, strugglers, storytellers, surfers and others: Images of self-identities in organization studies', *Human Relations*, **63** (2), 193–217.
Alvesson, Mats and Maxine Robertson (2006), 'The best and the brightest: The construction, significance and effects of elite identities in consulting firms', *Organization*, **13** (2), 195–224.
Armbrüster, Thomas (2004), 'Rationality and its symbols: Signalling effects and subjectification in management consulting', *Journal of Management Studies*, **41** (8), 1247–1269.
Ashforth, Blake E. (2001), *Role Transitions in Organizational Life: An Identity-based Perspective*, Mahwah, NJ: Lawrence Erlbaum Associates.
Atkinson, Robert (1998), *The Life Story Interview*, Sage University Papers Series on Qualitative Research Methods (Volume 44), Thousand Oaks, CA: Sage.
Bamberg, Michael (2004), 'Narrative discourse and identities', in Jan Christoph Meister, Tom Kindt and Wilhelm Schernus (eds), *Narratology beyond Literary Criticism*, Berlin & New York: Walter de Gruyter, pp. 213–238.
Benwell, Bethan and Elizabeth Stokoe (2010), 'Analysing identity in interaction: Contrasting discourse, genealogical, narrative and conversation analysis', in Margaret Wetherell and Chandra T. Mohanty (eds), *The Sage Handbook of Identities*, Thousand Oaks, CA: Sage, pp. 82–104.
Beyer, Janice M. and David R. Hannah (2002), 'Building on the past: Enacting established personal identities in a new work setting', *Organization Science*, **13** (6), 636–652.
Black, Stewart (1988), 'Work role transitions: A study of American expatriate managers in Japan', *Journal of International Business Studies*, **19** (2), 277–294.
Brown, Andrew D. and Michael Humphreys (2002), 'Nostalgia and the narrativization of identity: A Turkish case study', *British Journal of Management*, **13** (2), 141–159.
Brown, Andrew, Yiannis Gabriel and Silvia Gherardi (2009), 'Storytelling and change: An unfolding story', *Organization*, **16** (3), 323–333.
Bruner, Jerome (1994), 'The "remembered" self', in Ulric Neisser and Robyn Fivush (eds), *The Remembering Self: Construction and Accuracy in the Self-narrative*, Cambridge: Cambridge University Press, pp. 41–54.
Chreim, Samia, Bernie E. Williams and C.R. Bob Hinings (2007), 'Interlevel

influence on the reconstruction of professional role identity', *Academy of Management Journal*, **50** (6), 1515–1539.

Czarniawska, Barbara (1998), *A Narrative Approach to Organization Studies*, London: Sage.

De Fina, Anna and Alexandra Georgakopoulou (2008), 'Analyzing narratives as practice', *Qualitative Research*, **8** (3), 379–387.

Georgakopoulou, Alexandra (2006), 'Thinking big with small stories in narrative and identity analysis', *Narrative Inquiry*, **16** (1), 122–130.

Heracleous, Loizos (2006), *Discourse, Interpretation, Organization*, Cambridge: Cambridge University Press.

Horrocks, Aubrie and Jamie L. Callahan (2006), 'The role of emotion and narrative in the reciprocal construction of identity', *Human Resource Development International*, **9** (1), 69–83.

Humphreys, Michael and Andrew D. Brown (2002), 'Narratives of organizational identity and identification: A case study of hegemony and resistance', *Organization Studies*, **23** (3), 421–447.

Ibarra, Herminia (1999), 'Provisional selves: Experimenting with image and identity in professional adaptation', *Administrative Science Quarterly*, **44** (4), 764–791.

Ibarra, Herminia (2005), 'Identity transitions: Possible selves, liminality and the dynamics of career change', Working Paper Series. Fontainebleau: INSEAD.

Ibarra, Herminia and Roxana Barbulescu (2010), 'Identity as narrative: Prevalence, effectiveness, and consequences of narrative identity work in macro work role transitions', *Academy of Management Review*, **35** (1), 135–154.

Kärreman, Dan and Anna Rylander (2008), 'Managing meaning through branding: The case of a consulting firm', *Organization Studies*, **29** (1), 103–125.

Kenny, Kate, Andrea Whittle and Hugh Willmott (2011), *Understanding Identity and Organizations*, Thousand Oaks, CA: Sage.

Keupp, Heiner and Renate Höfer (eds) (1998), *Identitätsarbeit heute* (Second Edition), Frankfurt am Main: Suhrkamp.

Keupp, Heiner, Thomas Ahbe, Wolfgang Gmür, Renate Höfer, Beate Mitzscherlich, Wolfgang Kraus and Florian Straus (1999), *Identitätskonstruktionen: Das Patchwork der Identitäten in der Spätmoderne*, Reinbek: Rowohlt.

LaPointe, Kirsi (2011), 'Career change talk as a form of escape and resistance: An identity work perspective', paper presented at the 7th International Critical Management Studies Conference, Naples, Italy, July.

Louis, Meryl R. (1980a), 'Career transitions: Varieties and commonalities', *Academy of Management Review*, **5** (3), 329–340.

Louis, Meryl R. (1980b), 'Surprise and sense making: What newcomers experience in entering unfamiliar organizational settings', *Administrative Science Quarterly*, **25** (2), 226–251.

Maitlis, Sally (2012), 'Narrative analysis', in Gillian Symon and Catherine Cassell (eds), *Qualitative Organizational Research: Core Methods and Current Challenges*, London: Sage, pp. 492–511.

McAdams, Dan P. (1987), 'A life-story model of identity', in Robert Hogan and Warren H. Jones (eds), *Perspectives in Personality*, Greenwich, CT: JAI Press, pp. 15–50.

McAdams, Dan P. (2001), 'The psychology of life stories', *Review of General Psychology*, **5** (2), 100–122.

262 A guide to discursive organizational psychology

Meriläinen, Susan, Janne Tienari, Robyn Thomas and Annette Davies (2004), 'Management consultant talk: A cross-cultural comparison of normalizing discourse and resistance', *Organization*, **11** (4), 539–564.

Nicholson, Nigel (1984), 'A theory of work role transitions', *Administrative Science Quarterly*, **29** (2), 172–191.

Pentland, Brian T. (1999), 'Building process theory with narrative: From description to explanation', *Academy of Management Review*, **24** (4), 711–724.

Ricoeur, Paul (1988), *Time and Narrative (Volume 3)*, translated by Kathleen Blamey and David Pellauer, Chicago, IL: University of Chicago Press.

Ricoeur, Paul (1991), 'Life in quest of narrative', in David Wood (ed.), *On Paul Ricoeur*, London: Routledge, pp. 20–33.

Rossiter, Marsha (2009), 'Possible selves and career transition: Implications for serving nontraditional students', *The Journal of Continuing Higher Education*, **57** (2), 61–71.

Routledge, Clay, Jamie Arndt, Tim Wildschut, Constantine Sedikides, Claire M. Hart, Jacob Juhl, Ad J.J.M. Vingerhoets and Wolff Schlotz (2011), 'The past makes the present meaningful: Nostalgia as an existential resource', *Journal of Personality & Social Psychology*, **101** (3), 638–652.

Schein, Edgar H. (1978), *Career Dynamics: Matching Individual and Organizational Needs*, Reading, MA: Addison-Wesley.

Schein, Edgar H. (1990), *Career Anchors: Discovering your Real Values*, San Diego, CA: Pfeiffer.

Somers, M.R. (1994), 'The narrative constitution of identity: A relational network approach', *Theory and Society*, **23** (5), 605–649.

Steyaert, Chris and Bart Van Looy (eds) (2010), *Relational Practices, Participative Organizing. Advanced Series in Management (Volume 7)*, Bingley: Emerald.

Strauss, Anselm L. and Juliet M. Corbin (1990), *Basics of Qualitative Research: Grounded Theory Procedures and Techniques*, London: Sage.

Sturdy, Andrew and Christopher Wright (2008), 'A consulting diaspora? Enterprising selves as agents of enterprise', *Organization*, **15** (3), 427–444.

Sullivan, Sherry E. and Michael B. Arthur (2006), 'The evolution of the boundaryless career concept: Examining physical and psychological mobility', *Journal of Vocational Behavior*, **69** (1), 19–29.

Taylor, Stephanie (2007), 'Narrative as construction and discursive resource', in Michael Bamberg (ed.), *Narrative – State of the Art, Benjamins Current Topics 6*, Amsterdam: John Benjamins Publishing Company, pp. 113–122.

Turner, Barry A. (1981), 'Some practical aspects of qualitative data analysis: One way of organising the cognitive processes associated with the generation of grounded theory', *Quality and Quantity*, **15** (3), 225–247.

Weick, Karl E. (1995), *Sensemaking in Organizations*, Thousand Oaks, CA: Sage.

Wise, Amelia J. and Lynne J. Millward (2005), 'The experiences of voluntary career change in 30 somethings and implications for guidance', *Career Development International*, **10** (5), 400–417.

PART V

Intervention and change

12. De-normalizing subject positions in diversity interventions: how different can differences be(come)?

Anja Ostendorp and Chris Steyaert

INTRODUCTION

Over the last two decades, notions of diversity have travelled around the organizational landscape. As 'global ideas', they are repeated, imitated and translated through a broad range of corporate social interventions (Czarniawska and Sevón, 2005). Some of these interventions are explicitly labelled as 'diversity concepts', while others relate to various areas of commonly recognized HR practices. For instance, Swiss-based organizations increasingly initiate practices that involve 'multicultural teams' (Blom and Meier, 2002) and different language groups (Demont-Heinrich, 2005), or target older (Eberherr, Fleischmann and Hofmann, 2007) or disabled (Jens and Piazza, 2007) employees. Their efforts focus on people of different 'sexual orientations' (Räss, 2004), call for 'gender equality' (Nentwich, 2004) and engage in measures to 'balance' what is called 'work' on the one hand and 'life' on the other (Esslinger and Braun, 2007). But the target of these interventions is also extended into 'caring' about the 'health' of their employees (Ulich and Wülser, 2004), and 'corporate volunteering' (Schubert, Littmann-Wernli and Tingler, 2002). And, finally, they promise efficient 'management' of all this 'diversity' of diversity interventions (Koall, Bruchhagen and Höher, 2007).

In this chapter, we argue that every single example of what can be broadly called 'social interventions' refers to possibilities of difference in one way or the other: each carries with it possible answers to the core question we pose, namely how different differences can be(come). At first glance, ideas of diversity already emphasize the value of difference. In a critical turn, however, Lorbiecki and Jack (2000) have appropriately questioned whether, by definition, diversity concepts bring with them more possibilities of differences. Diversity is often reduced to a few categories, such as culture, gender or age, or, more importantly becomes completely domesticated instead of being encouraged and accepted within many different versions (Benshop and Doorewaard, 1998; Steyaert and Janssens, 2003). Because discourses travel globally, we must carefully analyse what happens when 'ideas go places' (Czarniaswka and Joerges, 1996): How are they repeated locally and translated in specific contexts? How are the varieties of interventions connected to varieties of difference in organizations?

To answer these questions, we must consider the effects of normalization, power and control of difference that are inextricably linked to each of the current social interventions in organizations. Instead of seeing differences as catering to a priori individual variables and essences (Zanoni and Janssens, 2007), we study how they result from the complex discursive processes that underlie social interventions. Hence, our interest in the question of how different differences can be(come) aims at understanding the discursive processes through which negotiations occur over the kinds of difference that are accepted or rejected. Therefore, we will consider current social interventions as concepts-in-the-making which are enacted as professionals, as well as participants, make sense of them. Reconciling a Scandinavian institutionalist frame with a discourse psychological analysis, we examine data from interviews with people involved as professionals or participants in a broad range of corporate social interventions. Focusing on the varieties of difference, two analytic questions provide structure for our analysis: (1) Through which interpretative repertoires do people make sense of the corporate social interventions they are involved in? (2) How do these repertoires allow for or undermine the possibility of difference?

Before we present our analysis, we situate our problem formulation in the literature and introduce the conceptual framework and methodology that has guided our study.

DIVERSITY AS A DISCURSIVE PRACTICE OF (DE)-NORMALIZATION

The Translation of Diversity Concepts

Ideas of diversity are sweeping through the organizational landscape; organizations draw upon the various circulating ideas, practices, discourses and paradigms to produce 'their' version of diversity. The academic work on global ideas (Czarniawska and Sevón, 2005) explores how ideas can spread quickly and travel around the globe, while local realities may still develop very differently. It shows how processes of translation are initiated as other social actors adopt ideas in ways that modify both the adopted and the adopters.

At first glance, diversity management seems to present itself as a variegated practice which results from both homogenizing tendencies and contextual variations. As diversity has become a managerial buzzword and showcase (Prasad and Mills, 1997), it has sometimes been perceived as a homogeneous concept that can easily be adopted independent of any specific context. Analysts using an institutional theory perspective argue that, as a field, diversity management tends towards imitation: companies copy examples, borrow ideas and increasingly resemble each other (Hedmo, Sahlin-Andersson and Wedlin, 2005). Thus, as Süss and Kleiner (2007) point out, the worldwide diffusion of diversity management represents an isomorphic process; comparing German companies with German subsidiaries of US multinationals, they found that 'globalization widely blends out cultural and national diversity' (Süss and Kleiner, 2007, p. 1951).

However, Scandinavian institutional theory, informed by Actor-Network theory (Czarniawska and Sevón, 1996; 2005; Greenwood, Oliver, Sahlin and Suddaby, 2008), has argued that imitation is not a passive process but a performative act (Sevón, 1996). Diversity management, like other management concepts, is reinterpreted as it is taken up and practised in different contexts. To understand this translation process, several authors have inquired whether the national context is important in understanding how diversity management is disseminated: do most actors appropriate a dominant version (Süss and Kleiner, 2007) or does it move into a different, hybrid version, eventually becoming 'lost in translation' (Boxenbaum, 2006; Kamp and Hagedorn-Rasmussen, 2004)? For instance, Kamp and Hagedorn-Rasmussen (2004) combine critical discourse analysis with neo-institutional theory to argue that, although they can identify a general set of diversity discourses, diversity management is interpreted in a specific societal and organizational context. Similarly, Boxenbaum (2006), using Goffmanian frame analysis, studied the making of Danish diversity management as a translation of an American model; she found a hybrid version, accounted for by individual preferences, strategic reframing and local grounding. These studies point out the importance of understanding how global ideas of diversity are embedded in unfolding sensemaking processes where local repertoires are decisive for how social interventions are enacted.

Against this backdrop, we stress the process of translation that enables actors to virtually enter a reflexive observation and discussion of why and how to translate any of those 'fashionable' (Czarniawka, 2005) interventions in the context of the Swiss corporate landscape. Connecting notions of neo-institutional theory with discourse theory (Kamp and

Hagedorn-Rasmussen, 2004; Phillips, Lawrence and Hardy, 2004), it becomes possible to study translation as performative act through discourse analysis.

De-essentializing Difference

This study thus joins the group of recent discursive studies of diversity that look into more historical discursive changes (Prasad, 2001; Runté and Mills, 2006; Ahonen, Tienari, Meriläinen and Pullen, 2014) as well as into the organizational contexts of discourses (Tomlinson and Egan, 2002; Zanoni and Janssens, 2007).

Common to this range of discursive studies is the assumption that differences are not essential features of individuals but are actually produced in discursive practices. Discursive studies thus follow the critical turn (Zanoni, Janssens, Benschop and Nkomo, 2010) as they undertake a reflexive examination of 'the political, social and cultural conditions' in which possibilities of difference have been constructed (Lorbiecki and Jack, 2000, p. 829). Differences become themes in the discourses of diversity, which are contextually enacted; thus notions of difference must be studied empirically in specific contexts rather than understood as available a priori. Giving an account of each intervention, therefore, is understood as an active, productive process that draws upon and associates some culturally and historically produced resources of sensemaking while neglecting or failing to associate others.

This discursive approach helps to illustrate how currently popular interventions and their effects on difference can be conceived of as always 'in the making'. While translating global ideas of diversity, actors fluently reproduce or modify certain meanings of their diversity practices, while rejecting other possible meanings (Zanoni and Janssens, 2007). For instance, possibilities of difference can be limited by the norm of culturally provided images of the 'ideal worker', an image well-known in the literature (Benshop and Doorewaard, 1998; Tienari, Quack and Theobald, 2002). Therefore, the question of what constitutes an 'ideal worker' is always open to negotiation. Images of that worker can never be fixed once and for all, but are subject to context and change (Benshop and Doorewaard, 1998; Tienari et al., 2002). What these images have in common is their orientation to the norm, as they create and effect dichotomous and hierarchical categories. Though the term 'ideal worker' is rather ironic, it refers to underlying assumptions about quasi-objective organizational realities and hidden patterns of power and dominance.

Accordingly, scholars have illustrated how 'the diverse person' and his or her 'difference' is complementarily constructed as a 'minority' (Ely and

Thomas, 2001; Steyaert and Janssens, 2003). In this light, the effects of diversity interventions cannot be ripped out of their context but need to be studied as elements of ongoing micro-political processes (Foldy, 2002). A discursive understanding of power helps us see that 'as power operates through everyday ways of sensemaking that are more or less institutionalized in disciplinary knowledge, the normalcy of the normal becomes constructed as such' (Hardy and Clegg, 2006, p. 769). Analysing the discursive construction of diversity concepts enables us to look empirically at how various interpretative repertoires operate in the sensemaking process and what consequences this process has for the different possibilities of difference.

The Politics of Discursive Sensemaking

We conceive of the different social interventions as depending on currently available discourses that allow specific ways of 'sensemaking' (Weick, 1995) while disguising others. While there are various ways to conceptualize discourse and undertake discourse analysis (Wood and Kroger, 2000), we follow an approach developed in discursive psychology (Hepburn and Wiggins, 2007; Potter and Wetherell, 1987). Crucially, this approach aims at the verbal toolboxes or interpretative repertoires (Potter and Wetherell, 1987; Wetherell, 1998) of social life. Potter and Wetherell (1987, p. 138) circumscribe interpretative repertoires as 'a lexicon or register' that people fluently use 'for characterizing and evaluating actions, events and other phenomena' (p. 149). Therefore, we do not conceive of repertoires as ideal-typical but as simultaneously available tools (Ostendorp, 2009).

Ely and Thomas (2001, p. 270) emphasized this idea, pointing out the need for research into the very dynamics of the ideal-typical perspective on diversity: 'Finally, we need to learn more about how and under what conditions work groups develop and change their perspectives on diversity, in particular, how they change to the more promising one of integration and learning.' In response to this challenge, Kamp and Hagedorn-Rasmussen (2004) examined how a set of discourses they derived from the literature is mixed in a specific organizational context, but they warned against overestimating the stability of these discourses; they suggested studying how actors mobilize discourses of diversity in interaction with other local discourses as they make sense of diversity management.

In order to follow up on these suggestions, we stress what Potter and Wetherell (1987, p. 168) call the 'basic theoretical thrust of discourse analysis': that the use of each repertoire has very different functions and effects on the process of constructing difference, revealing the political dimension of discursive sensemaking. By analysing the repertoires of social interventions, then, we can understand the ways that open up or close off different approaches to difference. As themes about difference arise in discourses, bringing with them different constructions of reality, we can see how, within a specific discourse, a subject's position (Davies and Harré, 1990) is constructed as a combination of knowledge and power and how the range of their diverse identities is established (Bruni and Gherardi, 2002).

METHODOLOGY

Sample and Data Collection

Seeking a variety of contemporary answers to the question of how different differences can be(come) within the local context of the Swiss corporate landscape, we first conducted a document analysis, collecting written material from Swiss organizations about their current social interventions. These interventions were not easily delineated; they related to diversity in its broadest sense, including neighbouring fields like health and social care and (corporate) volunteering. This broad approach seemed promising, because we found emerging practices rather than established interventions on diversity. Our approach to this variety was twofold. We selected three organizations that explicitly offered 'diversity management' and analysed their various social interventions. We also included three organizations that were discussing similar interventions but not referring to a special diversity concept and thus not drawing explicitly upon the global ideas of diversity. These six major Swiss firms were situated in the food, pharmaceutical, and industrial sectors as well as financial services.

In order to consider a variety of personal experiences with the selected interventions, we included accounts that would reflect the perspectives of professionals setting up interventions for organizations, as well as those of participating employees. First, we conducted nine interviews with so-called 'representatives' or 'professionals' of the six different firms, who were active in the areas of diversity, health, and volunteering. Second, we conducted sixteen interviews with employees who narrated their experience of participating in the selected interventions. Thereby, we tried to include the widest possible range of experiences, mixing differences in age, ethnicity, gender, family background, job position, and employment contract.

To provide enough balance between unrestricted narration and a strong focus on the core research questions, we followed the script of a narrative 'problem-centred' interview (Witzel, 2000). Each interview took from one to one and a half hours. Because the languages used in the interviews were German and Swiss-German, we conducted our data analysis in the language of the interviews; one of the authors translated the selected interview passages presented below in order to illustrate our findings. This translation of interview fragments adds to the complexity of discursively translating diversity concepts (Marschan-Piekkari and Reis, 2004; Steyaert and Janssens, 2013).

Data Analysis

The analytic goal was to identify those interpretative repertoires that people draw on to enable social practices (Potter and Wetherell, 1987) and to discuss the notions of difference they imply. The analytic process consisted of several stages. As a first integral part of the analysis, we fully transcribed all the interviews. Next, we fed the material into the electronic data processing program ATLAS/ti (Kelle, 2000) which makes it possible to edit passages in each interview and refer to them by line number (for instance, interview 8, lines 20–50).

In search of patterns in the text, we read the variety of materials repeatedly, and categorized and reconnected it with a high degree of curiosity and patience; we aimed to avoid hasty applications, circular identifications or generalizations about particular passages (Antaki, Billig, Edwards and Potter, 2003). Our key criterion for each of the four interpretative repertoires we identified was that it had to provide consistent patterns, which did not overlap with the central terms and descriptions of other emerging repertoires. Consequently, we traced back the implicit and explicit effects of each repertoire (Potter and Wetherell, 1987, p. 149; Wood and Kroger, 2000, p. 95). For each of the four repertoires, we systematically went through the material again, asking how each one allows for difference. In the following section we introduce these repertoires as *luxury*, *emergency*, *interest*, and *inclusion*, and discuss how each may allow or undermine possibilities of difference. Table 12.1 provides a summary overview of our findings.

RESULTS

Difference as Taboo: The *Luxury Repertoire* and the Construction of an 'Ideal Worker'

When the *luxury repertoire* is in play, social interventions are geared to a homogeneous, well-functioning workforce that is participating in some enriched and unnecessary, hence luxurious, service. Anyone operating from this repertoire is strictly oriented to the culturally-provided images of the 'ideal worker'. Drawing upon contemporary discourses of well-being, for instance, fashionable facilities from gyms to swimming pools are conceived of as luxurious offerings that do not interfere with everyday business: 'It takes place during lunch time, which makes it absolutely legitimate for employees to leave their offices' (Health and social care professional, interview 17, lines 218–220).

Other interventions, such as programmes that aim to sensitize employees about otherness and to improve their social competence, also can be constructed as luxurious offers. For instance, one professional set up a volunteering programme which aims to facilitate new experiences with otherness as an expensive 'pleasant perk', one that is not expected to entail any long-term effects for the company: 'Once the participants are back, then [the intervention] is over, it is finished on the last afternoon' (Volunteering professional, interview 20, line 359). A manager who had participated in that programme, volunteering for a week with people with disabilities, made a similar distinction. While he used other repertoires to speak affirmatively about his new experiences that made him become 'different' (Participant in volunteer programme, interview 7, line 358), in the context of business he switched to the *luxury repertoire*, stressing that this impact must be conceived of as very much a luxury and strictly separate from business:

> This is totally on a private basis . . . I am sure the program is an enrichment for the candidate, but not for the company . . . it is personal, for me it is personal. (Ibid., lines 592–784)

As a consequence, this manager pointed out that he would never voice his new perspective on difference with his colleagues in the office. Likewise, a young father who had started using his company's childcare services created a strict division between the spheres of private life and of business:

> The one thing is my job, and I am a hundred, hundred and fifty percent there for it, and the other is my family. The one has nothing to do with the other. (Participant in diversity programme, interview 4, lines 125–127)

Whenever he draws on the first repertoire, the organizational offer becomes a sheer luxury that he and his company can currently afford. As an 'ideal' husband (Simon, 1995) and father, he is willing to make use of it. Drawing on the *luxury repertoire*, however, this does not challenge the standard image of an 'ideal worker'. In a meeting, for instance, he would never mention that he has to leave at a certain time to pick up his son: 'This does not look good. It is kind of unprofessional' (Ibid., lines 123–124).

Perhaps ideas of diversity can be seen to make a company more attractive and its workforce more committed, but when they are oriented to the *luxury repertoire* these interventions are not designed to address differences which would challenge the norm of the organizational centre. Since no further connection is made, such interventions just become disposable, a luxurious 'side issue' (Volunteering professional, interview 21, p. 150). When it comes down to a careful cost-benefit analysis, therefore, the professionals understand that fashionable luxury is doomed to failure:

> As long as our company has to publish its quarterly results four times a year, then every single person is simply focused on the numbers. (Diversity professional, interview 16, lines 333–334)

People embrace the topic of diversity (in a politically correct way) as a pleasant perk; meanwhile they literally cannot mention fundamental deviations from the norm, which thus become a taboo. As a consequence, employees turn out to have fundamental reservations when it comes to talking about any kind of 'vulnerability':

> I think it always takes a not-so-simple step to somehow admit something. A weakness or whatever ... Well ... in the business world one does not easily admit to being burned out. Because that can also be easily explained as not being able to meet the demands or as overestimating oneself. (Health and social care professional, interview 17, lines 126–133)

In this vein, a manager who suffered from Ménière's Disease, which includes tinnitus and dizzy spells, spoke of his fear of 'giving himself away'. Thus, he strictly avoided talking about his 'personal problems' at work:

> Although my wife and the doctors had warned me again and again – at work there was no opportunity to deal with my critical physical and psychological condition. . . . I wanted to show everybody in the firm that I knew the important goals. I didn't want to seem weak. (Participant in health care programme, interview 12, lines 317–322)

No spaces exist for differences as they become normalized within the centre of an organization and its given images of an 'ideal worker'. Difference is moved out of the picture. While strategic considerations to keep up with a trend form the starting point, the respective interventions preserve homogeneity and confirm the dominant voice of the centre.

In summary, the *luxury repertoire* proves to be mainly constituted by terms such as standard, image, performance, and strength. A fashionable diversity intervention, then, is kept strictly apart from what really counts in the ordinary course of business. It acts as a sweetener during good times. Difference becomes a taboo and, in reverse, the image of an 'ideal worker' is strengthened.

Difference as Need: The *Emergency Repertoire* and the Construction of Minorities

We use the word *emergency* for the second repertoire, as it recognizes that outside of the firm's centre, some people are in need and therefore lack the attributes of the 'ideal worker'. Complementing the first repertoire, this one makes sense of social interventions by explicitly noting that some people have specific needs; for instance, they do not fit the expected conceptions about physical standards, are foreign to the country, have parenting obligations, and so on. Interventions oriented to the second repertoire are addressed to 'the world of minorities or to people with certain characteristics' (Diversity professional, interview 19, lines 10–11). The aim of these interventions is to help people cope with the more severe conditions, to provide for their needs, and to lessen their suffering. Therefore, the interventions explicitly address 'emergency cases' that arise whenever employees appear not to be up to the standard. In this vein, an organizational endeavour regarding diversity often proves to be associated with the notion of 'women in need':

> Diversity in Switzerland – here we are already moving away from the clean and shiny topics – is still . . . directed towards women who need support. (Diversity professional, interview 16, lines 9–12)

In this repertoire, the talk is about practicalities like balancing working hours; instead of bringing up images of a glamorous sabbatical, a fancy world tour, or innovative job-sharing, it is more about the mere compatibility of work and parenting, often about surviving in a stable half-time job. Thus, an initially open term like diversity becomes laden with particular needs, as a single mother states:

> Yes, I think that is great work that is done there. . . . Because the women who need such things, well, they are becoming more numerous. (Participant in diversity programme, interview 2, lines 319–322)

For those using the second repertoire, the various interventions are not conceived of as extraneous luxuries but rather as responses to serious social concerns. Though the repertoire entails requests to support 'the weak', it does not aim to enter the homogeneous centre and make different voices heard. Quite the contrary, differences become ascribed to the people who are seen to be different. By being grateful that they are getting special treatment out of sight of the centre and by pointing at clear-cut target groups and their needs, the argument turns out (often implicitly) to create a strict distinction between those who are and are not affected. As one participant put it:

> [H]ealthy people do not use all these things . . . actually they do not want to talk about this, they are healthy and for them that is simply not their world. (Participant in age and disability programme, interview 9, lines 208–211)

As a consequence, those who are addressed by the social interventions in the second repertoire understand their own situation as dependent. They speak of themselves as a 'case' that otherwise would fail or even drop out, as the single mother illustrates:

> I am basically dependent on this. . . . When you are dependent on this, as in my case, then you have no other choice, then there is no other possibility for yourself, unless the company tries to meet your needs. (Ibid., lines 325–330)

Likewise, an older employee who had surgery for a hernia stresses her dependence on special provisions such as an ergonomically designed workplace and the possibility of working half-time:

> I was very happy at that time, since I was really dependent on this, because things no longer went as quickly, and there were extra appointments and exercises and this kind of thing, and it was already difficult enough to get back into an everyday rhythm after all these changes. But for me it was very important to be able to work again. (Participant in age and disability programme, interview 9, lines 125–130)

The employee becomes an emergency case, as she can no longer work full-time (at least in the way the firm constructs that category). As a burden to the organization, an employee with a disability would, ideally, be laid off. But since this employee needs her wages, the company demonstrates its sense of social responsibility according to the *emergency repertoire*. Within this repertoire, the special offers represent the only chance for those involved to come to a suitable arrangement and for the firm to 'integrate' them as well as possible: 'If it is really needed, we can arrange things like that' (Health and social care manager, interview 17, lines 190–191). Affected employees are grateful for specific support and anticipate that there is simply no other workspace where their concerns would receive attention. Together with the extent of neediness, then, the concept of gratitude becomes a crucial element of the *emergency repertoire*. Thus, the older woman above points out that she is 'very happy that this has been made possible, that they are concerned with the weaker or elder ones' (Ibid., lines 144–145).

The various interventions act as a well-meaning pro-social way for 'those who give' to support 'those who take'. Calling on the social consciousness of singular actors, they provide no connection to 'the real business' and are silently displayed on the margins. In this light, those who are affected rarely talk about what they might be able to give to their organization, but instead about what they unfortunately take away from it. Differences become fixed, marginalized, and stigmatized as features that reside within those people who are different in regard to specific needs ('*the* single mother') or qualities ('persons with disabilities'). At best, then, when seen in terms of the *emergency repertoire*, difference is something that can co-exist on the fringes. This repertoire might facilitate a silent emergency solution, but it is not in a position to encourage other actors in the organization to hear different voices.

In summary, the *emergency repertoire* displays the linguistic kit of voiceless minority needs and refers to the 'diverse person' who is being constructed in the margins. The terms that constitute the *emergency repertoire* turn out to include weakness, need, dependence and gratitude. Acting on the assumption that real business is something strictly separate from the social agenda, differences become fixed as a deviation from the norm, leaving the minority dependent and powerless.

Difference as Dispute: The *Interest Repertoire* and the Construction of Interest Groups

Within the third repertoire, the specific interventions are said to be concerned with raising the issues of a particular interest group. When oriented to this repertoire, social interventions are not merely conceived of as silent favours for grateful people in need. On the contrary, when actors draw on the *interest repertoire*, they rather self-confidently stress the importance of being able to relate to the same interests and values, because – as one interviewee put it – 'birds of a feather flock together':

> And this plays a really important role, namely that you know, that you share a common platform to fall back on. . . . As I am always saying: Birds of a feather flock together. Then you are driven to take initiative, as you feel supported, and as you know, we have the same interests. (Participant in health care programme, interview 10, lines 176–304)

Thereby, the theme of difference and the positioning of various initiatives become serious political concerns as groups work to develop different voices and challenge the current image of the 'ideal worker'. Whenever speakers use this repertoire they are prepared to voice their issues not just in terms of an emergency, but rather systematically. Thus the third repertoire is associated with a call for those with the same interests to come together and fight for them:

> [I] know simply that here I have fellow-combatants. I told you about the woman responsible for equal opportunities . . . she is totally dedicated, there is a real involvement there, one can easily see that. This is not just her job, this is also about, yes, about the political, this is obviously about equal opportunities. (Participant in gender programme, interview 2, lines 304–315)

Currently, in the context of Swiss-based organizations, interest groups that can be linked to the subject of either gender or culture tend to come in first. When asked about the contents and target groups, diversity experts did not hesitate to list the well-known diversity categories:

> [F]rom the perspective of the company, cultural projects are definitely important since we have [a large variety of] nations here.. . . Of course gender is also important. (Diversity professional, interview 19, lines 108–110)

In addition to these interest groups that are almost classics to those in diversity management, another increasingly influential pillar is older employees: '[I]t is a demographic trend, the baby-boomer generation, a high percentage of old people; this is a long-term issue' (Diversity professional, interview 16, lines 370–372). Fighting for each of their particular interests, supported by trans-organizational fellow combatants, marks an important goal. Thus, speakers are less inclined to refer to difference in general, but instead try to lobby for their own interest group, emphasizing power positions and aiming to empower particular groups.

Organizations, in turn, tend to feel overloaded by the large number of requests. While they present themselves as willing to 'pick up' a limited number of the major trends cited above, they continue to stress that they cannot meet each specific interest on every issue. Consequently, one diversity professional pointed out how she had to 'fight on two fronts' when implementing a special programme to support 'employability' for older employees. She had to win over enough of the participants who saw themselves as 'fellow combatants', and also had to manage organizational distrust, justifying her (resource-consuming) efforts to the management and coping with resistance from the centre itself when some started 'speculating about what' she was 'up to now' (Diversity professional, interview 15, line 229).

Contention arises when several groups with different interests must share the same resources. Thus, difference moves as a conflict of interest between different groups. Each interest group opposes its particular interests to the interests of 'the rest' of the company. Ultimately, they compete

both with the image of the 'ideal worker' in the centre of the organization and with each other in the margins. For instance, male employees
working part-time due to parenting obligations prefer not to talk about
their experiences:

> Last year I had a request from a newspaper on the topic of men and fathers
> working part-time. I had identified a list of participants and in the end there
> were only two who wanted to testify. The others said, I had to fight for this and I
> had all these discussions with my colleagues, I simply do not want to go through
> this again. No, I am not eager at all to get in the paper with my story. (Diversity
> professional, interview 16, lines 170–181)

To make particular groups and their interests the focus of an intervention
also implies excluding everyone who is not a member of that group. And
the firm risks bringing back the image of 'the different person' through
the back door, but this time on an intergroup level. Whereas agreement
(or even collusion) exists within one group, other groups become 'the
opponent', provoking an 'Oppression Olympics' (Berdahl and Moore,
2006): a contest between diverse groups over who is more oppressed.

   In summary, the *interest repertoire* is used to create special interest
groups whose representatives are combative. Its main terms are rights,
fights, commonality, and fellow combatants. Lobbying about specific
interests often leads to a much-discussed ranking of the most powerful
minorities. Differences can actually be as different as their lobby groups
are powerful.

Difference as Sine Qua Non: The *Inclusion Repertoire* and the Construction of Otherness

The fourth repertoire provides a fairly comprehensive approach that aims
to connect different concerns and make them heard in all directions. In this
vein, there is an explicit quest for *inclusion*. As one diversity professional
put it, 'This means everyone. Therefore we say, "Diversity: inclusion!"'
(Diversity professional, interview 19, line 591).

   Instead of adopting well-defined categories that apply to single groups or
themes, current interventions apply to broader organizational issues, including 'agency, a holistic leadership, and the work atmosphere', according to
one health care professional, who added that 'it is always about the whole
system' (Health care professional, interview 18, lines 41ff.). Consequently,
diversity professionals stress their concern about dissolving the distinctions
between doing core business on the one hand and doing public relations,
charitable acts, or representations of interests on the other:

> We are intentionally not building out a diversity management group, because otherwise . . . every manager and top manager will say: 'That is perfect; we are doing diversity in our company. They are doing diversity, and I am doing "business"'. That is what we explicitly want to avoid. (Diversity professional, interview 19, lines 209–212)

In this context, the different constructions are supposed to lead to 'ongoing processes that basically concern everybody' (Diversity professional, interview 14, lines 275–276). Then, no one can conceive of a diversity practice as separated from other organizational practices. This understanding also begins to erase the gap between diversity management on the one hand and a volunteering programme that aims to increase awareness of difference. In this vein, an interviewee responsible for volunteering programmes stresses:

> [W]e will emphasize more and more that [our programme] stimulates diversity and thus teaches one to deal with diversity. (Volunteering professional, interview 21, lines 597–598)

Thus, the interviewee refuses to define his job description under any one concept such as 'corporate volunteering':

> [M]y position in the company is not as someone in personnel or HR, I am so to speak an internal expert on various themes . . . of a social nature; which in the broadest sense can be seen as corporate social responsibility. (Ibid., lines 13–17)

According to the inclusive approach implied in this repertoire, there is no point in distinguishing between different well-defined (and thus easily stigmatized) target groups. Viewing the company as one of many spaces in which different voices can interact in multiple ways, it stresses its quest to attend to and address vital cultural issues within the organization. This quest entails a call to be courageous and creative, as another professional from the field of diversity management explains:

> And this is our ambition. . . . To build up courage and also to give support, or simply to say . . . one has to get a bit creative and cunning. It is about working differently! (Diversity professional, interview 16, lines 190–202)

Likewise, employees are not only asked to reflect upon their differences 'in private', but are also challenged 'to talk about things . . . and to open up taboos' (Diversity professional, interview 21, p. 240). Consequently, the *inclusion repertoire* tries to overcome the rather homogeneous voice of the centre by making room for a variety of lives, experiences and horizons. Such a radical shift, for instance, can be noticed in the story of another successful manager who started volunteering with persons with disabilities:

> I used to walk in a wide circle around every wheelchair. . . . I earned a lot of money, I had a big office like most people can only dream of, a car, my own parking place, and, and, and . . . (Participant in volunteering programme, interview 6, lines 5–50)

As he became involved with persons with disabilities, he understood that he had to set aside his fear of contact, and he started to question what is considered normality and recognized the limits of his world:

> I realized how different the world actually is, how differently everything can work out . . . I don't know what else will happen. There are still many interesting things to come . . . I am curious. (Ibid., lines 652–654)

As the *inclusion repertoire* explicitly strove to disseminate difference within the overall organization, it moved differences, so to speak, to the centre of the organization. Consequently, difference is multiplied as the basis of organizational everyday life that stimulates people to open up to new connections and relations. In this light, difference becomes a sine qua non of organizational life, something that makes people start to move in the direction of an unknown part of themselves, an otherness.

This kind of destabilizing position is also illustrated in the life-changing experience of the above-cited 'ideal worker' who lives with Ménière's Disease. Here, otherness becomes a new (and strange) condition this manager has to learn to understand and express. Operating in the *luxury repertoire* and its threatening counterpart, the *emergency repertoire*, he emphasized that he worked hard at covering up his 'failure'. Initially he tried to make up for his 'deviations' from the norm within what he considered his 'private life'. More and more, he started to make use of organizational interventions about stress management, which he saw as a first step towards developing a new right to speak about himself differently within the organization. He appreciated such interventions as a building block that can support the entry of marginalized concerns into public and thus into everyone's focus, multiplying the views of how to act as an employee and bringing about a more hybrid organization:

> This can only be a small building block, one cannot expect too much. But for me personally this was really significant . . . that you learn that these problems are not to be tackled privately, but there, where they actually emerge, at one's work. Because time pressure comes from there, and it doesn't help me much when I work on it during the weekend in some expensive private workshop, and then come back here on Monday morning and go on without making the connection. (Ibid., lines 365–390)

Table 12.1 Synoptic overview of the interpretative repertoires and their possibilities of difference

Repertoire Functions, effects	I The luxury repertoire	II The emergency repertoire	III The interest repertoire	IV The inclusion repertoire
Main terms	standard; image; performance; strength	weakness; need; dependence; gratitude	rights; fights; commonality; fellow combatants	voicing; participation; curiosity; change
Focus on	the image of an 'ideal worker' in the centre of the organization	minority groups on the margins	special interest groups and their position in the organization	fluid differences as part of a hybrid organization
Aim	offering luxury for the 'ideal workforce'	soothing the most pressing needs of those who are 'different'	lobbying for special interest groups	overcoming categories and accepting a variety of differences
Hierarchies between business and personal/ societal sphere	are reproduced	are complementarily reproduced	are at stake	are rejected
Differences	as a taboo	are addressed in terms of particular needs	are narrowed down to particular interests	are addressed as plurality in terms of a 'sine qua non' of social interaction
Further impacts on power relations	are not intended	are not intended	are stressed for special interest groups	are stressed within the overall organization

Although this might also constitute an important experience, his participation was not only a matter of fulfilling urgent needs (as in the *emergency repertoire*), a matter of finding like-minded people (as it is within the *interest repertoire*), or a matter of how a specific health care offering could support his coping strategies (in terms of the *luxury repertoire*). As he emphasized, it 'became a matter of seeing things differently and voicing difference as a cultural contribution' (Ibid., lines 162–170). By challenging the rather homogeneous standard, he not only 'outed' himself and tried out other images of himself but also added to the images of people at work in a more hybrid organization.

In summary, within the *inclusion repertoire*, the various interventions are no longer conceived of as isolated, exclusive, or even private matters, but as concerns that are potentially salient for everyone. Its main terms are voicing, participation, curiosity, and change. Seeing difference as sine qua non requires people to take unsettling journeys along uncertain trajectories. It implies that the centre of an organization can include 'different' differences by distributing diversity as everyone's responsibility and affirming its own multiplicity, giving priority to a hybrid organization.

DISCUSSION AND CONCLUSION

In this study, we aimed to understand the discursive processes through which corporate social interventions are made sense of and to shed light on the consequences for the construction of difference. We started with the observation that diversity management in Swiss-based organizations (implicitly or explicitly) is related to and enacted by a wide variety of interventions. While some of them are categorized as interventions from the field of 'diversity management', others show a somewhat hidden connection. Thus, the effect of this variety proved to be rather small: both professionals and participants drew upon the same restricted range of interpretative repertoires. Whether they were talking about a cultural initiative, a disability intervention, or a new experience of themselves, they gave priority to the *luxury*, the *emergency*, and, sometimes, the *interest repertoire*. However, as we tried to trace the fourth repertoire, our open choice approach proved especially useful. In examining the *inclusion repertoire* it became clear that to make sense of diversity interventions, people did question the organizational and institutional boundaries, arguing that difference needs to be dealt with in the overall organizational context rather than strictly limited to a group of diversity professionals.

Thus, our study shows that diversity is an open and partially fluid term: some aspects of diversity are fruitfully adopted and modified while others are less happily embraced or often kept out of sight. In this vein, we did not find any interviews that were completely oriented to the *interest* or the *inclusion repertoire*. But we found several passages where interviewees left behind the first two common repertoires and repeatedly explored the alternatives. We believe that by using a discourse psychological analysis, which looks for variations in repertoire use rather than ascribing exactly one repertoire to one speaker, we can better understand and theorize how differences are fluently extinguished or emphasized during accounts of social interventions.

This brings us to our central question concerning how different differences can be(come). We have documented how each of the repertoires has different implications for the way that difference becomes acknowledged, modified or completely erased. Difference is thus positioned as taboo, as need, as dispute, and as necessity. Depending on the respective repertoire in use, it may be seen as not important to the organization, or be linked to the identification of specific minorities, related to conflictual interaction between interest groups, or be included in the overall, hybridized organization. For instance, talking about currently 'typical' diversity ideas in terms of a showcase, both professionals and participants would draw on the *luxury repertoire* and thus position differences as irrelevant to the daily business of the overall organization. While most of the (global) organizations we worked with can be seen as practising 'distant cheerleading' (Dick and Cassell, 2002), our more detailed examination of sensemaking practices shows that interventions often are not transformed into a broader organizational frame where difference has various meanings. Expensive investments in cultural training programmes, childcare services, or fashionable gyms do not necessarily increase the possibilities of difference but often remain the eternal bridesmaids: side issues far from the core of the organization. At the other end of the spectrum, we found building blocks such as the *inclusion repertoire* that translated a specific measure as a way to infuse a particular experience into the overall organization: when a manager becomes involved in the care of people with disabilities, which at first looks like a rather modest and unspectacular initiative, it can lead to a radical reframing of how difference is understood. The mere existence of different social interventions says nothing about the way people use interpretative repertoires and make sense of difference. In this light, the meaning of a diversity concept becomes less dependent on the features of a special intervention. Instead, it presents itself as a consequence of the interpretative repertoires by means of which actors give meaning to the interventions and their related varieties of difference.

Our study helps to explain the dilemma of managing diversity (Prasad and Mills, 1997): the more diversity management tries to nurture differences exclusively – as in the *emergency repertoire* – the more it becomes impossible to give them voice within the centre of the organization. Therefore, repertoires that cannot question the normalcy of the 'ideal worker' within the centre of an organization, that situate their actions in the margins, or that run the risk of setting up the norms of one interest group against those of another, systematically hinder the possibility of making (new) sense of difference.

This shows that it is political processes (Ahonen et al., 2014) that create or destroy the possibility of differences being tried out and create the possibility of multiplicity in everyday organizational life, eventually making it more hybrid (Styhre and Eriksson-Zetterquist, 2008).

In this sense, we agree with Foldy (2002, p. 109) that 'diversity programmes that downplay or ignore issues of dominance or subordination cannot succeed in making even superficial changes in organizations; they are sidestepping the elephant in the room'. The production of difference as the proverbial elephant of diversity management research can only be understood as an effect of power. To counter the normalcy of tabooing the variety of difference, the repertoires of *interest* and *inclusion* offer new meanings, making it possible to negotiate differences as a form of conflict or as a form of resistance against the norm of the 'ideal worker'. We thus conceive of them as two complementarily important sources to foster varieties of difference. Sensitive oscillations between those sources might enable a 'language of negotiation' (Northcraft, Polzer, Neale and Kramer, 1996, p. 69), which balances the (concrete, but often too fixed) building blocks of the *interest repertoire* and the fluid (but often too vague) building blocks of the *inclusion repertoire*.

Although the most powerful repertoires we identified were still those that focused on the 'ideal worker' and marginalized minorities, we also found traces of emerging interpretative repertoires which contribute to the idea of difference by overturning the dominant logic of general sameness and its counterpart of the 'diverse' person. We suggest that further studies become more aware of this simultaneous variety and its enabling effects on difference, no matter through which of the various old or new interventions they start filtering into workplace discourses. This would continue the search for avenues to move beyond current images of the 'ideal worker', to no longer essentialize people and normalize their positions but instead multiply their possibilities.

REFERENCES

Ahonen, Pasi, Janne Tienari, Susan Meriläinen and Alison Pullen (2014), 'Hidden contexts and invisible power relations: A Foucauldian reading of diversity research', *Human Relations*, **67** (3), 263–286.
Antaki, Charles, Michael Billig, Derek Edwards and Jonathan Potter (2003),

'Discourse analysis means doing analysis: A critique of six analytic shortcomings', *Discourse Analysis Online*, 1 (1).

Benshop, Yvonne and Hans Doorewaard (1998), 'Six of one and half a dozen of the other: The gender subtext of Taylorism and team-based work', *Gender, Work & Organization*, 5 (1), 5–18.

Berdahl, Jennifer L. and Celia Moore (2006), 'Workplace harassment: Double jeopardy for minority women', *Journal of Applied Psychology*, 91 (2), 426–436.

Blom, Herman and Harald Meier (2002), *Interkulturelles Management*, Berlin: Herne.

Boxenbaum, Eva (2006), 'Lost in translation: The making of Danish diversity management', *American Behavioral Scientist*, 49 (7), 939–948.

Bruni, Attila and Silvia Gherardi (2002), 'En-gendering differences, transgressing the boundaries, coping with the dual presence', in Iiris Aaltio-Marjosola and Albert J. Mills (eds), *Gender, Identity and the Culture of Organizations*, London: Routledge, pp. 21–38.

Czarniawska, Barbara (2005), 'Fashion in organizing', in Barbara Czarniawska and Guje Sevón (eds), *Global Ideas: How Ideas, Objects and Practices Travel in the Global Economy*, Malmö: Liber and Copenhagen Business School Press, pp. 129–146.

Czarniawska, Barbara and Bernward Joerges (1996), 'Travels of ideas', in Barbera Czarniawska and Guje Sevón (eds), *Translating Organizational Change*, Berlin: De Gruyter, pp. 13–48.

Czarniawska, Barbara and Guje Sevón (eds) (1996), *Translating Organizational Change*, Berlin: De Gruyter.

Czarniawska, Barbara and Guje Sevón (eds) (2005), *Global Ideas: How Ideas, Objects and Practices Travel in the Global Economy*, Malmö: Liber and Copenhagen Business School Press.

Davies, Bronwyn and Rom Harré (1990), 'Positioning: The discursive production of selves', *Journal for the Theory of Social Behaviour*, 20 (1), 43–64.

Demont-Heinrich, Christof (2005), 'Language and national identity in the era of globalization: The case of English in Switzerland', *Journal of Communication Inquiry*, 29 (1), 66–84.

Dick, Penny and Catherine Cassell (2002), 'Barriers to managing diversity in the UK constabulary: The role of discourse', *Journal of Management Studies*, 39 (7), 953–976.

Eberherr, Helga, Alexander Fleischmann and Roswitha Hofmann (2007), 'Altern im gesellschaftlichen Wandel: Alternsmanagement als integrative organisationale Strategie', in Iris Koall, Verena Bruchhagen and Friederike Höher (eds), *Diversity Outlooks. Managing Diversity zwischen Ethik, Profit und Antidiskriminierung*, Münster: LIT, pp. 82–96.

Ely, Robin J. and David A. Thomas (2001), 'Cultural diversity at work: The effects of diversity perspectives on work group processes and outcomes', *Administrative Science Quarterly*, 46 (2), 229–273.

Esslinger, Adelheid Susanne and Nadine Braun (2007), 'Möglichkeiten der Integration älterer Arbeitnehmer in der Arbeitswelt', in Adelheid Susanne Esslinger and Deniz B. Schobert (eds), *Erfolgreiche Umsetzung von Work–Life Balance in Organisationen. Strategien, Konzepte, Maßnahmen*, Wiesbaden: Deutscher Universitätsverlag, pp. 123–144.

Foldy, Erica G. (2002), 'Managing diversity: Identity and power in organisations', in Iiris Aaltio-Marjosola and Albert J. Mills (eds), *Gender, Identity and the Culture of Organizations*, London: Routledge, pp. 92–112.

Greenwood, Royston, Christine Oliver, Kerstin Sahlin and Roy Suddaby (eds) (2008), *The Sage Handbook of Organizational Institutionalism*, London: Sage.

Hardy, Cynthia and Stewart Clegg (2006), 'Some dare call it power', in Stewart Clegg, Cynthia Hardy, Tom Lawrence and Walter R. Nord (eds), *The Sage Handbook of Organization Studies*, London: Sage, pp. 754–775.

Hedmo, Tina, Kerstin Sahlin-Andersson and Linda Wedlin (2005), 'Fields of imitation: The global expansion of management education', in Barbara Czarniawska and Guje Sevón (eds), *Global Ideas: How Ideas, Objects and Practices travel in the Global Economy*, Malmö: Liber and Copenhagen Business School Press, pp. 190–212.

Hepburn, Alexa and Sally Wiggins (2007), 'Developments in discursive psychology', *Discourse & Society*, **16** (5), 595–601.

Jens, Nils and Katrin Piazza (2007), 'Behinderung als Chance zur Bewältigung von Komplexität', *HR Today – das Schweizer Human Resource Journal: Gesundheitsmanagement – Strategien ohne Label*, July/August, 41–42.

Kamp, Annette and Peter Hagedorn-Rasmussen (2004), 'Diversity management in a Danish context: Towards a multicultural or segregated working life?', *Economic and Industrial Democracy*, **25** (5), 525–554.

Kelle, Udo (2000), 'Computergestützte Analyse qualitativer Daten', in Uwe Flick, Ernst von Kardoff and Ines Steinke (eds), *Qualitative Sozialforschung: Ein Handbuch*, Reinbek: Rowohlt Taschenbuch, pp. 485–501.

Koall, Iris, Verena Bruchhagen and Friederike Höher (eds) (2007), *Diversity Outlooks. Managing Diversity zwischen Ethik, Profit und Antidiskriminierung*, Münster: LIT.

Lorbiecki, Anne and Gavin Jack (2000), 'Critical turns in the evolution of diversity management', *British Journal of Management*, **11** (1), 17–31.

Marschan-Piekkari, Rebecca and Cristina Reis (2004), 'Language and languages in cross-cultural interviewing', in Rebecca Marschan-Piekkari and Catherine Welch (eds), *Handbook of Qualitative Research Methods for International Business*, London: Sage, pp. 224–243.

Nentwich, Julia C. (2004), Die Gleichzeitigkeit von Differenz und Gleichheit: Neue Wege für die Gleichstellungsarbeit, Königstein i.T.: Ulrike Helmer.

Northcraft, Gregory B., Jennifer T. Polzer, Margaret A. Neale and Roderick M. Kramer (1996), 'Diversity, social identity, and performance: Emergent social dynamics in cross-functional teams', in Susanne E. Jackson and Marian N. Ruderman (eds), *Diversity in Work Teams. Research Paradigms for a Changing Workplace*, Washington, DC: American Psychological Association, pp. 69–96.

Ostendorp, Anja (2009), 'Konsistenz und Variabilität beim Reden über "Diversity": Eine empirische Untersuchung diskursiver Spielräume in Schweizer Großunternehmen', *Forum Qualitative Sozialforschung/Forum: Qualitative Social Research*, **10** (2), Art. 1.

Phillips, Nelson, Thomas B. Lawrence and Cynthia Hardy (2004), 'Discourse and institutions', *Academy of Management Review*, **29** (4), 635–652.

Potter, Jonathan and Margaret Wetherell (1987), *Discourse and Social Psychology: Beyond Attitudes and Behaviour*, London: Sage.

Prasad, Anshuman (2001), 'Understanding workplace empowerment as inclusion:

A historical investigation of the discourse of difference in the United States', *The Journal of Applied Behavioral Science*, **37** (1), 51–69.

Prasad, Pushkala and Albert J. Mills (1997), 'From showcase to shadow: Understanding the dilemmas of managing workplace diversity', in Pushkala Prasad, Albert J. Mills, Michael B. Elmes and Anshuman Prasad (eds), *Managing the Organizational Melting Pot: Dilemmas of Workplace Diversity*, Thousand Oaks, CA: Sage, pp. 3–27.

Räss, Daniel (2004), *Offenheit über die sexuelle Orientierung am Arbeitsplatz bei schwulen Männern in der deutschen Schweiz*, Bern: Edition Soziothek.

Runté, Mary and Albert J. Mills (2006), 'Cold war, chilly climate: Exploring the roots of gendered discourse in organization and management theory', *Human Relations*, **59** (5), 695–720.

Schubert, Renate, Sabine Littmann-Wernli and Philipp Tingler (2002), *Corporate Volunteering: Unternehmen entdecken die Freiwilligenarbeit*, Bern: Paul Haupt.

Sevón, Guje (1996), 'Organizational imitation in identity transformation', in Barbara Czarniawska and Guje Sevón (eds), *Translating Organizational Change*, Berlin: De Gruyter, pp. 49–68.

Simon, Robin W. (1995), 'Gender, multiple roles, role meaning, and mental health', *Journal of Health and Social Behavior*, **36** (2), 182–194.

Steyaert, Chris and Maddy Janssens (2003), 'Qualifying otherness', in Svante Leijon, Ruth Lillhannus and Gill Widell (eds), *Reflecting Diversity: Viewpoints from Scandinavia*, Göteborg: BAS Publishers, pp. 41–55.

Steyaert, Chris and Maddy Janssens (2013), 'Multilingual scholarship and the paradox of translation and language in management and organization studies', *Organization*, **20** (1), 131–142.

Styhre, Alexander and Ulla Eriksson-Zetterquist (2008), 'Thinking the multiple in gender and diversity studies: Examining the concept of intersectionality', *Gender in Management: An International Journal*, **23** (8), 567–582.

Süss, Stefan and Markus Kleiner (2007), 'Diversity management in Germany: Dissemination and design of the concept', *The International Journal of Human Resource Management*, **18** (11), 1934–1953.

Tienari, Janne, Sigrid Quack and Hildegard Theobald (2002), 'Organizational reforms, "ideal workers" and gendered orders: A cross-societal comparison', *Organization Studies*, **23** (2), 249–279.

Tomlinson, Frances and Sue Egan (2002), 'Organizational sensemaking in a culturally diverse setting: Limits to the "valuing diversity" discourse', *Management Learning*, **33** (1), 79–97.

Ulich, Eberhard and Marc Wülser (2004), *Gesundheitsmanagement in Unternehmen*, Wiesbaden: Gabler.

Weick, Karl E. (1995), *Sensemaking in Organizations*, London: Sage.

Wetherell, Margaret (1998), 'Positioning and interpretative repertoires: Conversation analysis and post-structuralism in dialogue', *Discourse and Society*, **9** (3), 387–412.

Witzel, Andreas (2000), 'Das problemzentrierte Interview', *Forum Qualitative Sozialforschung/Forum: Qualitative Social Research*, **1** (1), Art. 22.

Wood, Linda A. and Rolf O. Kroger (2000), *Doing Discourse Analysis: Methods for Studying Action in Talk and Text*, Thousand Oaks: Sage.

Zanoni, Patrizia and Maddy Janssens (2007), 'Minority employees engaging with (diversity) management: An analysis of control, agency, and micro-emancipation', *Journal of Management Studies*, **44** (8), 1371–1397.

Zanoni, Patrizia, Maddy Janssens, Yvonne Benschop and Stella Nkomo (2010), 'Unpacking diversity, grasping inequality: Rethinking difference through critical perspectives', *Organization*, **17** (1), 9–29.

13. The coaching conversation as a discursive HRM intervention

Florian Schulz

INTRODUCTION

Today, human resource management (HRM) has become the 'preferred international discourse to frame employment management issues' (Delbridge and Keenoy, 2010, p. 799). In addition to recruitment practices, HRM encompasses a number of performance management and evaluation operations through which the workforce is organized (McKenna, Richardson and Manroop, 2011). Historically HRM has always merged elements of psychology and management, and has been influenced through many psychological theories and practices (Huselid, 2011). It is here that organizational scholars have taken an interest in exploring the precise dynamics of HRM interventions and called for process-based research which allows analysts to discuss the mechanisms and dynamics of interventions in a critical-reflexive manner (Janssens and Steyaert, 2009).

One major trend in the field of HRM over recent decades has been the development of soft skills (Boltanski and Chiapello, 2005) such as emotional intelligence (Goleman, 1995), social and communicative skills (Payne, 2005), empathy (Kellett, Humphrey and Sleeth, 2002) and motivational forms of leadership (Bruch and Ghoshal, 2003). Improving 'human resources' in these ways has been associated with improvements in worker performance (Boselie, Dietz and Boon, 2005), thus giving companies a competitive advantage. Particular individual-centered interventions, that is, planned actions which are 'deliberate and presumably functional' (Cummings and Worley, 2009, p. 750), such as mentoring, supervision and coaching, have begun to play an important role in the development of soft skills.

Surveys, like those from the Chartered Institute of Personnel and Development (2015), report that three quarters of UK companies are already making use of coaching and mentoring and that most companies plan to further increase this practice, especially coaching. Importantly these coaching interventions are organized and funded by the company of the employees being coached; thus I refer to them as management coaching (Schulz, 2013) to distinguish them from other forms of coaching such as personal coaching, sports coaching, and health coaching. At its core, management coaching consists of one-on-one conversations in an intimate setting between an in-house or externally contracted professional coach and an employee with managerial responsibilities.

Given that management coaching has grown into a worldwide, multi-billion-dollar industry (Passmore and Fillery-Travis, 2011) we might well ask what happens during the intervention and what effects the intervention brings about. On the latter question, most publications suggest that coaching 'has proven to be one of the most powerful one-on-one management techniques for getting the best out of every employee' (Fournies, 1999, p. 244) and can unlock the potential of employees and 'maximize their performance' (Whitmore, 2009, p. 10). While such claims partly reflect the marketing rhetoric of an upwardly-striving profession, they also show how coaching is positioned as a new HRM practice for managing workforce productivity. A review of recent literature in management and organization studies (Schulz, 2013) suggests that most empirical research uses functional-quantitative approaches to measure the effectiveness of the intervention via self-report questionnaires (Ely, Boyce, Nelson, Zaccaro, Hernez-Broome and Whyman, 2010) and that we still know little about the concrete practices coaches use in their everyday applications, the dynamics in which the conversations unfold, and the relational processes that occur between coaches and managers.

Thus, Feldman's (2005) suggestion that coaching is a 'black box' still seems to apply today. This is somewhat astonishing, given the ongoing debate in the coaching literature around how far coaching utilizes psychotherapeutic techniques. Indeed, while many publications explicitly distinguish coaching from psychotherapy (Hart, Blattner and Leipsic, 2001) and place management coaching close to sports coaching (Peltier, 2001) others highlight the proximity of the two interventions (Gray, 2006; Gray, Ekinci and Goregaokar, 2011) and point out that coaching and psychotherapy are based on similar theoretical constructs (Barner and Higgins, 2007) and have functional similarities (McKenna and Davis, 2009). If coaching were indeed an 'isopraxism' (Erlingsdottir and Lindberg, 2005) – a practice that is given a new name when translated into a new context, but otherwise remains relatively unchanged – this would become evident in the ways workers are positioned and their concerns interpreted. Moreover, in my review of the literature I found little critical-reflexive discussions of coaching, as the intervention is generally scripted in a positive manner.

Following calls for process-based research in HRM interventions (McKenna et al., 2011; Thompson, 2011; Wright and Boswell, 2002) I set out to explore management coaching as a timely representative of current developments in the larger field of HRM. Concretely, I will critically explore the dynamics of the coaching conversation as well as some of its immediate effects on the manager. I will focus especially on how far psychotherapeutic practices play a role in these interventions and whether and to what extent coaching, like psychotherapy, places the psyche of the individual at the center of attention.

FRAMEWORK: COACHING AS DISCURSIVE HRM PRACTICE

To open the black box of coaching, I first develop a theoretical framework for studying conversations between coach and manager in a critical-reflexive manner. As the core discussions on coaching are only slowly opening up toward models that serve as alternatives to functional-quantitative frameworks, the more established field of HRM will serve as a source of inspiration as it already offers several processual approaches that offer ways to investigate its actual practices.

In particular discourse analysis has established itself as a method for engaging in critical reflection on HRM interventions. Advocates of discourse analysis point out that it 'provides a theoretical and methodological framework for exploring the social production of organizational and interorganizational phenomena' (Phillips, Sewell and Jaynes, 2008, p. 549) and that it offers a way to investigate the local and contextualized practices used in HRM interventions (Lawless, Sambrook, Garavan and Valentin, 2011). One well-established stream of discourse analysis particularly questions the taken for granted, performance-driven, managerial logic of HRM and considers its contextual, individual and collective effects, while concurrently suggesting alternative modes of organizing (Paauwe and Boselie, 2005). Paradigm-type discursive studies (Alvesson and Kärreman, 2011) have also been used to contemplate the relationship between power, history and ideology; in the case of HRM they look into the development, mutation and proliferation of HRM as an ideological formation (for an overview see Barratt, 2003).

Here, analysts have particularly drawn upon Foucauldian terminologies and ideas, which focus on concepts of power/knowledge regimes, disciplinary power, and technologies of the self (Townley, 1993). A second stream, one that might be described as text-based discursive studies (Alvesson and Kärreman, 2011), has framed HRM as a body of discursive practices and has taken particular interest in how psychological and emotionalized discursive practices have and are shaping management culture through text and talk (Cullen, 2009; Doorewaard and Benschop, 2003; Fineman and Sturdy, 1999). Finally, more recent discursive approaches have emphasized the processual nature of discourse (Ainsworth and Hardy, 2009; Martin, Beaumont, Doig and Pate, 2005).

This take on discourse bridges the two discursive traditions outlined above by taking seriously the idea that paradigm-type discourses 'must be embodied, materialized or even incarnated in [text-based] discourses, that is, tokens of text or talk, in order ... to be reproduced, sustained and transported from one point to another' (Cooren, Matte, Taylor and Vasquez, 2007, p. 155). Following this notion it becomes possible to empirically explore how HRM interventions constitute and perform paradigm-type discourses on a local, daily basis (Francis and Sinclair, 2003; Lawless et al., 2011). Thus, process-oriented discursive research might ask how HRM practices come into being, how managerial discourses are performed through concrete practices, and how the politics of these practices shape everyday interactions (Watson, 2004, p. 447). I aim to contribute to this processual approach by asking how specific discourses are mobilized in the coaching conversation and what immediate effects that mobilization has for the manager.

METHODOLOGY

Analytical Strategy

The attempt to trace the discursive dynamics in management coaching conversations 'involves yet another struggle for the researcher: how to connect feasible empirical studies to the complex reflections on the ontological and epistemological role of discourse and provide new explanations of organizational structures and processes' (Grant and Hardy, 2004, p. 9). To study the way discourses were mobilized in these conversations, I had to address three specific challenges. The first challenge was to identify the relevant discourses enacted in and through the intervention. Coaching conversations, like other interventions such as psychotherapy, medical counseling or business counseling, can be understood as professionalized problem talk between a manager as lay person and a coach as expert facilitator (Watzlawick, Weakland, Fisch and Erickson, 1974). Problem talk 'consists of portrayals of (and interactions about) aspects of people's lives as undesired and, perhaps, warranting change in behavior or perspective' (Miller, Gale and Silverman, 2005, p. 725). Moreover, it is argued that people draw upon specific discourses to construct the problems and the aims of the intervention. These underlying discourses are crucially important as they draw attention to some interpretations while marginalizing others; in so doing, they legitimate specific (discursive) actions which have considerable consequences. In this study, therefore, I focused on how agents construct the problem and the aims of the conversation.

The second methodological challenge was finding an analytic concept that makes it possible to understand how discourses are used to construct the problems and aims within coaching conversations. Here, the orientation toward the rich methodological spectrum of discursive psychology offers a possible approach (Potter and Wetherell, 1987). Discursive psychology assumes that discourse is constructed, constructive, and action-oriented. Importantly, because it is a constituent of social reality, talk itself is seen as a form of action, an action that is often readily accessible to empirical investigation. Furthermore, discursive psychology assumes that discourse is always situated within a set of interacting conditions and that to understand discourse better, one must examine it in situ as it occurs within its situational context.

Moreover, scholars of discursive psychology advocate that the construction of discourse happens via various types of linguistic building blocks, a claim which makes the following analysis feasible. Based on these premises, a so-called interpretative repertoire analysis (Potter and Wetherell, 1987) is suggested for the analysis of problem constructions in management coaching conversations because it can capture the central discourses around which people structure their actions. Concretely, interpretative repertoires (IRs) have been defined as 'broader elements' than 'words and grammatical structures'; they signify 'clusters of terms organized around a central metaphor, often used with grammatical regularity' (Wiggins and Potter, 2008, p. 74). Analysis using the concept of IRs is oriented toward tracing the multiplicity of accounts in order to be able to show how different constructions of social reality compete with each other, and are negotiated and challenged, leading to a variety of effects (p. 74). Thus, in this study I examined the use of discourses by examining IRs.

The third challenge is how to interpret and describe change processes in conversations. Here I suggest that a difference in the use of discourses over the course of a session is a relevant change. When people vary the intensity with which they use discourses, making one discourse dominant and marginalizing others, or when they introduce new discourses or no longer mobilize earlier ones, this has effects on people (Heracleous and Barrett, 2001). Such a discursive change is relevant because people interpret their lives, their feelings, and their actions on the basis of discourses (Boje, 1994).

Following these methodological considerations, I first ask how agents discursively construct the problem and the associated aims of the intervention by using interpretative repertoires. In a second analytical step I then look into the temporal processes and ask how the use of IRs changes over the course of each of the three sessions I analyzed. Finally, to look for potential variation in the ways different individuals use IRs, I consider the relational processes by asking how coaches and managers negotiate the IRs in each case.

Data Collection, Sample Selection and Analysis

In response to these research interests, I analyzed three initial conversations between one coach and three different managers working in the financial industry. While the coach has no traditional training in counseling methods, she is specialized in 'emotional intelligence coaching' (Sayers, 2010; Graf and Pawelczyk, 2014) and also offers workshops and a training programs for coaches. My data source stems from a corpus of nine cases with nine different managers. Each case had between three to nine individual sessions and each session lasted between two to three hours, totaling 115 hours of recorded and transcribed material distributed over 46 individual sessions. For this study three sessions from three different cases, representing a total of 460 pages of verbatim transcript, were selected along the following selection criteria.

First, though each client's coaching process lasted between three and nine sessions, the initial sessions were the most important for understanding how both parties constructed and negotiated both the problems of the managers and the aims of the coaching. Essentially, once the first session was over the protagonists would implicitly follow what they had negotiated in the first session. This is in line with the argument that Graf and Pawelczyk (2014) make: that the problem construction is a central part of the first session of coaching processes and mainly happens during this phase of the intervention.

Second, for the analysis I present here, I chose to examine three cases with three different managers yet always the same coach. Two cases seemed inadequate to show enough variation in the relational and temporal processes, but using four cases could over-complicate the analysis. Also, I based my selection of the three cases on a first close reading of the transcripts of all nine different coaching sessions in the entire data corpus. I selected these three cases because they gave an indication of the varying dynamics in the relationships between the coach and the managers. Moreover, while it would have been tempting to offer a comparison between different coaches, such a comparison would have added yet another layer of complexity and thus widened the scope of the study. Finally, in this chapter I look at a coach specialized in 'emotional intelligence coaching'. Graf (2015, p. 101) says this approach 'applies the core features of Emotional Intelligence as formulated by' Daniel Goleman (1995); these are 'self-awareness, self-regulation, self-management, empathy and relationship management'. Having chosen to focus on this style of coaching, I cannot make a claim about all forms of coaching, but this selection does seem highly appropriate as I aim to study how new forms of HRM practices can unfold in the work context, and their effects. Overall, I argue that these selection criteria best reflect my interests in looking into the discursive construction of problems and their effects in the context of work.

I should also mention several circumstances which embed the intervention in a specific organizational context. All the coaching sessions were funded by the managers' host firms and were organized through those firms' HRM departments. The managers whose sessions I chose to analyze are Josef, the department head in an insurance company; Julia, a senior finance consultant in an insurance company; and Richard, the head of a branch office in a bank. All names are pseudonyms. While Richard and Josef had had no previous contact with the coach or with emotional intelligence coaching, Julia had participated in an emotional intelligence workshop some months earlier. Monica, the coach who conducted the coaching sessions, has a background in business administration and has received training in various coaching methods. She has also worked as a freelance coach for several years.

Following the theory and method outlined above, I began my analysis by first asking how individuals construct linguistic representations of problems with the help of IRs, and oriented my analysis toward tracing a multiplicity of IRs (Wiggins and Potter, 2008, p. 74). I undertook the analysis of conversation transcripts using Atlas.ti as well as a multi-level text program called Scrivener. The first reading allowed me to become familiar with the text; thus I summarized semantically coherent fragments. In a second step I analyzed data in a recursive process involving open interpretations, coding episodes and categorizing similar text fragments. In order to find categories that would allow variation and coherence in the statements, I had to move through several 'models', which I validated, tested and reworked by analyzing and re-analyzing the empirical material until it was possible to link the accounts to one or more of the repertoires I was building.

During the recursive coding process, I tagged the texts, discussed my primary interpretations with a group of colleagues, recoded texts, built meta-categories, and then discussed it again in various iterative cycles. In particular, the repeated reviews helped me focus and calibrate the interpretation of the materials and align my overall focus. Finally, to investigate the temporal and relational processes I looked over all the transcripts again after I had stabilized the analysis of IRs. Through this processual form of analysis I looked for a change in the patterns of people's use of IRs.

INTERPRETATIVE REPERTOIRES USED IN THE COACHING CONVERSATIONS

In this section I present the results for the analytical problems and construct the aims of the intervention with the help of IRs. Building on these findings, in the next part I then follow up on the processual inquiry into the temporal and relational processes that developed within the conversations and across the three cases, thus answering the larger question of what happens in coaching. My analysis revealed three IRs which the managers and the coach repeatedly used as they constructed the problem. I call them unconscious psychic dynamics, organizational politics, and personal entanglements. Table 13.1 offers a summary of the central motives of the IRs as well as the effects connected to them.

To illustrate how these IRs were enacted and to show the coherence between the individual statements within one IR, I now describe them in more detail, offering vignettes from the conversations. The conversations were conducted and analyzed in German while the vignettes were translated into English.

Table 13.1   Key characteristics of the three interpretative repertoires

Interpretative Repertoire	How is the problem constructed?	What effects result from the problem construction?
Psychic dynamics	Manager lacks adequate understanding of unconscious motives and traumata which trigger reactions and emotional responses.	Manager needs to work through the psychic problem causing the anachronistic reactions in order to better control his/her emotions.
Organizational politics	Manager is subjected to organizational power struggles and political games as well as tensions resulting from economic constraints.	Manager must position self towards these dynamics and find ways to cope with personal values and aims in the face of them.
Personal entanglements	Manager struggles with, and is drawn into, issues resulting from intense personal relationships where the appropriate responses are unclear.	Manager must shape relationships so they are less associated with stress and personal needs can be addressed and fulfilled.

Unconscious Psychic Dynamics

The construction of the problem through the IR of what I call 'unconscious psychic dynamics' depicts managers as lacking awareness about the measures they can use to control inadequate, primarily emotional, responses. The psyche is given a quasi-independent agency which does not follow everyday rational logic but needs to be understood:

> . . . and this 'Why' coming from your head never really gets you anywhere. And often it's like this: as long as something stays hidden, as long as something is not emotionally comprehended you don't have any orientation at all about what really goes on inside of you, it runs through automatically. So, sometimes, or very often, you can better control such patterns, such automatic reactions, once you understand what really is reacting in a sensitive way inside of you. (Monica, speaking to Josef)

As the extract suggests, rational analysis 'from your head' cannot liberate the individual from automatic (re-)actions. Only when the managers understand 'what really is reacting' are they able to control themselves adequately. When they achieve a certain state of emotional awareness, they can solve the problem, as the coach suggests in the next extract:

> My experience is that when you arrive in a state of being in which you can feel yourself more lucidly, also the pain, only then will the emotions no longer overwhelm you. What overwhelms you almost always has to do with – what I mean by overwhelming is that emotions flood you – this is connected to the fact that you have not understood them yet. Somehow you do not understand, or have suppressed something, or have not accepted it. (Monica, speaking to Julia)

While the first part of the comment again suggests that people need a more-than-rational understanding to overcome their automatic reaction to emotions, the second part of the comment explains this relationship more deeply as it suggests that the individual has suppressed something and not accepted it. Moreover, the IR argues that the inability to control this inner psychic dynamic then leads to automatic, and inadequate, behaviors:

> . . . in our everyday lives, right?, we are often required to take action quickly, right? There our routines run automatically or such an automatism runs through, like you described, right? There the tension comes up automatically, something controls, yes. You can't influence that at all, that just happens . . . (Monica, with Josef)

Here the sore spot is the leftovers from earlier experiences which Josef is not able to access and control and which thus haunt him so that he inevitably feels helpless in interactions with his boss. Indeed, two central metaphors of this IR are the idea of a wound and of something that has gotten under one's skin, so that one is 'thin skinned'. Following on this idea, Monica suggests that Josef needs to learn to process emotions without reacting negatively to them; thus, acquiring a 'thicker skin' is seen as a personal development step. In fact, in her case Julia describes herself as having failed at this developmental task: 'I think I am insecure deep inside. I was very insecure as a child. I also had, never had, didn't have such outstanding self-esteem.'

These statements describe the problem as a missed step in development, one that for Julia goes back to her childhood and is now something of a 'psychic handicap'. It is also suggested that the deficit developed through past experiences of trauma which are burned into, and then stored in an 'emotional experience memory'. According to this IR, upsetting events, whether from decades earlier or the day before, will become internalized, embodied and stored in deep layers of the self but will sometimes surface and haunt the person and thus affect current activities. Essentially, as these traumatic events are reactivated through current situations, the old emotions are transferred into current situations: 'Something is, this sounds as if something is really, almost traumatic. In any case it seems to have shaken you to the very core' (Monica speaking to Julia).

The next extract also hints at this idea of a sore spot. Richard describes an episode in which he was overruled in an important decision by his boss. And Monica responds: 'And there, you can't reach the sore spot, right? So, with your boss there is just this sore spot of powerlessness.'

In total, this first IR can be understood as a form of 'psy-talk', a form of conversation saturated with psychological terms in which people analyze themselves and others in search of a supposedly liberating insight. This IR mainly seems to mobilize psychoanalytic concepts like the unconscious, and the suppression of emotions or childhood traumata which then direct the conversation to finding ways to overcome the problems thus constructed.

Organizational Politics

The problems represented in the IR I call 'organizational politics' are caused by power games, politics, bad organizational routines, and economic constraints. In reaction, the manager is drawn into these organizational dynamics and has to position him/herself. The situation builds up great pressure for which the manager becomes an involuntary valve. The manager's problems are thus reactions to organizational conditions. Julia explained the reasons for her stress:

> I had a really exhausting time and I had a lot of bad luck with the projects I have been working on over the last two years, projects that have pushed me to the limit for various reasons. In the first half year my project partner, a new recruit, experienced but new to the project, simply quit. I had to give more to the project than I got out of it and could not find a replacement. And for several weeks I worked 170 percent, and 30 percent was still missing.

As we see, she describes her work situation as exhausting and pushing her to her limits. More specifically, she says this is because she had to overcompensate in order to complete project work for missing colleagues. Underlying her statement seems to be an expectation that despite the shortage of employees the project had to be fulfilled as originally planned. This construction of the problem shows that she is situated in a larger context. Generally, this IR often refers to the organizing dynamics of the larger work organizational setting in which a manager's work situation is embedded. In the next quote, for example, Richard explains the impact on his individual situation of an increase in the everyday work load and expectations:

> Well, of course the pressure has now been adjusted and increased since then [due to the financial crisis]. Actually the required performance, the goals given to us, to every employee, to me, are exaggerated. The way things are working is not in perspective and we already know that we will not be able to meet the goals by the end of the year.

The real problems, we learn here, are the unrealistic expectations set out by senior management which the individual manager can no longer fulfill. In addition, Richard places his employer's increased expectations into an even larger frame: his bank has to react to the financial crisis. This perspective of the manager embedded in and part of a larger organizational dynamic is also brought up by Julia, who says she struggles with the performance-driven corporate culture in her firm:

> He [my boss] gave me the feeling that I have to do it all alone, that, that it's my, my job, my job and that, that it's part of the job to do the project alone. And he spiced it up with anecdotes from a project where the senior consultant got fired because they blew a project, which wasn't even their fault, but they were sacrificed anyway.

A common motif is that managers have to cope and position themselves toward performance-driven expectations, a situation that affects not only their own lives but also those of others, as Richard explains:

> I have a strong sense of justice and in the context of such a company this can be quite stressful. You are there to do what your superiors and the board of

executives say you should do. But if you have a strong belief or opinion, I'll say it like that, then it can collide every now and then. Especially when it concerns things that are not only about general ideas . . . I am in charge of employment issues in [this company]; I also authorize new positions and so on, just so you know what I do. And then for example when I find it important, like it always was at [this company], that we do not fire people and therefore do not hire too many people at once, when the board of executives sees this differently then that can really get to you and that is a problem for me and costs me a lot of energy.

Thus Richard shows us the problem of having responsibility for others without having the power to act freely and thus being subjected to constraints placed upon him by superiors. In summary, in texts that relate to this IR, individuals constitute the problem as being produced outside of the manager. They point to the tensions that they have to endure because they are embedded in a larger organizational dynamic over which they have limited control.

Personal Entanglements

The last of the three IRs is 'personal entanglements'. I chose that term because this IR constructs the problem through reference to the struggles the manager has with personal relationships to family members, friends or close colleagues. The central theme is that managers have to make decisions which emotionally affect them as well as other people they care about. For example, Julia talks about a relationship breakup and the stress it has caused:

Well, what really got to me was that a few weeks back I broke up a wonderful but long-distance relationship which was unfortunately hopeless because of the distance. That was really, let's say a burden I had to end because it really had no future but that really hurt a lot and that was really bad.

The burden for the manager here is the loss of a relationship. While this is surely an extreme, the focus in this IR is mostly relational, as it places the manager in connection to others; when personal needs are not sufficiently fulfilled and relationships do not go smoothly it is suggested that this affects the manager. A common issue is how boundaries, and close emotional bonds, can be maintained despite ambivalent circumstances. A typical remark is this one from Josef, where he speaks of his position in relation to his son:

Yes, well, what really gets on my nerves is that he takes everything for granted, ahm, he often takes advantage of my time or my, well yes, money, that really annoys me. It's less the money, more important is the time. And, what especially annoys me is this taking things for granted – things I do for him like cleaning up the apartment, moving his things, being of service for something.

Another variation focuses on struggles with marital issues, again around the issue of how the manager can balance and maintain these relationships to others:

> And it's always a question of how much I tell my wife, because, how is she going to react? Because sometimes when I turn down a request too quickly she takes sides and says 'Hey, you are always opposing him' or 'What more do you want from him?' (Josef)

Navigating personal relationships is the core of this IR when people use it to construct the problem the coaching is to address. Moreover, this IR states that problematic and strong emotional responses are a consequence of personal interdependencies, entanglements of needs and one's personal space.

Once again, considering how language is used to construct the problems through all three IRs, one might suggest that each IR places the problem at a different spatial level in relation to the coach. The psychic dynamics IR constructs the problem as something inside of the manager. The organizational politics IR places the problem outside the manager with the manager being part of a larger context to be navigated. Finally the personal entanglements IR places the problem in-between the manager and intimate others. Consequently, the attention of the conversation shifts in relation to these different constructions. It may focus to the inside, to the outside context, or to the manager's relationships.

TEMPORAL AND RELATIONAL PROCESSES

Having described the IRs, I can now analyze the processes in which they were used over the course of the conversations (temporal process) and across participants (relational process). A more detailed analysis of temporal and relational processes is available in Schulz and Steyaert (2014). Looking first at the relational dynamic, the three managers each reacted differently to the coach's interpretations; in a recursive manner, Monica reacted differently with each of the managers. The overall dynamics are summarized in Table 13.2.

I now offer brief outlines of the relational dynamic in each case, beginning with Josef. He gradually moved from using the organizational politics IR and personal entanglements IR to the psychic dynamics IR; meanwhile Monica consistently used the psychic dynamics IR through all

Table 13.2   Development in use of IRs over time across cases

Case 1 The complicit client (Josef)		Case 2 The experienced client (Julia)		Case 3 The resistant client (Richard)	
Josef OD & PE → PD		*Julia* OD, PE, PD → PD		*Richard* OD → OD	
Coach PD	→ PD	**Coach** PD	→ PD	**Coach** PD → PD	
Joseph: gradually adopts PD **Coach**: interprets narrations and anticipates Joseph's feelings along PD		*Julia*: fluently adopts PD **Coach**: interprets narrations and reinforces Julia's use of PD		*Richard*: stays with OD and resists coaches interpretations **Coach**: highlights her expertise and attempts to define the setting	

Note: OD = organizational politics; PE = personal entanglements; PD = psychic dynamic.

phases of the conversation. Josef's behavior might be seen as complying with her interpretative program. Moreover, working with Josef, Monica very strongly defined the setting and the aims of the intervention at the beginning of their first session to establish her interpretative authority. Once Josef began to narrate emotional experiences and adopt the psychic dynamics IR, Monica oscillated between reinterpreting his narrations and anticipating his experiences; this seemed to be her preferred mode of interpretation.

The extract cited in Table 13.3 exemplifies this dynamic. In it, Monica attunes toward Josef's narration, brings in her preferred interpretation and reinforces it once Josef begins to use it. The extract takes place around minute 24 of the two-and-a-half hour conversation. Josef had just spoken about a crucial meeting with a senior manager, Hubert, in which he tried to prevent his superiors from downsizing the unit he is responsible for. He said Hubert simply ignored his important arguments that opposed the decision to downsize. He suggested that since Hubert seemed to lack any grounded arguments, his true motives were personal interest and involvement in organizational power struggles. Thus Josef formulated his problem through the organizational politics IR. Just before this extract Monica had asked him how he felt in the situation.

In the beginning of the episode, Monica anticipated what Josef might feel in the situation. She said, 'and that's a situation where you would say "Aha, this could be an example of a feeling where you are disappointed, baffled"' (lines 723ff.). She followed this with an assessment: 'in situations

Table 13.3   Extract from the coaching conversation with Josef

722	M:	. . .I didn't get agitated, I was simply baffled and bitterly disappointed.
723	C:	Exactly, ahm, and that's a situation where you would say 'Aha, ahm, this could be
724		an example for a feeling where you are disappointed, baffled, right?
725		Other situations might be annoying, but in situations like this one, where there
726		are strong emotions, (Yes). – you can't express those.
	M:	Exactly, Hhm
727	C:	because it seems as if it were, when you don't
728		express them – as you probably know, you're probably aware,
729		that they ferment inside of you, right, Yes.
	M:	That builds up inside. (Hmh) And it is also
730		It becomes, ahm, the, the same old story
731		of discontent and insecurity,
	C:	Yes, yes, sure.
	M:	that's simply not good.
	C:	Yes, yes.
	M:	that's unpleasant.
732	C:	Exactly. Yes, ahm, and it also is connected to . . . you are a very
733		emotional person, ahm, well the feelings are simply there, they move you
734		yes? (Hmh) Maybe a bit more than for others, ahm,
735		but there is some sort of / some sort of mechanism inside of you, ahm, through which
736		emotions are suppressed, maybe more than to the normal extent.
	M:	Yes, too much suppressed, Yes.
737	C:	And in those situations you don't see a way, ahm, to adequately express the emotions.

like this one, where there are strong emotions, [Josef: Yes]. You can't express them' (lines 725ff.). Through these statements she suggests that Josef is overwhelmed by emotions, making it impossible for him to adequately express them. Also notable is her remark 'you are probably aware – right? – that it ferments inside of you' (line 728). Her statement that suppressed emotions are viewed as a common reality makes it hard for Josef to reject the interpretation: he would need both to contradict a 'common truth' and to challenge her authority. Furthermore, she assesses his problem: he is more emotional than others and has built up a mechanism that suppresses emotions 'more than the normal extent' (line 732), suggesting another internal problem. And he confirms (line 729) her assessments, taking on her proposed interpretations.

The relational dynamic between Monica and Josef in the example above also resembles that in her interaction with Julia. But Julia's case differs as she already used all three repertoires at the beginning of the session. In addition, Julia very fluently adopted Monica's interpretative scheme, so that Monica neither explained her methods in detail nor grounded the intervention in her professional expertise. In the cases of both Josef and Julia, through large portions of the session, Monica took up their narrations and directed them toward her own views; she also reinforced their interpretations once they were in line with hers.

A different dynamic occurred with Richard and Monica. He countered her interpretations and attempted to use the coaching session as an opportunity to reflect on his work context and routines. Richard consistently used the organizational politics IR and Monica first reacted by reinterpreting his experiences through the psychic dynamics IR. As he resisted these interpretations she then reacted by highlighting her experiences as a professional coach and by suggesting that Richard would use the coaching to reflect on his emotional topics rather than organizational ones. Thus, in Richard's case it appears that the coach used a stronger, more direct form for negotiating the problems and aims of the coaching, in an attempt to regain interpretative authority. Yet, Richard maintains to keep the focus of the conversation on the organizational politics IR, which is, over the next sessions, eventually also accepted by Monica.

DISCUSSION

In the above analysis I first aimed to understand how the participants in the conversation constructed a work problem and developed ideas about what should be done to resolve it. The analysis showed that the conversations were structured around three IRs that focus the attention of the conversation. The psychic dynamics IR focuses the attention of the conversation onto the inside of the manager, and the organizational politics IR onto the outside work context into which the manager is integrated. Finally, the personal entanglements IR focuses on the manager's relational connectedness, or the area between inside and outside.

The second analysis, which was built on the first one, asked how the temporal and relational dynamic unfolded within the conversations. The managers seem to show different degrees of responsiveness to the psychic dynamics IR, with Richard resisting it somewhat, Joseph gradually adapting to it, and Julia, who had already been using it somewhat from the beginning of the session, intensifying her use of it over the session. While the managers showed variations in their behaviors, the coach showed very little variation in her use of IRs. Her discursive actions thus seem to suggest that she persistently promotes the psychic dynamics IR, attempting to persuade the managers to accept it as well. The sample interaction provided in Table 13.3 shows some of the positioning mechanisms through which she attempts to promote her preferred IR (Schulz and Steyaert, 2014).

Instead of relating to the managers' own constructions of their problems and looking for possible solutions within the work context for the organizational politics IR, or for help with maintaining difficult relationships in the personal entanglements IR, the coach put her dominant focus on the inside of the manager. It might therefore be suggested that though the managers initially presented quite a wide variety of concerns, the coach enacted the sessions in a routinized form, in which the problems were internalized and emotionalized and the focus moved away from contextual circumstances.

Looking more closely at the psychic dynamics IR one can argue that it actually represents a classical psychotherapeutic framework. This argument is supported by linguistic research on psychotherapy which has yielded several factors which differentiate psychotherapy from other forms of talk. In a summary of 30 years of linguistic research on psychotherapy, Pawelczyk (2011, p. 126) suggests that psychotherapists use linguistic actions that press patients 'to present (traumatic) facts that the therapist, in turn, helps him/her to comprehend'. Moreover, psychotherapists directly interpret meanings and behaviors, using questions to probe the client's narration and reinforce the client's desired narration which 'clearly manifests that their function is to press the client to continue his/her disclosive talk' (p. 101). Pawelczyk concludes that it is typical of psychotherapy talk for the therapist to focus on 'feeling-talk' and encourage the client to continuously evaluate emotions, for example by pointing out that some emotional reactions are not socially accepted – and by allowing the client to express emotions, such as crying. Given these descriptions of psychotherapy, my argument here reflects the nature of the psychic dynamics IR, which puts emotions on center stage and focuses on psychic trauma and the negative social and anachronistic effects of both emotions and trauma. Though I might seem to be arguing that coaching is psychotherapy, I do see them as different. The difference is not in the practices themselves, but in the context and framing of the intervention. Thus coaching may in fact be an isopraxism. If so, psychotherapeutic practices may have been translated into the realm of work while the initial health-oriented aims have been dropped and replaced with managerial, performance-driven aims.

A central question arises now: What effects does the intervention have when promoting the psychic dynamics IR? Here, the proponents of management coaching might argue that if managers internalize and emotionalize their problems, they can more efficiently change and improve their (work)life. Also, doing so may be effective because it is easier to change one's own emotions, perceptions and behaviors than to change the dynamics in relationships or organizations. While changing an individual's discourses might indeed be 'efficient', the focus here lies on a critical reflection which should not be limited to the individual effects but should also include the organizational and socio-cultural effects attached to the practice of promoting the psychic dynamics IR in such a way. As we see in the case of Richard, who resists the coach's interpretative attempts, the coach's sole focus on one IR might not adequately meet the needs of the manager. By suggesting that the problems are inside the manager, the coach makes it harder to follow up on alternative options the manager could use to position him/herself in relational and organizational dynamics. This limits possible interpretations and solutions. Moreover, the idea that the problem and the solution are inside the person is connected to the assumption that every person is the (sole) architect of his/her own fortune. Clearly this assumption can be problematic because it places on the individual the responsibility for change and the burden to endure hardship, as it rigidly fails to account for contextual circumstances.

It is here that we must also place coaching into an organizational perspective: it is not only a confidential one-on-one conversation but also an HRM intervention. Management coaching is funded and organized by a company and embedded in the context of work. Thus, coaching conversations do not stand outside of organizational dynamics and politics but are essentially an instrument through which the workforce is managed (Alvesson and Willmott, 2002). The form of management coaching encountered in this analysis attempts to pull employees into what Costea, Crump and Amiridis (2008) call a 'therapeutic habitus' by promoting problem descriptions and solutions which focus on the necessity to work on oneself and manage one's own emotions. While this hybrid between intimate emotions and the management of performance may seem paradoxical at first, I argue that this is exactly what the current ideology of HRM promotes.

An intervention in this form indeed promotes an ethics of self-work along a 'supposedly caring, sharing ethos' (Thrift, 2005, p. 11). By suggesting that the intervention is confidential and all about the manager, it attempts to manage the workforce from the inside. While the organization has no direct influence on the course of the conversation, it does buy into a very specific form of conversation which, as these three cases show, is highly coherent in the use of its interpretative regime. It is such practices that Kärreman and Alvesson (2004) associate with what they call socio-ideological control which aims to modify employees' behavior indirectly, by influencing their systems of beliefs. Such socio-ideological interventions then target 'social relations, emotions, identity formation and ideology' (Kärreman and Alvesson, 2004, p. 152) instead of watching and assessing employees directly. Following this argument, the form of management coaching portrayed here, practiced on the company's behalf, attempts to indirectly shape employee behaviors by controlling the ways they interpret their intimate constructions of self.

CONCLUSION

The ideas I have presented here connect to ongoing discussions in several ways and attempts to make contributions toward these. Primarily this work responds to calls to explore how HRM practices are manifested and play out at work (Janssens and Steyaert, 2009; Paauwe and Boselie, 2005). The question I have addressed, through an empirical analysis of management coaching conversations, is what happens in such conversations and how its effects can be interpreted. Thus I aim to understand the inner workings of coaching and help shed light into the 'black box' (Feldman, 2005) of this tremendously popular HRM intervention. By using a discursive approach to investigate dynamics within the conversations, this analysis helps to understand the dynamics of HRM interventions like management coaching by illustrating that the parties negotiate with various IRs within the sessions and that these discourses carry specific implications for how the managers' experiences, thoughts and feelings are to be interpreted.

Methodologically, this study takes a step in developing the processual discursive frameworks that can study talk-at-work (Cooren, 2004; Francis and Sinclair, 2003; Watson, 2004). The two-step analysis first analyzes the central discourses, operationalized as IRs, used in the conversations and then looks into how the participants relationally position themselves and the other along these IRs as well as how their use of these practices varies over the course of the conversation. Such forms of analysis, I suggest, help to explain the ways that management practices constitute and are constituted by larger ideological social discourses (Cooren, Vaara, Langley and Tsoukas, 2014) and help bridge the gap between paradigm-type and text-based discursive studies (Bamberger, 2008).

This study also connects to discussions about how new management ideologies increasingly aim to mobilize emotions and foster socio-ideological forms of control (Costa, Duarte and Palermo, 2014; Lindgren, Packendorff and Sergi, 2014). Here, I showed that the coach, as the facilitator of the coaching intervention, mainly promoted a discourse which scripted the managers' problems along individualized and emotionalizing interpretations. I therefore argue that this analysis provides reason to support those voices (Graf and Pawelczyk, 2014) in the ongoing debate on the nature of coaching which state that many of its practices are essentially psychotherapeutic.

Moreover, I emphasize that coaching follows the current paradigm of HRM which can be understood as a 'network of expert knowledges, based particularly on the "psy" disciplines that have developed around the emotions, seeking to measure and survey emotional response and to counsel people on how best to deal with and express their emotions' (Lupton, 1998, p. 6). With this, I do not want to suggest that the form of management coaching studied here only produces more intense regimes of the self, as Fogde (2011) has suggested in a study of a group-based career coaching intervention with students, and that it thus succumbs to what one can consider a one-sided criticism of the intervention. After all, many clients will surely recount positive experiences connected to their coaching conversations and simply reflecting on their work experiences may feel freeing.

Instead, what I suggest is the need to explore and discuss the concrete workings of HRM interventions on the basis of empirical materials and to replace the often one-sided discussions on the effects of HRM with more in-depth and critically informed materials. Thus, in this chapter overall, I have worked to expand a critical-reflexive understanding of how the workforce is managed through new forms of HRM interventions and how discourse-oriented organizational psychology can offer valuable theoretical and methodological resources which make this undertaking feasible.

REFERENCES

Ainsworth, Susan and Cynthia Hardy (2009), 'Mind over body: Physical and psychotherapeutic discourses and the regulation of the older worker', *Human Relations*, **62** (8), 1199–1229.

Alvesson, Mats and Dan Kärreman (2011), 'Decolonializing discourse: Critical reflections on organizational discourse analysis', *Human Relations*, **64** (9), 1121–1146.

Alvesson, Mats and Hugh Willmott (2002), 'Identity regulation as organizational control: Producing the appropriate individual', *Journal of Management Studies*, **39** (5), 619–644.

Bamberger, Peter (2008), 'Beyond contextualization: Using context theories to narrow the micro-macro gap in management research', *Academy of Management Journal*, **51** (5), 839–846.

Barner, Robert and Julie Higgins (2007), 'Understanding implicit models that guide the coaching process', *Journal of Management Development*, **26** (2), 148–158.

Barratt, Edward (2003), 'Foucault, HRM and the ethos of the critical management scholar', *Journal of Management Studies*, **40** (5), 1069–1087.

Boje, David M. (1994), 'Organizational storytelling: The struggles of pre-modern, modern and postmodern organizational learning discourses', *Management Learning*, **25** (3), 433–461.

Boltanski, Luc and Eve Chiapello (2005), 'The new spirit of capitalism', *International Journal of Politics, Culture, and Society*, **18** (3–4), 161–188.

Boselie, Paul, Graham Dietz and Corine Boon (2005), 'Commonalities and contradictions in HRM and performance research', *Human Resource Management Journal*, **15** (3), 67–94.

Bruch, Heike and Sumantra Ghoshal (2003), 'Unleashing organizational energy', *MIT Sloan Management Review*, **45** (1), 45–51.

Chartered Institute of Personnel and Development (2015), *Annual Survey Report. Learning and Development*, London: CIPD.

Cooren, François (2004), 'Textual agency: How texts do things in organizational settings', *Organization*, **11** (3), 373–393.

Cooren, François, Frédérik Matte, James Taylor and Consuelo Vasquez (2007), 'A humanitarian organization in action: Organizational discourse as an immutable mobile', *Discourse & Communication*, **1** (2), 153–190.

Cooren, François, Eero Vaara, Ann Langley and Haridimos Tsoukas (2014), *Language and Communication at Work: Discourse, Narrativity, and Organizing*, Oxford: Oxford University Press.

Costa, Tiago, Henrique Duarte and Ofelia A. Palermo (2014), 'Control mechanisms and perceived organizational support: Exploring the relationship between new and traditional forms of control', *Journal of Organizational Change Management*, **27** (3), 407–429.

Costea, Bogdan, Norman Crump and Kostas Amiridis (2008), 'Managerialism, the therapeutic habitus and the self', *Human Relations*, **61** (5), 661–685.

Cullen, John (2009), 'How to sell your soul and still get into heaven: Steven Covey's epiphany-inducing technology of effective selfhood', *Human Relations*, **62** (8), 1231–1254.

Cummings, Thomas and Christopher Worley (2009), *Organization Development & Change* (Ninth Edition), Mason, OH: Cengage Learning.

Delbridge, Rick and Tom Keenoy (2010), 'Beyond managerialism?', *The International Journal of Human Resource Management*, **21** (6), 799–817.

Doorewaard, Hans and Yvonne Benschop (2003), 'HRM and organizational change: An emotional endeavor', *Journal of Organizational Change Management*, **16** (3), 272–286.

Ely, Katherine, Lisa A. Boyce, Jonathan K. Nelson, Stephen J. Zaccaro, Gina Hernez-Broome and Wynne Whyman (2010), 'Evaluating leadership coaching: A review and integrated framework', *The Leadership Quarterly*, **21** (4), 585–599.

Erlingsdottir, Gudbjörg and Kajsa Lindberg (2005), 'Isomorphism, isopraxism, and isonymism: Complementary or competing processes?', in Barbara Czarniawska and Guje Sevón (eds), *Global Ideas. How Ideas, Objects and Practices Travel in the Global Economy*, Copenhagen: Liber & Copenhagen Business School Press, pp. 47–70.

Feldman, Daniel (2005), 'Executive coaching: A review and agenda for future research', *Journal of Management*, **31** (6), 829–848.

Fineman, Stephen and Andrew Sturdy (1999), 'The emotions of control: A qualitative exploration of environmental regulation', *Human Relations*, **52** (5), 631–663.

Fogde, M. (2011), 'Governing through career coaching: Negotiations of self-marketing', *Organization*, **18** (1), 65–82.

Fournies, Ferdinand F. (1999), *Coaching for Improved Work Performance*, McGraw-Hill Professional.

Francis, Helen and John Sinclair (2003), 'A processual analysis of HRM-based change', *Organization*, **10** (4), 685–706.

Goleman, Daniel (1995), *Emotional Intelligence*, Westminster, MD: Bantam Dell Pub Group.

Graf, Eva-Maria (2015), *The Discourses of Executive Coaching. Linguistic Insights into Emotionally Intelligent Coaching*. Habilitation, Alpen-Adria-Universität Klagenfurt.

Graf, Eva-Maria and Joanna Pawelczyk (2014), 'The interactional accomplishment of feelings-talk in psychotherapy and executive coaching', *Discourses of Helping Professions*, **252**, 59–90.

Grant, David and Cynthia Hardy (2004), 'Introduction: Struggles with organizational discourse', *Organization Studies*, **25** (1), 5–13.

Gray, David E. (2006), 'Executive coaching: Towards a dynamic alliance of psychotherapy and transformative learning processes', *Management Learning*, **37** (4), 475–497.

Gray, David E., Yuksei Ekinci and Harshita Goregaokar (2011), 'Coaching SME managers: Business development or personal therapy? A mixed methods study', *International Journal of Human Resource Management*, **22** (4), 863–882.

Hart, Vicki, John Blattner and Staci Leipsic (2001), 'Coaching versus therapy: A perspective', *Consulting Psychology Journal: Practice and Research*, **53** (4), 229–237.

Heracleous, Loizos and Michael Barrett (2001), 'Organizational change as discourse: Communicative actions and deep structures in the context of information technology implementation', *Academy of Management Journal*, **44** (4), 755–778.

Huselid, Mark A. (2011), 'Celebrating 50 years: Looking back and looking forward: 50 years of human resource management', *Human Resource Management*, **50** (3), 309–312.

Janssens, Maddy and Chris Steyaert (2009), 'HRM and performance: A plea for reflexivity in HRM studies', *Journal of Management Studies*, **46** (1), 143–155.

Kärreman, Dan and Mats Alvesson (2004), 'Cages in tandem: Management control, social identity, and identification in a knowledge-intensive firm', *Organization*, **11** (1), 149–175.

Kellett, Janet B., Ronald H. Humphrey and Randall G. Sleeth (2002), 'Empathy and complex task performance: Two routes to leadership', *The Leadership Quarterly*, **13** (5), 523–544.

Lawless, Aileen, Sally Sambrook, Tom Garavan and Claire Valentin (2011), 'A discourse approach to theorising HRD: Opening a discursive space', *Journal of European Industrial Training*, **35** (3), 264–275.

Lindgren, Monica, Johann Packendorff and Viviane Sergi (2014), 'Thrilled by the discourse, suffering through the experience: Emotions in project-based work', *Human Relations*, **67** (11), 1–30.

Lupton, D. (1998), *The Emotional Self: A Sociocultural Exploration*, London: Sage.

Martin, Graeme, Phillip Beaumont, Rosalind Doig and Judy Pate (2005), 'Branding: A new performance discourse for HR?', *European Management Journal*, **23** (1), 76–88.

McKenna, Douglas D. and Sandra L. Davis (2009), 'Hidden in plain sight:

The active ingredients of executive coaching', *Industrial and Organizational Psychology*, **2** (3), 244–260.

McKenna, Steve, Julia Richardson and Laxmikant Manroop (2011), 'Alternative paradigms and the study and practice of performance management and evaluation', *Human Resource Management Review*, **21** (2), 148–157.

Miller, Gale and David Silverman (2005), 'Trouble talk and counseling discourse', *The Sociological Quarterly*, **36** (4), 725–747.

Paauwe, Jaap and Paul Boselie (2005), 'HRM and performance: What next?', *Human Resource Management Journal*, **15** (4), 68–83.

Passmore, Jonathan and Annette Fillery-Travis (2011), 'A critical review of executive coaching research: A decade of progress and what's to come', *Coaching: An International Journal of Theory, Research and Practice*, **4** (2), 70–88.

Pawelczyk, Joanna (2011), *Talk as Therapy: Psychotherapy in a Linguistic Perspective*, Berlin: Walter de Gruyter.

Payne, Holly J. (2005), 'Reconceptualizing social skills in organizations: Exploring the relationship between communication competence, job performance, and supervisory roles', *Journal of Leadership and Organizational Studies*, **11** (2), 63–77.

Peltier, Bruce (2001), *The Psychology of Executive Coaching – Theory and Practice*, Ann Arbor, MI: Sheridan Books.

Phillips, Nelson, Graham Sewell and Steve Jaynes (2008), 'Applying critical discourse analysis in strategic management research', *Organizational Research Methods*, **11** (4), 770–789.

Potter, Jonathan and Margaret Wetherell (1987), *Discourse and Social Psychology – Beyond Attitudes and Behavior*, London: Sage.

Sayers, Pete (2010), 'Emotional intelligence coaching', *Industrial and Commercial Training*, **42** (2), 116–118.

Schulz, Florian (2013), *The Psycho-Managerial Complex at Work: A Study of the Discursive Practices of Management Coaching*, St. Gallen, Switzerland: University of St. Gallen.

Schulz, Florian and Chris Steyaert (2014), 'Studying talk-at-work: An analysis of the discursive processes of management coaching conversations', in François Cooren, Eero Vaara, Ann Langley and Haridimos Tsoukas (eds), *Language and Communication at Work: Discourse, Narrativity and Organizing, Perspectives on Process Organization Studies (Volume 4)*, Oxford: Oxford University Press, pp. 173–196.

Thompson, Paul (2011), 'The trouble with HRM', *Human Resource Management Journal*, **21** (4), 355–367.

Thrift, Nigel (2005), *Knowing Capitalism* (First Edition), London: Sage.

Townley, Barbara (1993), 'Foucault, power/knowledge, and its relevance for human resource management', *Academy of Management Review*, **18** (3), 518–545.

Watson, Tony J. (2004), 'HRM and critical social science analysis', *Journal of Management Studies*, **41** (3), 447–467.

Watzlawick, Paul, John H. Weakland, Richard Fisch and Milton H. Erickson (1974), *Change: Principles of Problem Formation and Problem Resolution*, New York: W.W. Norton.

Whitmore, John (2009), *Coaching for Performance: Growing Human Potential and Purpose – The Principles and Practice of Coaching and Leadership* (Fourth edition), London: Nicholas Brealey Publishing.

Wiggins, Sally and Jonathan Potter (2008), 'Discursive psychology', in Carla Willig and Wendy Stainton-Rogers (eds), *The Sage Handbook of Qualitative Research in Psychology*, London: Sage, pp. 73–90.
Wright, Patrick M. and Wendy R. Boswell (2002), 'Desegregating HRM: A review and synthesis of micro and macro human resource management research', *Journal of Management*, **28** (3), 247–276.

14. Discourse analysis as intervention: a case of organizational changing

Pascal Dey and Dörte Resch

INTRODUCTION

In recent years, researchers in management and organization studies have devoted considerable attention to discursive research, so it is hardly controversial to claim that discourse analysis is one of the field's most popular research methodologies. At the risk of simplifying, a key assumption underlying much of the available literature is that discourse analysis is primarily an excellent tool for producing knowledge (Heracleous, 2006) and more generally an analytic mentality (Phillips and Hardy, 2002). This interpretation is noteworthy as it consigns discourse analysis to its epistemological function.

Although we agree that discourse analysis is inextricably connected to questions of epistemology (knowledge), in this chapter we seek to transcend this position by demonstrating that it can also be used productively as a means of intervention. Conflating the epistemological and interventionist trajectories of discourse analysis, we build on prior work that conceives of 'method' and 'research' quite generally as a means for enacting and changing reality instead of 'only' representing or interpreting it (Law, 2004; Steyaert, 2011). Following this vein of thinking, we tentatively outline the interventionist potential of discourse analysis against the backdrop of organizational changing. Thereby, drawing on Tsoukas (2005), we define organizational changing as the process through which multiple discursive practices unfold, allowing members of organizations to give meaning to the organizational reality of which they are part. Using this approach, and analysing a consultancy project in a large German voluntary organization, we reveal how discourse analysis can be used to intervene in discursive practices that are characterized by tensions and struggle. To this end, we pinpoint how the results from one such analysis were used to break up a contracted conflict via two interrelated steps. First, discursive spaces were created that offered members of the organization an opportunity to vent their frustration and to create awareness of the antagonistic discursive practices that triggered the tensions and conflict. Second, generative dialogue allowed them to foster more affirmative re-interpretations of organizational changing.

This chapter is organized as follows. First, we advance a discursive understanding of organizational changing. Then, we offer an interventionist conceptualization of discourse analysis. In the third section we discuss the context, the case organization, and the design of the consultancy project. The fourth section offers a schematic outline of how discourse analysis was used to engage members of the case organization in new meaning-making practices by gradually shifting from 'talking tough' to a more generative mode of exchange. We draw the chapter to a close by identifying some areas for future research.

FROM ORGANIZATIONAL CHANGE TO ORGANIZATIONAL CHANGING

Organizational change is a central topic of Management and Organization Theory, and has been advanced from behavioural, cognitive and discursive perspectives (Tsoukas, 2005). At its simplest, a discursive perspective, which has risen to prominence over the last two decades (Heracleous and Barrett, 2001; Phillips and Oswick, 2012) emphasizes how discourses bring organizations and organizational phenomena into existence. In spite of the variety of interpretations of discourse, the notion of discourse mostly attends to how language works, not as a medium of representation but as an 'ordering force' of reality (Alvesson and Kärreman, 2000). Primarily concerned with the constitutive role of spoken and written language, discourse is commonly envisioned as the meaning-making practices which constitute the social reality which they ostensibly only describe. Discursive practices comprise such diverse phenomena as talk, text, metaphor, myth, narratives and images (Grant, Michelson, Oswick and Wailes, 2005).

Transposed to the topic of organizational change, a discursive perspective calls attention to how organizations are both constituted and changed via discursive practices. A discursive perspective sees organizational change less as a one-time, episodic event than as an ongoing process of discursively co-constructing meanings. As Hodge (2010, p. 34) points out, change 'is never final, but is always subject to changes, appearing and disappearing arbitrarily'. In line with research that sees organizational change as a process of 'becoming' and not as a 'momentary disturbance that must be stabilized and controlled' (Graetz and Smith, 2010, p. 136), Tsoukas (2005) suggests that we speak of 'organizational changing' instead of organizational change in order to stress the processual aspect of the phenomenon, the fact that it can never really be finalized. Embracing Tsoukas' conceptual twist, in this chapter, we speak of organizational changing to allude to instances where members of organizations invoke different and sometimes contradictory discourses to redefine, re-label, and reinterpret what happens within their organization, what their organization stands for, or what is considered to be its raison d'être (Jian, 2011). Organizational changing as an ongoing process of meaning-making thus encompasses the interweaving of different discourses, conceived as relatively coherent and (temporarily) stable patterns of meaning, which give rise to our experience of 'organization'.

DISCOURSE ANALYSIS AS INTERVENTION

It follows from the above that organizational changing involves tensions and struggle triggered by competing discourses. Tensions thus occur as certain discourses might reinforce the status quo of an organization, whereas others might transform established meanings. Although organizations rarely attain a state of complete discursive domination (or what Grant and Marshak (2011) call 'discursive closure') struggles do ensue over the question of who is given the opportunity to determine the 'what' and 'why' of organizational changing (Grant and Marshak, 2011). As organizational changing comprises competing discourses vying for dominance, the question, then, is how different, and often incompatible, discursive practices can be dealt with in ways that prevent open hostility, violence or deadlock. The managerial answer would be that managers must ensure the consent of their employees by making sure that they comply with and thus act according to the strategic desideratum of organizational cadres.

And yet, we are reluctant to accept that executives and managers are the only people in organizations who are entitled to 'destroy existing meaning systems and establish new ones in an effort to set strategic direction' (Sonenshein, 2010, p. 477). Instead, envisioning organizational changing less as a hierarchical (that is, top-down) endeavour and more as a dialogic one (Marshak and Grant, 2008a), we contend that all members of an organization should be given the opportunity to participate in defining the 'what' and 'why' of organizational changing (Grant and Marshak, 2011). Granting all members an active role in the process of changing is in line with accounts which advocate that 'change recipients' (that is, ordinary employees) should also be granted voice in solving existing conflicts and in deciding on the organization's future direction (Ford, Ford and D'Amelio, 2008). The question that emerges here is how to best conceptualize such an inclusive prospect of organizational changing.

It is here that discourse analysis has an important role to play. As a start, let us reiterate that discourse analysis can be productively used to intervene in (the making of) realities instead of merely representing reality (Law and Urry, 2005). Based on this premise, the overarching aim of discourse analysis as a vehicle for intervention is to engage members of the organization in generative dialogue (Scharmer, 2001) geared towards opening up less conflict-ridden, more affirmative ways of co-creating organizational reality. Such a shift towards generative dialogue fosters an openness to engage in a collective process of re-negotiating what the organization should stand for and how it should develop going forward. A crucial step towards generative dialogue is creating discursive spaces (Hardy and Maguire, 2010) where all members of a group, team or the organization at large can meet, describe their experiences and concerns, and learn to listen to other people's points of view. Whilst such encounters permit actors to exchange their dissenting viewpoints and gather a better understanding of how the struggles and tensions within their organization emanate from competing discourses, discourse analysis serves the purpose of making palpable the antagonistic discursive practices upon which a given organization is premised. Overall then, a crucial merit of discourse analysis is its ability to create minute insights into the ways that competing discourses spark tensions and conflict, which in turn can be fed back into a generative dialogue that gives all those in the organization a say in determining the purpose and prospect of organizational changing.

It is not difficult to see that the interventionist usage of discourse analysis involves an epistemological endeavour as a first step. That is, the results of a discourse analysis, which essentially reveal the different meaning-making practices that underpin a given organization, sensitize the organization's members about the 'open-ended micro-processes that' underlie 'the (changing) trajectories' (Tsoukas and Chia, 2002, p. 570). In other words, by making transparent how the breadth of meaning-making practices engenders tensions and conflicts (Grant and Marshak, 2011) discourse analysis allows all involved to understand that their organizations change in particular ways, experience turmoil and crisis, or become stagnant because of the specific discursive practices in which people engage (Thomas, Sargent and Hardy, 2011).

The actual intervention, then, is a matter of creating discursive spaces (Hardy and Maguire, 2010) to which all members of an organization have access and which do not privilege or exclude certain meanings and modes of speaking. Discursive spaces constitute democratic spaces which allow employees to freely express their 'truth', their vision of how things pertaining to the change-at-hand are or should be. The overarching aim of a discursive space is to provoke a generative dialogue geared towards the 'reweaving of actors' webs of beliefs and habits of action as a result of new experiences obtained through interactions' (Tsoukas and Chia, 2002, p. 570).

Before offering a vignette showing how we used discourse analysis as an interventionist tool, we first provide some background information on our empirical case material.

CONTEXT

This chapter had its beginning when our team, led by Annette Kluge, at the Research Institute for Organizational Psychology at the University of St. Gallen received an email invitation from one of the largest German voluntary organizations to partake in a tendering process. The focal attention of the organization, which we refer to using the pseudonym Subvenio, was, and still is, to support families and children in need. The project in question was resolving a protracted conflict which had become intense enough that the board of Subvenio sought external assistance. Two representatives of Subvenio visited us in St. Gallen to explain the mandate of the project and the conditions of the tendering process. During that meeting, it became obvious that the mandate was still very inchoate and that what the representatives told us strongly reflected their own interpretations of the reasons for the crisis at Subvenio.

In their view, the crisis was caused by the introduction of new managerial arrangements such as financial forecasting, budgeting, portfolio planning, and so on, which had estranged Subvenio's employees, because they ostensibly undermined values deeply entrenched in the organization such as spending time with and caring for their clientele. The new accounting systems took so much time to operate that people found it increasingly difficult to engage with others, be they colleagues or clients. By implication, the managerial arrangement had a direct negative effect on employees' ability to pursue the organization's social mission. Though Subvenio had overcome its precarious financial situation within less than two years, the struggles between the promoters of the reforms (read managers) and its sceptics had worsened as more and more employees raised their concerns over the value-disrupting effects of the new managerial arrangements.

Shortly after the initial contact, we were invited to come to the organization's headquarters in Germany to present our team to the two directors and select members of the board. On the sidelines of this gathering, the directors gave us a very different interpretation about the sources of the conflict at Subvenio. Although they agreed that the conflict was between management and employees, the directors did not frame the introduction of managerial tools and technologies as a sheer necessity in the face of looming financial misery. In their account, Subvenio traditionally had little understanding of, and hence control over, its financial flows and expenditures, and that had led to a precarious financial situation caused by a slump in donations. Adhering to the idea that financial transactions at Subvenio had to be made more transparent, both directors were eventually dumbfounded by the amount of resistance their reforms produced among their employees.

Informal talks with members of the board revealed a third interpretation which occupied a middle ground between the two previous interpretations. Asserting that the managerial reforms were inevitable if Subvenio was to return to a sound financial foundation, members of the board maintained that the reforms jeopardized the organization's culture; in their view that made it crucial to engage in an open dialogue on issues related to values and tradition.

METHODOLOGY: DESIGNING THE INTERVENTION

Not long after our trip to Germany the board of directors notified us that they had given us the mandate, in large part because of our team's methodological expertise. Thus they granted us considerable liberties in designing the project and in choosing a methodology to address the hardened conflict at Subvenio. A steering committee, consisting of 12 volunteers (including both directors), was formed and given the task of serving as a 'sounding board' for our tentative ideas. Our basic thinking at the time was that the conflict was characteristic of those at many voluntary organizations that were pressured to become more businesslike (Maier, Meyer and Steinbereithner, 2014). In concrete terms, we believed that the incorporation of practices and instruments from the corporate realm was causing value-subverting effects (Eikenberry and Kluver, 2004) at Subvenio, also referred to as 'mission drift' (Minkoff and Powell, 2006). Framed in a discursive perspective, the conflict was due to discursive struggles triggered by competing discourses. Put bluntly, different groups at Subvenio promoted different interpretations of the managerial reforms, and different opinions on what the organization should be(come). Our working assumption was that the first step in getting a grip on the conflict would be identifying the various actors involved in shaping particular discourses, and pinpointing the extent to which these discourses clashed. Furthermore, our team was strongly convinced that to mitigate the conflict at Subvenio we would have to create opportunities where the quarrelling parties could express their concerns and gradually shift from 'talking tough' to a more affirmative mode of collective meaning-making (Scharmer, 2001).

The steering committee suggested framing the project as a 'cultural change' intervention; in their view, this term best resonated with the employees' perception of the conflict. We agreed to embrace the label, but insisted that we would use 'culture' as a proxy for 'discursive practice' (Alvesson, 2004). As we refused to see culture as a static property of Subvenio, 'culture' in our logic meant the heterogeneous discursive practices which ultimately engendered the conflict there. Stated this way, the main task going forward was to develop a design that would permit us to render palpable the ways that particular meanings were constructed in and through discursive practice (Wood and Kroger, 2000).

To this end, our team suggested various methods to illuminate the meaning-making practices at Subvenio. We presented a list of four methods to the steering committee. One was 'serious play' where people used Lego as a means for experimenting with organizational culture(s). The second was a 'force field' analysis which would represent the various forces affecting organizational culture(s) in either positive or negative ways. The third was the 'value square' which visualizes the tensions between different (cultural) values, and the fourth was the OCAI (Organization Culture Assessment Instrument; Cameron and Quinn, 1999), an empirically validated questionnaire representing four ideal-type profiles of specific cultural types: family/clan, hierarchy/bureaucracy, market, and adhocracy.

The OCAI was the only quantitative method. It had gained few adherents during the committee's previous discussions, but recurrent claims about the need to involve as many people as possible in the project and to create a more or less 'representative image' of Subvenio's cultural (read discursive) practices paved the way to use it across the organization. The OCAI was broadly promoted as the method of choice.

The steering committee agreed that the results of the OCAI should be used mainly to visualize Subvenio's different cultural practices. Most importantly, these visualizations should be fed back to the members of Subvenio during workshops in which at least one director would be present. In this way, the results of the OCAI formed the stimulus for the discursive spaces (Hardy and Maguire, 2010) to which all members of the organization were invited and which were presented as an opportunity to get together and exchange dissenting opinions and points of view. Apart from the results of the OCAI, which was completed by more than 400 people at Subvenio, we also gleaned valuable information from the innumerable corridor conversations and emails with people from different functional areas and hierarchical levels. Moreover, a source of surprisingly insightful information was the open question at the end of the OCAI where respondents were given the opportunity to post comments. They often gave lengthy descriptions of personal ordeals and other experiences, suggested ways to deal with the conflict, and offered both positive and negative appraisals of the worthiness of our project. Lastly, we chose to include in our analysis insights from formal meetings with Subvenio's managers and board of directors. These encounters provided insights into Subvenio's strategic considerations, offering important claims about how things were supposed to be done within the organization.

Subvenio's employees filled out the OCAI questionnaire online, but our analysis proceeded somewhat unconventionally. We had decided at the outset of the project that our team should not use any recording devices, to preclude the impression that we were simply pursuing our own (research) agenda, so we had to get by with taking notes and, most importantly, memorizing the formal and informal discussions, telephone conversations, and group discussions the three of us were involved in. Our analysis began right after the meetings and workshops at Subvenio; we used the long car rides back to St. Gallen from various German cities to make sense of our experiences.

In line with our own research (Dey, 2007; Resch, 2006), which was largely inspired by the discourse analysis developed by Potter and Wetherell (1987), we tried to rephrase our experiences at Subvenio in the language of interpretative repertoires: relatively stable sets of conversational schemas, or 'bounded units', built around specific terms (Wetherell and Potter, 1988, p. 172). By identifying the different interpretative repertoires which people invoked to make sense of what was going on in Subvenio, we were able to grasp the divergent logics circulating within the organization and potentially fuelling the conflict. Attempting to better understand how different actors used language to portray the purpose and prospect of Subvenio in particular ways, our attention focused on how to foster sensitivity for the competing discourses that had spurred the conflict (Buchanan and Dawson, 2007).

Our encounters with various people within the organization confirmed that employees and management held largely incompatible views about Subvenio's purpose and its future prospects. Once we were back in Switzerland, one of us checked our initial results against the backdrop of other available texts, and formalized the analysis in a Word document. This was followed by iterative discussions of the results between the two authors, the overarching aim being to corroborate our observations. The last step, then, consisted of the first author writing up the case narrative. The results of our analysis were transmitted via workshops which were set up either directly at Subvenio offices or in convention centres all across Germany.

Participants in the workshops were social workers, caretakers and administrators of various branch offices as well as a varying number of managers and board members. We began each workshop by presenting the results of our discourse analysis of the commentaries from the open questionnaire question, along with the corridor conversations, emails and formal meetings, as well as the results of the OCAI. In the section below, we first present the results of our discourse analysis and then, in a second step, outline how we used these insights to spark a generative dialogue between the quarrelling parties.

COMPETING DISCOURSES: THE SOCIAL VERSUS MANAGERIAL REPERTOIRE

Our discourse analysis revealed a myriad of meanings at play at Subvenio, but the discussion below is limited to the two competing discourses which had the greatest power in explaining the conflict at Subvenio: the social and the managerial repertoire.

The Social Repertoire

We chose the name social for the first interpretative repertoire. Summoned mainly by social workers and caretakers to hint at relational and axiological aspects of their work, the organization or its mission, the social repertoire is largely wedded to notions such as 'empathy', 'caring for others', 'companionship' and 'conviviality'. Importantly, the repertoire does not so much advance a descriptive account of the social reality of Subvenio. Rather, it provides a normative script delineating how things at Subvenio should be, ideally. This normative script about the social is established through a temporal division between, and juxtaposition of, Subvenio's 'golden past' (the time before the managerial reforms), its present (where the negative ramifications of the managerial reforms are plain for everyone to see) and its possible future (which essentially means a return to the cherished past).

Discussing the temporalities in turn, a first point worth noting is that the past of Subvenio, that is, the time before the funding gap, was portrayed in a unanimously positive light as the 'good old days' or the 'heydays' of Subvenio. Thus this repertoire conjures a nostalgic image of the past. This longing for the past results in large part from idealized portrayals of the organization's founder – we will call him Jakob Busch – who had passed away almost two decades earlier. In stories conveyed by employees, in brochures, and on the organization's homepage, and in images on display at Subvenio's premises, Busch is characterized as a genuinely 'compassionate', 'generous' and 'charismatic' individual, and as someone who 'cared more about others than about himself'. Often referred to as the 'father' of the organization, Busch is positioned by the repertoire as the originator of Subvenio's social outlook and culture. Thus, he is portrayed as both an extraordinary individual and a symbol of Subvenio's core values and culture 'back in the day'.

Clearly, the focus of the social repertoire is placed squarely on how Busch endowed Subvenio with a sense of purpose predicated on a common set of humanistic values. Busch is seen as a role model for Subvenio's values, which were still diffused through rituals and festivities which were presented as essential for cultivating solidarity among members of the organization.

The social repertoire suggests that in the past a particular emphasis was placed on beneficiaries – families and children in need – who were unanimously envisioned as the essence of Subvenio. Whilst beneficiaries ostensibly used to be at the very centre of Subvenio, accounts of the past further stress that employees were then treated by both their superiors and their colleagues not as means to certain ends but as ends in themselves. 'Respect', 'authentic trust' and 'informality' were mentioned as key features of the way that employees, their direct superiors and Busch himself, as well as his immediate successor, interacted in the past. A key contention in accounts of the past is that all people at Subvenio, regardless of their status, function and role, were treated with dignity and respected as human beings.

This ideal situation is contrasted with the sombre presence of Subvenio. The current disenchantment is attributed directly to the managerial reforms which ostensibly weakened the bonds among employees, as well as between employees and beneficiaries. As we mentioned earlier, people challenged the managerial reforms because they saw them as diverting both time and money away from the organization's social mission. A decisive point in this argument is that these reforms have transformed Subvenio from a family-oriented and solidarity-based organization to one mainly concerned with financial forecasting and budgeting. This shift towards valuing managerial prowess was presented as an extremely problematic caesura of Subvenio which threatened to marginalize its cultural heritage and core values. The push towards managerialism was causally linked to the two current directors whose appointment coincided with Subvenio's precarious financial performance at that time. This explanation of the crisis that followed the reforms made the two directors appear as 'culprits' who bore responsibility for the nuisances the employees were experiencing.

In turn, accounts of Subvenio's future indicated how to deal with the current impasse and how to go forward. Accounts of its future were largely concerned with re-establishing the situation that existed before the reforms. Paradoxically, the quest towards the future eventually formed a backwards-oriented gesture. This longing to return to a bygone era was expressed, for example, by a caretaker who claimed that 'the "real work" with the residents should again be appreciated more and employees should be adequately supported'. Further, 'we must stop focusing too much on our own (economic well-being) as well as the pressures engendered by the newly introduced entrepreneurial language and thinking'. This quote is indicative of how the social repertoire eulogizes the past by pinpointing its myriad of merits. Presenting the managerial reforms as posing a threat to Subvenio's core values and social mission, the social repertoire essentially marks an attempt to re-establish the pre-eminence of social workers and caretakers (over managers) by stressing that they are ultimately the ones working 'at the frontiers of Subvenio's social services'. Further, the social repertoire demands that more time should be reserved for working with Subvenio's beneficiaries who, as the same caretaker maintained, are the ones 'who really count'.

The Managerial Repertoire

In contrast, the managerial repertoire was used almost exclusively by the two directors and by select members of the board. In sharp contrast to the social repertoire, the managerial repertoire represents the managerial reforms as unalterable and rational, and as being in the best interest of the organization. A persistent theme of this repertoire is that the reforms were instrumental in improving Subvenio's performance and, most importantly, in ensuring it would survive. Relating the reforms to efficiency and performance, the main emphasis of the managerial repertoire is on how the reforms noticeably increased Subvenio's ability to plan and control its activities based on financial information. In this way, the managerial repertoire chiefly echoes the now widespread belief that practices from the private sector have great potential for making voluntary organizations more sustainable and financially self-sufficient (Maier et al., 2014).

Thus the discursive justification of the managerial reforms at Subvenio is predicated on two distinct registers: pragmatism and urgency. Specifically, those using this repertoire hold that the reforms are pragmatic as they offer an efficient, objective and rational solution to the financial turmoil Subvenio had witnessed some years earlier. Central to the conception of management reforms as pragmatic is the belief that given the right management techniques, it should be possible to eliminate the current frictions and troubles (Morozov, 2013). And yet, in signifying managerial reforms as pragmatic, the managerial repertoire glosses over the fact that such interventions do not necessarily offer a value-free approach to organizational changing, since changing always has to do with contesting and negotiating values, interests and, potentially, relations of power.

The second justificatory regime conjures a sense of urgency by framing the managerial reforms at Subvenio as 'necessary', 'inevitable' and 'indispensable'. Underlying this justification is the assumption that Subvenio had no other option but to implement the reforms – that it could not have survived without them. This invites the conclusion that the managerial repertoire establishes a 'do-or-die' mentality by highlighting that refusing to implement the reforms would have irrevocably led to Subvenio's demise.

FROM TALKING TOUGH TO LISTENING CLOSELY

After they had listened to the presentation about the two repertoires, the workshop participants were divided into groups and asked to discuss and comment on what they had just heard. The groups were set up to facilitate encounters between people who did not work in the same area or team, and would rarely meet while at work. Participants were assured that they could speak openly about things at Subvenio that concerned or upset them without having to fear any negative consequences.

By and large, our general impression was that workshop participants had little difficulty in relating to and making sense of the results of our discourse analysis. During the early stages of the discussion we noted a tendency amongst participants to merely reproduce the two repertoires. That is, they often affirmed that their preferred repertoire was correct and legitimate, and denigrated the value of the rival position. To simplify somewhat, we noted that social workers and caretakers stressed that the social mission and values formed the centrepiece of Subvenio, and that the reforms created a major obstacle to realizing that mission. Managers, on the other hand, maintained that Subvenio's social mission had been jeopardized precisely because it had lacked proper mechanisms to steer and control its finances. Managers thus contended that there was no way around becoming more business savvy, whatever the temporary repercussions such a shift might cause.

What we can see here is that the rival parties enacted the two repertoires as irreconcilable. The early stage of the dialogue was underpinned by a zero-sum logic: the belief that one party's gain would inextricably lead to a loss by the opponent. The exchanges between the two groups – the managers, and the social workers and caretakers – were in fact polarized, reactive and at times even hostile. Still, we remained mindful that it was imperative for the participants to experience such a moment of 'talking tough' (Scharmer, 2001), using the two discourses which had caused the conflict in the first place. At the same time, though, it was clear that a dialogue premised on 'talking tough' was insufficient to overcome the conflict because it obstructed any appreciation of the other party's perspective.

Hence, we saw the need to gradually shift the perspective of the dialogue so participants could move to a more affirmative and constructive mode of exchange. So, after they had expressed their viewpoints and worries, and vented their frustrations, our team instructed them to temporarily suspend judgement and to pay close attention to what their 'opponents' actually had to say. Listening closely to the perspective of the others had a distinct effect: it redirected their attention so they could see the situation at Subvenio through the eyes of their counterparty.

To help each group foster a proper appreciation for the perspective adopted by their opponents, our team tried to shift their perception of the conflict at Subvenio by moving their focus. Instead of focusing solely on the people (that is, managers, caretakers, social workers) who invoked the respective repertoires, we suggested they see the repertoires as tightly related to the organizational roles and responsibilities bestowed upon these people. Making it clear that the two repertoires chiefly reflected people's positions and functions within the organization rather than their private proclivities and interests, we also drew on existing research to underscore that managers of voluntary organizations typically emphasize issues related to strategy, mission and organizational purpose whereas employees tend to focus more on cultural issues, including values and practices. Our aim with this instruction was to de-individualize the conflict at Subvenio by helping them all see that any individual's appraisal of the two repertoires would be a function of their own position.

Moving against the tendency to appraise the two repertoires as either 'black or white', we acquainted the participants with the idea that any attempt to judge the opposing repertoire would be incomplete unless they also considered the roles, duties, practical constraints and goals associated with the perspective of the other. Once we created a heightened acceptance of the opponent's point of view and a better awareness of the organizational position from which each side enunciated its repertoire, we were then able to move away from gridlocked interpretations of the two repertoires, and towards generative dialogue where both sides could sense and actualize new possibilities (Jaworski and Scharmer, 2000).

GENERATIVE DIALOGUE AND THE RENEGOTIATION OF MEANING

A key insight transmitted during the various workshops was that the two repertoires which had triggered the conflict at Subvenio were contingent and thus could be changed. This revelation was crucial for nudging changes in individuals' casual way of making sense of their organizational reality (Brown and Humphreys, 2003). To allow them to tap new ways of making sense of the 'what' and 'why' of organizational changing (Grant and Marshak, 2011), we then asked them to analyse closely which aspects of the two repertoires were supporting or hindering their everyday work specifically and their sense of purpose and commitment more generally. We then divided them into small groups and instructed them to share their individual appraisals with their colleagues and try to establish, via extended discussions, a tentative consensus around which aspects of the two repertoires should be retained and which ones should be changed.

We also called on them to treat the inputs of their colleagues with respect. And we stressed that they should try to engage as constructively as possible with the rival repertoire by trying to understand it in detail and redefine it instead of merely rejecting it. This instruction mostly fell on fertile ground: the caretakers and social workers readily elaborated how the managerial repertoire could be altered to better fit their everyday realities, whilst managers reflected on ways the social repertoire could be adapted to minimize frictions with the newly implemented accounting systems. The outcomes of the group discussions were captured on flip charts and later presented in a plenary session. Table 14.1 reproduces one such flip chart, recorded as a group evaluated the two repertories in terms of their respective advantages (the dimensions 'to be sustained') and disadvantages (the dimensions 'to be changed').

A striking observation was that, after some brief hesitations, both employees and managers increasingly shifted from defending their preferred repertoire to engaging in generative dialogue that led to new interpretations of both repertoires. Flexibly removing aspects of the two repertoires whilst adding others, the participants gradually transformed the two repertoires based on the insights and experiences gathered during the group conversations. In this way, generative dialogue permitted groups to re-imagine what Subvenio stands for in largely novel ways. The generative dialogue had a pacifying effect as it dissolved the antagonism between the two interpretative repertoires. The tensions between the two groups were reconciled as the intervention changed the two repertoires, thereby disrupting the strict correspondence between group and repertoire, that is between the social repertoire and the social workers and caretakers and,

Table 14.1 Example of a generative dialogue at Subvenio

Social		Managerial	
To be sustained	To be changed	To be sustained	To be changed
– Humour	– 24-hour	– Power	– The weak and
– Lived values	availability	– Responsibility	vulnerable
– Emphasis on	– 'We are all	and	have no right
relations	nice with	accountability	to exist
– Valuing the	each other'	– External per-	– People are
individual	climate	ception in terms	positioned as
– Tolerance of failures	– Inability to	of efficiency	inferior once
– Patience	perform vis-	– Competitiveness	they are not
– Inclusiveness	à-vis donors	– Goal orientation	able to trigger
– Relevance to the			their full
identity of Subvenio			potential

on the other hand, between the managerial repertoire and the managers. It became clear that engaging organizational members in generative dialogue had the distinct effect of dissolving the root of the conflict: the competing discourses.

Cursory though this discussion has been, the key insight to be gleaned from our consultancy project is that organizational changing, to be successful, presupposes a thoroughgoing dialogue between managers and employees where competing discourses are 'interpreted and further reinterpreted by those' they address, 'depending on the interpretative codes and the local circumstances of its addressees' (Tsoukas and Chia, 2002, pp. 579–580). Such iterative interpretations eventually change antagonistic discursive practices and allow rival parties to incrementally experience each other as 'allies' in a quest towards redefining the purpose and prospect of organizational changing.

CONCLUDING DISCUSSION

Traditional accounts of discourse analysis conceive of the subject matter more or less exclusively as an epistemological tool – that is, a tool for studying how meaning is created through language (Wood and Kroger, 2000). In contrast, our central contention in this chapter has been that discourse analysis can serve as a means to intervene in the ways that organizational reality is created and changed. Based on a consultancy project at Subvenio, one of the largest German voluntary organizations, we have explored the interventionist possibilities of discourse analysis by attending to how it can be employed to steer organizational members towards a more affirmative mode of exchange. Perhaps this work's most important contribution is showing that discourse analysis does in fact have practical value (Oswick, Grant, Marshak and Cox, 2010).

Discourse analysis has practical value to the extent to which it works to engage people in generative dialogue (Gee, 2005) so it instigates movement where tensions and conflict had prevailed. By fostering generative dialogue amongst members of an organization, an interventionist usage of discourse analysis suggests that those people move from talking tough to actively participating in the process of organizational changing. Hence, what is crucially at stake in an interventionist usage of discourse analysis is the question of how competing discourses within an organization can be made palpable for all involved, and how, in turn, people can learn to re-evaluate these discourses with an eye towards suspending organizational conflicts.

To be sure, any consulting team needs to remain impartial with regard to defining the 'what' and 'why' of organizational changing (Grant and Marshak, 2011). Although impartiality can prove difficult to sustain in practice, as one might develop sympathies for some discourses more than for others, impartiality nevertheless becomes an indispensible part of any intervention that tries to confront competing discourses in largely affirmative ways. In this light, a central merit of an interventionist usage of discourse analysis is precisely that it fosters impartiality by supporting those involved in cultivating a more inclusive way of interpreting organizational reality that relaxes antagonistic discursive practices. In saying this, of course, we do not suggest that certain voices and interests might remain more authoritative than others in shaping an organization's trajectory and purpose (Tsoukas and Chia, 2002). It remains true that power will always play a role in determining who can speak and who is heard in the context of organizational changing (Marshak and Grant, 2008b), but in this chapter we have tried to raise awareness that generative dialogue has great potential to prevent an existing discourse from becoming dominant by rendering organizational changing democratic and non-hierarchical.

Our objective was to show how existing relations of power at Subvenio were temporarily neutralized through the process of establishing discursive spaces that were bracketed away from everyday action, and that offered the possibility of creating alternative interpretations that could, in turn, alter the general outlook of the organization (Howard-Grenville, Golden-Biddle, Irwin and Mao, 2011). Thus our intervention at Subvenio helped keep the influence of existing hierarchies and relations of power in check by ensuring that none of the discourses were excluded or marginalized

(Deetz, 1992). We believe our intervention had a positive effect at Subvenio, at least during the time we were active there, because people we spoke to readily acknowledged that moving the organization out of its crisis presupposed that everyone would adopt a 'democratic spirit' (Eisenberg, 1994). Conceding that it made little sense to view managers as the only legitimate 'change agents' in the organization (Sonenshein, 2010), board members in particular encouraged our team to overcome the existing hierarchies, thereby placing managers and employees on a level playing field. Using workshops as a contact zone where opposing vistas and interests could meet proved helpful for curbing partisanship, fostering sympathy with opposing views and, most significantly, allowing for alternative visions of Subvenio to materialize.

Whilst this work casts a positive light on the interventionist potential of discourse analysis, we must also bear in mind that discourse analysis plays a marginal role in 'real-life' consultancy projects dealing with organizational changing. Indeed, while we were preparing this chapter, we simply could not find published guidance on analysing discursive practices that have not been tape-recorded. Whereas scholarly texts on discourse analysis mostly stipulate methodological techniques ('first this, then that') and standards of quality and rigour, these discussions, although significant in their own right, have very little practical significance for projects in which the consultants cannot record and transcribe conversations and interviews. To address this lacuna, we believe that future researchers should attune discourse analysis to the particular needs and conditions of (consulting) practice.

Thus we see a particularly urgent need: to address in sufficient depth the ways that discourse analysis can support consultants in implementing organizational changing in a more participatory and democratic way. Moreover, we deem it important to establish analytic conventions and principles for dealing with non-recorded discursive practices (Hammersley, 2005). If researchers and practitioners accept that an interventionist approach to discourse analysis enacts reality in largely new ways (Grant and Iedema, 2005), then it may be possible to use whatever kind of data are available to complete a given task. We have tried to take a first step in this direction by opening up discourse analysis to sources of information which typically exceed the scope of textbooks on discourse analysis. We are well aware that this task is far from completed, and that the interventionist usage of discourse analysis can be extended in several directions. At this decisive point in time, we are curious to see if and how others relate to this debate and move it forward.

REFERENCES

Alvesson, Mats (2004), 'Organizational culture and discourse', in David Grant, Cynthia Hardy, Cliff Oswick, and Linda L. Putnam (eds), *The Sage Handbook of Organizational Discourse*, London: Sage, pp. 317–335.

Alvesson, Mats and Dan Kärreman (2000), 'Varieties of discourse: On the study of organizations through discourse analysis', *Human Relations*, **53** (9), 1125–1149.

Brown, Andrew D. and Michael Humphreys (2003), 'Epics and tragic tales. Making sense of change', *Journal of Applied Behavioral Science*, **39** (2), 121–144.

Buchanan, David and Patrick Dawson (2007), 'Discourse and audience: Organizational change as a multi-story process', *Journal of Management Studies*, **44** (5), 669–686.

Cameron, Kim S. and Robert E. Quinn (1999), *Diagnosing and Changing Organizational Culture*, Reading, MA: Addison-Wesley.

Deetz, Stanley A. (1992), *Democracy in an Age of Corporate Colonization: Developments in Communication and the Politics of Everyday Life*, New York: State University of New York Press.

Dey, Pascal (2007), *On the Name of Social Entrepreneurship: Business School Teaching, Research, and Development Aid*, unpublished doctoral dissertation, Basel, Switzerland: University of Basel.

Eikenberry, Angela M. and Jodie D. Kluver (2004), 'The marketization of the nonprofit sector: Civil society at risk?', *Public Administration Review*, **64** (2), 132–140.

Eisenberg, Eric M. (1994), 'Dialogue as democratic discourse: Affirming Harrison', in Stanley A. Deetz (ed.), *Communication Yearbook 17*, Thousand Oaks, CA: Sage, pp. 275–284.

Ford, Jeffrey D., Laurie W. Ford and Angelo D'Amelio (2008), 'Resistance to change: The rest of the story', *Academy of Management Review*, **33** (2), 362–377.

Gee, James P. (2005), *An Introduction to Discourse Analysis: Theory and Method*, New York: Routledge.

Graetz, Fiona and Aaron C.T. Smith (2010), 'Managing organizational change: A philosophies of change approach', *Journal of Change Management*, **10** (2), 135–154.

Grant, David and Rick Iedema (2005), 'Discourse analysis and the study of organizations', *Text: An Interdisciplinary Journal for the Study of Discourse*, **25** (1), 37–66.

Grant, David and Robert J. Marshak (2011), 'Toward a discourse-centered understanding of organizational change', *The Journal of Applied Behavioral Science*, **47** (2), 204–235.

Grant, David, Grant Michelson, Cliff Oswick and Nick Wailes (2005), 'Guest editorial: Discourse and organizational change', *Journal of Organizational Change Management*, **18** (1), 6–15.

Hammersley, Martyn (2005), 'Ethnography and discourse analysis: Incompatible or complementary?', *Polifonia*, **10**, 1–20.

Hardy, Cynthia and Steve Maguire (2010), 'Discourse, field-configuring events, and change in organizations and institutional fields: Narratives of DDT and the Stockholm Convention', *Academy of Management Journal*, **53** (6), 1365–1392.

Heracleous, Loizos T. (2006), 'Images of discourse: Interpretive, functional, critical and structurational', in Loizos Heracleous (ed.), *Discourse, Interpretation, Organization*, Cambridge: Cambridge University Press, pp. 1–27.

Heracleous, Loizos T. and Michael Barrett (2001), 'Organizational change as discourse: Communicative actions and deep structures in the context of information technology implementation', *Academy of Management Journal*, **44** (4), 755–778.

Hodge, Bob (2010), 'Oedipus and the CEO: Ambiguities of change in myth, discourse and practice', *Culture and Organization*, **16** (1), 23–35.

Howard-Grenville, Jennifer, Karen Golden-Biddle, Jennifer Irwin and Jina Mao (2011), 'Liminality as cultural process for cultural change', *Organization Science*, **22** (2), 522–539.

Jaworski, Joseph and Claus O. Scharmer (2000), 'Leadership in the new economy: Sensing and actualizing emerging futures', working paper, Society for Organizational Learning, Cambridge, MA.

Jian, Guowei (2011), 'Articulating circumstance, identity and practice: Toward a discursive framework of organizational change', *Organization*, **18** (1), 45–64.

Law, John (2004), *After Method: Mess in Social Science Research*, New York: Routledge.

Law, John and John Urry (2005), 'Enacting the social', *Economy and Society*, **33** (3), 390–410.

Maier, Florentine, Michael Meyer and Martin Steinbereithner (2014), 'Nonprofit organization becoming business-like: A systematic review', *Nonprofit and Voluntary Sector Quarterly* (online first).

Marshak, Robert J. and David Grant (2008a), 'Organizational discourse and new organization development practices', *British Journal of Management*, **19** (1), 7–19.

Marshak, Robert J. and David Grant (2008b), 'Transforming talk: The interplay of discourse, power, and change', *Organization Development Journal*, **26** (3), 33–40.

Minkoff, Debra C. and Walter W. Powell (2006), 'Nonprofit mission: Constancy, responsiveness, or deflection?', in Walter W. Powell and Richard Steinberg (eds), *The Nonprofit Sector: A Research Handbook*, New Haven, CT: Yale University Press, pp. 591–611.

Morozov, Evgeny (2013), *To Save Everything, Click Here: Technology, Solutionism, and the Urge to Fix Problems that Don't Exist*, London: Allen Lane.

Oswick, Cliff, David Grant, Robert J. Marshak and Julie W. Cox (2010), 'Organizational discourse and change: Positions, perspectives, progress, and prospects', *The Journal of Applied Behavioral Science*, **46** (1), 8–15.

Phillips, Nelson and Cynthia Hardy (2002), *Discourse Analysis: Investigating Processes of Social Construction*, Thousand Oaks, CA: Sage.

Phillips, Nelson and Cliff Oswick (2012), 'Organizational discourse: Domains, debates, and directions', *Academy of Management Annals*, **6** (1), 435–481.

Potter, Jonathan and Margaret Wetherell (1987), *Discourse and Social Psychology*, London: Sage.

Resch, Dörte (2006), *Soziales Miteinander in Organisationen – Diskurse und Funktionen zwischen individueller Kompetenz und organisationaler Metapher*, unpublished doctoral dissertation, Neuchâtel, Switzerland: University of Neuchatel.

Scharmer, Claus O. (2001), 'Self-transcending knowledge: Sensing and organizing around emerging opportunities', *Journal of Knowledge Management*, **5** (2), 137–150.

Sonenshein, Scott (2010), 'We're changing – or are we? Untangling the role of progressive, regressive, and stability narratives during strategic change implementation', *Academy of Management Journal*, **53** (3), 477–512.

Steyaert, Chris (2011), 'Entrepreneurship as in(ter)vention: Reconsidering the conceptual politics of method in entrepreneurship studies', *Entrepreneurship & Regional Development*, **23** (1), 77–88.

Thomas, Robyn, Leisa D. Sargent and Cynthia Hardy (2011), 'Managing organizational change: Negotiating meaning and power-resistance relations', *Organization Science*, **22** (1), 22–41.

Tsoukas, Haridimos (2005), 'Afterword: Why language matters in the analysis of organizational change', *Journal of Organizational Change Management*, **18** (1), 96–104.

Tsoukas, Haridimos and Robert Chia (2002), 'On organizational becoming: Rethinking organizational change', *Organization Science*, **13** (5), 567–582.

Wetherell, Margaret and Jonathan Potter (1988), 'Discourse analysis and the identification of interpretative repertoires', in Charles Antaki (ed.), *Analysing Everyday Explanation: A Casebook of Methods*, Newbury Park, CA: Sage, pp. 168–183.

Wood, Linda A. and Rolf O. Kroger (2000), *Doing Discourse Analysis. Methods for Studying Action in Talk and Text*, Thousand Oaks, CA: Sage.

Index

342 A guide to discursive organizational psychology